A People's Court?

A People's Court?

A Bottom-Up Approach to Litigation Before the European Court of Justice

Jos Hoevenaars

eleven
international publishing

Published, sold and distributed by Eleven International Publishing
P.O. Box 85576
2508 CG The Hague
The Netherlands
Tel.: +31 70 33 070 33
Fax: +31 70 33 070 30
e-mail: sales@budh.nl
www.elevenpub.com

Sold and distributed in USA and Canada
International Specialized Book Services
920 NE 58th Avenue, Suite 300
Portland, OR 97213-3786, USA
Tel.: 1-800-944-6190 (toll-free)
Fax: +1-503-280-8832
orders@isbs.com
www.isbs.com

Eleven International Publishing is an imprint of Boom uitgevers Den Haag.

ISBN 978-94-6236-829-3
ISBN 978-94-6274-827-9 (E-book)

Printed in The Netherlands

Contents

PART II

PART IV

Acknowledgements

This book has been made possible with the help, support, collaboration and guidance from a number of people who I wish to mention here.

First and foremost, I wish to thank my supervisors for giving me the trust to work on this topic, despite of my initial lack of knowledge and expertise in either law in general or the world of Euro-litigation in particular, and for supporting me in making this project my own. Thank you Tetty Havinga for your keen eye, constructive supervision and for the pleasant discussions during our weekly meetings, and professors Betty de Hart and Leny de Groot-van Leeuwen for your structural guidance, your often well-timed encouragement and valuable feedback. In addition, I would like to thank the members of my doctoral committee, professors Henri de Waele, Ashley Terlouw and Antoine Vauchez for kindly agreeing to take on the task of reading this thesis and for their constructive evaluation.

I am indebted to the many respondents who agreed to be interviewed and who shared their experiences with me. Without their collaboration this project would not have been possible. I thank the law students of the Radboud University for contributing to parts of the data collection. Additionally, This work has benefitted from the help of numerous scholars I've met during seminars, workshops and summer schools throughout the years, whom I thank for the helpful discussions and their constructive comments on different parts of this book.

I wish to thank the Institute for Sociology of Law and the Centre for Migration Law of the Radboud University Nijmegen for the opportunity to conduct this research and all my former colleagues for the pleasant and stimulating work environment throughout the years: Anita Böcker, Maria Bruquetas Callejo, Mary Dickson, Dario Dzananovic, Kim Gildeman, Kees Groenendijk, Carolus Grütters, Madeleine Hoctin Boes, Sandra Mantu, Paul Minderhoud, Alex Jettinghoff, Amélie Poméon, Asuncion Fresnoza-Flot, Nadia Sonneveld, Wouter van der Spek, Tineke Strik, Hans den Tonkelaar, Karin Zwaan, and the many visiting researchers that have all contributed to making my time at Radboud a pleasant one. Hannie van de Put deserves special thanks for taking care of the layout of the book and putting up with my last minute adaptations. And many thanks to Beverley Slaney for the language editing.

A special thanks to my new fellow researchers Alexandre Biard, Alina Ontanu, Erlis Themeli, Emma van Gelder and Georgia Antonopoulou at Erasmus School of Law for a very welcoming new work environment and the promise of very fruitful future collaborations, and especially to professor Xandra

Kramer for giving me the chance to further develop as an academic and for allowing me the time to finish this project.

The greatest of gratitude goes to my former colleagues and fellow PhDs Tamara Butter, Jos Vleugel, Marija Davidović, Ralph Severijns and Reyer Baas for making this experience not only intellectually enriching but also a lot of fun. With special thanks to my former roommates Anoeshka Gehring and Ellen Nissen, firstly for providing me with an often much needed sounding board but moreover for putting up with my occasional rants and other attempts at distraction.

My final words of gratitude are for my friends and family, who made my decision to stay in Rotterdam, and put up with the substantial commute back and forth to Nijmegen, one I have never regretted. Thank you Irene van Oorschot for being my fellow traveller for the demanding first years of this project. Thank you to my fellow editors of Het Potentieel, Shivant Jhagroe and Tuur Ghys for our ever-fun meetings. I thank my friends and fellow musicians Arnold van de Velde, Rene van Lien, Youri Seidler, Rob van Gameren, Marjoleine Molenaar, Jaap Rovers, Friso van Wijck, Edwin Willemen, Vincent van Duin, Frank Jonas, Jasper den Dulk and many others for the much needed musical distractions and the great projects I was honoured to be part of throughout these years. Finally, thank you Choca Alcazaba for being my friend and teaching me many lessons in life. Thank you Caroline for tirelessly putting up with my moods in the final challenging stages of this PhD, but above all for continuously making me laugh throughout it all. Thank you Bart, Maartje, Rutger, Mies, Fos and Roek for being my family and so much more.

To my parents, Truusje and Mari, who have always supported me in many more ways than one, I dedicate this book.

Rotterdam 2017

1 Introduction

"What citizen of Europe has not been assisted in some way by the rulings of the European Court in Luxembourg? As long as the Court goes on handing down judgments that enable ordinary men and women to savor the fruits of integration, it will continue to demonstrate its usefulness."[1]

1.1 Individual Litigants Before the European Court of Justice

Over the past sixty years, the integration of Europe has exceeded many expectations. Among other accomplishments, the European Union (EU) has completed its common market, created a common currency and has expanded to include twenty-eight Member States. European political and economic integration has been to a great extent a legal process with an important role for the European Court of Justice (ECJ).[2] Among legal scholars and political scientists alike, there is general agreement that the dynamics of that process have in large part relied on the critical influence the ECJ has exerted through the preliminary reference system. The latter allows national judges in national proceedings to refer questions regarding the interpretation of EU law to the ECJ. The judgments of the ECJ in such preliminary reference cases have been transformational in European legal and political dynamics. Not only have preliminary rulings by the ECJ been responsible for significant integration of the national legal systems, the procedure has been the main means by which individual rights can be and have been invoked, consolidated and expanded. The preliminary reference procedure is therefore widely considered the backbone of the European legal system, and the ECJ as a catalyst in the integration of the European Union.[3]

1 Mancini & Keeling 1995, 413.

2 The *Court of Justice of the European Union* (CJEU) is the collective term for the European Union's judicial arm, but the single institution consists of separate courts, each enjoying its own specific jurisdiction. Established in 1952 as the *Court of Justice of the European Coal and Steel Communities*, renamed in 1958 the *Court of Justice of the European Communities*, and with the entrance into force of the Treaty of Lisbon on 1 December 2009, the Court's official name became *Court of Justice of the European Union,* officially designating the institution's two main courts, the *Court of Justice* and the *General Court*, along with its former specialised court, the *Civil Service Tribunal,* which ceased to exist on 1 September 2016. This study deals almost exclusively with preliminary reference cases, which are dealt with by the *Court of Justice*, colloquially known by its former name: the *European Court of Justice*. From here on I will use both the acronym *ECJ* as well as *the Court* (with a capitalised C) as synonyms to denote the institution.

3 Vauchez 2008b.

Although the ECJ's case law, and therefore litigation, is recognised as an essential element in the process of European integration, the litigation process in itself has remained a rather unexplored topic. A large body of research into the integration of Europe has given special weight to the role of private litigation in activating the preliminary reference system and by extension fostering integration dynamics in Europe. However, while there is strong consensus about the pivotal role the procedure has had in the transformation of Europe, there remains significant disagreement on why the system is used, and who is primarily responsible for its success. While private litigants are seen as central actors in this integration dynamics there is still little insight into who goes to Court in Europe, and why. As such, so-called 'Euro-litigation' remains somewhat of a black box.

1.2 Changing Power Relations in Europe

In studying European integration dynamics, a voluminous body of scholarship deals with the institutional make-up of the EU and recognises EU law, the preliminary reference procedure and the ECJ as essential features of European integration.[4] The new legal constellation changed power relations within Europe, shifting the political centre from the national to the supranational and making citizens subject to new international norms, with far-reaching implications for the (legal) position of the citizen. The rise of the ECJ itself stems from the perceived 'reciprocal empowerment', the linking of the Court with various groups and institutions that sought to profit from further integration.[5] On the one hand, these developments have resulted in critical evaluations of the EU's democratic deficits, focusing particularly on the lack of popular representation.[6] On the other hand, a growing narrative sees this federalizing aspect of the EU as transforming the relationship between citizen and state, possibly in favour of the former.[7]

Each year, over a thousand decisions are made by the ECJ on the basis of EU legislation that affects governance in the Members States as well as the lives of their citizens. These citizens now are no longer citizens only of their countries but also European Union citizens. This status is reflected in the way EU law is formulated. The 'language of rights' or 'rights based regime' – the notion that the EU legal system functions predominantly by formulating (enforceable) rights – stands at the basis of much change within Europe through the jurisprudence of the ECJ.

4 For a comprehensive literature review see Conant 2007.
5 Burley & Mattli 1993.
6 Forst & Schmalz-Bruns 2011.
7 Cichowski 2006.

Box I: A Union Based on Law[8]

The European Union started out as an economic endeavour aimed at integrating a single economic market in which the free movement of goods, services, capital and workers were to be ensured. This undertaking slowly but surely progressed into a political integration of the Member States aimed at 'an ever closer union of the peoples of Europe'. In essence the economic consortium of the Member States of the first hour has evolved into a multinational economic and political union of federal-like proportions. This process has from the earliest instances on been facilitated by a body of legal rules and regulations aimed at ensuring uniform application of the Treaties agreed upon. At first, this legal body focused exclusively on matters of transnational movement of goods, workers and capital and the establishment of a single market in Europe. Over the past decades, this European body of rules has transformed into a fully-fledged federal-like system of law, binding all Member States, and its peoples, to a plethora of supranational laws and regulations in a vast number of policy areas. At the top of this European legal system stands the European Court of Justice (ECJ), the final arbiter when it comes to interpreting European legislation. Through its judgments the ECJ has had a fundamental influence on the European legal as well as political landscape. Many of the Court's most transformative judgments have come from cases that reached the Court through the preliminary reference system, which allows and sometimes requires national judges to refer national cases to the ECJ.

Established as early as 1952, the ECJ has been of seminal importance in the creation of this federal-like union of European nation-states. Not only by being mandated with ensuring uniform application of the Treaties across Member States, but moreover by constitutionalising EU law, and by making EU legislation directly applicable in a national context through the now famous decisions in *Van Gend & Loos v Nederlandse Administratie der Belastingen* in 1963, and in *Flaminio Costa v E.N.E.L.* in 1964, two of the very first preliminary references to the ECJ. With these judgments the Court formally enshrined the semi-constitutional character of EU law and, moreover, gave private parties, including individual citizens, a stake in the application of EU law.[9] The doctrine of supremacy stipulates that whenever there is a conflict between national laws and EU laws, the former shall be subordinated to the latter. According to the direct effect principle, rights conferred on individuals by EU legislation should be enforceable by those individuals in national courts.

The analysis of this jurisprudence, and the influential precedential function and ground-breaking effects thereof, have led scholars to conclude that EU law and the preliminary reference procedure give individuals and civil society a stake in the transformation of Europe's political and legal order. The authority of the ECJ to interpret EU legislation combined with a growing focus on individual rights seems to signal a shift towards greater empowerment of the individual

8 Paragraphs on the general institutional design of the EU will be presented in textboxes.
9 Stein 1981. See also Micklitz 2012.

within the European legal system. This 'empowerment-through-law' narrative focuses mainly on the preliminary reference procedure with the assumption that it gives firstly, the possibility of having government legislation, policy and acts reviewed by a higher judicial authority, the ECJ, and secondly, the power to influence the course and pace of European legal and political development.

1.3 Euro-Litigation: A View from the Inside

The aforementioned legal and political dynamics give rise to questions of how and to what extent individuals are able to profit from the changing legal landscape. The position of individuals in the European legal system, and their opportunities for invoking rights under EU law, has been the subject of debate ever since the ECJ became operative. The general lack of empirical substantiation of the claims underpinning narratives about the ECJ and EU law raises questions about the tenability of this idea and forms the starting point of this research. We still know very little about who actually goes to court in Europe. As will be discussed further in Chapter 2, the individual is given centre stage as a 'subject' in the discourse on the 'European project', and as a 'private litigant' in scholarly analysis of the European legal system, yet the individual as an 'actor' has only sparsely been the serious focus of research. As once concluded by Friedman, "[i]ntellectual debate does not make case-law; cases are controversies, and they presuppose conflicts, not to mention people and groups who take steps to set the legal process in motion".[10] Following earlier studies that have focused on the legal system from the perspective of those who make use of it,[11] this research will focus on the preliminary reference system by placing the actors that feature in Euro-litigation at the centre of attention.

In this light Banakar stresses the need to combine both top-down and bottom-up approaches, and argues that the contextualization of laws in comparative studies of law is necessary in order to transcend the understanding of law as (merely) a body of rules and doctrines, and to situate "legal action, behavior, institution, tradition, text and discourse in specific time and socio-legal space, thus, revealing law's embeddedness in societal relations, structures, developments and processes".[12] Where a top-down perspective characterizes most studies on the European legal system, this study aims to add a bottom-up approach to reveal how EU law is embedded in and manifests itself at different levels of

10 Friedman 1975, 2.

11 See for instance Bouwen & McCown 2007; Bruinsma 2010; Felstiner, Abel & Sarat 1980; Fitzgerald & Dickins 1980; Friedman 1989; Galanter 1974; Harding 1980; Kritzer 1980; Macaulay 1963; and Miller & Sarat 1980.

12 Banakar 2009, 71.

European society. It critically examines the image created of the ECJ as an arena for change, and the preliminary reference procedure as an opportunity for empowerment. It approaches the preliminary reference procedure from a bottom-up perspective in order to reveal what actors are involved in these procedures, what their aims and strategies are, the opportunities these actors have in the deliberate use of it, and moreover, what relative power relations exist in the exploitation of these legal avenues.

The spirit of this study, with a particular focus on the individual's stake in EU law and politics, results in a necessarily narrowed view. The focus on individuals and the preliminary reference procedure has a twofold, though interrelated, theoretical foundation. Firstly, the important role of preliminary reference cases before the ECJ in shaping and steering European integration raises the important question of their origins (hence the intensive focus in European integration studies on the relationship between national courts and the ECJ as well as efforts to try to understand the variation in the number of references between Member States, as discussed in Chapter 3). And secondly, the purported empowerment through law – as well as the agreement in the political science literature that business interests are much better represented in 'Brussels' when it comes to lobbying and access to the policy process at the EU level[13] and in sociology of law literature when it comes to litigation opportunities and strategies,[14] – raises the question of the means and relative success of the 'have-nots' in mobilising EU law and Euro-litigation.

In other words this study focuses on: whose interests, whose actions and what possibilities, challenging a notion of individual empowerment by critically examining access to justice in the European context. By looking in depth at cases brought before the ECJ and investigating the motives of the parties involved, this study aims to open the 'black box' of Euro-litigation and provide an answer to the central research question:

To what extent can EU law in general and specifically the preliminary reference procedure be considered an opportunity for empowerment and who is (most) likely to use it?

In order to provide an answer to this central research question, different parts of this study aim to answer the following sub questions:

13 Coen & Richardson 2008.

14 Galanter 1974.

- Who goes to court in Europe, and why?
- Who is (most) likely to make use of the opportunities in EU law and which legal strategies are effective?
- To what extent can Euro-litigation be considered empowering to individual litigants?

1.4 Methodology

In order to answer the main research question of this study, and with the practical limitations of in-depth research in mind, this study focuses on preliminary references from one Member State in particular; the Netherlands. With respect to the judicial review function of EU law – the possibility of having government legislation, policy and acts reviewed by a higher judicial authority – the Netherlands provides an interesting case study. As compared to a country like France, that has a rich history of constitutional review in its domestic system, and was therefore classified by Lijphart[15] as a country with a 'medium-strength' judicial review, the Netherlands shares no such history and more closely resembles the British model of parliamentary sovereignty. The Dutch system, wherein the balance between courts and politics leans more firmly towards the legislator, was therefore considered by Lijphart as a country with 'no judicial review'.[16] However, as Koopmans has pointed out, while the Dutch system does not allow the courts to review the constitutionality of legislation, they have progressively come to scrutinize legislation for compatibility with international norms, thus moving closer to a system of legal review that resembles that of countries like France and Germany.[17] The Dutch legal system has been, since its constitutional reform in 1956, 'monist' in nature, in the sense that national and international law are considered as forming a single legal order. Therefore the Dutch case is one where international law to a significant extent performs the role played by constitutional law in other countries. Historically, the Netherlands has been in the top three Member States making the most use of the possibility for referral to the ECJ, together with Germany and Italy.[18] Additionally, in their analysis of the different 'worlds of compliance', the domestic political cultures related to the implementation of EU legislation, Falkner et al. label the Netherlands under the header of 'world of domestic politics'.[19] This category includes Member States

15 Lijphart, A. 1999, 229.
16 Lijphart, A. 1999, 229.
17 Koopmans 2003, 84.
18 See *Appendix B,* which includes the number of references according to Member States, both in absolute numbers as well as for the period studied for this research.
19 Falkner, Hartlapp and Treib 2007.

making cost-benefit calculations when it comes to the implementation of EU legislation, in which conflicts between EU obligations and national political interests will more frequently lead to non-compliance. Consequently, the Netherlands is a Member State that finds itself before the ECJ on a regular basis.

Selection of cases

This study focuses on preliminary reference cases from the Netherlands that involve individual litigants, and thus excludes cases where the litigants are businesses and institutions. The case selection covers all Dutch references dealt with by the court in the period 2008-2012. Given that the procedure for the ECJ alone takes on average up to two years to conclude, selecting more recent cases increased the chances of vivid recollection of the procedures by the individuals involved. Selecting to the end of 2012 provided a long enough period since the ruling by the ECJ for the cases to have been further adjudicated by the national court. The cases under investigation in this study were selected using the search form on the ECJ's website[20] and selecting 'Reference for a preliminary ruling', 'Preliminary reference – urgent procedure', and selecting 'Netherlands' as the 'Source of a question referred for a preliminary ruling'. The selected period spanned five years, from January 1st 2008 up to December 31st 2012. The date on which a judgment was delivered (or the case was otherwise dealt with) was used as a selecting criterion. This search resulted in a total of 114 separately registered cases concerning preliminary references originating from Dutch courts during the selected five years. These 114 included fourteen cases that did not result in a separate judgment. These were either joined with other cases, withdrawn prematurely or dealt with by reasoned order. As a result the baseline number of cases was a well-rounded 100.

The focus on individuals requires some clarification. A distinction is made between 'natural persons' and 'legal persons'. This distinction is necessarily somewhat arbitrary for the simple reason that determining the actual subject of the procedure is a matter of definition – typically one grounded in legal terminology. For example, this study excludes small businesses (that may in fact be individual enterprises) but includes farmers (even though, similarly, these may be subject to a procedure as the owners of an enterprise) based on the fact that the law in the selected cases addresses the former in terms of a legal entity and the latter as individuals. For the purposes of this study, the distinction is justified by the fact that when discussing the relationship between the ECJ and European society and especially when considering the 'individual rights narrative' we are not discussing businesses but individuals. Additionally, it is safe to assume mo-

20 http://curia.europa.eu/.

tives of individually affected litigants to be of a different nature than motives in the case of a business.

Since there was no option in the Court's database to select cases based on types of litigant (no possibility of selecting either natural persons, businesses or institutions), the only way was to go over the Court's documents case by case. Any case in which at least one individual was mentioned as a party in the proceedings was selected. This excluded cases involving only institutions, corporations or other organizations.[21] This method of selection resulted in a total of forty-six different preliminary reference cases that involved an individual litigant (out of a total of 100 references). Of these cases six were joined with other cases by the ECJ,[22] resulting in a total of forty separate cases, as dealt with by the Court. Of these forty cases thirty-six received an actual judgment (of which two were by way of reasoned order[23]) and four cases were removed from the register because at some point in the proceedings the request for a preliminary ruling had been retracted. These forty cases thus constituted all of the ECJ cases involving individual litigants originating from Dutch courts and tribunals over the selected five-year period. They form the basis of analysis in this study.

The description of cases and quotes has been anonymised as much as possible without losing the context of a case or subject. Where cases are dealt with without anonymisation or where complete anonymity could not be guaranteed (through the context of a case) respondents have been asked for their explicit consent. In order to facilitate readability throughout the book and in order to improve anonymisation of respondents, the twenty-six cases studied have been given nicknames in order to be able to refer back to them without having to describe continuously their context and subject and without using the official names assigned to the cases by the ECJ, which may refer back to the names of individual litigants. *Appendix A* includes nicknames and short descriptions of the

21 This process of selection was not always straightforward. For instance, some cases, which in first instance showed an individual as party to the proceedings, had to be excluded on closer inspection due to the fact that the individual mentioned turned out to be an appointed liquidator, managing the assets of a corporation that had become insolvent. As a guiding principle of selection those individuals involved had to be a natural person. This thus excluded individuals acting in other than a personal capacity.

22 Typically, the Court joins references cases that are filed by the same national judge, on or around the same day, involving the same legal dispute (although each reference involves a separate litigating party). In my analysis I treat these joined cases as a single reference.

23 Article 99 of the Rules of Procedure of the Court of Justice of the European Union: 'Where a question referred to the Court for a preliminary ruling is identical to a question on which the Court has already ruled, where the reply to such a question may be clearly deduced from existing case-law or where the answer to the question referred for a preliminary ruling admits of no reasonable doubt, the Court may at any time, on a proposal from the Judge-Rapporteur and after hearing the Advocate General, decide to rule by reasoned order.'

cases to help the reader when needed. In the text, cases will be referred to by their nickname, while *Appendix A* includes the official case number for reference.

Interviews

The aim was to interview actors involved in these cases in order to both reconstruct the case trajectories, as well as get the participants' perspective on the procedures. A total of forty-five semi-structured interviews were conducted, of which thirty-five interviews were with the parties directly involved in the selected cases: twenty-three with counsellors (lawyers and advisors), eleven with individual litigants and one counsellor for the opposing party. An additional ten of the total of forty-five interviews were conducted with other actors involved in the preliminary reference, including academic experts (four), one staff member of the European Commission's legal department (one), one former agent of the Netherlands before the Court of Justice (one), additional counsellors with experience of preliminary references falling outside the selection period (two), and representatives of a labour union (one) and an NGO (one) involved in litigation before the ECJ. Additionally, several informal conversations and meetings with counsellors, union representatives and EU law scholars took place, which were used as reference material. These supplementary interviews were conducted with lawyers involved in proceedings that fell outside the selected period and several informal interviews at a meeting aimed at working out supranational litigation strategies with regard to the rights of asylum seekers and refugees.

In addition to my own fieldwork, a number of interviews were conducted by law students of the Faculty of Law of the Radboud University Nijmegen in the context of the course 'Sociology of Law in European Perspective', which served as an exploratory phase of this research. A total of eight cases were dealt with, and related to these a total of thirteen interviews were conducted by students. They also included interviews with several parties in cases that fell outside the selected period for this research. The quality of these interviews varied considerably, from very brief surveys by email to extensive in-depth interviews. These cases included, next to the preliminary references, direct actions and cases not involving individuals, but small businesses or organizations. For the purposes of this study, most of these additional interviews were used to explore the viability of the research design and as complementary data in analysis.

Respondents were traced by different means. Information on parties directly involved in the ECJ proceedings were collected using ECJ documentation, especially judgments, wherein in most cases the names of the litigants were mentioned, occasionally including place of residence, and in most cases including the names of their legal representatives. On occasion, national court documents had to be consulted in order to trace counsel because, depending on whether the counsel had been physically present at the ECJ hearing,[24] they were not always listed in ECJ documents. This was especially the case where a court hearing had not taken place and the counsel had submitted no written observations. Because of their professional registration, counsel was generally easier to trace than individuals for whom usually only a name was available. Most counsellors were approached directly, some via intermediaries. Individuals were approached directly or via their lawyer.

As part of the fieldwork for this study, in twenty-six out of the forty selected cases at least one of the parties involved (litigant, lawyer and/or third party) was traced and interviewed. The larger part of the analyses is based on these interviews. In the remaining fourteen out of forty cases, none of the parties directly involved were successfully traced, either due to a lack of personal information, respondents living abroad, in two cases because the litigants were now deceased, or those involved were unwilling to participate. With the exception of one interview that was conducted via online videoconference with a respondent abroad, and one interview over the phone, all interviews were carried out face to face. The choice for the location of the interview was left to the respondents. In the case of legal professionals this was usually at their office, and in the case of the individuals this was at their home. The average duration of the interviews was approximately 1.5 hours, ranging from forty minutes to two hours and forty-five minutes. The interviews were conducted between the spring of 2013 and the summer of 2016, with the majority in 2013 and 2014. Most respondents were interviewed separately. In two instances both individual and counsellor were interviewed simultaneously. Forty-five semi-structured interviews were subsequently transcribed verbatim and analysed using qualitative data analysis software Atlas.ti.

Case studies

The starting point for the case studies was four of the ECJ judgments that were part of the research selection. The aim of the in-depth case studies was to reveal their genesis and evolution from the perspective of those behind the legal action and place them in their larger legal and political context. By tracing the way in which these cases had originated and evolved, the case studies reconstructed the events and actors' efforts that led to these four specific ECJ judgments. The case studies allowed for further investigation into the consequences and further de-

24 Not all ECJ cases include a court hearing. Therefore the names of counsel are only available in the court's documents whenever there has been a hearing, and the counsel in question actually attended.

velopments surrounding the subjects of the cases and provided a substantive account of the different ways in which EU law had been mobilised at the local level.

The four case studies are included separately and are scattered throughout the book in-between the chapters. The selection of these specific cases from among the broader case selection was partly based on theoretically informed *a priori* criteria. Among these was the aim to ensure empirical variety of both legal subjects and types of litigants, and a prerequisite of having more than one respondent available who had been part of the litigation effort. However, not all criteria were formulated prior to the actual case selection. Since many relevant aspects of the cases studied surfaced only after the initial phase of empirical work (exploration, reading and interviewing) a number of criteria were more emergent and unforeseen. Substantively, these cases were selected based on their ability to illustrate varying themes that were relevant to the analyses throughout the book. The cases should therefore be read as illustrative with regard to certain subjects. The choice for such themes was based not on their prevalence, but on their salience with respect to certain themes. For example, the last case study (*Integration Abroad*) is used mainly to illustrate Member States governments' ability to influence and obstruct certain legal developments and prevent unwelcome judgments by the ECJ.

The abundance of both legal and non-legal perspectives and materials in these case studies necessitated certain selection. The methodology used for the focus of analysis can be considered abductive. Abduction is the method through which the researcher follows the questions, puzzles and problems as they present themselves during analysis. Following particular themes and issues (informed by preliminary analysis and further conceptualisation), analysis focused more on certain aspects while other (in other respects possibly interesting) elements remained less developed. Consequently, empirical materials for the different cases were selected and collected based on a combination of induction and deduction, rather than being driven by an aspiration to be comprehensive. Below is a short description of the types of sources that were used for the different case studies.

Case Study A: Catering Employees

The analysis in *Case Study A* on the rights of employees is based on newspaper articles, legal academic literature on the court cases, as well as information available on a website set up by the employees to inform all those involved of relevant developments, including correspondence with their former and current employer, court documents and online discussions among the employees.[25] Ad-

25 http://www.bierkater.nl/ [last accessed 2 November 2017]; the website is no longer updated.

ditionally three semi-structured interviews were conducted with the employee largely responsible for the legal action, the lawyer in the court proceedings and a legal expert from the labour union who supported the employees.

Case Study B: Pensioners Abroad
The analysis in *Case Study B* on the pensioners is based on newspaper articles, secondary legal analysis, as well as information retrieved from the website created by the association for the purposes of informing the large membership and other affected pensioners of the developments surrounding their (legal) actions.[26] The extensive information available on this website included correspondence of the association with government officials, relevant decisions by government bodies and insurance companies, court documents and online discussions among the members of the association. Additionally, four semi-structured interviews were conducted with two of the leading members including the chair of the association and two of the involved individual litigants.

Case Study C: Fees in Migration Law
The analysis in *Case Study C* on the fees in migration law is based on documentation provided by two key actors: the files of the Consultative Council of Turkish Migrants in the Netherlands (*Stichting Inspraak Orgaan Turken in Nederland*, IOT) as well as the personal dossier of one of the academics involved in the working group that was responsible for the legal action. These files were provided to the Institute for Sociology of Law of the Radboud University for the purposes of this research. The dossiers, consisting of five binders and a CD-ROM with documents, contain collections of legal documents such as the judgments, opinions and memoirs of relevant court cases as well as minutes of meetings of the working group responsible for the litigation efforts and internal communications and emails. Additionally, several semi-structured interviews were conducted with the actors involved, including the previously mentioned academic, the lawyer central to the court cases, three lawyers laterally involved in the working group, a representative from the IOT as well as the individual litigant.

Case Study D: Integration Abroad
The analysis in *Case Study D* on the Dutch policy on integration abroad is, apart from the study of newspaper articles and secondary legal analysis of the court cases, mainly based on four semi-structured interviews conducted with the academic involved in the effort to put pressure on the Dutch policy, the lawyer in

26 http://www.vngsint.com/ [last accessed 15 February 2016]; the website is no longer available and has been replaced by https://vbngb.eu/ [last accessed 2 November 2017].

the case, a representative of the Dutch Refugee Council and a former representative of the Netherlands before the ECJ.

1.5 Aims and Limitations

Before moving on to a discussion of the literature on the Court and Euro-litigation, I want to make clear what one should and should not expect from this study. By looking at litigation before the ECJ through the preliminary reference procedure from the ground up, this study aims to offer a better understanding of the relationship between local interests, litigation and judicial politics from a relatively understudied perspective, namely the micro and local level, connecting the EU and its legal system to its constituents.

This study thus aims to understand and explore the *how* of Euro-litigation through the preliminary reference procedure. The focus is on one particular element: the practice of references and the position of the individual within litigation dynamics. Admittedly, when approaching the subject of Euro-litigation in this way, this study has some inherent limitations. The social realities of qualitative, in-depth study make for a reduced number of bases to potentially cover. Firstly, a lack of base line comparison limits the possibility of projecting findings of this analysis on to possible long-term trends. We will be looking with a microscope, which we cannot use to look at the stars. Secondly, the focus will be on only one Member State. A comparison with other Member States lies beyond the scope of this study, and therefore insights will vary in their generalizability to other Member States or other contexts. Thirdly, not all actors potentially involved in litigation will be part of the analysis. The explicit focus on the perspective of the litigating parties runs the risk of underestimating the relevance of other actors and factors: i.e. national judge, opposition parties, structural dynamics etc. A further limitation, the focus on only 'individual litigants' as subject of study, requires some further clarification. This study includes a tentative assessment of the salient question of whether EU litigation is "monopolized by the powerful or open to participation by the marginalized".[27] And while the effort to provide a full picture of the structural imbalances in EU law litigation would advocate for inclusion of businesses as well, the set-up of this research – only spanning a five-year period and having a small-n case selection – does not allow for structural comparison over a longer period of time and would run the risk of over-essentializing certain differences. Alternatively, a more focused approach on certain of these features – e.g. the type of legal representation of litigants: specialized in EU, large versus small law firms, international orienta-

27 Pavone 2016.

tion etc. – would be more fruitful in trying to uncover structural imbalances. In that respect, differently structured studies, like the novel spatio-temporal approach by Kelemen and Pavone trying to explain temporal and spatial variation in the use of the preliminary reference procedure,[28] are promising in discerning meaningful structural comparisons. As for this study, its theoretical contribution should be sought not in testing such hypotheses, but in raising new questions and suggesting new narratives for the study of the role of law in Europe, as well as to critically approach some existing ones.

The aim of this study is therefore ambitious in one sense and modest in another. The ambition lies in trying to connect the local with the supranational; the micro with the macro. By utilizing in-depth methodology and bringing out the micro perspective, the aim is to contribute to a more 'embodied' understanding of Euro-litigation. The modest aim lies in the fact that the analysis as well as the results will be limited when it comes to discerning general trends or giving a comprehensive account of the phenomenon under study. However, a distinct advantage of in-depth study is that elements are revealed that may go unnoticed or that become obscured when one aims for the largest possible variance in predetermined factors. The trade-off is therefore that the micro approach offers the distinct advantage of revealing details that help to better understand the complexities and context of Euro-litigation, which in macro approaches remain underexposed or even entirely invisible. When taking into account these caveats and acknowledging them here wholesale, the insights gained from such an approach should outweigh its shortfalls at least by the fact that these methods are the only way to break into the world of litigation at the ground level. It is submitted that these insights are invaluable when questioning the underpinnings of the more meta-narratives on European integration and the relationship between European law and democracy.

1.6 Structure of the Book

The book is divided into four parts. Part I (Chapters 2 and 3), starts with a description of the theoretical position of the individual in the European legal system, and reviews the literature on the ECJ and litigation. Chapter 2 deals with the narratives surrounding the Court and the way in which it is portrayed as an ally to civil society and European citizens. Chapter 3 goes deeper into the theories of European integration that have sought to explain the dynamics of the European legal system, and exposes some of the inherent dead angles in both

28 Kelemen & Pavone 2016.

legal and political science approaches to the topic of European integration and the ECJ.

Part II (Chapters 4, 5 and 6) presents the results of the empirical analysis, guided by the question: who goes to court in Europe, and why? Chapter 4 deals with the assumptions of rational action and interest in previous studies on Euro-litigation, gives a tentative typology of individual litigants in the Dutch context and analyses the various ways in which national court cases reach the ECJ. Chapter 5 focuses further on how individual cases may be proxies for larger interests, either by organised collectives or due to the transformative effects of a reference to the ECJ. It deals with how lawyers aim to have cases referred to the ECJ as well as the tensions that arise between litigants and lawyers aiming to serve more collective interests. Chapter 6 directs our attention to the practical aspects of 'lawyering a reference' and focuses on the ways in which legal practitioners deal with the challenges in exercising their professional duties when confronted with a reference to the ECJ.

Building on the insights about the potential in preliminary reference cases for the championing of collective interests, Part III (Chapters 7 and 8) deals with the more strategic aspects of Euro-litigation and places the actors in a field of opportunities and constraints, pitting them against other interested parties in order to map out the legal arena at the supranational level. Chapter 7 aims to answer the question of the strategic employment of EU law, and dissects who is (most) likely and able to use the preliminary reference procedure as a means to an end. Chapter 8 subsequently focuses on two other actors that feature prominently in the supranational legal arena – the European Commission and the Member States – and analyses the ways in which litigating parties may be confronted with extra opposition or how they may find allies or opponents before the ECJ.

Part IV reflects on the analyses presented in Parts II and III. Chapter 9 returns to the main question of this study and reflects on the main findings in light of the theoretic frame sketched out in Chapters 2 and 3. The final chapter concludes with an impetus for further research by offering several new avenues for inquiry.

The four more in-depth case studies are included throughout the book to provide substantive and illustrative material for analyses in the various chapters. They are written in a largely descriptive manner and can be read separately from the main chapters of the book. Conversely, the analyses in the chapters draw on insights from the case studies but recapitulate where necessary; therefore the main chapters can be read without examining the case studies.

Part I

2 Promises and Expectations

2.1 Introduction

When it was founded, the European legal system was not particularly integrated, and the position the ECJ now enjoys, as an important adjudicator in an impressive supranational legal constellation, was not evident from the outset. The creation of an integrated community in Europe was a contested project from the very early days. As a first step towards a better understanding of the relationship between the Court and Europe's citizens, this chapter deals with the way in which the European legal system evolved and how the relationship between the ECJ and the citizens of Europe developed over time. It discusses the narratives on the ECJ as a 'people's court' and the ways in which the Court has tried to draw legitimacy directly from the peoples of Europe, mainly by pointing especially to the benefits its judgments created for European citizens. I will describe the tensions that exist between the ideological position of the European citizen as a 'subject of EU law', the 'emancipatory functionalism' that is seen as legitimizing the ECJ itself, and the institutional position of the citizen within the European legal system.

2.2 The Promise of the European Court of Justice

The interlinked processes of juridification – the increase in laws that permeate more and more spheres of social life, and the related judicialization – the increased inclination by people to regulate social relations by settling disputes within the sphere of law, give rise to an augmentation of the political weight of judicial decision-making. It is in this light that some describe how judges in general increasingly view themselves as the 'keepers of promises'.[1] Because of this trend of judicialization "judges will be called upon more and more to uphold not just the law but moral standards, legitimate expectations, fairness: to keep everyone's promises".[2] The waning of the nation-state as a national collective and more or less clearly demarcated political entity has, in the international sphere, amplified the role of law as an instrument of governance as well as the curbing of state power. The growing distrust in government and administration purportedly has propelled the judge into the position of what Shapiro has called

1 Garapon 1996.
2 Schepel & Blankenburg 2001, 9.

the 'anti-bureaucratic hero'.[3] This curbing of state power is inscribed in the possibility of judicial review of legislation and administration. In the European context, through the doctrines of 'direct effect' and 'supremacy' of EU law, the ECJ effectively affirmed the possibility of judicial review of national administrative action at the supranational level, and with it itself as the arbitrator with final jurisdiction. The ECJ, according to legal sociologists Schepel and Blankenburg, is the keeper of this 'greatest of promises', the protection of citizens against the abuse of power by the state.[4] By placing the individual (and not the peoples, or states) 'at the heart of its activities',[5] the EU has formulated its objective of 'the creation of an area of freedom, security and justice' for its citizens,[6] and by effect the ECJ acts as the 'conscience' of the peoples of Europe.

Sticking to this 'language of promises' the ECJ has made significant promises to the European citizen. The landmark decision of the Court in *Van Gend & Loos* in 1963 was not only a first step in effectively establishing the political union as a legal unity, it also expressed a clear vision by the Court of the stake European citizens were to have in this 'ever closer union of the peoples of Europe'. Against the explicit objection of the Member States,[7] the Court proclaimed that:

> "[T]he Community constitutes a new legal order [...] for the benefit of which the states have limited their sovereign rights, albeit within limited fields, and the subjects of which comprise not only Member States but also their nationals. Independently of the legislation of the Member States, Community law therefore not only imposes obligations on individuals but it also intended to confer upon them rights which become part of their legal heritage. These rights arise not only where they are expressly granted by the Treaty, but also by reason of obligations which the Treaty imposes in a clearly defined way upon individuals as well as upon the Member States and upon the institutions of the Community."[8]

Van Gend & Loos constituted recognition of the interests of individuals in EU law and transformed the EU legal system, by formally including the citizens of Europe, who were now able to assert EU law rights before national courts. Arti-

3 Shapiro 1993, 47.
4 Schepel & Blankenburg 2001, 9.
5 European Commission 2010.
6 Article 67 of the Treaty on the Functioning of the European Union (from here on: TFEU). With respect to the ambitions of the European Union, see the famous quote by Jean Monnet, one of the 'founding fathers' of the European Economic Community: "Nous ne coalisons pas les états, nous rassemblons les hommes." Thus, heralding at once the renewed focus on the individual and the diminishing of state sovereignty.
7 Craig & De Búrca 2003, 204.
8 Case 26/62, *Van Gend & Loos v Tariefcommissie* [1963], ECR I, 12.

cle 67(1) of the Treaty on the Functioning of the European Union (TFEU) furthermore provides for the constitution of "an area of freedom, security and justice with respect for fundamental rights and the different legal systems and traditions of the Member States".[9] And through its case law the ECJ contributes to "[the creation of] a legal environment for citizens by protecting the rights, which European Union legislation confers on them in various areas of their daily life".[10] The Court itself does not shy away from this message, and emphasising the significance of its work for the benefit of 'the people'. For instance, one of the Court's press releases announcing its annual report reads: "The cases dealt with [...] once again demonstrate the importance of Community law in the day-to-day life of citizens of the Union".[11] And on its website the Court recurrently relates its case law to the purported benefits this has brought to Europe's citizens, especially stressing the 'fundamental freedoms' of the EU, the protection of fundamental rights, social and equality rights and citizenship. Thus, the ECJ presents itself, and draws legitimacy from, the idea of a court for the benefit of the peoples of Europe.[12]

2.3 The Promise of EU Law

The legal order of the EU functions as an important unifying factor in European society, regulating relations between Member States, EU institutions and citizens as subjects of EU law. European governance is 'legalized' to a high degree. The EU is not merely created by law; it also pursues its objectives by means of law. The common economic and social life of the peoples of Europe is governed to a large degree by the law of the Union. In this sense, European society is above all a 'community based on law'. According to the so-called integration-through-law narrative, law has succeeded in Europe where 'iron and blood' have failed in the past.[13] Through the proliferation of binding legislation at the EU level, more and more aspects of life in Europe are regulated at the supranational level and ultimately fall under the jurisdiction of the Court of Justice of the European Union, which has the task to 'ensure that in the interpretation and application of the Treaties the law is observed'.[14] An important characteristic of this

9 Article 67(1) TFEU.
10 https://curia.europa.eu/jcms/jcms/Jo2_7024/en/ [last accessed 7 November 2017].
11 ECJ Press release 18/99, 18 March 1999, available at http://curia.europa.eu/en/actu/communiques/cp99/cp9918en.htm [last accessed 7 November 2017].
12 Wernicke 2007.
13 Vauchez 2008b.
14 Article 13 TEU.

system of law is that not only the Member States, but also individuals, are subject to that law. The expanding scope of EU law, penetrating national legal systems and framing national policy to a large extent, has increased the significance of the EU legal system in the lives of EU citizens. Article 2 TEU states:

> "The Union is founded on the values of respect for human dignity, freedom, democracy, equality, the rule of law and respect for human rights, including the rights of persons belonging to minorities. These values are common to the Member States in a society in which pluralism, non-discrimination, tolerance, justice, solidarity and equality between women and men prevail."

Furthermore Article 3 TEU stresses that the Union not only promotes the well-being of its peoples, but it shall also offer its citizens an 'area of freedom, security and justice without internal frontiers'. This formulation of the promise made by the European Union directly to the peoples of Europe highlights the nature of the Union as going beyond mere intergovernmental politics.

In addition, a strong focus on individual rights manifest in the EU's legislation was reiterated in 2010 in the so-called 'Stockholm Programme' which states that "[p]riority should be given to mechanisms that facilitate access to justice, so that people can enforce their rights throughout the Union".[15] This European 'language of rights' or 'rights based regime' – the notion that the EU legal system functions by formulating (enforceable) rights – stood at the basis of much change within Europe. Through the jurisprudence of the ECJ in judgments on preliminary references and the efforts of the European Commission in holding Member States accountable for their failure to comply with EU law, the EU has been able to extend the reach of supranational influence on national policy. Schepel describes this idea of 'emancipatory functionalism' as one of the apparent self-legitimating descriptions of the role of EU law by the earliest lawyers of the 'European persuasion'.[16] These Europeans of the first hour saw in European law the next step in the expansion of social life beyond the nation-state and saw law as "liberating civil society from the shackles of parliamentary democracies".[17] This self-description, according to Schepel, is essential in understanding, on the one hand, the success of the European legal system (in that it effectively worked as described, most notably in curtailing the power of the nation-states), but on the other hand, also in the ways in which this system has been justified and legitimized by its propagators, by reference to the individual empowerment and benefit that allegedly resulted from it. The generous assumption is that "[l]aw belongs to civil society, and civil society finds in European law the

15 European Council 2010, 4.
16 Schepel 2004, 3.
17 Schepel 2004, 2.

framework for its cross border dynamism".[18] The sole authority of the ECJ to interpret EU legislation combined with a growing focus on individual rights seems to signal a shift towards greater empowerment of the individual within the European legal system, by giving him or her a voice at the supranational level. In the famous words of Federico Mancini – one of the most influential ECJ judges in the history of the institution – "[taking] law out of the hands of bureaucrats and politicians and [giving] it to the people".[19] As such, Schepel views this legitimizing rhetoric as "a spectacularly unsubstantiated claim to the loyalties of Europe's citizenry".[20] Apart from an attempt to shield the nascent legal system from criticism and drawing legitimacy directly from the peoples of Europe, European law also needed the citizen for another purpose, as I will describe in the next paragraph.

2.4 Giving the Citizen a Role in European Law Enforcement

Apart from making a promise to European citizens, the European legal system also has a more functional role reserved for private parties in the enforcement of EU rules. Private enforcement of EU law through the courts has been an essential element in the functioning of the European legal system. In fact, the EU, with its significantly limited administrative capacity, has always struggled to ensure compliance by the Member States. One of the ways this has been offset has been by relying on the legal system to reveal and address breaches of EU law obligations by Member States. As a result, the enforcement of EU law relies in large part on private parties invoking EU law before national courts. With this in mind, the European Commission calls upon citizens to actively enforce their rights under EU law and it is a fervent proponent of private standing to enforce EU legal norms.[21] For example, Kelemen describes what he calls the 'Passenger rights saga', wherein the European Commission sponsored posters featured at European airports informing passengers of their right, under EU law, to compensation for delayed flights.[22] The passenger rights saga not only encompasses these efforts by the Commission but includes a strain of litigating efforts before the ECJ that has served to both establish as well as expand individual rights, which, according to Kelemen, illustrate a new trend of practices throughout

18 Schepel 2004, 2.

19 Mancini & Keeling 1994, 183.

20 Schepel 2004, 2.

21 European Commission 2008.

22 Similarly, the 'Citizens First Initiative' launched by the European Commission aimed at increasing people's awareness of rights conferred upon them by EU law and to help those who have difficulty in exercising those rights.

Europe. He concludes: "The emphasis on the language of rights – EU rights no less – and the courtroom battles between regulators and the regulated would have been out of step with the more cooperative and decidedly less judicialized approaches to regulation that prevailed across Europe [well into the 1980s]."[23]

Box II: The Enforcement of EU Law

The European Union and its courts cannot alone ensure the effective application of European Union law. It depends strongly on domestic courts, individuals and organisations that initiate proceedings before these courts to enforce their rights under European Union law. The domestic judge must apply European Union law because it enjoys precedence over domestic law. Any conflicting provision of national law is inapplicable. The domestic judge can apply European Union law because it has direct effect, if it is sufficiently clear and unconditional. The provisions of the Treaties and of Regulations as such do not require any additional measures by Member States to become effective. In contrast, Directives require transposition into national law by Member States within a certain time limit. Nevertheless, once the time limit for their implementation has expired Directives, too, can have direct effect. European Union law can also have indirect effects because all provisions of domestic law must be interpreted, as far as possible, in order to achieve the result sought by the relevant European Union law, its effet utile. Finally, European Union law requires effective judicial protection, which means that if European Union law creates rights, Member States must provide access to courts to enforce these rights.

This judicialized approach has been part and parcel of governance in Europe and in practice diminishes the enforcement burden on European public authorities.[24] Moreover, this form of mobilisation of EU law by private actors through litigation above and against their state is a symbolic and potentially real shift of power from the states towards their citizens, and is a weapon in the hands of those aiming to further integration.[25] In this sense, litigation opportunities can be seen as an "attempt to extend the types of juridical checks found at the domestic level to the international governance level",[26] and an effort to extend the scope and enhance the power of EU law. On the impact of European integration on the lives of European citizens, Mancini and Keeling write: "And let there be no mistaking the impact of Community law on the citizens of Europe. Natural and legal persons are intimately involved in the application of the Treaty by the Community institutions and the Member States. They are the ones who profit directly by an unhindered flow of goods, services and capital throughout the common market; they are the beneficiaries of the rules on labour mobility and of

23 Kelemen 2011, 5.
24 de Waele 2010, 65.
25 Mancini & Keeling 1994, 183.
26 Alter 2010, 22.

the right to share, on a par with local workers, the social advantages available in the country to which they move."[27]

Within this narrative, the role of the ECJ is seen as having been invaluable for promoting and ensuring individuals' rights. EU law, in this line of reasoning, has not only transformed the face of Europe but also actively promoted the rights of the European citizen. At the same time, the citizen, as a 'private enforcer', has been integral to the application of EU law at the national level. The next paragraphs deal with the ways in which this new role for the European citizen can also be seen to expand his or her power in the political realm.

2.5 EU Law and the New 'Public Power'

The supremacy and direct applicability of EU law have served as federalizing instruments, altering the status of states in international law and introducing private parties as subjects of international law.[28] By granting access to the Court, the EU legal system contributes to expanding the public power of private parties, who are now able to subject government acts to judicial scrutiny.[29] And this in turn implies the establishment of a 'European rule of law', with a common judicial tribunal with sole jurisdiction over EU law: the ECJ. Alongside the doctrines of *supremacy* and *direct effect*, more recent developments in EU citizenship case law and the area of freedom, security and justice are giving more and more substance to the idea of European rule of law, protecting the fundamental values listed in the Treaties, including democracy and fundamental rights.[30] One element strongly connected with the idea of the rule of law is what is called 'public power', which entails the possibility of non-state actors, including individuals, to invoke judicial authority against the abuse of power by the state.

A public power approach to the institutional role of the ECJ as 'supreme court' of the EU postulates that, since the Court has jurisdiction over the interpretation of EU law especially where it relates to national governmental action,

27 Mancini & Keeling 1994, 182.

28 Cf. Weiler, who critically examines the actual status of individuals as 'subjected' but not 'subjects'. On understanding the relation between law and democracy in Europe he writes: "Individuals, not only States, are thus subjects. Semantically, in English, 'subjects' is often synonymous with citizenship. The Queen's subjects of old are the present citizens of the Realm. It could seem, thus, that in the very articulation of one of the principle 'constitutionalizing' doctrines – direct effect – the condition was provided by elevating individuals to the status of full subjects alongside Member States." [...] "But note, individuals are 'subjects' only in the (direct) *effect* of the law. In this sense alone is Europe a new legal order. [...] Enjoying rights created by others does not make you a full subject of the law." Weiler 1998, 380.

29 With restrictions of course, see Scheingold 1965.

30 Micklitz 2012.

it effectively enforces the power of constitutional judicial review.[31] Access to courts from a supranational rule of law perspective thus brings with it elements of scale and impact not found at the national level.[32] Access to justice in this supranational setting is seen by some as empowering citizens to influence national policy, and by extension the scope of international constitutionalism, through the opportunity to invoke the reviewing powers of a higher judicial authority. [33] In the case of the EU, this judicial authority is the ECJ, which is charged with the task of ensuring a uniform interpretation and application of EU rules and norms. Access to the ECJ might thus provide the individual a stake in a game in which he or she is structurally disadvantaged. As stated by Dalton, Cain and Scarrow: "From a strictly governmental perspective, the expansion of the opportunity for citizens [to influence legislative and administrative decisions] alters the administrative structure in very important ways, and might have significant long-term effects on systemic performance and policy legitimacy."[34]

This expansion of the public power of citizens through the legal system is of course predicated on the accessibility of judicial institutions. However, the *locus standi* of individuals before the ECJ has been shaped only restrictively, as will be explained in the next section.

2.6 Access to the European Court of Justice

As we have seen, the Court portrays its own role within European society as a protector of citizens' rights, and the reviewing powers of the Court are seen by some as the best example of citizens' empowerment against their national government. Although the Court presents itself as the "embodiment of a new European *Volksgeist*, one that emphasizes the emancipatory power of legal rationality over (national) politics and judicial process over political debate",[35] such celebratory proclamations should be approached with some scepticism. For one, the European citizen has never enjoyed full and direct access to the Court. As Costa's critical study of direct litigation before the Court reveals, there is no mention of the terms 'citizens' or 'individuals' in any of the texts, projects and reports of the ECJ.[36] Neither term exists in any rules and regulations that address the procedures of the Court, which Costa takes to be a token of the gap between

31 Shapiro 1998.
32 It should be noted that – while not in the Netherlands – a number of EU countries have constitutional courts that have similar institutional positions.
33 Kumm 2011.
34 Dalton, Cain, & Scarrow 2003, 265-6.
35 Schepel & Blankenburg 2001, 11.
36 Costa 2003, 750.

the Court's self-portrait and the concrete possibilities for any private litigant to go to court.[37] The official denotation of parties is by the word 'person' and the rules of procedure only distinguish between 'natural' and 'legal' persons on one occasion.[38] Costa concludes on this point that the Court's judges consider the Court to be the guardian of the respect for Union law (as is its mandate through Article 19 TEU) in order to further European integration, "but not as a means for citizens to be involved in the governance of the Union, or to be protected from excesses from Community institutions. Legal practice and judges' opinions lend little credit to the possible advent of a 'judicial democracy', which would go beyond the mere judicialization of European politics."[39]

For a court that has presented itself as being 'for the people'[40] it is not the most accessible institution for Europe's citizens. In reality, direct access to the ECJ by private parties is limited to contesting the validity of EU measures, and, from an individual's perspective, to the relationship between the citizen and the EU. Furthermore, the strict interpretation of standing rules for private parties by the ECJ means that EU measures can only be contested if and when they *directly* affect the individual. In practice, this means that only a small minority of private parties may be eligible to access the ECJ via this route. Individual claimants therefore make up only a fraction of these direct actions.[41] Based on interviews with its judges and clerks, and by studying the Court's case law as well as its internal structural reforms, Costa concludes that "[t]he [ECJ] seems to consider that broader dissemination of the Court's jurisprudence and the principle of supremacy of Community law over national law contribute more to democracy in the Union and better protection of fundamental rights than easier access to the Court".[42] This is in line with the conclusion drawn by Rasmussen decades earlier that the Court made efforts to channel questions of judicial review through preliminary references.[43] When looking at the possibility of direct petitioning of the Court's authority vis-à-vis the EU there is therefore a strong discrepancy between the restrictive access to the ECJ, limiting the possibilities of bringing

37 The only mention of the term individual is in Article 104§6 on the possibility of judicial aid by the ECJ.

38 Costa 2003, footnote 34. The selection of cases for this study also quickly revealed this lack of distinction in any of the Court's information, neither in any of the official documents of specific cases, nor in the statistics provided on the Court's judicial activity.

39 Costa 2003, 756.

40 Lecourt 1976, 309.

41 Additional to strict standing rules, Costa describes a few elements that can be dissuasive for potential litigants in deciding to start these kinds of proceedings: Length of the proceedings, legal costs and needed expertise combined with the risks of losing.

42 Costa 2003, 754.

43 Rasmussen 1986.

direct actions to a privileged minority, and the ambition of furthering legitimacy of the Court by directly addressing the European citizen.[44]

Box III: The Preliminary Reference Procedure

The responsibility for ensuring the enforcement of EU law in large part falls upon the national courts. In their capacity as 'decentralised EU judges' national judges are tasked with applying EU law in national proceedings. The Treaties have provided for a mechanism that allows national courts to usher in the assistance of the ECJ. Under Article 267 TFEU a national judge may request the ECJ to provide an interpretation of EU law that is needed to resolve a dispute pending before its court. Whenever there is doubt as to the interpretation and applicability of EU law in any case, national judges can (and in some instances must) refer the matter to the ECJ through a so-called request for a preliminary ruling.

The preliminary reference procedure performs three separate functions. Firstly, and most importantly, it ensures a uniform interpretation of EU law. Secondly, the procedure facilitates the application of EU law at the national level by offering national courts a 'helping hand' in resolving the problems that may accompany the application of EU law. And finally, the preliminary reference procedure may serve as a means to protect the rights that citizens derive from EU law.

Although formally the ECJ does not concern itself with the interpretation of national law, having jurisdiction only over the interpretation of Union law, the nature of preliminary rulings is often that of a veiled form of review. These rulings given by the Court, on the constituent elements of the reference made by the national judge(s), effectively function as vertical precedent in that the Court's decision provides an explanation on the basis of which the cases at hand are to be decided by the national judge. They also have horizontal effect in that the Court's decisions apply to all Member States and its rulings establish the principles on which courts in all Member States are to rule in similar cases in future.

During the examination of the question before the ECJ, proceedings before the national court will be suspended. Having received clarification from the ECJ, the national court then resumes its proceedings leading to its final judgment.

Critical literature more generally reveals, on the one hand, a discrepancy between the 'promise' of the Treaties and of the ECJ, and on the other hand, the practical impossibility of challenging legislative and administrative action, especially of EU institutions, by private parties.[45] On judicial protection and individual rights in a European context, Ward concludes that effective judicial protection and individual rights have been used in the European legal order to justify the 'federal-type' constitutional design as crafted over the years by the ECJ. The need for effective judicial protection and protection of individual rights has been expansively – yet selectively – addressed by the preliminary reference procedure

44 Costa 2003, 755.

45 Biernat 2003; Schepel & Blankenburg 2001; Costa 2003. And for a more fundamental critique of the empowering function of the European legal order see Weiler 1998.

in order to ensure the uniform enforcement of EU legislation at national level.[46] She finds that these imperatives have been actively addressed by the ECJ in anchoring EU law in the legal systems of the Member States but private parties have had little success in challenging EU institutions to the same degree, thus signifying the double standard developed over the years that constrains Member States but insulates EU institutions from similar judicial accountability for their actions. The growing role of EU regulations in the everyday life of citizens gives great significance to the question as to what possibilities citizens have in mobilising the authority of the Court, especially when considering the emphasis of the ECJ itself on ensuring an area of freedom, security and justice. To conclude, the opportunities for citizens to profit from this system seems to be limited to a large extent to the profits they may enjoy from EU law, and forcing compliance by their national government, by invoking EU law in national courts and by activating the preliminary reference procedure.

2.7 An Infringement Procedure for the European Citizen?

Over the years the ECJ has been fairly successful in enforcing compliance with EU legislation and its judgments. One structural ally for the Court in this respect has been the European Commission, that is tasked with ensuring compliance with EU law by Member States, and that can bring Member States before the Court on charges of not fulfilling their obligations under EU law. Since *Van Gend & Loos* it has become clear that the Court also, and arguably predominantly, relies on private parties to enforce EU law by mobilising their rights. The success, or relevance, of the preliminary reference procedure is reflected in the number of cases brought before the ECJ, which has been increasing steadily since the first reference in 1961, to upwards of 400 a year since 2011. The workload has increased to such an extent that in 2011 the Court requested that the rules of procedure be recast to reflect the predominance of the ECJ's caseload of preliminary rulings.[47]

Whereas the European Commission and the Member States can resort to Articles 258 and 259 TFEU, private parties are provided no 'European level' judicial control over Member States' violations of Treaty obligations. [48] They in turn have to rely on 'national level' control by invoking the direct effect of EU law in

46 Ward 2000.

47 Council of the European Union 2011.

48 In practice, due to the obvious political sensibility of such proceedings, Member States have proven very reluctant to use Article 259 against another Member State. To date, this has in fact only occurred four times. ECJ cases: C-141/78, C-388/95, C-145/04, C-364/10.

national court proceedings. While the enforcement function of the European Commission was clearly marked out in the Treaty from the outset, the second route to rights enforcement was developed some years later by the ECJ itself in *Van Gend & Loos*. In its judgment, the Court effectively established the legal means for private parties to hold Member States accountable for any violation of the rights conferred upon them by the Treaty, albeit in a less direct form than the procedures available for Member States and the European Commission. In addition, addressing objections by Member States, that argued that Articles 258 and 259 (then 169 and 170) TFEU already provided a system for exercising supervision of Treaty violations, the Court proclaimed: "The vigilance of individuals concerned to protect their rights amounts to an effective supervision in addition to the supervision entrusted by Articles 169 and 170 to the diligence of the Commission and of the Member States." Thus, a second avenue for challenging the breach of EU law, one that included private parties as possible benefactors of EU law, was called into existence.

This 'dual vigilance',[49] of both the European Commission and the population at large, not only made it more likely for Treaty provisions to be observed by contracting states, it also stood at the basis of the transformation of the entire European legal system. Private parties were now able to invoke EU law and rights conferred upon them before national courts. With regard to the main functions of the preliminary reference procedure[50] in particular and the ECJ's mandate in general, the ensuring of a uniform application of EU law in all Member States, it must be stressed that formally the ECJ does not have constitutional review powers. It has jurisdiction over international – and not constitutional – law. A true European constitution never made it beyond the 2005 referenda in the Netherlands and France, and the authority of the ECJ as the highest court of Europe, trumping national constitutions has not gone unchallenged.[51] On the other hand, although Member States do remain sovereign states with their own constitutions, the principles of direct effect and supremacy of EU law and the way the ECJ has interpreted and applied EU legislation has resulted in a body of higher order norms that has substantially constrained the manoeuvrability of the national legislature. In this respect Mancini and Keeling conclude:

> "[A]ware of the difficulties faced by the national judge, the Court does not confine itself to interpreting the Community rule; instead it enters into the heart of the conflict submitted to its attention, but it takes the precaution of rendering it abstract, that is to say it presents it as a conflict between Community law and a hypothetical

49 Weatherill 2014, 86.

50 See textbox at paragraph 2.6.

51 Mattli & Slaughter 1998, 191.

> national provision having the nature of the provision in issue before the national court. The technique thus described, which is formally impeccable and of great use to the national court, results in the Court of Justice acquiring a power of review which is analogous to – though of course narrower than – that routinely exercised by the Supreme Court of the United States and the constitutional courts of some Member States."[52]

Even though formally the Lisbon Treaty is not the constitutional document it was designed to be, in reality the practical design of the EU legal system has the effect as if it were. In this respect former ECJ judge Pierre Pescatore refers to the preliminary reference procedure as having effectively "become the infringement procedure for the European citizen".

The doctrines of direct effect and supremacy of EU law established by the Court in the early 1960s, transformed EU governance and paved the way for a decentralized form of enforcement. With EU law since then having direct effect at the national level, citizens, companies and groups were provided the means to challenge Member States' compliance with EU law. These parties are now able to invoke EU law directly before national judges and the preliminary reference procedure (now Article 267 TFEU) provides the means to activate the reviewing powers of the ECJ. The doctrine of supremacy of EU law has dramatically diminished public authorities' possibility of relying on national law to justify national policy and national judges, in their capacity as EU judges, are required to resolve any conflict between national and EU law by ruling in favour of the latter. For individuals, the preliminary reference procedure is as of now the principal route to the ECJ for supranational contesting of government action.[53] With reference to Dworkin, a report published by the European Parliament expresses this view on the preliminary reference procedure: "Thus, individuals may use EU law both as a 'shield' (to defend themselves from action by national authorities which infringes EU rights) and as a 'sword' (to challenge national measures on the grounds of incompatibility with EU laws). Consequently, the preliminary ruling procedure provides an opportunity for individuals and national courts to question governmental actions".[54] Considering that more and more areas of law are governed by EU rules and regulations, national governments' actions increasingly fall within the realm of EU law.

52 Mancini & Keeling 1994.

53 That is, apart from the direct review by national judges. See Claes & de Witte 1998.

54 European Parliament 2007, 13.

2.8 Conclusion

The relatively limited enforcement capacity of the EU in combination with the emergence of powerful courts encourages the EU legislator to "introduce directives and regulations with strict substantive and procedural requirements and to encourage judicial enforcement – including by private parties – of these legal norms".[55] Judicialization has thus formed a solution to the principal-agent problem in power delegation as a result of political fragmentation and the extremely limited administrative capacities of the EU. In others words, legislators "have an incentive to frame policies as rights and to encourage private parties to enforce them on their own through the courts".[56] Kelemen thus not only foresees a continuing increase in the judicialization of the political sphere but he gives much weight to the potential of private action in producing systemic change in the political structure. International regimes throughout the world are witnessing an increase in judicial authority and with it an "increase in the opportunity for individuals to bring rights claims, and a liberalization of legal standing rules enabling wider citizen and interest group participation in the development, monitoring and enforcement of laws".[57] International law in general, and EU law in particular, in effect functions as a form of restriction of the lawmaking power of national governments. Moreover, overcoming this restriction by changing legislation imposes a higher threshold on national governments when routine lawmaking is undesirably restricted by a higher order law, since changes must be effectuated by a different lawmaking body, namely at the supranational level. These changes are thus beyond the powers of the national lawmaking bodies to unilaterally alter. From a rule of law perspective this results in more effective limitations on lawmaking powers.[58] The involvement of private actors in the exercise of political power greatly influences the form of public power and with it the legitimacy of public institutions. The Court has effectively created a quasi-bill of rights in several countries that had previously not known such a body of judicially enforceable rights.[59]

The extension of the competence of the EU granted by earlier Treaties, beyond the purely economic, has increased the influence of the EU on domestic policy, and with it its significance in the lives of the European people. With the entry into force of the Lisbon Treaty, generally expanding the jurisdiction of the ECJ to interpret and review the EU 'area of freedom, security and justice' (AFSJ) legislation and policies, and by transforming the EU charter of funda-

55 Kelemen 2012, 58.
56 Kelemen 2012, 58.
57 Cichowski 2006, 6.
58 Tamanaha 2007.
59 The Netherlands is a notable example, see Claes & de Witte 1998.

mental rights into a legally binding 'bill of rights'[60] it can be expected that the ECJ will be called upon more often to review the implementation of EU legislation and practices in accordance with the EU charter. The role and function of the ECJ can thus be expected to change, as well as the relative position of both Member States and EU citizens. Earlier studies have shown how domestic policy terrains falling within these competences, under the influence of litigation before the ECJ, have been put under pressure and eventually conceded. Examples include consumer protection,[61] environmental policy and equal treatment,[62] and domestic commercial policy.[63]

The private access to the ECJ, channelled through the preliminary reference procedure, has potential impact on the whole of the EU and on domestic governance. As Alter has shown, private access to the compulsory jurisdiction of an international court as a tool for individuals to challenge the national implementation of supranational rules is a trait found only in Europe (ECJ and the ECtHR).[64] Although it is not clear whether in this respect EU courts are in fact the model or the exception, it seems that Europe provides a unique test case for this role played by courts and private parties in an international setting. Kelemen has described how increasing judicialization of the policy process serves as a solution in a constellation characterised by fragmentation and a principal-agent problem. It has incentivised lawmakers to frame policies as rights and to encourage private parties to enforce them on their own through the courts. It has encouraged judicial independence, strengthening courts to "act as a check against bureaucratic drift enforcing legal norms against bureaucratic agents who may seek to deviate from them". Not only has this process made both courts and citizens as litigants part of the institutional make-up of the European Union, framing policies in the language of individual rights has been thrust forward rhetorically as a promise to enhance the EU's legitimacy and show that it is serving the interests of its citizens.[65] This interrelation between court litigants and international governance is thus an important element in the EU legal structure that is bound to develop further. The rhetorical promise to European citizens gives reason for critical examination of the usage of European law by individuals and the preliminary reference procedure, connecting individuals with the ECJ, and allows for study of the way in which European law has found its way into the fabric of European society.

60 Guild 2010.
61 Kelemen 2011.
62 Cichowski 2007.
63 Rawlings 1993.
64 Alter 2006.
65 De Búrca 1995.

3 The Political Role of the ECJ

3.1 Introduction

Arguably, the most captivating feature of the ECJ as an international court is the pivotal role it performs at the intersection of the legal and political spheres. As a central actor in transforming the European legal system, the ECJ came to play an unmistakable part in the integration of Europe, with legal integration succeeding where political integration proved more difficult. As Scharpf concludes: "[B]y the end of the 1970s, European integration had reached a highly asymmetric institutional configuration: attempts to remove national barriers to trade through legislative harmonization continued to be severely impeded by the 'joint decision trap', whereas 'integration through law' was able to move forward without political interference through the seemingly inexorable evolution of judicial doctrines protecting and extending the Treaty-based rights of private individuals and firms."[1] The ECJ, through its doctrinal development, has thus been a central arena of political development in Europe. And although this idea of the Court as embodying one of the essential spaces where the government of Europe is being produced[2] is now well established, the scholarly interest in the Court did not get off to a flying start. This chapter outlines a brief historical overview of how and why the Court has gained scholarly interest over the last half a century, followed by a critical review of what has generally remained an underexplored element in the study of the Court; individual litigants and the very notion of 'interests'. Finally, I will outline how this study will contribute to taking the lid off this 'black box'.

3.2 Early Scholarly Interest in the Court of Justice

Before the 1980s, studies on European integration were characterised by their legalism and formalism and the Court attracted little attention from other than the legal disciplines in the first decades of its existence. As Snyder concluded: "[I]t has often been regarded (and taught) simply as a highly technical set of rules, a dense doctrinal thicket into which only the ignorant or the foolish would 'jump in and scratch out their eyes', still less try to understand in terms of social

1 Scharpf 2010, 220. The 'joint decision trap' refers to the idea that the requirement of unanimous decisions will systematically generate sub-optimal policy outcomes unless a 'problem-solving' (as opposed to a 'bargaining') style of decision-making can be maintained. See Scharpf 1988.

2 Vauchez 2007.

theories of law".[3] Stein's seminal 1981 article ushered in a new focus on a contextual analysis of the Court's case law. He described how the ECJ, while functioning 'under the radar' of the mass media and scholarly interest, in the first decades of its existence, transformed the traditionally international law methodology of the European Community Treaties and fashioned an essentially 'constitutional framework for a federal-type structure' in Europe.[4] Weiler furthered Stein's analysis by showing how this newly formed 'interstate government structure defined by a constitutional charter' transformed the relationship between the Member States and the Community. This was made possible by the ECJ's constitutional doctrines of supremacy and direct effect and the strengthening of legal ties of Member States to the Community's constitutionalized framework, effectively limiting Member States' options for non-compliance.[5] Weiler played an essential part in giving academic credentials to this theory, now known as the 'integration-through-law' theory, or more critically the 'Europeanization-though-law-narrative'.[6] He argued that the dwindling political push for integration during the 1960s and 70s was counterbalanced by the European legal system, with the European Court of Justice taking on the role of an integration actor.[7]

With this increasing awareness of the politically significant role played by the ECJ, the Court attracted attention as well as criticism, being deemed an activist court that usurped legislative functions. Contrary to the prevailing belief by EC legal scholars that the Court's case law encountered little resistance, Rasmussen famously argued in 1986 that numerous examples of attempts by the 'countervailing powers' (most notably the Member States) to curb the Court's power showed how the Court was stretching its legitimacy to the limit by encroaching on the legislative branch.[8] Although the Court had not been wholly immune from attacks by politicians, the criticisms did not pose a sustained challenge. Yet, with the ensuing debate,[9] Rasmussen's work did bring about an important impetus to the scholarly attention paid to the ECJ by both legal scholars with a normative approach to the Court's legitimacy, as well as a contextual ap-

3 Snyder 1987, 180.
4 Stein 1981. See also Mancini 1989, 596.
5 Weiler 1991.
6 *Integration-through-law* was the title of a large-scale research and multi-volume publication project launched at the European University Institute, Florence in 1981. For a critical analysis of the support which this concept had received early on from an enthusiastic Euro-law community, see Vauchez 2008b.
7 Integration is defined as the "*process*, leading gradually, with the passage of time, to an increase in the exchanges between the various societies concerned and to a more centralized form of government". Dehousse & Weiler 1990, 244. Emphasis in original.
8 Rasmussen 1986.
9 See especially Weiler 1987 as well as Cappelletti 1987.

proach 'beyond doctrine' that started to focus on judicial developments in relation to the reception of the Court's case law by other actors. In this new wave of interest the Court started attracting increased attention from political scientists interested in the relationship between law and politics.

3.3 Competing Political Science Perspectives on European Integration

With the notable exception of Scheingold,[10] who very early on recognised the Court's contribution to integration, political scientists were remarkably late in recognising the ECJ as an important political actor.[11] This changed after the aforementioned contributions by Stein and Weiler. Political researchers subsequently tried to explain how the ECJ's legal doctrines had become politically transformative within the social and political context. Within this new 'law in context' approach to the role of law in European integration, two contending paradigms – intergovernmentalism and neofunctionalism – battled over explaining the dynamics of legal integration, largely focusing on the relationship between the Court and the 'Masters of the Treaties'; the Member States.[12] As Conant describes, for political scientists "the spectre of a supranational court eliciting the obedience of states was puzzling from the perspective of traditional international relations theories".[13] The big question was how the ECJ had played a role in transforming Europe from an international free-trade constellation into a supranational polity, transcending state sovereignty. The two competing interpretative paradigms subsequently started quarrelling over the best explanation for the dynamic towards integration and supranationalization without the backlash of the nation-states who saw their sovereignty gradually diminish.

The first paradigm, the intergovernmentalist 'camp', most famously propagated by Garrett, contended that the ECJ encouraged compliance by aligning its decisions with the preferences of the most powerful states.[14] Based on a rational choice institutionalist approach, the Court in this view is seen as strategically positioning itself in relation to the preferences of the most powerful 'principals'. Basing his conclusions on traditional rational choice analysis and game theory, Garrett argued that the ECJ tends to uphold Member States' interests, being influenced by the reaction it expects from national governments, placing the Court under the Member States' ultimate control. The Court's mandate in this view derives from its "collective utility in enforcing pre-established bargains

10 Scheingold 1965.
11 Burley & Mattli 1993.
12 Alter 1998.
13 Conant 2007, 47.
14 Garrett 1992; 1995.

related to trade liberalization and efficiently filling gaps in the 'incomplete contract' of European law".[15]

The dismissal of judicial autonomy in the intergovernmentalist approach sparked a challenge by neofunctionalists who argued that legal integration did indeed erode the dominance of states, including the more powerful ones. This second paradigm, contrary to the intergovernmental view, submitted that legal integration was the result of the activity of both sub- and supranational actors that pursued their own interests. The neofunctionalist view accorded much more weight to the mechanism for dialogue between national judges and the ECJ, the preliminary reference procedure, and the resulting possibilities for judicial review of government acts. In their seminal contribution in which they outlined their 'political theory of legal integration', Burley and Mattli stressed the importance of the structures of opportunity that were created by the ECJ.[16] In a reasoning that ventures close to the ideal of the European legal system as described in Chapter 2, the neofunctionalist account described 'integration-through-law' in three constitutive elements.

The first element consists of the 'constitutional' doctrines of the European legal system that were created by the ECJ in a series of transformational judgments. As a second element, they identify, on the one hand, the mobilisation of EU law by multinational companies, transnational interest groups and EU institutions, seizing the newly formed institutional opportunities, and on the other hand, the national courts' progressive (yet turbulent[17]) acceptance of the general principles established by the ECJ. The final element of their theory sees the resulting dynamic, the support by private and national actors that in turn offers new opportunities for the Court to assert and extend the scope of its case law, thus creating a self-reinforcing mechanism that catches interest groups, multinationals, EU institutions, Member States and the ECJ in a virtuous circle of Europeanization.[18] This system has thus not been designed by any specific actor, has no principals and agents, but everybody contributes in its own way. The fact that national governments have accepted this transfer of power and undermining of their sovereignty is due to legal justifications masking the implications of rulings and as a result shielding the ECJ from attack.[19]

15 Conant 2007, 47.
16 Burley & Mattli 1993.
17 Mattli & Slaughter 1998, 191.
18 Stone Sweet 2004.
19 Burley & Mattli 1993; Mattli & Slaughter 1998.

3.4 The Magic Triangle of the Legal System

The competition between intergovernmentalist and neofunctionalist views of European integration to this day remains an instructive partition in the analysis of the tensions between supranationalization and more entrenchment on the part of Member States. However, the mechanism as described by the neofunctionalist account of integration has become widely accepted as an explanatory mechanism for how Europe's legal system and the ECJ have contributed to integration. The European political and economic integration has been to a great extent a legal process, the dynamics of which do not rely exclusively on some inherent force of EU law, or on the activism of the ECJ and the boldness of its rulings, but more widely on the way sub- and supranational actors have used the 'supremacy' and 'direct effect' doctrines of EU law in pursuit of their own interests. According to this theory of the dynamics behind this process of 'integration-through-law', it unfolded predominantly through the dynamics of the European legal system, and the activation of that system by various actors. Vauchez, analysing the genesis of 'integration-through-law' as a theory, describes how the 'magic triangle' of the EU legal system – the doctrines of direct effect and supremacy of EU law combined with the preliminary reference procedure – has come to be regarded as the explanatory mechanism for how Europe became more integrated through the functioning of its legal matrix: "Despite being possibly deterring for non-lawyers, ['direct effect', 'supremacy' and 'preliminary ruling'] have become crucial keywords for grasping the specific nature of the EU polity. Taken individually, any of these notions is merely a legal principle utterly incapable of founding a political order on its own. Taken together, their effects appear to beget a dynamic of circular reinforcement."[20] The combination of 'supremacy' and 'direct effect' with the preliminary reference procedure is thus considered the essential channel, if not the real engine, of integration itself. The subsequent rise of the ECJ itself stems from this 'reciprocal empowerment' linking the latter with all those various groups and institutions.[21]

The neofunctionalist account spawned a host of new strands of research, focusing especially on the preliminary reference procedure as an essential cog in the 'integration-through-law' machinery. Over the last two decades this link between Europe's legal matrix and the building of the European polity has become more and more evident as abundant literature started documenting the examples of the use of the legal opportunities by a host of actors, in pursuit of their own interests.[22]

20 Vauchez 2008b, 1.

21 Burley & Mattli 1993; Vauchez 2007.

22 For an overview of literature see Conant 2007.

3.5 Integrationist Dynamic: The Inter-Court Dialogue

Early literature on integration and the ECJ remained largely theoretical and descriptive, with next to no systematic empirical testing of competing claims. The neofunctionalist theory inspired new research agendas that aimed to empirically underpin its foundational elements. Subsequent waves of scholarship began to test competing claims against empirical evidence and specify theoretical expectations.[23] Much of the literature exploring legal integration was framed to speak to the international relations debate and a lot of emphasis was placed on the relative power of EU and national institutions. The literature trying to specify the nature of interaction between law, politics and society started to analyse ECJ case law and focused especially on the relationship between national courts and the ECJ. The idea was that it was in this ongoing 'inter-court cooperation' that the integration mechanism is activated, with preliminary references providing the ECJ with the possibility to enhance the scope of its case law, and in effect foster further integration. Analysing the interaction between international courts, governance and democracy, the 'dialogue' between national courts and the ECJ became an important and much studied subject with respect to European integration. Over the decades, a lot of scholarly work has gone into explaining the striking differences in the number of preliminary references sent by different courts in different Member States.[24] As his or her role is crucial in referring cases, the analyses have mostly focused on the national judge as the central actor. The most notable example is the work done by Stone Sweet and Brunell who, in order to do a rigorous analysis, created a database of all cases starting from the earliest preliminary reference originating in the Netherlands in 1961 up until 2006.[25]

Since then, a number of authors have made use of this dataset with the aim of clarifying the unequal distribution in references between Member States and between different referring courts. Subsequent research has employed quantitative analysis of ECJ case law and the participation of national courts in the EU legal system in attempts to explain the variable degrees of 'responsiveness to EU Law', or 'societal demand for integration'. Using mainly econometric methods, authors have tried to find causal links between preliminary reference rates and as diverse variables as 'density of EU legislation', 'intra-EU trade', 'size of EU migrant worker populations', 'monist or dualist legal traditions' and 'the pub-

23 Conant 2007.

24 Judges in Belgium, for instance, call on the ECJ approximately ten times as often as do judges in Portugal.

25 Dataset available at: http://www.nuff.ox.ac.uk/Users/Sweet/datapage.htm [last accessed 10 November 2017].

lic's political awareness'.[26] Other research has started to focus more on the role of national judges in the integration dynamic and has approached the cooperation between courts as an opportunity for national lower courts to empower themselves vis-à-vis the national high courts.

Tridimas and Tridimas for example, use a so-called 'public choice model' to examine factors that influence the use of the preliminary reference procedure by national judges.[27] The authors put forward a rational action based model as a tool for the analysis of national judges' motives for referring to Luxembourg. Using their 'public choice' model, defined as 'the principles of optimizing behaviour and equilibrium on political outcomes', they analyse the process of legal integration as the equilibrium outcome of demand and supply factors in the interaction between individual litigants, national judges and the ECJ, wherein each decision maker is modelled as pursuing its own interests under the relevant sets of constraints. They argue that the 'market' for rulings based on this procedure is not a direct interaction between consumer and producer, since demand and supply, by the nature of the procedure itself, are channelled through the intermediation of national courts. In this view, courts, like other organs of government, are assumed to have their own preferences over policy. Courts are seen as pursuing, using their judgments, preferred policy outcomes. Reference to the ECJ for national courts is seen to have two benefits. The first is the 'judicial empowerment' of national judges as a result of this newly formed legal order, as described by Weiler, who stated that "[l]ower courts and their judges were given the facility to engage with the highest jurisdiction in the Community and thus to have de facto judicial review of legislation".[28] The second benefit is the protection of judgments, through ECJ rulings, against reversal by a higher national court. With this the authors describe the national courts and their decisions whether or not to refer, not as mechanical conduits but as 'eclectic agents', and therefore conclude that the preliminary ruling mechanism has empowered the ECJ to deliver judgments that would not have been possible in the absence of the mechanism.[29] In return, ECJ rulings "enhance the power of national courts in their own legal systems *vis-á-vis* the executive and legislative branches by

26 Wind Martinsen & Rotger 2013; Broberg & Fenger 2013; Carrubba & Murrah 2005.

27 Tridimas & Tridimas 2004.

28 Weiler 1991, 2426.

29 Other institutionalist analysis of law and courts: Shapiro & Stone 1994; On judicial empowerment: Golub 1996; On the judicial empowerment of national judges Alter earlier added the important insight that the integration dynamics did not empower all judges equally, and that it were mostly lower judges who had the strongest incentive to refer, she demonstrated that the stream of references from lower courts led higher courts to begin to send their own references in an effort to control the case law of the ECJ. Alter 1996.

providing the opportunity for review of national legislation".[30] This empowerment narrative subsequently found its continuation in a focus on what these developments meant for the relationship between the EU and European society, and for the relative position of the individual in this legal system.

3.6 Connecting the Citizen to EU Law

Within the search for explanatory theories on the dynamics of integration, the significance of the transforming relationship between law and society became obvious. Legal instruments formulated at the Union level are binding upon the Member States as well as on their citizenry. By the increase in the amount of EU legislation as well as its expansion into more and more areas of law, the Union's legal order directly affects daily life to a seemingly ever-increasing extent. It accords rights and imposes duties on the individual, so that as a citizen of both Member State and of the Union he or she has become subject to a hierarchy of legal orders — a phenomenon resembling federal constitutional systems. Like any legal order, that of the European Union provides a system of legal protections for the purpose of recourse to as well as the enforcement of Union law. The Member States are obliged to take all appropriate measures to ensure fulfilment of the obligations arising from the Treaties or resulting from action taken by the institutions of the European Union, facilitating the achievement of the EU's tasks and to abstain from any measure that could jeopardise the attainment of the objectives of the Treaties. Member States are answerable to their citizens for any harm caused by violations of their Treaty responsibilities.

The ECJ's case law has potential impact on the way national governments act and on the room for manoeuvring available to them, and the set-up of the legal system provides opportunities for various state (and non-state) actors, including national judges, individuals and societal groups. The neofunctionalist model has stressed this point by incorporating non-governmental actors into the system and process of European governance through litigation before the ECJ. Neofunctionalist approaches, although focusing on different aspects and different actors in the integration dynamics, all underline the pivotal role played by litigation as an essential part in the reciprocal mechanisms of the EU legal system. Alter, in a quest to explain when and how international legal authority is constructed and how the ECJ's legal doctrines have become politically transformative within a social and political context illuminates how the Court has gained influence and has encouraged greater respect for and adherence to Euro-

30 Cichowski 2007, 249.

pean rules by allying itself with societal actors.[31] With this Alter refers to the occasions where the Court has been able to assert its authority and expand the scope of EU law through the mobilisation of EU law by private litigants bringing cases through the preliminary reference procedure, as well as through attempts to activate the European Commission. Wernicke describes the broadening range of litigants able to participate in the Court's proceedings and the ECJ's own efforts to reformulate EU law into individual rights, in pursuit of direct democratic legitimacy.[32] In this way, the ECJ and private parties find themselves in a relationship of mutual interest. More generally, Alter states that "it is clear that private access to [international courts] to challenge supranational actors can help facilitate rights claiming, international organization's accountability, and the rule of law within supranational governance systems".[33]

As part of the functioning of the 'magic triangle', the activation of the legal system is indeed critical for keeping the integrationist train running by providing the ECJ with the means to expand its case law. As such, preliminary references provide the fuel for the integrationist machinery of the European legal system. Therefore the European Union is not only a 'community based on law', but moreover a 'community built on case law'.[34] Although the bulk of the studies has focused on the institutional interconnection between the national and supranational level, giving more or less weight to the role of purposeful actors, including national judges and societal groups, the integration theory gives a clear and important role to litigation.

3.7 Participation Through Law Enforcement

The question of the wider connection between law and European society has given more recent studies cause to focus on the interconnection between the legal sphere and civil society. The peculiar nature of the EU legal system, with an elevated role for private parties leads to an emphasis on the possible influence society has on the scope and direction of European integration. In the words of Cichowski: "In the EC, individuals can activate transnational adjudication processes on their own. In virtually all other international regimes, individuals must rely on intermediaries, usually representatives of governments, to press their claims and to pursue their other interests. But in the EC, the operation of the legal system has progressively reduced the capacity of national govern-

31 Alter 2009.
32 Wernicke 2007. See also: De Búrca 1995; Wigger & Nolke 2007; and more critically discussed by Schepel & Blankenburg 2001.
33 Alter 2010, 45.
34 Vauchez 2008; Kelemen 2011.

ments to control policy outcomes, while it has enhanced the policy influence of the EC's supranational institutions, national judges, and private actors."[35] It is at these crossroads of European governance and litigation that theories of empowerment of individuals and civil society are focusing. This strand of research, therefore, places its emphasis on the so-called 'participation-through-law-enforcement'.[36]

This approach takes the idea of an increase in opportunities for private action within a newly structured supranational sphere as having far-reaching consequences for power structures and for the democratic nature of this political constellation. Litigation before the ECJ as a result acquires a more significant role in EU governance and new possibilities for individuals to invoke EU law and appeal to individual rights beyond the nation-state emerge.[37] Cichowski concludes that legal integration operates to diminish Member States' control and therefore empowers individuals. This empowerment is not limited however to the possibility for judicial remedy beyond the domestic legal system. Cichowski's argument goes further by claiming that "[t]he EU is a most likely case for courts to enhance (democratic) participation in international governance". To support this claim she points to the fragmentation of political authority in the EU, which has led to a relative increase in the power of nonmajoritarian institutions, such as the European Commission and the European Court of Justice.[38] This increase in power has in turn been reinforced by the aforementioned supremacy of European law and its direct effect, which provides citizens, firms, and societal groups with the legal opportunity to plead in national courts for the enforcement of European law.[39] Cichowski concludes that the possibility for disadvantaged individuals and groups at the domestic level to obtain rights at the national and EU level through EU law and litigation before the ECJ can be seen as "giving civil society a voice and place in EU politics".[40] This is possible through the mobilisation of transnational public interest groups that provide new power and a voice to EU citizens who may be excluded from domestic political deliberation.

Cichowski argues that not only are the ECJ and civil society of integral importance to the process of creating a European polity, but that the balance of

35 Cichowski 2006.

36 Börzel 2006. Wind, Martinsen & Potger 2013; Cichowski 2006; Cichowski & Stone Sweet 2003.

37 These developments have enticed questions as to whether there is a need for reformulation of the way we view the primacy of parliamentary legislature in the light of a growing democratic deficit of policy-driven delegated legislation. See Van Gestel 2013.

38 See also Börzel 2003; Tallberg 2003; Kelemen 2011.

39 Cichowski 2006; Conant 2002.

40 Cichowski 2007.

power in EU politics between national governments, EU organizations and civil society have shifted under the influence of institutional and organizational change, making the ECJ a site of democratic empowerment for individuals and civil society. Cichowski explicitly voices an idea of democratic enhancement defining it as "greater accountability, transparency and individual participation in political processes". She claims that her studies illustrate how supranational legal mechanisms can provide increased accountability "through enforcing the law, rights claiming and greater legal protection for individuals".[41] In this view, EU law, the legal system and the opportunities provided by the ECJ create a situation of empowerment for individuals and civil society.

3.8 Token Cases and Selecting on the Dependent Variable

Because of the ground-breaking effects of preliminary rulings in the history of the ECJ, the preliminary reference procedure is widely considered the central mechanism, or backbone, of the European legal system and moreover is put forward as the main means by which individual rights can be (and have been) invoked, consolidated and expanded. This model of a dynamic and relatively autonomous system of integration gives an important role to litigants as providing the 'demand for integration', as well as promotes the idea of law as a particularly powerful tool against national governments. As Schepel and Blankenburg conclude, the model "fits nicely with the court's self-styled role as liberator of European civil society".[42]

In the development of the empowerment and participation narratives on the EU legal system, the *Defrenne* cases (I, II and III), the so-called 'Sunday Trading Saga', and the case of the British Equal Opportunities Commission are famous examples frequently used to illustrate the successful exploitation of the opportunities provided by the EU legal system to put pressure on national policies. The first revolved around the non-implementation of the equal pay provision in the Treaty of Rome (Article 141). While not one national government had undertaken domestic policy changes to implement the provision since the signing of the Treaty, Article 141 was 'brought to life' as a result of the strategic action and activism of a Belgian lawyer. Eliane Vogel-Polsky, who specialized in social and labour law, regarded Article 141 as a stepping-stone to expanding

41 However this accountability seems to be only directed towards national policies vis-á-vis EU law, and thus in no way enhances the accountability of EU legislators and policy-making. Furthermore, and this might be Cichowski's single most important assertion, rights claiming and the following supranational legal mechanisms supposedly constitute a form of democratic participation.

42 Schepel & Blankenburg 2001: 31.

women's labour rights. Through a series of test cases involving Miss Gabrielle Defrenne, a flight attendant with a Belgian national airline, Vogel-Polsky was able to solicit ground-breaking judgments that expanded the scope of the provision and began to provide real situations in which Article 141 was applicable.[43] The second famous example showed the recourse to Community law by British retailers who set out to attack the British ban on Sunday trading in the UK, after running into the limitations of a court strategy in domestic law.[44] These large retailers were successful in what Rawlings called playing 'the Eurolaw game', which entails the "sounding in [of] Community law, to challenge the product of the national legal and political order".[45] In other words, the 'outflanking' of the domestic legal system. Especially when the national arena is characterized by a deadlock in doctrine, breaking out of the confines of the national legal system can be a very attractive option. In the third example British equal opportunity groups used the EU legal system to force a conservative British government to make considerable reforms to its equality policy. The reforms included extending work benefits to part-time workers, eliminating the cap on the size of discrimination awards, and stopping the policy of dismissing women from the military because of pregnancy.[46]

These cases are used repeatedly to highlight the empowering aspects of EU law, and the ways in which EU law strategies have been transformative in the past. However, in focusing on such cases one runs the risk of a confirmation bias, and the meaning of certain cases is transformed into a token of a certain narrative. As Börzel argues, "research on litigation and participation in the EU tends to suffer from a selection bias on the dependent variable. Cases in which citizens and groups fail to bring claims against their governments for non-compliance with international law are hardly considered".[47] Focusing on single judicial events, such as a particular court case, obviously provides incentives to select those that stand out in some way, as most such cases of litigation are highly uneventful from the perspective of integration. Not only are we not seeing failed attempts, or non-attempts, these studies also fail to consider that references may not always constitute a 'demand' for a ruling, or an attempt at participation or expecting a net gain from invoking EU law. A related critical observation is the fact that these studies have a significant methodological problem in focusing on past examples of successful mobilisation of EU law. In other words, research on Euro-litigation has a tendency to focus on results and what is visible,

43 Havinga & Hoevenaars 2015.
44 Rawlings 1993.
45 Rawlings 1993, 332.
46 See Alter & Vargas 2000; Barnard 1995; Harlow & Rawlings 1992; Mazey 1998.
47 Börzel 2006.

thus looking merely at 'successful' litigation. Those who have lost, or have not litigated, for lack of resources or other reasons, are not part of the equation. And in the case of the debate on empowerment and democracy on the other hand, the issue is only dealt with *in abstracto* and *in posse*. As a result, the presented model of European integration creates a narrative in which private parties (and when focusing on rights specifically individuals) are particularly well off. The emancipatory functionalism of EU law is expected to benefit the citizens of Europe, and those citizens are expected to grasp the opportunities in EU law whenever it serves their interests. While the cases often used to underscore this idea provide a particularly strong case for such model of empowerment, this selective presentation of success stories is unsatisfactory when trying to understand Euro-litigation as a phenomenon in its own right.

3.9 Playing the Eurolaw Game: Indications of an Uneven Playing Field

The assumption of the equality of power between participants in the legal system was challenged by Galanter's work on the structural disadvantage of 'one-shotters' before the courts.[48] Galanter described a way of analysis that defines positions of structural (dis)advantage between contending parties in a legal system that, although formally neutral, may perpetuate and reinforce advantages of the 'haves' over the 'have-nots'. Distinguishing between rules, courts, lawyers and parties as the essential elements of contemporary legal systems he reverses the usual legal analysis that takes rules as a starting point and works to see what effects these rules have on the parties concerned, by starting with those parties and examining what effect different kinds of parties may have on the system of law. He identified two key players in the legal system – one-shotters and repeat players. A one-shotter is a person, or organisation that deals with the legal system only infrequently. These actors tend to have few resources at their disposal. Repeat players on the other hand, have had, and anticipate having repeated litigation. They tend to be institutions and tend to have more resources at their disposal. Moreover, repeat players have the opportunities to establish and develop lasting facilities and informal relationships with institutional officials, and their 'bargaining reputation' serves as a resource. They are able to calculate risks of maximum loss and deploy strategies to maximize gains over a long series of cases, thus 'playing the odds'.[49] Galanter argues that these repeat players

48 Galanter 1974.

49 Playing for the rules can also be done outside the courtroom, mainly by lobbying for the creation, adaptation or adoption of certain relevant rules. This is of course a focus on the 'input side' of legislation – the main focus of the debate on the purported democratic deficit of EU legislation. The argument being that people of Europe directly or indirectly →

have the ability to "play the litigation game differently from [a one-shotter]"[50] and this ability affords them substantial advantages and benefits. His central proposition is that even though 'haves' and 'have-nots' are formally equal before the law, social mechanisms lead to a structural advantage for the 'haves'.

Within European integration studies, the exclusive focus on the judicial dimension of legal integration, underscored by the profusion of quantitative analysis on judicial proceedings and on the fact that supranational case law is considered almost automatically a by-product of 'civil society', leaves us with a particularly rosy picture of the work done by the ECJ. In the words of Vauchez: "[A] very optimistic vision of the contribution of law and of Courts to the emancipation of citizens from the allegedly close and exclusive circuit of majoritarian institutions."[51] The fact that the legal system in itself is not a level playing field is a critical element in such considerations.

Rawlings' article on the 'Sunday trading saga' is one of the exceptions that do pay attention to dimensions of power. He describes how Euro-litigation can be part of political action campaigns by powerful actors that play what he calls the 'Eurolaw game'.[52] Rawlings' article shows how such legal strategies cannot be understood as separate from the social, economic, political and legal conflict surrounding them, both in terms of the objectives and strategies of the litigating parties, and in terms of the responses of courts and authorities. Rawlings stresses that the Sunday trading saga is an exceptional example of litigating efforts and political pressure through law. The sheer scale and complexity, ranging across the domestic legal system as well as several trips across the continent, make this a great example of the ways in which litigation is used as a successful strategy for change. At the same time the scale and complexity make this story just that: exceptional. It reveals political struggle, extensive strategic use of the legal system and it shows the different actors involved in such a process, as well as their relative power and incentives for action. However, it can hardly be seen as exemplary for strategic Euro-litigation per se. As Rawlings acknowledges: "For Britain, it is without doubt the most considerable Community law litigation to date, and it has only a few serious rivals across the Community as a whole".[53] The Sunday trading saga was a very exceptional example of a lengthy coordinated legal campaign by a large number of retailers, and by all accounts very powerful repeat players.

---

have too little say in what is developed and implemented as EU law. In this field it is of course even more obvious that those with the numbers, resources, experience and expertise, in short agency, are 'coming out ahead'.

50 Galanter 1974, 98.

51 Vauchez 2008.

52 Rawlings 1993, 332.

53 Rawlings 1993, 331-2.

Similarly, the oft-cited *Defrenne* cases were revealed to be part of a long battle by one particular activist lawyer. Éliane Vogel-Polsky, the cause lawyer behind the *Defrenne* cases, was by no means an average litigator. She was at the time a young law professor at the Université libre de Bruxelles, trained under the patronage of former Belgium Minister of labour and former president of the WTO Board Léon-Eli Troclet and a member of the milieu of Brussels' Euro-lawyers, including Michel Waelbroeck, one of the major repeat players of the ECJ, and Jean-Victor Louis, a well-established authority in the field of European law.[54] Vogel-Polsky would later become an expert advisor to the European Economic Community (EEC) and the European Council. Looking at such contextual factors should lead to the preliminary conclusion that examples like these could be therefore more likely the exception than the rule. The cases of Ms Defrenne are a famous example of how individual cases may disguise the existence of cause lawyering or interest group activity behind an individual façade. The proverbial 'straw man' has been used in this sense to describe cases where individual interests are actually merely the 'vehicle' by which a more strategic game is played.[55]

Such insights direct our attention to the maxim that the legal system has a tendency to be favourable to 'the haves', and should trigger sensitivity to this misbalance. When it comes to the European legal system there are still more questions than answers, which is why Alter and Vargas conclude that "EC law litigation strategies are one way that European integration is changing domestic politics. But the argument we make—that domestic groups can pull in EC law in a strategy to shift the domestic balance of power—raises almost as many questions as it answers" and that it is therefore "time to move beyond vague statements that actors following their interests further integration". Presumptions based on rational considerations by actors that are "purported to have a clear and unbiased perception of the various opportunities offered in the European arenas",[56] give very limited insight into what transpires at the ground level before a reference is made to the ECJ and which actors are most able and likely to use the EU legal system to their advantage. This research will therefore analyse the

54 Vauchez 2008. Cichowski does mention Vogel-Polsky's strategic endeavour including the fact that Vogel-Polsky also published an article in a Belgian legal journal suggesting the direct effect of Article 119, but does so only in a footnote. Evidently, this aspect of the *Defrenne* saga was not the main focus of Cichoski's analysis, however, the underestimation of the capital and credentials necessary for such strategic mobilisation to work undermines Cichowski's final and optimistic conclusion of Euro-legalization as the democratisation of a European public sphere.

55 This phenomenon traditionally makes it particularly difficult, from a research standpoint, to assess the amount of organised litigation without using more pervading (and with it more time- and resource consuming) methodology.

56 Vauchez 2007, 2.

specific ways in which, next to an opportunity, the preliminary reference procedure has its own specific obstacles that have to be overcome by strategic actors, and I will focus on the coping strategies some actors have developed to navigate the specific characteristics of the European legal system.

3.10 The View from a Distance

As has already been pointed out early on by Mattli and Slaughter, there is more to litigation before the ECJ than a mere case judgment relationship.[57] A host of different legal, procedural and political variables and 'a community of actors above and below the state' can be distinguished.[58] The statistical and case-centred approaches to the analysis of supranational litigation goes a long way in showing the results and consequences of such legal action and can be seen to show the resulting macro shifts in power relationships. However, this approach does not reveal the ways in which these cases are brought before the Court, or the strategies and goals behind litigation at a micro level. The approaches using econometric methods and those focusing on the interaction between national courts and the ECJ are not erroneous in their attempts to come to grips with integration dynamics; however there is a lot that remains invisible that way. Moreover, while the aim is to understand the role of law in the dynamics of integration, there is a lot that gets swept up in such analyses that strictly has nothing to do with the integration of Europe,[59] and therefore these models include spurious correlations and various studies produce contradictory results.[60]

The 2005 article by Carrubba and Murrah is an excellent example of a macro-theoretical approach and the testing of hypotheses by econometric methods. Not surprisingly they conclude after analysis "that no single, mono-causal argument is sufficient for explaining the development of European legal integration".[61] As their findings suggest, "future study of the preliminary ruling system needs to incorporate and control for all steps in the legal process, *from case generation to actual reference*".[62] The authors also signal the important oversight of the role of the European public at large in the top-down study of European legal integration, which has focused largely on elite actors, i.e. the ECJ, national courts, and organized business interests. Numerical analyses like Stone Sweet and Brunell's database provide information on the relative distribution of

57 Mattli & Slaughter 1996. See also Slaughter, Stone Sweet, & Weiler 1998.
58 Mattli & Slaughter 1995.
59 Chalmers 2000; Schepel & Blankenburg 2001, 31.
60 Conant 2007.
61 Carrubba & Murrah 2005, 414.
62 Carrubba & Murrah 2005, 414 my emphasis.

preliminary references, according to subject area, country and referring court; however they give little insight into *how* cases reach the Court and the role played by different actors involved in the process. If the objective is to say anything about Euro-litigation and the relationship between EU law and society, we have to look at cases in depth, especially from the perspective of private parties, as will be done in the study at hand. Only then will we be able to identify meaningful characteristics that are not evident in quantitative analysis. That is, for example, the involvement of interest groups, test cases, the need for financial support and significant expertise, all of which have some bearing on the nature of Euro-litigation and the position of individuals in this 'Eurolaw game'.

As to the macro-level analysis, in most research Conant argues that "[i]n-depth qualitative research has generally yielded more compelling findings than efforts to explain aggregate national trends in references".[63] Similarly, Alter concludes that "[c]ase study analysis risks being more impressionistic than quantitative. But given the over-aggregated nature of the ECJ's reference data, and the current impossibility of determining the number and content of national court cases that are not referred to the ECJ, it may be the only way to capture the many factors shaping judicial behavior".[64] The atomized, disembodied understanding of action gives general indications of trends and differentiations but it reduces actors to rational and unified units and fails to account for the social complexity in which the cases in practice arise and unfold. Generally, the research on preliminary references based on econometric methods starts with the methodologically necessary premise that under the same circumstances all actors will act alike. It fails to account for possible constraints, independent of direct interaction.

3.11 Materialising the Individual Litigant

In studies on Euro-litigation, the motives of the litigating parties are often implicitly (and sometimes explicitly) assumed, as is customary to rational choice theories, to be based solely on an assessment of (financial) gain. Such assumptions of rational choice and 'demand for ECJ rulings' runs counter to insights from socio-legal studies, sociology of law and litigation and mobilisation studies that reveal the complexity of the world of litigation and the use of the legal system.[65] When the role of individual litigants is discussed, the rational choice basis of their model shines through: "Private litigants will resort to litigation and in-

63 Conant 2007, 54.
64 Alter 2000, 501.
65 A selection: Galanter 1986, Felstiner, Abel & Sarat 1980, Fitzgerald & Dickins 1980, Macaulay 1963 and Rosenthal 1974. For an overview, see Friedman 1989.

voke EC law if they expect a net gain, financial or otherwise, from doing so".[66] The success stories of the use of the ECJ are repeatedly put forward as examples that affirm a certain idea of empowerment of the less powerful by means of EU law.[67] However, these much-repeated examples may lead to an overstatement of the opportunities provided by the EU legal system.

As pointed out by Börzel, the selection bias possibly blinds us to the less fitting findings we may encounter when looking beyond the success stories. In similar vein, Shaw concluded earlier that "there is very little authoritative or non-anecdotal evidence to buttress claims for the centrality of individual rights as the key to the connection between so-called 'Community citizens' and the EC constitutional order. The only evidence which has been collected takes as its model litigants (rather than potential litigants, or a class of aggrieved citizens)".[68] With the latter she points to work done by Harding. Indeed, Harding was one of the few examples of attempts at an empirical approach to the dynamics behind litigation. In 1980, Harding pioneered an approach to the ECJ's case law by not only focusing on the legal significance of adjudication and its transformative power within the legal sphere but also by looking at who actually gives *acte de presence* in Luxembourg.[69] The most significant result flowing from Harding's preliminary statistical analysis is that most questions can only be answered by directly confronting the litigants themselves as to their strategies, objectives and hopes when engaging in litigation before the ECJ. However, his work was not met at the time with a lot of subsequent in-depth research.[70]

The general agreement that cases brought by private litigants continue to play a central role in the EU legal process stresses the need for more insight into the dynamics behind litigation. As Alter concludes: "The question remains, however, whether the ECJ's success at transforming the system with the help of private litigant cases means that a never-ending process of legal expansion has been set in motion. When do private litigants and national court actions help to advance legal integration? To answer this question, we need to better understand the interests of the ECJ's key intermediaries (private litigants and national judges) and thus the factors shaping where, when, and why they use the EU legal system to promote their objectives".[71] Similarly, Kelemen and Schmidt con-

66 Tridimas & Tridimas 2004, 132.

67 Cichowski 2007.

68 Shaw 1996.

69 Harding 1980, followed by Harding 1992 and Rawlings 1993, shows the usefulness of a focus on litigants and strategies in explaining litigation before the ECJ. Notable exceptions focusing on socio-legal dynamics: Harlow and Rawlings 1992 and Chalmers 2000.

70 In 2005, Harding still concludes that a non-qualitative inquiry into litigation gives no insight into motivation and strategies of litigants. See Harding & Gibbs 2005, 368.

71 Alter 2000, 492.

clude, "we still know far too little about the conditions under which private litigants actually claim their European rights in front of national courts".[72]

Harding, as one of the few legal scholars to adopt a different approach, argued that systems of judicial review of actions taken by public authorities are usually solely assessed on the basis of purely judicial criteria, i.e. the judicial framework as provided by the constructors of the system, rather than in the subjective sense based on the strategies, motivations and habits of the private individuals that may take these kinds of actions. Similar critique has been voiced by Harlow and Rawlings, who concluded: "Doctrine and case analysis we possess; research into *who* litigates, how *often*, and in respect of *which* governmental activities, has been singularly lacking."[73] Moreover it can be said that there is a tendency to analyse litigation in isolation from alternative non-judicial or non-legal, usually political strategies. These tendencies can probably be ascribed to the all too ready assumption that litigious behaviour is primarily determined by legal opportunities, a misconception that was exposed earlier.[74] To their credit, in their early work Mattli and Slaughter professed that "[t]he next generation of scholarship on EC legal integration, as with European integration more generally, will require far more nuanced attention to the identification of both interests and constraints in very specific contexts. It will move away from contending paradigms such as realism and neofunctionalism and toward the development of mid-range hypotheses that are both theoretically sophisticated and empirically informed".[75]

3.12 Conclusion

There seems to be a disciplinary bifurcation between legal and political science perspectives on the preliminary reference procedure. Where the former perspective emphasises the procedure as a technical dialogue between courts, potentially under-estimating the political aspects inherent in the procedure as an enforcement mechanism, the latter takes the procedure as the focal point of European integration, running the risk of unduly assuming purposeful action by interested actors. Jurisprudence of the ECJ, and especially the influential precedential function and ground-breaking effects thereof, leads to the conclusion that the preliminary reference procedure gives individuals and civil society a stake in the transformation of Europe's political and legal order. Not only are they active participants in the enforcement of EU law, it also provides them with the oppor-

72 Kelemen & Schmidt 2012.
73 Harlow & Rawlings 1984, 257.
74 Macaulay 1963.
75 Mattli & Slaughter 1996.

tunity to defend their rights, leading some scholars to conclude that this is in fact an avenue for empowerment for individuals and civil society.[76] The ultimate promise to the European citizen in this narrative can be formulated as follows: the fragmentation of political power transforms democratic structures and diminishes national sovereignty. When political power is mediated to a large extent by legal structures, access to these structures is seen as a way of influencing the political process. The ECJ is seen as the place where citizens and civil society can challenge national policy and are thus in a sense 'empowered' against their government, because this mechanism enables them to 'outflank' the national jurisdiction. This scenario sounds attractive, yet for legal sociologists it poses some important questions about the realities of legal mobilisation.

The common point between the aforementioned approaches is that they tend to be ontologically rationalist. They emphasize material aspects over ideational ones and assume the rationality of agents without much regard for structural influences and actors' relative agency. This rational choice approach also shines through in a positivist tendency to try to establish strong causal links between actors' actions and outcomes, as well as a predominant reliance on quantitative research strategies and tools (e.g. statistics and econometric models). Finally, deductive approaches tend to prevail over inductive ones, selecting and interpreting events and facts to test and support the explanations of European integration. Econometric methodology, macro-approaches and the remnants of rational action theory all contribute to the continuing disembodied nature of the study of the role of law and litigation in the integration of Europe. It is submitted that such reductions can impair the explanatory virtues of these analyses, to the extent that they are likely to overestimate the purposefulness of actors while underestimating the complexities involved in litigation and judicial decision-making.

A host of unanswered questions thus remain when it comes to Euro-litigation and the role of the parties in these proceedings. Apart from some general assumptions with regard to the motives and capacity of non-institutional actors, there is little insight into how and why both individual and organised interests bring cases before the national courts, as well as whether or not these litigants play a role by pushing the national court towards making a reference. Especially when looking at the democratic empowerment of citizens suggested by some, a study into the objectives of and constraints on litigation from the perspective of the litigant will be a vital contribution to interrelated debates on juridification, empowerment, democracy and the legitimacy of the ECJ. Although some of the more vocal judges of the ECJ paint a positive picture, one of

76 Cichowski 2007.

the ECJ as a 'people's court',[77] the actual possibility for citizens to address legal issues at the ECJ might be a significant overstatement.[78] However, individual cases do reach the Court, and so citizens are actors within the judicial system of EU law. An in-depth approach with regard to power relationships between the actors involved in litigation will reveal the ways in which politics and law coincide in this arena of political development.

77 Wernicke 2007.

78 Schepel & Blankenburg 2001.

Part II

4 A Look Below the Surface

4.1 Introduction

A number of unanswered questions remain when it comes to the role of individuals in the European legal system. While neofunctionalist theories of integration stress the role played by private actors, they do not differentiate between individuals and other actors. From the theories of participation- and empowerment-through-law we may expect significant participation of individuals, while other researchers with more critical examinations of the practical position of individuals in the EU legal system suggest that the individual has been largely left out of the 'Eurolaw game', by being excluded from legal arenas that would allow them to challenge suspect government practices.[1] Based on such literature one would expect the number of cases including individual litigants to be marginal. On the other hand, the number of high-impact rulings in individual preliminary reference cases suggests that the idea of EU law as solely managing the internal market, and thus being a field where only economic actors are able to participate, may be insufficient, or at least outdated. The true extent to which individuals play a part in the EU's legal system remains a marginalized discourse. To fill this gap, this chapter sets out to investigate what kinds of cases involving individuals are brought before the ECJ, who are the litigants and what are the motives behind litigation.

The following paragraphs analyse the Dutch preliminary references in the selected period of 2008-2012 and compare them on a number of characteristics for which statistics are available. Firstly, the number of individuals' cases is compared to the total number of references. Secondly, the cases are differentiated according to the referring national court. And finally, the subject matter is used to differentiate cases and give an idea of the areas of EU law that are most prominent when it comes to individual litigation. These numbers will give us some general characteristics of both the types of cases and the types of litigants before the ECJ. Such numerical analysis of case law only get us so far in understanding litigation dynamics; they give little insight into why and how cases reach the Court and the role played by different actors. Therefore, after the numerical scrutiny of these cases, this chapter will go further into the question of who in fact are individual participants in the EU legal system. For that purpose it is necessary to disaggregate the concept of 'individuals', which encompasses a wide range of actors with various interests as well as resources. Therefore the second part addresses these questions and delves deeper into the possible ex-

1 Costa 2003; Conant 2002.

planatory factors that help understand the trajectory of the cases. I focus on the litigants, the motives behind litigation and take a closer look at the behavioural factors of the litigating parties and interests that lie behind these legal actions.

4.2 Preliminary References in Numbers

Individual Involvement in ECJ case law

Looking at Dutch preliminary reference cases in the period 2008-2012, the first relevant observation to be made is that while a majority does not include any individual party, the percentage of cases that does, more than a third, is substantial.[2] While the number of preliminary references is only indicative of the total range of national cases wherein matters of EU law come to the fore, this percentage is a testament to the extent to which individuals are in fact involved in the European legal system, are impacted by the application of EU law and potentially the course of integration. This observation thus nuances the assumption by some that the EU's legal system remains heavily market-driven, mainly addresses matters of trade and that the role and stake of the individual in EU law is thus very limited.[3] Especially when considering the preliminary reference procedure from a legal remedy perspective, these numbers of cases involving individuals at first glance seem to paint a slightly more inclusive picture than we would expect following critical literature.[4] A quick survey of a previous period of five years of preliminary references from the Netherlands, judgments between January 1st 1988 and December 31st 1992, reveals that at least for the Netherlands this is not at all a recent trend. Out of a total of seventy-three adjudicated cases in that period, thirty-three, or 45% involved individual litigants.

Private v Public

When looking at the total of 114 references in the selected period, two out of 114 cases were disputes between two private parties, but not necessarily individuals. All other ninety-two cases were disputes with public or (semi-)public institutions.[5] When we further selected for individuals this relative amount increased. A total of thirty-nine out of the forty cases including individual litigants

2 Forty cases out of a total of 114. One caveat is in place here. As stated, all figures and conclusions are based on analysis of Dutch cases only. Comparisons to other Member States fall outside of the scope of this study.

3 An idea not lastly brought forward by the ECJ's judges themselves. See Costa 2003, 752.

4 Conant 2003, 13.

5 Harding found that over half of all references included a dispute with a public authority. Harding 1992, 105.

involved a dispute between (a number of) individual(s) and a public institution. These included predominantly ministries, administrative bodies (such as the Immigration and Naturalisation Service) and the tax authorities. Only one case was an exception to this rule showing a dispute between two private parties. This case involved a group of former employees (supported by a labour union) and a catering firm in connection with the outsourcing by their former employer of its catering activities to the latter and the resulting substantial loss of wages and fringe benefits.[6] One other case, while in fact a dispute between an individual and a public authority, was not a matter of administrative law. This case revolved around the question of whether Community law required a lessee, on the expiry of the lease, to deliver to the lessor the leased land along with the payment entitlements accumulated thereon or relating thereto, or to pay him compensation. And although the opposing party was in fact a municipality, it was part of the proceedings as lessor of a number of parcels of agricultural land and not as a public authority.

This distribution of cases is a reflection of the nature of EU rules. The applicability of EU rules, as litigated in national courtrooms, concerns mainly the relationship between private parties and public authorities; the 'horizontal' effect of EU legislation remains limited. The remaining disputes between two corporations mostly concern trademark disputes, regulated by EU intellectual, industrial and commercial property regulations.[7] When it comes to individuals, the vast majority of cases fall within the category of public law. It is thus almost entirely in disputes with national public authorities that individuals may find themselves and their case being decided upon by the ECJ. This confirms the idea that where EU law touches upon the lives of individuals in a national context it does so predominantly by setting administrative standards and boundaries to national governance as well as providing individual rights that may be invoked in citizens' dealings with the authorities.

Referring Courts

Out of the total of forty individuals' cases under study, thirty cases were brought by the four highest courts in the Netherlands: either the Supreme Court (*Hoge Raad*: ten cases) that has exclusive final jurisdiction over civil and criminal matters, or one of the three highest courts in administrative law; the Council of State (*Raad van State*: eleven cases), the Central Board of Appeals (*Centrale*

6 This case is included as one of the case studies (*Case Study A*) in part to juxtapose it with other disputes, based on this private-private dimension.

7 In fact, almost half of the twenty-two cases not involving a public authority also are about questions of intellectual, industrial and commercial property.

Raad van Beroep: five cases) or the Trade and Industry Appeals Tribunal (*College van Beroep voor het Bedrijfsleven*: four cases). The remaining ten cases were either brought by lower courts (*Rechtbanken*: seven cases), or courts of appeal (*Gerechtshoven*: three cases). In comparison to the other, non-individual, references the number of cases referred by the highest court was similar, with 78.5% of cases in the same period. These numbers were a little higher than, but not greatly out of step with the general statistics for the Netherlands with two-thirds of all references coming from the highest courts and one-third from lower courts.[8] These numbers are brought together in Figure I.

Figure I: Dutch references according to referring court in the period 2008-2012[9]

	Individuals 40	**Other 74**	**Total 114**
Highest Courts	**30 (75%)**	**58 (78%)**	**88 (77%)**
Supreme Court *(Hoge Raad)*	10	44	54
Council of State *(Raad van State)*	11	8	19
Central Board of Appeals *(Centrale Raad van Beroep)*	5	0	5
Trade and Industry Appeals Tribunal *(College van Beroep voor het Bedrijfsleven)*	4	6	10
Lower Courts	**10 (25%)**	**16 (22%)**	**26 (23%)**
Courts of appeal *(Gerechtshoven)*	3	6	9
Lower courts *(Rechtbanken)*	7	10	17

8 Statistics from the first Dutch reference in 1961 up until 2015. *Hoge Raad*: 29%, *Raad van State*: 11%, *Centrale Raad van Beroep*: 16% and *College van Beroep voor het Bedrijfsleven*: 7%%. Including 4% by the (former) *Tariefcommissie*, the referring court in *Van Gend en Loos,* which no longer exists.

9 Derived from http://curia.europa.eu/. Note of criteria selected: Procedure and result = "Reference for a preliminary ruling", "Preliminary reference - urgent procedure" Source of a question referred for a preliminary ruling = "Netherlands" Period or date = "Date of delivery"; period= "from 01/01/2008 to 31/12/2012".

Duration

Excluding the cases that are dealt with through the urgent procedure (PPU) the average duration of the proceedings before the ECJ amounts to over one and a half years,[10] with the shortest just under a year[11] and the longest over three and a half years.[12] This average is a little longer than the Court's most recent accomplishment in keeping the procedure as short as possible, averaging at fifteen months in 2015.[13]

The total duration of the proceedings, including the national procedure, is significantly harder to determine, because establishing the start of a case can be somewhat arbitrary. One could start counting at the date of the first lodging of actual legal proceedings, or, and from a litigant's perspective this is arguably more accurate, one should start counting from the start of the actual dispute. Taking the first official decision (the declaration or, for instance, tax notice that sparked the proceedings) as a starting point, the average time these cases spend before being referred to the ECJ is over two and a half years,[14] with outliers of as much as five and a half years.[15] Of course, these numbers vary widely and drawing any general conclusions from it would be tentative; however, it does underscore the fact not often acknowledged that although the ECJ does a remarkable job in working its way through the ever increasing number of preliminary references within reasonable time frames, the time a case spends in Luxembourg is added onto an often already lengthy domestic procedure.

Subject Matter

In recent years, a lot of effort in the study of the ECJ and the preliminary references has gone into explaining the variation in references between different Member States, the different courts and tribunals filing a reference request and different areas of EU law. Categorical differentiation points in the direction of some general characteristics in cases that get referred, as is also apparent in the cases under investigation in this study. Due to the multitude of EU rules that may be the subject of references, it is not straightforward distinguishing between general areas of law. Stone Sweet and Brunell have, however, devised a way to

10 18 months and 17 days.

11 11 months and 8 days.

12 43 months and 16 days.

13 From the ECJ's own reporting, available at: https://curia.europa.eu/jcms/upload/docs/application/pdf/2016-08/rapport_annuel_2015_activite_judiciaire_en_web.pdf [last accessed 10 November 2017].

14 31 months and 17 days.

15 67 months and 13 days.

subdivide cases into thirteen 'meta-categories' that account for 80-90% of all references made to the ECJ, regardless of country of origin.[16] The dataset created by Stone Sweet and Brunell has been the basis for many studies trying to explain variations in the usage of the preliminary reference procedure.[17]

It should be noted that these categories were defined based on the numbers available up until 2006, and based upon a categorization as provided by the ECJ. Between 2006 and 2012 EU law developed significantly (the Lisbon Treaty of 2009 is a case in point) and consequently some categories that are ascribed to the cases in this study did not exist as such in the previous period. There are further inherent limitations to the method devised by Stone Sweet and Brunell, as some cases may fall into two or more categories which means the total scoring is somewhat skewed. Stone Sweet and Brunell were interested in the EU law side of references, and not necessarily in litigation as such, which provides an explanation for the inherent lack of precision and nuance in these numbers from that perspective. With George Canning's maxim in mind that 'nothing is so fallacious as facts, except figures',[18] applying it to the cases in this study gives a tentative insight into their distribution and the dimension of the subject matter, and it reveals some striking contrasts when differentiating between individuals and other litigants.

A comparison is made between the number of cases according to subject matter, between the number of cases including an individual litigant and the total number of cases from the Netherlands in the period 2008-2012. Figure II shows the distribution of cases, using the categories as employed by Stone Sweet and Brunell. The first column shows the number of cases (to be precise the number of scorings on a specific category) per area of EU law for the cases including individual litigants, with the second column specifying those cases for which at least one of those involved was interviewed. The third column shows the same scorings for the remainder of cases in the selected period. Comparing these numbers gives insight into the relative weight of different areas of EU law

16 Stone Sweet and Brunell differentiate cases along several dimensions, including the following: date, Member State, court of referral, legal domain or subject matter (meta-categories include *Agriculture, Free Movement of Goods, Competition and Dumping, External Relations, Social Security, Social Provisions, Environment, Establishment, Free Movement of Workers and Persons, Taxation, Transportation, Commercial Policy, Approximation of Laws)* and the official European Court Reports citation.

17 Among others: Stone Sweet & Brunell 1998; Stone Sweet & Caparoso 1998; Cichowski 1998; and Carrubba and Murrah 2005.

18 See also the critical remarks by Felstiner, Abel & Sarat with regard to the inclination to view court cases as things and the subsequent temptation to count them. Felstiner, Abel & Sarat 1980, footnote 1. Galanter states that "figures like litigation rates *are* theories, especially slippery ones because the assumptions embedded in them are hard to see and especially persuasive ones because they are disguised as mere facts." Galanter 1986, 15.

when differentiating between individuals and the remainder of the cases. In order to facilitate comparison, the categories in bold are the meta-categories as defined by Stone Sweet and Brunell.

Figure II: Dutch references according to area of EU law

Categories	Individual Cases		Other cases
	All 40 cases	26 (interviews)	
Free movement of workers	**9**	**8**	**0**
Agriculture	**6**	**5**	**6**
External[19]	**6**	**6**	**1**
Social security	**5**	**4**	**0**
Freedom of Establishment	**4**	**3**	**12**
Free movement of goods	**3**	**3**	**15**
Taxation	**3**	**2**	**14**
Social Provisions	**2**	**1**	**0**
Approximations of laws	**1**	**0**	**13**
Environment	**1**	**0**	**2**
Common policy	**0**	**0**	**1**
Competition	**0**	**0**	**13**
Transport	**0**	**0**	**13**
Area of Freedom, Security and Justice[20]	5	2	5
Citizenship of the Union	4	2	0
Visa, Asylum, Immigration	4	4	0
Principles of the treaties	3	2	0
Border Control	2	0	0
General Provisions	2	1	0
Cooperation in civil matters	1	0	5
Fundamental Rights	1	1	0
Human Rights	1	0	0
Right of Entry and Residence	1	1	0
Other	0	0	3
Total	100% (64)[21]		100% (108)

19 A miscellaneous category including all EC economic policies affecting the *European Free Trade Area*, the *GATT*, and *Association Agreements* with non-EC states.

20 Categories not in **bold** are categories that as such did not yet exist before 2006, the end of the existing dataset. The categories used here are the same as used by the ECJ.

21 Although most references are limited to a single subject matter of EC law, some references contain claims based on as many as five subject matters. This accounts for the dif- →

Some general conclusions can be derived from these numbers. While substantively preliminary references may concern a very broad range of issues, from the interpretation of general principles derived directly from the Treaties to the specific meaning of certain words in Directive texts, a number of patterns are visible in the types of cases in the selection. When considering the preliminary reference procedure with respect to individuals, we observe that the number of individuals involved in a preliminary reference procedure concentrates around certain areas of EU law.

Just as businesses and states are subject to certain kinds of legislation, for individuals to become involved in a procedure before the ECJ there is the obvious but necessary precondition of an EU rule to which they or their situation is subject. In other words: without a rule no dispute, without a dispute touching upon an EU rule no reference to the ECJ is possible. Simply stated, we would not expect to find preliminary references including individuals that cover for instance the area of the 'Nuclear common market'. The individuals thus belong to specific groups that broadly change along with newly emerging or changing EU legislation. As shown in Figure II, the areas of EU law that were the subject of Dutch individuals' cases before the ECJ were, most notably, the areas of 'freedom of movement for workers', 'agriculture', 'social security', cases concerning the category 'external' and (outside the meta-categories of Stone Sweet and Brunell) cases relating to the 'area of freedom, security and justice', 'citizenship of the Union' and 'visas, asylum and migration'.[22] We can conclude that the bulk of these individuals are therefore farmers (agriculture), workers (freedom of movement for workers, social security) and migrants and asylum seekers (visas, asylum and immigration).

The category 'external', while in fact a combination of areas of law (all EC economic policies affecting the European Free Trade Area (EFTA), the General Agreement on Tariffs and Trade (GATT), food aid, and special agreements with non-EC states), in this selection consist solely of cases pertaining to the Association Agreement of the EU with Turkey. These cases involve individuals with Turkish nationality with rights derived from the Association Agreement. These Turkish nationals can be added to the group of migrants. Together with the areas of 'border control', 'area of freedom, security and justice', 'fundamental' and 'human rights' as well as 'right of entry and residence' and 'citizenship', that are all cases involving non EU migrants, the cases involving migrants (excluding

ference between the number of selected cases and the total number of subject matters invoked in references.

22 The category of 'asylum policy' appears separate in the Courts administration as of 2010. For the sake of comparability I have added cases with this label to the general category of 'visa, asylum and immigration' as used by Stone Sweet & Brunell.

double scorings) amount to a little over 25%, making it the largest category in this selection.

When comparing these numbers with the remaining cases not involving individuals there are some striking contrasts. The area of taxation is among the lowest in individuals' cases but among the highest in the totality of cases. Other areas that score high when it comes to companies as litigants are: *competition*, *freedom of establishment*, *free movement of goods, approximation of laws* and *transport.* The meta-categories provided by Stone Sweet and Brunell are indeed very accurate in capturing the bulk (84%) of the references when it comes to companies. When selecting only individuals, however, these meta-categories account for only little over 60% of all cases. Notable areas that fall outside these categories are 'area of freedom, security and justice', 'visas, asylum and immigration' and 'citizenship of the union'. These areas of EU law are fairly recent additions to the *Acquis* with the introduction of the area of freedom, security and justice covering the harmonisation of private international law, extradition arrangements between Member States, policies on internal and external border controls, common travel visas, immigration and asylum policies and police and judicial cooperation. Additionally EU law has seen a significant increase in the amount of (secondary) legislation in the areas of asylum and migration in the first decade of this century.

4.3 Intermediate Conclusion

The aforementioned numbers on the selection of references from the Netherlands between 2008 and 2012 provide us a general sense of the subjects of individual litigation before the ECJ, what the sources of the references were and what the average duration of the proceedings was. Almost all cases concern disputes between individuals and government institutions and the relative distribution of the subjects suggests three main groups of litigants – farmers, workers and migrants – that make up the bulk of court cases that involve an individual as litigant. When considering the following quote by Conant, it is striking to see the relative number of cases addressing issues in exactly those areas mentioned: "Both the need to appeal through the national judicial hierarchy and the relative disinclination of most courts of last instance to make references create obstacles to individual legal action on issues related to visas, asylum, immigration and the free movement of persons."[23] Essentially, Conant expects little participation by individuals in the EU legal system on the whole. The relative number of individual cases, as well as the number of cases falling within areas relating to mi-

23 Conant 2003, 248. See also Conant 2002, 85 and 235.

grants, as well as the free movement of workers runs counter to Conant's expectations on effective access to justice for individuals.[24] Newly emerging EU legislation indicates an increase in EU legislation that potentially (more) directly affects individuals, and these numbers suggest that this results in increasing participation by individuals in Euro-litigation as well. Although these findings do not necessarily contradict Conant's assertion about the obstacles to individual legal action, it shows that these obstacles do not prevent individual participation altogether.

A pertinent question this study aims to answer is the question of who in fact are the individual participants in the EU legal system. For that purpose it is necessary to disaggregate the concept of 'individuals', which encompasses a wide range of actors with various interests as well as resources. Especially when considering litigation in the light of themes like active rights claiming, judicial review of government acts, litigation as political participation and notions of empowerment-through-law, it is imperative to look beyond the surface of what is visible from court documents and statistics in order to discern what disputes and motives lie behind the legal action and which parties and other actors are involved in the litigating effort. The next section addresses these questions and delves deeper into the possible explanatory factors that help understand the trajectory of these cases. For the remainder of this chapter, I investigate where these cases originate by focusing on the litigants and looking more closely at the behavioural factors of the litigating parties and the motives and interests that lie behind these legal actions.

4.4 On Proactive and Reactive Litigation

The described tendency in studies on Euro-litigation to adopt an ontologically rationalist approach to litigant preferences results in the implicit assumption that preliminary references constitute legal action by parties that have an interest in pursuing this course of action. Only rarely does inquiry venture further than what can be deduced from court documents, general statistics, and into behavioural aspects that play a role in the course of legal proceedings. The question is what role the litigating parties have in the trajectory of their case from the domestic to the supranational level. Selecting cases based on their reaching the ECJ through a reference captures both successful attempts at harnessing the procedure as a judicial strategy, as well as cases where neither party was actually seeking a referral. Therefore when considering references from a litigation

24 See Alter & Vargas 2000 and Burley & Mattli 1993 for similar reasoning and expectations.

perspective, first of all, a distinction has to be made between 'proactive' and 'reactive' litigation.[25] Whether or not parties are actively pushing for a reference gives further insight into the meaning of a reference from the perspective of the litigating parties. In this respect, Chalmers and Chaves found in their study on the role of EU judicial politics in the UK, that the decision by the national judge to refer relied in large part on the actions of the litigating parties.[26] They concluded that in the UK national judges rarely refer questions to the ECJ without one of the parties in the national proceedings proactively 'pushing for it'. The cases that were studied in depth in this study show considerable variation when it comes to the question of to whom the choice for a reference can be ascribed, and whether or not the reference may have been the result of the purposeful action of the litigants 'pushing for it'. Of course, given that the ultimate decision to refer lies squarely in the hands of the national judge, establishing whether a judge has in fact been convinced by the litigating party to refer a question, or whether he or she is motivated on his or her own, is not always possible. However, from the interviews with litigants and their counsel we do have insight into the degree to which litigating parties have tried to pressure a judge into considering a reference.

On the whole, in ten out of the total twenty-six cases studied in depth, respondents claimed it was the explicit aim to reach the ECJ and a reference was thus seen as a goal that would help serve their interests. In these cases of 'proactive' Euro-litigation, either from the outset, or developed during national proceedings, the litigants had their express wish and aim to have their case adjudicated by the ECJ, and implored the national court(s) to refer their case. The reasons behind this aim vary. Some cases simply revolved around a question of EU law for which there was no clear precedent in either national or ECJ jurisprudence and therefore the road to the ECJ was an anticipated and logical one, and litigants and their counsel saw the ECJ as the body best qualified to clear up the uncertainty. In other cases the wish to reach the ECJ was more informed by a deadlock in national doctrine, making the road to the ECJ a particularly viable opportunity to 'outflank' the national system. A good example of the latter is the case between catering employees and their employer, as described in detail in

25 The distinction between pro- and reactive litigation is used often in the context of legal mobilisation studies in order to make a distinction between strategies of pressure groups either proactively using the filing of lawsuits as part their strategy, or reactively employing court cases, such as criminal proceedings against, for instance, participants in protests, and incorporating them as part of their strategy. See Harlow and Rawlings 1992. Here, I use the distinction to draw attention to the fact that the preliminary reference procedure could be seen as a viable part of legal strategy but can also be an unexpected result of the considerations of the national judge.

26 Chalmers & Chaves 2011.

Case Study A. In this case the ECJ's interpretation of the Directive regarding the safeguarding of employees' rights in the event of the transfer of an undertaking allowed for possible protection for the employees that was different from the prevailing doctrine in Dutch jurisprudence. In such cases, aiming for a reference can prove a useful strategy where success with national judges, who are inclined to apply prevailing national doctrine, is unlikely.

In seven of the twenty-six cases, the litigating parties put forward a deliberate focus on EU law yet had no explicit aim of eliciting a referral to the ECJ. In these cases the dispute did revolve around questions of EU law, but neither litigants nor their counsel had the intention of having the national judge refer their case to Luxembourg. They were simply aiming for, and expecting a resolution by national courts. Even in cases that were explicitly set up to clear up legal or practical questions pertaining to EU law, the aim was not necessarily to have these questions adjudicated by the ECJ. For example, in the *Self-Employed Tax Deductions* case, although the small tax consultancy firm behind the litigation explicitly used the case to 'test the waters' of EU law, the preliminary reference procedure was initially not even considered as a possible avenue. The aim and expectation was that the Dutch Supreme Court would give a principle ruling on the matter of non-discrimination according to nationality in the matter of tax deductions for the self-employed. The consultant explained discussing the moment preliminary questions were asked by the Dutch High Council:

> "At first, I hadn't even considered that that could happen. I thought, the legal question is pretty clear. But given the structure, how the court of appeal had framed its ruling, the Supreme Court felt like, there are some nuances here that I want to submit to the Court of Justice."

In such cases, the choice for referral of the case to the ECJ thus lies expressly with the national court. Similarly, in *Case Study C* of the organised Working Group of lawyers, academics and an NGO using EU law in order to challenge the Dutch policy on fees for residence permits (discussed in detail later in the book), a reference to the ECJ was seen as an unnecessary and unwanted delay. Even the Working Group's lawyer explicitly did not mention a possible reference to the ECJ and presented the matter as "clear and already decided by the Court". The Dutch Council of State (*Raad van State*, the highest Dutch court in administrative law) nonetheless decided to refer the case. So, even when a case serves to get a judgment on principle based on EU rules, the ECJ is not always the intended target. In light of assumptions of purposefulness behind litigation before the ECJ, it is thus important to note that even when the result of a case may be that the ECJ provides a principle judgment, the aim of the litigating party can still be very much focused on the national legal system.

In the remaining nine out of twenty-six cases, there was no express aim on the part of the litigating party with regard to questions of the interpretation or application of EU law, and the reference came as a complete surprise to them. Whether or not a reference is part of a legal strategy has a bearing on the way a case is litigated, and especially when it is not, this has repercussions for the parties involved. Lawyers as well as their clients may be completely blind-sided by the decision of a judge to refer a case, and are forced to adapt to a course of action with which they (usually) have no experience.[27] Also, from the perspective of the litigants a reference to the ECJ is far from always welcome because it amounts to further prolongation of their uncertainty, considering the average time of eighteen months it takes the ECJ to decide these cases. In this sense, the preliminary reference procedure itself may actually be considered a procedural obstacle in a practical sense, which can lead litigants to drop their case due to the extended duration of the proceedings. The fact that cases reach the ECJ and do receive a judgment on principle should thus not automatically lead to the conclusion that this was the express goal of (one of) the litigating parties. Moreover, as I will discuss below, the referral of a case to the ECJ may transform it in ways that were not intended (or always desired).

4.5 Litigant Characteristics

The court statistics have shown that the bulk of individuals involved in preliminary reference procedures are farmers, workers and migrants. Further typologies can be made based on the individual characteristics of litigants. In general, two types of litigants can be distinguished; falling into categories according to how active the litigants themselves were in pursuing a legal claim. The first category is made up of individual litigants who seek to employ every avenue possible in their legal claim. In such cases they play a very active personal role in their case. Rosenthal defined 'active' clients as those who express special wants to their lawyer, make follow-up demands for attention, provide additional information to aid the lawyer, seek a second legal opinion, etc.[28] He found that such 'active' clients were drawn disproportionately from those of higher social status, which presumably provided both the confidence and the experience to conduct themselves in this active manner. Since in these cases the litigants' claim includes an EU law element, the referral of the case to the ECJ is one possible outcome. Among the very active individuals, the ones taking legal action without any

27 This aspect of preliminary references will be discussed in more detail in Chapter 5, which will focus on the perspective of these practitioners.

28 Rosenthal 1974.

legal support, and thus acting *pro se*, constitute a very small group; only three such examples were found.[29] Also included in this category of active litigants are the more collective actions, brought by multiple individuals sharing the same interests. The cases of the catering employees as well as the pensioners (*Case Study A* and *Case Study B* respectively) are prominent examples. Such cases, with truly active litigants in fact constitute a minority, and most litigants belong to the second, and largest category, which covers the more passive or even more or less completely absent litigant. Out of the twenty-six cases studied in depth seven included actively involved litigants, while the remaining litigants were either passively involved (nine) or more or less absent (ten).

The more passive litigants, consistent with Rosenthal's expectations, are found especially in asylum and migration law cases, where clients often are completely reliant on their lawyer, and show limited involvement in the course of the proceedings. The more or less completely absent litigants are found in cases where another actor or collective is responsible for the legal action. These cases include accountancy firms seeking to get a judgment on principle on matters of interest to their clientele, so-called 'cause lawyers' individually seeking to get an answer to a principle question, and the more strategically motivated alliances of interest groups, lawyers and academics proactively contesting national policy. Such categorisation and the relative lack of involvement of the individuals whose case is brought before the courts hints at an inherent difficulty in determining the interests that lie at the basis of legal action. As we will see later, it is not always straightforward to determine with any precision who the 'real' litigant is.

Building on the insight that reaching the ECJ was the aim in a minority of cases, I will focus on the various contexts, motives and origins of litigation and relate these to the assumption of interests, strategies and questions of purposefulness. The next sections will deal with different litigant characteristics, ask to whom motives and aims behind litigation can be ascribed, and investigate the extent to which these aspects have explanatory value for the trajectory of these cases.

4.6 The 'Irrational' Litigant: Dealing with Assumptions of Interest

The majority of studies about the behaviour of litigants before the ECJ are based on ontologically rational approaches and assumptions of cost-benefit calculations. Whenever the role of litigants' behaviour is taken into account it is usually assumed that litigation is initiated where people expect material benefit in so

29 For a typology of *pro se* litigants see Vago 2006, 391.

doing, and people are expected to refrain from initiating legal proceedings when the outcome of cost-benefit calculations is negative. When immersing ourselves in the world of litigation, one is immediately confronted with its complexity and compounded nature, and getting to grips with the varying interests and motives behind litigation can be a daunting task, due to the multiplicity of relevant factors, as well as the transformations that may occur during legal action. This was a point famously made by Felstiner et al. who argued that "[e]ven in ordinary understanding, disputing is a complicated process involving ambiguous behavior, faulty recall, uncertain norms, conflicting objectives, inconsistent values, and complex institutions. It is complicated still further by attention to changes in disputant feelings and objectives over time."[30]

A closer look at motives behind these court cases indeed reveals a far more complex picture when it comes to the considerations of litigants for legal action than a rationalist approach suggests. Although an important incentive for legal action and a distinct element in the considerations of litigants, motives for legal action are not solely based on an assessment of the expected (financial) gain. The motives for engaging in legal action are neither straightforward nor always based on cost-benefit calculations. In fact, from both the interviews and substantive analysis of these cases it is clear that in more than a third, ten out of twenty-six cases, the cost-benefit ratio for the individual claimant was such that following a clear-cut rational action approach we would not expect these cases to have resulted in litigation in the first place.[31] The question then arises, what other considerations on the part of the litigant may serve as an explanation for these cases reaching the ECJ.

4.7 Reaching for that 'Final' Judgment

The different areas of law that potentially fall under the jurisdiction of the ECJ result in a complex combination of the types of disputes that end up before the Court. While many areas of EU law are concerned especially with establishing restrictions on governmental practice through substantive and individual rights (in the case of workers' protection or asylum procedures, for example), other areas have the character of conferring obligations upon individuals. The area of

30 Felstiner, Abel & Sarat 1980, 638.

31 Of course, this form of weighting costs and benefits is somewhat arbitrary in the sense that determining actual costs nor determining actual gains of a case is clear cut, especially when the possible gains are not of a financial nature. However, these conclusions are based on the personal judgments of litigants and their lawyers. One case, for example, resulted in a difference in tax deduction from 330 euro to 253 euro annually, a difference of only seventy-seven euro.

agricultural law is a prime example in this respect. As one of the oldest areas of EU legislation, it has permeated much of the national legislation on agricultural practice. Such rules cover, among others, rural development, animal welfare, food safety and agricultural subsidies. As a result, a substantial portion of the rules and regulations to which farmers are subject are EU rules. The significant portion of agricultural cases dealt with by the ECJ (both in general as in the selection for this study) can in part be ascribed to this pervasiveness of EU law in this area. With regard to individuals, this also has consequences for the type of dispute that is the basis for litigation before the ECJ. Without exception, the cases of farmers that end up before the ECJ start with a purported violation by these farmers of EU rules and regulations, and possible related cuts in subsidies as a result.

One example is the case of a farmer whose (EU) subsidies were withdrawn due to a purported violation of the relevant requirements for said subsidy. The amount of money he lost as a result of the withdrawal did not weigh up to eventual costs, financial as well as personal, of the litigation effort. Yet he chose to fight the decision for a full eleven years. When asked about the financial aspect of this case he emphatically states:

> "When we started, the opposition asked whether the money was that important to me. I said no, it's the principle that matters to me. It came down to about 1,100 euro reduction, and an 875 euro fine. And money is nice of course, but I thought that was more an afterthought. It became a matter of principle. I felt I was being treated unfairly. And in the end it took me eleven years to address that."

This farmer's story is a case of individual persistence. His motive for litigating lay in a personal sense of being wronged. In his quest for justice, he became increasingly dissatisfied with the result of the legal procedures and how in his view the whole process was riddled with unfairness, resistance and even corruption. He was considerably disadvantaged by a relative lack of knowledge about the proceedings, especially in the preliminary stage. Asked whether he was aware of the ECJ, he answers:

> "I did not know it. I had thought there would be some kind of umbrella organization, but I was not aware there was a court, no. I imaged it more like an official administrative organisation in Brussels. But I didn't know about the Court. I had never even heard the word preliminary reference before."

The fact that his case ended up before the ECJ can be ascribed more to the diligent national judge that saw a need for the ECJ to answer a question as to the right interpretation of the related EU Regulation.[32] Not knowing the ECJ, for the farmer, the Court had in no way been a target but simply became a step on the way towards personal vindication. Although he lost his case before the ECJ, he subsequently went on to start several national civil proceedings. Eventually, after eleven years and several thousands of euros of legal expenses, he reluctantly struck a deal with authorities, which ended the legal quarrel.

4.8 'Frivolous' Litigation

Another example, with a clearly negative cost-benefit result, is the *Tethered or Chained?* case of a farmer who was fined 500 euro for not complying with an animal welfare regulation based on EU Directives. This farmer, who was well known locally for his organic breeding style, received a fine for not keeping his young calves in accordance with the rules laid down in a Directive on the minimum standards for the protection of calves.[33] The fine, in his view was meant to set an example explicitly using a well-known local farmer like himself. His subsequent unwavering stance was his way of highlighting the absurdity of the strictness in the application of these rules by the agency that initially fined him. In his words:

> "Look, everything is filled with regulation these days, a lot of legislation that makes no sense. Rome perished due to its decadence and we are going to perish in regulations."

His reasons for litigation were a deliberately light-hearted response to the, in his view, bureaucratic stubbornness of the Dutch food and consumer goods authority. Never expecting to win, this farmer decided to make a point and play it out until the end. In response to the question whether he felt he had accomplished anything with his litigating efforts he responds:

> "Well, I've learned a lot. That's the point. I did not do it to gain something. But I did it just to know how it all works. An ordinary person just does not know, really. So I thought I'll take it. I told my wife, I'm going to drink this whole cup. I want to experience the whole circus. That joke, I just wanted to have."

32 In many respects the ECJ has been working on ways to temper such diligence, by encouraging self-restraint by national judges in referring too many questions to the Court. See Advocate General Jacobs' Opinion in case C-338/95 *Wiener S.I. GmbH v Hauptzollamt Emmerich* (para. 17) in which he discusses the limited value of some questions that are put before the Court.

33 Council Directive 91/629/EEC.

As an active board member of several livestock farming related associations, he was not unfamiliar with bureaucratic and rule related quarrels. Moreover, he was well aware of his chances of winning, or the lack thereof. The financial aspect of this case is striking. The costs of going to court far outweighed what winning the case was worth. He explains the costs of the whole proceedings:

> "I have not summed it all up, I don't know. It took a lot of money, yes. I should have just paid that fine. [Laughs] That would have been only 200 euro, and this has cost thousands. No, you do not have to try achieving justice in the Netherlands, that usually costs more than you get."

Considering that he expected beforehand that he was not going to win, his motives for legal action can hardly be designated as a form of cost-benefit consideration. He even had to convince his own lawyer, who did not deem it necessary, to attend the hearing in Luxembourg, a trip that most lawyers in this study were more than willing to make and that was often described in terms of 'privilege' and 'once in a lifetime experience'. His lawyer, who had decided in another one of his cases that was referred to the ECJ to refrain from travelling to Luxembourg, confirms:

> "My experience with pleading before the Court of Justice is in large part thanks to my client's character and way of thinking and working. Nine out of ten people would not have done what he did, at least nine out of ten. Any other would have just paid the fine. But he is stubborn, so it is thanks to him that we have this judgment."

The unwavering disposition of the authorities is an important reason why his case went as far as it did. He himself described the point he wanted to make using the German proverb '*Jede Konsequenz führt zum Teufel*', which translates freely into 'consistent into hell'. One can debate the noteworthiness of the rights or obligations that were put before the ECJ to adjudicate in these cases. In the latter case, the central question to be answered by the Court was whether or not his practice of farming was in accordance with animal welfare regulations. Ultimately this boiled down to the interpretation of the word '*tethered*' vis-à-vis the Dutch translation '*aangebonden*' in the respective texts of the Directive upon which the initial fine was based. Although the question of the proper way of binding one's calves is one that could probably have been dealt with without the help of the ECJ, as a result of both these parties 'sticking to their guns' it is now settled case law that "where there is a divergence between the various language versions of an EU legislative text, the provision in question must be interpreted by reference to the purpose and general scheme of the rules of which it forms part".[34] So, with his stubbornness this farmer gave the ECJ an opportunity to add another building block, the proper way of settling language divergence in EU legislation, to the *Acquis*. In the end the farmer was convicted, but without punishment by the national criminal judge, who considered that it was 'thanks to his efforts that we now have an answer to this important question'. He did not have to pay the 500 euro fine.

Disputes like these illustrate some of the more mundane questions the ECJ is asked to answer with some regularity. Similarly, two more cases on agriculture-related matters (*Breeding or Fattening?* and *Suckler Cow Premiums*) were at least in part about the accuracy and applicability of certain terminology in EU legislation. In this regard, Schepel & Blankenburg refer to former ECJ judge Mancini who somewhat mockingly concluded, "if the Court ever acquires the power to indulge in agenda-setting, the customs classification of shoes and sandals will not be high on the agenda".[35] At the same time, they highlight the difficulties of constructing any type of cross-European or Euro-profile of litigation or considering litigation from a rationalist perspective. Rather than references all being 'demands for integration' or an attempt to profit from the acquired European freedoms for individual citizens, in fact, cases like these are more easily understood as examples of resistance against the application of EU rules than anything else.

4.9 Individual Persistence: Surviving the Legal System

Undoubtedly, the aforementioned case of 'frivolous' litigation is somewhat of an anomaly. Especially when considering the duration of the proceedings, the additional costs of the trip to Luxembourg, and the fact that this litigant continually described the affair in terms of 'a joke', it is unlikely that cases like this are widespread. However, what these examples highlight is how motives for litigation are not always as easily understood as being the result of cost-benefit calculations on the part of the litigating party. Since the potential benefit of winning their case did not weigh up to the cost of the proceedings, the trajectory of these disputes can in large part be ascribed to the unwillingness of these farmers to give in and their desire to take a stand. The main personal trait of the litigants to which the course of these cases can be ascribed is their persistence, often against the odds; a recurring theme among the active litigants in the case selection.

Similarly, the story of the catering employees (*Case Study A*) illustrates how such persistence by one individual can indeed be essential to litigation efforts. In

34 Opinion of Advocate General Sharpston referring to this case in C-554/13.

35 As quoted in Schepel & Blankenburg 2001, 40.

the case of their prolonged battle with their current and former employers, the employee leading the charge was advised on multiple occasions, by his lawyer and the workers union supporting them, to take a deal proposed by his former employer and discontinue the legal action. Despite this, he continued his quest and therefore became the main champion of the collective interests that were served by the eventual successful ECJ judgment. In part thanks to the financial and organisational capacity offered to him by the workers union, but also thanks to his own persistence, he became responsible for limiting the possibilities to circumvent worker protection under EU law, in the case of the transfer of an undertaking.

Especially the length of most of these legal actions underscores the requirement of personal perseverance. Two other illustrative examples, cases where the litigants acted *pro se,* help to underscore this point. These cases were both brought by individuals with considerable personal legal agency. One (*Mortgage Interest Deduction*) was a legal expert working as a public servant, and the other (*Proportional Tax Deduction*) a tax consultant who decided to start proceedings in his own name to address a Dutch VAT regulation that he saw as incorrectly implemented in light of European rules. While such a matter could have been addressed in any one of his clients' cases, he explains that his case would never be part of his regular practice, since the possible gains would not weigh up to the costs of his services:

> "For a client, you will never start such a procedure, because it costs them too much, and doesn't get you much in the end. So for me it was really more of a point of principle."

The ECJ eventually ruled in his favour, contrary to prevailing views among Dutch VAT specialists. Illustrative in this respect is that it took a legal professional to bring up a matter that through the ordinary course of legal practice would never have been addressed. Since he was able to act as his own consultant he incurred no extra costs. In the other case, the individual did in fact consider hiring a lawyer but was dissuaded by the high cost:

> "I have considered taking on a specialized lawyer. And I did find one who was very willing to help, because in the literature at the moment, professors left and right were debating my case. Everyone thought something else, so they were interested in my case. But then you're told beforehand that if they have to catch up completely on my case, after all those years, then just preparations will cost 8,000 euro. And then they haven't been to Luxembourg yet. That would run into tens of thousands of euros before you have a ruling. That's obviously not possible. For any ordinary citizen like me, that threshold to find your way to justice is terribly high. The financial interest I had did not outweigh the cost of a lawyer."

Ultimately he was able, through his own legal background and a lot of effort, to win his case. Although in many respects examples of an individual successfully employing EU law to further his or her interests before the national judge, these cases particularly illustrate the amount of effort needed to do so. Such examples suggest that we should not expect too many cases of this sort. Firstly, these litigants are legal professionals, thus able to draw from their own expertise and work a case without assistance. Therefore, both were aware of the role of EU law and the ECJ. And secondly, the duration of these cases (seven and eleven years in total) requires considerable persistence, especially in light of the relatively small financial stakes.

4.10 Stakes and Impact: Perspectives on Success

When considering the impact of the proceedings on individual motives for litigation, it is important to note the differences in potential personal impact of government decisions that are being disputed. These differences largely coincide with the different areas of law; for example, when we compare fiscal law cases to migration law cases. As explained by an asylum lawyer:

> "In immigration law it is black and white, you do or do not get a residence permit, whether that is regular or asylum. There are no consolation prizes, half-residence permits or the like, so typically there the cases will be brought to court."

In comparison, a tax advisor compared the general impact of fiscal cases to that of asylum cases, when asked for the involvement of her client in the case:

> "Not really excessively. But with tax law, that's always the case. The joy you'll get with an asylum seeker for example, whose life is completely changed, that is of an entirely different order. With us it is mostly just a nice bonus."

Indeed, it is not difficult to imagine that often the interests in migration and asylum law cases are of a different personal magnitude and the incentives for starting a case differ accordingly. In most cases concerning migrants, the government refused or revoked the residence permit of the individual, for reasons ranging from the non-payment of the accompanying administrative fees to people who were declared undesirable due to being convicted of a crime. During proceedings contesting the governmental decisions, these people lose most of their rights related to residence; the right to work, the right to social security and health insurance as well all forms of subsidies and/or fiscal returns. The migration lawyer in *Double Nationality,* where his client faced expatriation due to being convicted of a crime, discusses the toll such cases can take on his clients:

> "You have to imagine that in this case my client was glad he wasn't expelled from the country when he came out of prison. But we also had to sue again in order to get that preliminary injunction to prevent expulsion. He was lucky that he could go home to his wife and children. But in the meantime you have no entitlements, no health insurance or anything. The fees for the children, benefits, healthcare, etc., everything is affected. He could not work, so it also has a negative psychological effect on people. And that's the other side of the story of these kinds of issues that are challenged before the Court. And ultimately, in practice you have to litigate to the highest instance nationally, and then you also must await the judgment by the Court of Justice. That takes its toll on the lives of people."

For the individuals and their families the consequences of a government decision as well as the following legal proceedings can thus be enormous; having to choose between accepting the decision and leaving the country and thus their family and livelihood, or contesting the decision and enduring the loss of rights with all its consequences, including living in constant uncertainty over the outcome of one's case. For most this does not feel like a choice at all, and leaves these people between the proverbial Scylla and Charybdis. In such cases the efforts of the lawyer play a large role in assisting his or her clients both legally as well as psychologically. As one other lawyer specialized in migration law explains:

> "I really have to take them in tow. You have to consider it from the psychology of that one person. Because it eventually ends up at the Council of State, he lives for four years in a position you really do not wish on your enemies. Because you do not know what will happen, whether he can stay here? Because he is not allowed to work anymore. So those people are penniless, and they cannot claim benefits."

Such pressures are not reserved for cases of migrants and questions of residence, but are relevant in social security matters as well. In *Compulsory Insurance,* a labour union supported a litigant, who had been employed on an oilrig on the Dutch part of the continental shelf, in his effort to fight a cut in his disability allowance. The judgment in his case had repercussions for the treatment of people in similar situations, and stipulated that Dutch social insurance should not exclude employees from other Member States operating on the Dutch part of the continental shelf. Although the eventual ECJ judgment was in his favour, and his allowance was subsequently paid retroactively, he reflects on the impact the dispute had on his situation:

> "The whole situation has cost me a lot. I was stuck in social isolation and it was difficult to get out. My wife left me and suddenly I had to make do with much less money. At the beginning, I went into debt because I could not adjust to the fact that I

> suddenly had less than a third of my income. So, I still have to see what it all means for me. In any case, it is good for all those who do the same work as I did."

As such, the reference to the ECJ itself can become a prolongation of the dire situation in which litigants find themselves. Even in cases where the personal impact of the proceedings is not as high, lawyers often state that referral to the ECJ, from their perspective, is not always desirable due to the additional length of the procedure and the extra work involved. When neither litigant nor lawyer has an interest in getting a judgment on principle from the ECJ the prolongation of the proceedings is not met with great enthusiasm. Especially when a case, by reference to the ECJ may serve the interests of more than a single client, lawyers must make trade-offs between the interests of the client and the interest in answering the legal question. In asylum cases for example, the procedures have large consequences for those involved, they often not only have an interest in a positive ruling but sometimes also in a quick decision. As one asylum lawyer explains:

> "Well, it would have been great if the Council of State had decided in our favour without a reference. But you have no control over the court's decision. Of course, you can suggest questions, but that's always a bit awkward. Because you know it will take a lot of time so that your client has to wait a long time. And, of course, that is not in their favour because they can have a residence permit much faster. But if the court thinks that a reference is absolutely necessary, you cannot stop them."

When it comes to legal proceedings then, the notion of *interest* is usually connected more or less directly to the outcome of court decisions. It is not in all cases that the result of a case for the individuals involved is as easy to determine based simply on a court's judgment. A reference to the ECJ is not always strictly in the litigants' interest. When looking at the results of a case, it matters greatly whose perspective and what parameters for success one applies.

Illustrative is *Case Study C* (included later in the book), which describes the legal battle against unlawful increases in fees for residence permits. When viewing the ECJ case in isolation and based on the consequences of the Court's judgment for the Dutch policy only, it indeed suggests that an individual citizen was able to enforce his rights with the help of the ECJ, being in a sense empowered vis-à-vis his government.[36] It seems that here the ECJ in that sense fulfilled its role as a true 'people's court', curtailing Member States' trespasses.[37] The context reveals, however, that since this case was part of a conscious and collective effort with a number of central and more powerful actors, the actual role of

36 Cf. Cichowski 2007.
37 Wernicke 2007.

the individual involved in such a case is very limited. And with changing the perspective from the aims and experiences of the Working Group to those of the individuals involved, the parameters for success also change. The story of this individual's case is described mostly from the perspective of the parties behind the scenes who employed it for the purposes of challenging the Dutch policy on administrative fees. Telling that same story from the individual's perspective reveals the personal impact such proceedings can have, eventual success notwithstanding. In fact, from interviewing him and his wife, I found that they had little understanding of the procedure, or of the role of the ECJ and they appeared unaware of the collective interests that were being served by their case.[38] Their interests lay with simply obtaining a permit and ending the uncertainty. He had been in possession of a residence permit, which ran until November 2002, and had asked for an extension before it expired. However, the Dutch authorities maintained that this request was never received. In February 2003, when his stay had expired by two months, he submitted another extension request for which he received a payment slip for a fee of 169 euro. Due to a transfer problem, this payment was completed a week too late. The fact that these fees weren't paid in time meant that the request would not be considered, resulting in him receiving an order to leave the country. At this point he and his wife sought help from their lawyer. The lawyer recalls that it took three years before his case was eventually referred to the ECJ:

> "Well, the objection was deemed unfounded. We filed for appeal, which was granted in Court. That was very easy because I had relied on Association law arguments. Since the Immigration and Naturalisation Services (IND) in the decision on appeal had not addressed them that was just not a reasoned decision on that point. So then the case went back to the IND. Then the objection was declared unfounded again, this time with a tailored decision on the Association Agreement. We then filed a second appeal and then the Court of Rotterdam said that the action was justified because it was indeed contrary to the Association Agreement. To that decision the Minister of Justice appealed, and then in May 2006 the Council of State finally referred questions to the Court of Justice."

During the appeal process, his loss of residence was not suspended, and the reference to the ECJ added another three years and three months to his already lengthy endeavour. For him and his family the proceedings meant a prolonged period of substantial uncertainty and a loss of his work permit, his social securi-

38 Their already limited understanding of the procedure was in all likelihood not helped by the fact that he spoke no Dutch at all and his wife, also not a native speaker had to function as a translator between her husband and their lawyer.

ty and his health insurance. In response to the question whether they had expected it to take this long his wife, acting as his translator responds:

> "No, not really. For as long as seven years, he could not go abroad. He had no insurance, he could not work, so I had to do everything. So, seven years we were waiting, from 2002 to 2009. And I had just had my first child in 2002, so it was tough for me, and for him, too."

Apart from a loss of work, income and a social network, he was furthermore unable to leave the country, for, if he did, he would not be allowed back in. This meant he could not accompany his family on family visits to Turkey for over seven years. He described the whole period as feeling like "being imprisoned". The added three years of waiting for an ECJ judgment obviously made this aspect even worse. The collective interests being served by his case, effectively being employed as a test case, were thus not necessarily those of the individual. Even with eventual success the consequences for those directly involved were not entirely positive.

4.11 Promises and Expectations: (Mis)understanding the Court

The relatively small number of cases that reaches the ECJ on the express wish of the litigants raises the question of when and why litigants have a desire to have their case adjudicated by the ECJ, and how those with experience with the Court evaluate its adjudication. While only a minority of litigants can be considered truly active in their pursuit of justice (not leaving their case completely in the hands of their lawyer), this group can be used to evaluate litigants' expectations and evaluations of the ECJ in its treatment of their case. Among this small group, the perceptions of the Court and the way their case was handled differed considerably. While for many the referral to the ECJ initially felt like an improvement in their chances, perceiving the Court as a form of extended appeal beyond the national courts, attending the proceedings before the Court did not always serve to strengthen their belief in fair treatment.

In general, most litigants knew little about the ECJ before their case was referred, and they had high hopes going in. Especially where the preceding procedures within the national system had been particularly disappointing, the ECJ appeared to litigants as a promise of more neutral and expert treatment.[39] The litigant in *Mortgage Tax Deductions*, acting *pro se* recollects:

39 A good example of this perceived contrast between national judges, seen as extensions of government, and the ECJ as more neutral can be read in the case of the pensioners, described in *Case Study B*.

> "Every time I had to read again that they concluded I was wrong, I systematically indicated, listen, why don't we have this tested by the European Court. I always hoped that would be perceived as a kind, well threat goes too far, but as a kind of incentive for them to have it looked at truly objectively. I have always had a very good feeling about European law and the Court. I always had the feeling that in the Netherlands I would not be able to win, but I had good hopes that in Europe I was going to succeed. And that's the reason I've always consistently indicated that in the documents."

As discussed, this litigant was, due to his own legal background quite familiar with the work of the ECJ, and thus had a good grasp of the opportunity that lay in EU law, as well as how the ECJ might deal with his case. Often, however, the positive expectations of litigants are based not on a full grasp of the legal merits of their case but on a certain idea about the Court as the 'highest of courts'. As the farmer in *Suckler Cow Premiums* describes how he felt after his case was referred:

> "That's when I thought it was all going to work out. If even the appeals court has its doubts ... That strengthened me in my conviction. Now the 'supreme judge' is going to look at it. So that's when I thought it would turn out alright."

Thus, the mere referral of people's cases to the ECJ can provide a sense of validation of their claim. This is further confirmed in the interviews with lawyers, who explained that the procedure was difficult for the clients to understand. As discussed by one lawyer, it was not easy to explain to clients the role and significance of a reference to the ECJ:

> "Of course, I'm not going to discuss with clients all the technical procedures and so on. But what I explain to them is that the EU is not an appeals court. And I will try to explain that the Dutch judge is basically asking for clarification. That is always difficult to get across. Clients always have the idea that the Court of Justice is a higher appeal body."

The perceived obscurity over these proceedings resulted in some remarkable misunderstandings among litigants, most notably about the intervening of the European Commission and other Member States. As one of the pensioners, involved in the case described in *Case Study B*, recalls:

> "Some strange things happened at the Court of Justice. The Court asked the advice of other Member States. And which countries did they choose? Finland and the Czech Republic, where almost no Dutch people live, and France where there is no such problem. And they all disagreed with us and said we must participate in national solidarity. Because these countries, especially Finland, are very much focused

> on solidarity. In a previous case there were Spaniards and Portuguese and they are much more individualistic. I think simply by choosing these countries, they can steer the case in a certain direction. It does not mean that the EU court did not do its job correctly, but I have the impression that they influence it and that we are manipulated."

To be clear, the ECJ does not choose the intervening Member States; interventions by Member States occur on their own initiative. However, the attendance and intervention of specific Member States can thus result in a sense of disparity, due to different parties giving their opinions before the Court. In the most extreme examples this results in the perception by litigants that there has been evident foul play. One of the farmers discussed at the beginning of this chapter, remained frustrated after his experience with the ECJ. Since he had chosen not to consult a lawyer, his general lack of knowledge about the ECJ, and the peculiarities that come with a preliminary reference, weren't ameliorated. His lack of understanding is illustrated by the fact that he remembered that, apart from France, there was "a European commission that had been created for my case," that had also given its opinion in the case. This was of course *the* European Commission filing observations. He did not request a hearing before the ECJ and was unaware that this had been a possibility, although in hindsight he would have liked one. While he in many respects found the European Commission on his side, arguing in favour of his position, the Court nonetheless reached a different conclusion. This unexpected turn left him disillusioned and with the suspicion that something malicious had taken place:

> I: "So you had expected, following the views of France and the Commission, that it would turn out in your favour?"
> R: "Yes, and that's my conclusion, what I think about the Court. It's a totally unpredictable, and, yes, what word should I use for it, it's corrupt, that such a thing can happen. Through influencing by the opposition, while there was no formal possibility. They have been lobbying behind the scenes. And well, it worked. The beauty of that European commission was that they reviewed the facts very well, and came to a favourable conclusion. Apparently, that did not sit well with the Dutch Government. It is very corrupt, how that all went down."

Especially in such cases, where litigants are not assisted by legal counsel, the preliminary reference procedure can create significant confusion about the nature and purpose of the proceedings, particularly with other parties joining in the proceedings.

While litigants may have high expectations of the Court when it comes to neutrality and expertise, the ways of the Court do not always serve to strengthen their perceptions of fair treatment. Although the Court itself presents these proceedings clearly as a form of 'judicial cooperation', it can be questioned how the procedure impacts the original dispute from the perspective of the litigant. In line with the 'judicial cooperation' image of the procedure, the actual role for the individual in the proceedings before the ECJ is very limited. All communications between the Court and the parties are channelled through the lawyers, and during a hearing before the Court the individuals, unless they attend while representing themselves, have no role to play in the actual proceedings. Where lawyers are received at the Court, introduced to the judges and instructed about the procedures during the hearing, the litigants themselves are delegated to the public gallery. Although only a minority of litigants actually express an interest in attending the Court's proceedings, this raises questions about the nature of the procedure and the possible impact of this experience on the perceived (procedural) justice of the parties. The technical nature of the proceedings, with little to no role for the individual litigant left some with the feeling of being a spectator to their own dispute. As the coffee shop owner in *Free Movement of Cannabis* laments:

> "To begin with, as a party in a case I expect that I get the chance to be heard. And secondly, that I'm taken seriously and I can sit in the front. At the Court of Justice, I had to sit in the audience. The attorney of the Netherlands was allowed to speak, and my lawyer too, but I had to sit in the public gallery, and not show my disapproval. The usher had to urge me several times to remain calm."

This litigant was one of the few with a reasonably good grasp of the function of the preliminary reference procedure. More generally, only rarely did litigants, whether they had travelled to Luxembourg or not, have a good understanding of the reason for, and function of referral of their case to the ECJ for a preliminary ruling. Asked what she thought of the fact that the ECJ would rule in her case, one litigant responds:

> "Yes, it is a nice feeling. Especially that other countries found our story interesting enough and wanted to say something about it. They were behind us, I think."

In fact, in this case, none of the intervening Member States were on the side of the litigant, and the assumption about their opinions is illustrative of a general lack of understanding by litigants about the purpose and practice of the preliminary reference procedure.

When looking at the preliminary reference procedure from an institutional perspective, there thus appears to be a discrepancy between the function of the procedure – the interpretation of EU legislation in order for EU law to be uniformly applied in all Member States – and the occasion on or form in which this function is performed – namely in the resolution of an actual dispute. This discrepancy could be a partial explanation for a mismatch in perception of the

ECJ's practice and the experiences and aspirations of litigants. For those litigants who are 'confronted' with the ECJ's authority, its mere existence constitutes the 'promise' of another form of high court. Expectations are thus usually quite high. Litigants generally expect the 'highest court of Europe' to provide significant expertise and authority. The misunderstanding of the role of the Court and of the preliminary reference procedure contribute to either a sense of respect and support for the Court, in the case of a decidedly favourable outcome, or dismissal and distrust, in the case of a resulting loss.

4.12 Conclusion

From the subjects of the cases brought before the ECJ we can conclude that the largest share of individual litigants with cases before the ECJ is made up of migrants, workers and farmers, coinciding with some of the most salient EU policy areas: the Common Agricultural Policy, created in 1962 and covering a wide range of agricultural practices and a system of subsidies, as one of the oldest policies of the EU affecting farmers, free movement of workers and relatedly affected European and national social policies affecting workers throughout the EU, and the Association Agreement between the EU and Turkey as well as the more recent efforts creating a Common European Asylum System affecting migrants and asylum seekers. These areas thus form the bulk of individual cases that reach the ECJ. However, the counting of cases only gets us so far in understanding litigation before the ECJ, and gives little insight into the how and why of litigation through the preliminary reference procedure. The variation in the types of cases that reach the ECJ shows the complexity of litigation and should lead to an increased sensitivity in our analysis of developments and dynamics in litigation. Chalmers and Chaves rightfully conclude in this respect that "such heterogeneity makes it impossible to point to a single dynamic pushing forward the preliminary reference process".[40] While all these cases contribute in one way or another to the shaping and steering of the impact of EU legislation on a local and sometimes international level, *post hoc* conclusions as to the intentionality of these outcomes need to be based on an understanding of the goals and interests of the parties involved, which cannot readily be surmised by solely looking at the legal outcomes.

To add a new dimension to our understanding of the practice of preliminary references, I investigated the role of underlying motives and the background of litigants in explaining the trajectory of cases that end up before the ECJ. Behavioural aspects may influence the trajectories of cases that may or may not result

40 Chalmers & Chaves 2011, 35.

in European arbitration, depending not only on the willingness of the national judiciary to refer but also on the persistence of the parties involved. When taking into account that cases including references to the ECJ can take up to eleven years, it is not a stretch to assume that, from the point of view of the litigant, whenever the costs outweigh the possible benefits, motivation for continued legal efforts with accompanying costs (financial and other) originate somewhere other than in an assessment of possible (financial) gains. Indeed, the relatively small number of cases with active litigants, combined with the predominance of a particularly resilient stance by these litigants hints at the requirement of persistence by litigating parties in these, often lengthy, legal proceedings. In general, as Dehousse concluded in this respect, since litigation before the ECJ is usually a 'lengthy and cumbersome' affair, it favours large corporations and interest groups.[41]

We have seen that the degree to which cases are referred to the ECJ at the express wish of the litigants, or their counsel, is limited. The extent to which this is the case has repercussions for the practice of, as well as the way we view, the procedure; whether the procedure is considered merely a resource for national judges in deciding upon cases with an element of uncertainty with regard to EU law, or on the other end of the scale, we view the procedure as a legal resource for litigants, lawyers and interest organisations. Chalmers and Chaves concluded that British judges rely largely on litigating parties pushing for reference.[42] Based on data presented in this chapter we have to conclude that this is only partly the case. Not only is there a significant portion of cases without any such effort by the litigating parties, but even in cases with a focus on EU law 'pushing' may be formulating it too strongly. From the perspective of litigants and even their counsel, sometimes these references come as a complete – and in those cases often unwelcome – surprise. The purposefulness behind references to the ECJ should thus not be taken as self-evident.

41 Dehousse 1998.
42 Chalmers & Chaves 2011, 33.

Case Study A. Catering Employees

A.1 Introduction: Gaul v. the Romans

This case study focuses on the only case in the selection for this study that revolves around a conflict between two private parties. This case is a story of how EU legislation on the protection of workers' rights prevented large corporations in the Netherlands bypassing workers' protection granted under Directive 2001/23/EC in the event of a transfer of undertaking. A group of catering employees together with a Dutch labour union took a large catering company to court in connection with an outsourcing by their former employer, a large brewery and beer company. At issue was the use within the corporation of a so-called *special purpose vehicle* as the formal contracting party for all brewery employees and a social plan between the company and the labour unions stipulating that the outsourcing model used by the brewery did not qualify as a transfer of undertaking. After a long battle, which was ultimately brought before the ECJ, the employees were vindicated and their rights as employees under EU law confirmed. The case made headlines in the Dutch press as a victory for the little guy, and it is therefore also the story of the perseverance of one catering employee.[1]

A.2 The Dispute

At the time the dispute started, the catering employee who would lead the efforts against the brewery and the catering company had been working in the brewery's catering department for over twenty years. He and his colleagues were informed in 2002 that the company was planning to reorganise its activities in order to cut costs. One of the first measures was the outsourcing of catering activities. This stirred the pot among the employees who had been working at the company for a long time, felt part of 'the family' and were less than happy about the prospect of being outsourced to a different company. In 2003, their employer agreed with trade unions on a Social Assistance Scheme (SAS) that determined that employees had two choices with regard to the outsourcing. One of the two choices was resignation by mutual consent with payment of a fee by

1 'Europees Hof steekt stokje voor truc van werkgevers', *de Volkskrant*, 22 October 2010; 'Volgend jaar doceren ze dit op de universiteit', *De Gooi- en Eemlander*, 23 October 2010; 'Troebel brouwsel', *de Volkskrant,* 23 October 2010; 'Het wordt smullen voor de advocaten', *Misset Catering*, 11 November 2010.

the employer. The other choice was employment with the transferee, the catering company. In the latter case the new employer would add a temporary transition fee to the workers' lower income. Even though this would temporarily keep the workers' income at a comparable level, in reality this meant their loss of income was only postponed for a few years.

With the transfer of the catering activities it was arranged that everyone who had worked for the brewery could enter into the service of the catering company. However, as agreed in the SAS, this was without retaining their working conditions. The terms of employment that were offered to the staff were significantly less favourable than the relatively good benefits package they had enjoyed previously. Their new employer used the collective bargaining agreement (CAO) for the catering sector, which was at a significantly lower level. The employees could take up employment at the catering company, albeit, in the most extreme case, at 48% of their former salary.[2] On average, these employees lost approximately 35% of their wages. The transfer of catering operations and staff thus left the employees in a situation of significant deterioration in their working conditions. This was the result of a special construction the brewery employed in which catering activities were placed in one company, while the catering staff was placed in a personnel carrier, a so-called *special purpose vehicle*. The staff was seconded permanently to the various operating companies of the executive company. In 2005, the brewery transferred its catering activities, by virtue of an agreement, to the catering company. At the same time the staff was transferred from the personnel carrier to the catering company. Personnel and activities were thus transferred from two different companies. The brewery assumed that the existing contracts would have to be terminated and new contracts had to be signed with the new employer, so that the usual protection of workers' rights in the case of a transfer of undertaking, falling within the scope of Directive 2001/23/EG, would be essentially sidelined.

In response to the brewery's declared intentions to outsource the catering activities, one of the supervisors in the catering department went to the management of the company on behalf of the staff to discuss the situation of the workers. He proposed a die-out construction to at least help the long-term employees reach retirement age. However, the familial atmosphere and consultation culture had been under pressure in recent years, and the supervisor was well aware of the change in course of the management:

2 The huge difference in terms of employment was partly explained by the history of the company. According to the labour union, the brewery was 'a traditional company with traditional views and traditional workers'. Many employees working in the catering department of the company had ended up there at the end of their career, often because they could no longer cope with the work in the production department due to physical reasons. This way the company made sure its staff stayed employed.

> "It was a social company, but since the former owner died it was just restructured hard and cool. They had those plans ready. You felt it, the management was replaced, and directors were replaced. Directors of other companies were brought in. Well, if you Googled, you saw what they had done with other companies in the ports, they were substantially reorganized. So they were no 'gentle healers',[3] they were guys with a certain background. So we very quickly realized, they are looking for an entry into the catering, and once the Central Workers Council agrees, you can do the same within the rest of the company."

Indeed, his efforts to dissuade management from the chosen path did not yield any results. His concerns fell on deaf ears and he was told that 'all lawyers in the Netherlands agreed' that this construction was legally sound. This estimation, most likely corroborated by in-house lawyers, was correct according to settled Dutch case law at the time. Furthermore with, according to the supervisor, a 'callous tone' that would characterize the relationship that was to follow, he was told that the workers should be happy they went 'from work to work'.[4]

The supervisor, however, was not the type to sit down and be quiet. He was a member of the labour union and had taken up a position within the Central Workers Council within the company in order to at least be able to keep track of all the proposed reorganizations. He actively opposed the planned outsourcing. After his efforts to negotiate an alternative solution with the management of the company failed, he took the lead in organizing opposition and taking legal action.

A.3 Organizing Legal Opposition

The disquiet among the employees soon turned into anger when all attempts at negotiation and accommodation failed. The supervisor decided to find out whether or not there was a chance of fighting the transfer by legal means. As luck would have it, some of the temporary holiday workers in the catering department were students studying for a degree in labour law. The supervisor recalls:

> "We just hired them. We did the dishwashing and other things, so they could then figure it out for us with their law books. And they found it totally amazing, because they did not have to work. So then we found out fairly quickly that we would lose a

3 Original Dutch quote: "zachte heelmeesters".

4 A somewhat derisive reference to a policy adopted by the Dutch government to ensure civil servants would find new employment after reorganizations in a period of drastic cuts in government spending.

> case in the Netherlands, but then you would get the European Court. So the labour law student told us: well, I consider it very likely that you could win this."

Before legal action was actually taken, he went on to find as many employees as possible willing to go along and litigate together. In order to convince his colleagues (some of whom had already taken up their own legal counsel) he sought an independent expert opinion to corroborate this assessment of eventual success. For this purpose, he aimed high and called 'the best employment lawyer in the Netherlands'[5] at a leading international law firm.[6] However, because this law firm did not take on cases for individuals, he was referred to a smaller law firm in The Hague. The labour law specialist there presented them with an estimation of what they could expect legally:

> "He said, within Dutch law you won't win this. But when I think about it, you'll first have Dutch law, but then you go to Europe, because that's where you will end up, but it will take years. But when you get to Europe, I'll bet you a good bottle of wine that you will win. And he said, then 'your name will resound throughout Europe,' because that is going to change labour law [in the Netherlands]."

Furthermore, the lawyer advised that the labour union should litigate the matter, since they had good in-house lawyers, and also because the costs at an individual level would be immense.[7] Partly due to this helping hand, the supervisor stated that he was always "110% confident"[8] that they would eventually win the case. This conviction was important as the supervisor was in for an uphill battle and because he took the lead in an endeavour that was not without risk for those involved. About this responsibility, he says:

> "Basically, if it did not work out... Everyone went along [to work for Albron], so everyone lost a large part of his or her income. And people started going into debt, expecting money in the end. So everyone took a risk. So your sense of responsibility

5 An interesting detail, which the supervisor found out later, is that the lawyer he was trying to contact, was one of the lawyers who had advised the brewery on the personnel carrier construction. However, this was not the reason he was denied service, he never actually spoke to the lawyer himself, but was redirected by his secretary.

6 A high-end law firm that provides legal services mainly in business and finance transactions and commercial litigation. Their clients include among others: financial services institutions, logistics and transport companies, and supervisory boards.

7 For the same reason he declined taking up the case himself, explaining he would be too expensive for individuals to hire.

8 An ironic nod to the former director of the brewery who was said to be "110% certain" that this construction was legally possible, and that they did not stand a chance of winning.

> is like, well if this goes wrong… And I must honestly say that I have never doubted it. I've obviously thought about it, but I have never doubted it."

His motivation lay also in that, apart from the impact on his colleagues in the catering department, he felt that the planned outsourcing of catering activities would only be the first of a series of reorganisations within the company.

Of the seventy-three affected catering employees, forty either did not want to join the fight (not everyone was hit as hard in their working conditions) or, when employees were fifty-five years or older, they were seconded elsewhere and effectively could stay with the company.[9] Of the forty-seven employees who went on to work for the catering company, a group of thirty employees teamed up with the labour union and joined the legal proceedings. The union asked everyone to become a member so that their claims could all be litigated in one lawsuit.

A.4 The Legal Battle

As the law students and expert advice had assessed, the case revolved around the claim that in this situation the catering workers were protected by Directive 2001/23/EC (from here on: the Transfer of undertakings Directive) on the safeguarding of employees' rights in the event of a transfer of undertaking. This interpretation was contrary to the hitherto prevailing doctrine among Dutch labour law jurists, which did not consider the Transfer of undertakings Directive's protection applicable in the case of a construction as employed by the brewery. About this, the labour union affiliated lawyer[10] states:

> "The brewer and the catering company assumed this construction was perfectly legal, like everyone in the Netherlands really, except – and I always think of Asterix and Obelix, I do not know if you know those books: 'There is one village that stubbornly persists' – except a few people within the union, and yours truly."

---

9 About this distinction based on age, the group subsequently filed a complaint with the national Equal Treatment Commission (*Commissie Gelijke Behandeling*) because no account was taken of the length of employment of certain employees. Someone who had worked at the brewery for only a year, but was fifty-five years of age or older could stay, while someone aged fifty-four with thirty-five years of service was fired. The Equal Treatment Commission found that a distinction based on age was justified, provided that person was a long-term employee.

10 The lawyer in the case was not permanent staff but was regularly hired by the union at a reduced fee.

This conclusion was, in light of the prevailing doctrine, far from self-evident. The legal expert of the labour union who was on the case from the outset considered this a principle matter with little or no precedent in Dutch jurisprudence. She estimated that there was a possibility based on the ECJ's interpretation of the Transfer of undertakings Directive, but she still had to convince their lawyer it had a good chance of success:

> "I then just went around probing people I knew. Someone I know was professor of labour law and European law. I said, 'Well, I see it this way, am I crazy?' And he said, 'No, no, I agree with you'. The funny thing is, I remember when I came to our lawyer with the case, he said: 'No, I don't see any merit in this'. And I really had to use my powers of persuasion[11] to convince him we should do it."

The opening the labour union's legal expert saw, lay in the ECJ's interpretation of the Directive with regard to the transfer of undertakings and the safeguarding of employees' rights. The legal essence of the case was as follows: Article 3 of the Directive states: 'The transferor's rights and obligations arising from a contract of employment or from an employment relationship existing on the date of a transfer shall, by reason of such transfer, be transferred to the transferee'. This part of the Directive has been implemented in Dutch law by means of Article 663 of Book 7 of the Dutch Civil Code stating: 'By virtue of the transfer of an undertaking, the employer's rights and obligations, at the time of the transfer, under an employment contract concluded between the latter and an employee in that undertaking are automatically transferred to the transferee'. The text is slightly different. Where the Directive speaks of an obligation arising from a contract of employment or from an *employment relationship,* this latter part of the formulation does not appear in the Dutch implementation text. In the Dutch explanatory memorandum of 1980 to, among others, Article 7:663 of the Civil Code, the choice to omit the term employment relationship is explains as follows:

> "The directive refers to 'contract of employment or employment relationship' to tie in with the different legal systems in the Member States. Substantively it aims at only one thing. For Dutch law the use of the term 'employment relationship' is not necessary. From the wording of the directive it should not be concluded that there is an obligation to adopt further provisions in addition to the measures in respect of employment."[12]

11 Original quote: "*ik moest praten als Brugman*".
12 *Kamerstukken II* 1979/80, 15 940, nr. 3-4.

Apparently, the Dutch legislator decided to apply the Directive only to those working under an employment contract, interpreting the scope of the Directive in a narrow sense. It was further decided not to adopt the term used in the Directive: *transferor*, but instead went with *employer*. This choice of terminology gets to the heart of the case. In the dispute at hand, considering the construction used by the brewery, wherein activities and employees were essentially transferred from two different companies, the question was who could be deemed the transferor in terms of the Directive, and by extension, what this meant for the protection of the workers in the event of a change of employer.

Court Proceedings

Before initiating substantive proceedings, the employees unsuccessfully tried to stop the transfer by way of interim relief. Entirely in line with the prevailing Dutch doctrine, the judge decided to reject the claim of the labour union and the employees.[13] The interim judge considered that for their claim to be valid a formal contract must exist between the transferor and the employees, which was not the case. The labour union subsequently brought an action, on behalf of the employees, before the sub-district court seeking a declaratory judgment that the transfer of the catering business in fact constituted the transfer of an undertaking within the meaning of the Directive, and that the catering employees were therefore entitled to retention of their employment terms. They sought payment of unpaid wages and statutory interest from March 2005 onwards, to be increased by a statutory fine of 50%. The group was, in view of the prevailing opinion among Dutch labour law jurists, quite unexpectedly vindicated and the sub-district court upheld their claim. The court found clues in the *Botzen* judgment and the *D'Urso* judgment of the ECJ to assume that the employees were certainly entitled to the rights as laid down in the Directive. It reasoned (controversially) in the first place that the Court of Justice in its *Botzen* judgment had discussed transfer of undertaking within the context of concerns, or 'group' companies. The judge considered that although this judgment was not directly applicable, it indeed gave an indication as to how the ECJ could be expected to review the matter at hand. According to the court, it was conceivable that the ECJ would actually associate the term 'material employer' with 'employment relationship', of which the latter was essentially characterized by the link between the employee and the part of the business where he or she was employed. This would, according to the judge, have as a result that the role of the *formal* employer (by contract) could be marginalized. Thus, in the court's view, this

13 Rechtbank 's-Gravenhage 22 February 2005, ECLI:NL:RBSGR:2005:AS7198, par. 3.3-3.5.

should be considered an *acte éclairé*. The judge decided therefore, despite the employees and the labour union pressing for a preliminary reference to the ECJ, to consider the question as asked and answered.

This was an important and promising victory for the employees. However, because the court, recognizing that this case still had a long way to go, declared its judgment 'not automatically enforceable', it yielded no direct results for those involved. The judge reasoned that, if it would declare the ruling immediately enforceable, those concerned would be entitled to the wages they had previously enjoyed, something that could result in great personal problems in case of loss in the long run. As expected, the catering company appealed against this ruling before the Amsterdam Court of Appeal. The Amsterdam Court of Appeal subsequently considered that the hitherto prevailing Dutch (*Heidemij*) doctrine on the transfer of undertakings could constitute a circumvention of the rights conferred on workers by the Directive. The workers were in fact employed by the brewery and not by another company. The court thus posited that within this doctrinal understanding, workers lost their protection because of the structure within the company, and it felt compelled to bring the matter before the ECJ. The Amsterdam Court then, in consultation with all parties, formulated questions that were referred to the ECJ. On whether a reference to the ECJ had been the actual goal, the lawyer states:

> "Well, I have always thought that, given the fact that it was a principled explanation of a European directive… I had actually already suggested to the sub-district judge that this case perhaps lent itself for the submission of questions to the ECJ. But he never addressed this, I do not know why. But he did suggest in his judgment that it would be a possibility at some point. And in the plea at the Amsterdam Court I have vehemently suggested it, even in the comments. Since it concerns the interpretation of a European directive, we have to let the ones who are the experts decide. And they indeed referred the case. The opposition was not very happy with this. Because the case was submitted to the ECJ it was more likely that they would lose. So they were not very happy with it, and with good reason, as it turns out. So yes, I've always had in mind and suggested it in all instances."

Oddly enough, after the formulation of the questions, the Amsterdam Court waited for almost a full year before sending the questions to Luxembourg in July 2009. A very unwelcome development, of course, for those involved whose adverse situation was not helped at all by more delays.

The ECJ Judgment

Luckily for the supervisor and his colleagues, the judgment of the ECJ followed relatively quickly, in October 2010, bringing an end to the uncertainty. In its answer the Court held that, in the context as was the case at the brewery, the Directive's protection of workers' rights also applied. The Court concluded that a company belonging to a group in which workers were permanently employed could be considered as a transferor within the meaning of the Directive. The judgment thus implied that the catering workers, even though they had no employment contract with the operating company to which they were permanently seconded, were to be transferred along with the catering operations, while retaining their work benefits. The Court also concluded that the effect of the judgment was not limited in time to the future, stating that it did not do more than explain the Directive and that this interpretation also applied to matters that had already occurred before the date of this judgment. In summary, the Court stated: "Transferor is he who loses his contractual or non-contractual employer status. So even a non-contractual employer can be transferor". This judgment caused much uproar in labour law circles in the Netherlands, since it effectively put a stop to constructions like that of the brewery, and essentially went directly against Dutch doctrine.[14]

Returning from the ECJ

After this European law question was answered by the ECJ, the question that remained before the Amsterdam Court was whether the Dutch legal text, in line with this ECJ judgment, could be interpreted in conformity with the Directive. The catering company (or actually the brewery) unsuccessfully appealed against it and, after the Amsterdam Court judgment, appealed to the Supreme Court. If the Supreme Court concluded that Dutch legislation was not in conformity with the Directive, this would have led to the conclusion that the Dutch government had not implemented the Directive correctly, and thus the Dutch State (and not the catering company) would have been liable to the employees. From the per-

14 The ensuing debate focused especially on the impact of the judgment on other constructions like pay rolling. A selection: Grapperhaus, A. 'Annotatie bij de uitspraak van de Kantonrechter Utrecht', *Ondernemingsrecht* 2006-7, 87; Knipschild, E. 'Permanente detachering in concernverband en overgang van onderneming', *Arbeidsrecht* 2008-12, 63; Wiersma, K. 'Enkele recente ontwikkelingen inzake overgang van een onderneming', *O&F* 2009-4, 65-85; Rutgers, D.J. & Noordoven, T.L.C.W. 'Hof van Justitie: permanent gedetacheerde werknemers worden beschermd bij overgang van onderneming', *Bedrijfsjuridische berichten* 2010-53, 197-201; Verburg, L.G. 'Europese invloeden op het Nederlands arbeidsrecht: de overgang van onderneming', *ArbeidsRecht* 2010-53, 33-37; Kote, C.J.M.W. 'Permanent gedetacheerde werknemer in concernverhoudingen niet meer vogelvrij bij overgang van onderneming, *Nederlands tijdschrift voor Europees recht* 2011-1, 20-26; Zwemmer, J.P.H. 'Het Albron-arrest, de contractuele werkgever versus de niet-contractuele werkgever en de mogelijke gevolgen voor andere uitzendvarianten', *Tijdschrift Recht en Arbeid* 2011-4, 16-20; Witteveen, A.P.P. 'Annotatie bij: Hof Amsterdam 25 oktober 2011, LJN BU1290', *JAR Geannoteerd* 2011-8, 219-221.

spective of the brewery and the catering company, it was, therefore, understandable that they advocated in this direction in order to lay the blame on the legislature, since, based on Dutch law (and prevailing doctrine at the time), they had acted in good faith. However, from the perspective of the employees, this was not desirable, as this would then mean that the procedure would again be extended. As the lawyer states:

> "Well, fortunately it did not come to that, because then we would have spent another eight years in court. Then I would have made it to my retirement [laughs]."

The Supreme Court did not follow the catering company's reasoning and ruled on April 5th 2013 that the Dutch implementation was in fact correct. Its judgment finally established definitively, after eight years, that the catering employees, who until March 1st 2005 had been employed by the brewery and then by the catering company, were retroactively to that date entitled to the benefits they had previously enjoyed.

A.5 Effects of the Ruling

The ECJ judgment effectively closed the door on the construction that would have made it relatively easy for larger companies to outsource certain activities while effectively bypassing workers' rights. On the effects of the ECJ ruling the union's legal expert states:

> "Awaiting this verdict, several large corporations were in the starting blocks to implement the same construction. By the ruling of the ECJ they are now prevented from doing this."

That the brewery was not the first company to go down this road was underlined by the fact that former employees of other companies, workers who had been in a similar situation, contacted the supervisor to congratulate him on his victory. The many responses showed that several companies had used such a construction, but the workers affected had never had the means, confidence or courage to litigate the matter. This was the result of an important and illustrative theme in the case of the catering employees that concerned the employment relationship which, in comparison with the other cases, made the situation for those directly affected that much more complex and trying. The supervisor and his colleagues were probably not the first to be confronted with the detrimental effect of these constructions, but taking one's employer to court is an arduous task that not many will choose. As the supervisor recalls:

> "Later on, I also got people from other companies who wanted to know how to fight reorganizations. I got a lot of comments on the internet of people who said, we were outsourced in the past, and that was a dirty trick, and I am glad you're doing what you are doing. They had never dared to take that step. That felt good. The same with journalists, who were kicked out at media companies, who said, it is good that you have raised this because I haven't. So you noticed that there were more people with the same problem, but no one dared to take that step. Because it was a fight that was going to last for years."

Taking legal action against one's (former) employer creates complications, especially when workers still remain with the company with which they have a dispute. The supervisor indicated that, as a result of the transfer, his colleagues had all sorts of personal troubles: some had to sell their homes because they were no longer able to afford their mortgage on their new wage, the wife of one of the employees had to return to her country of birth because her husband, with his lower income, no longer met the income requirements in migration law and several employees were on sick leave for extended periods due to psychological problems. Partly because of this, many workers were willing to accept the settlement proposals by the brewery made before as well as after the ECJ decision.[15]

A.6 Deductions from a 'Victory for the Little Guy'

The eventual success of the supervisor and his colleagues was described in the Dutch press as 'a victory for the little guy'. In this story however, that little guy was in fact a man with remarkable resilience and stamina. The interests involved in this legal battle were significant. The catering company had undoubtedly offered highly attractive commercial terms in order to win the brewery's catering contract. Since labour was one of the major cost components for catering, the wage factor would weigh heavily. Taking into account that the average difference in compensation between the brewery and the catering company was 35%, the savings the catering company could offer the brewery were substantial. But even more significant was that such constructions, if left unchecked, could be rolled out on a much larger scale. The employees' claim thus stood in the way of a potentially very profitable construction.

The fact that at the time of writing (four years after the ECJ judgment) the supervisor and the brewery were still trying to work out the details of his settle-

15 Of the thirty claimants eventually twenty-three reached a settlement, so in the final stage before the Supreme Court only seven employees were left, most of who still worked at the catering company.

ment exemplifies the pressure exerted on him and his colleagues, as evidenced by how few were eventually left and the acrimonious relationship between the supervisor and his former employer. The relevance of the individual persistence of the supervisor cannot be overstated. He took on the role of champion of workers' rights in the face of significant opposition. Not only did he face financial challenges, he also took it upon himself to take the lead on behalf of his colleagues. His leading role and uncompromising stance made him the target of extra-legal pressures as well. He often found himself in staunch opposition to both the catering company and the brewery's leadership. At one point he was even put on leave because of statements he had made in the press, something that was eventually reversed by the intervention of a judge. Subsequently, the catering company tried to fire him, which again was prevented by a court ruling.

A.7 ECJ to the Rescue

Another important element in this case is that the interpretation of EU law was clearly the 'redeeming' element. The prevailing view among labour lawyers, as well as in Dutch judicial doctrine, was that such constructions were legally possible. The ECJ ruled that such a construction could not mean that the workers and their working conditions did not fall under the protection of the Transfer of undertakings Directive. It took an ECJ judgment to break this deadlock in the interpretation of EU law by the Dutch legislature, and the companies, as well as the Dutch judiciary. That this was a typical Dutch matter is illustrated by the fact that no other Member State joined in the proceedings before the ECJ. The Dutch government and the representatives of Luxembourg had a position less obvious than in most other cases where the Netherlands to a great extent was the defendant. This case therefore had a rather different dynamic in Luxembourg than the more common administrative issues. It is the only case in the selection for this study in which the Dutch representation before the ECJ did not take an oppositional stance to that of the individual litigant. During the hearing in Luxembourg, the Dutch agents did call for an exception to the application of the Directive for temporary workers because it would have serious consequences for the Dutch labour market. The European Commission was clearly on the side of the employees and expressed gratitude to the supervisor for bringing a case that allowed a gap in EU legislation to be filled. As the supervisor describes the stance of the Commission before the Court:

> "There was a lawyer, a Belgian, on behalf of the European Commission. That said, I'm thankful to the claimant for bringing this matter before the court. It is a gap in the European legislation. And it is difficult to raise such an issue, because it takes years. And no one has done it yet, so we are very happy. But if this is what happens

> with employees, then tomorrow I am attorney again with a private law firm and I'll advise all multinational companies in Europe to adopt such a construction. I will be rich overnight. And after the hearing they came to me, to congratulate me. On behalf of the European Union and all Member States, I thank you for this case, he said. So we were like, what is going on? He says, no, no, I am being serious. This was a gap in the legislation, which will be fixed. And I'm going to congratulate you that you have won this case."

A.8 Collective versus Collective

The supervisor's victory for himself and many of his direct colleagues was also a victory for the larger collective of workers in the Netherlands, who in these corporate constructions would be left outside the protection of the Directive. The legal expert of the union concludes in this regard:

> "It is really by virtue of his determination that we were able to win this. Even with all the opposition and hassle, he still continued. Which is his Achilles' heel as well sometimes, because he is still litigating at the moment, and I wonder how happy that makes you. But we succeeded by the grace of his perseverance."

Obviously the support of the employees by the labour union that took care of the costs of the lawsuit was indispensable. Although on paper the catering company was their opponent, in fact the battle was waged against the brewery that was planning to apply this construction more frequently. The costs for the labour union ran into hundreds of thousands of euros and, according to the union's legal expert "possibly up to a million on the other side". There were rumours from people higher up at the brewery that employers' organisations were helping them pay for it. The fight thus became employers against workers. As the supervisor realised:

> "At some point you just felt that we did not matter. It was at one point just to the principle they were fighting for, and large corporations, like as the 'Unilevers' and the 'Shells' of this world, and all major European companies work this way."

Without the support of the union, both financially as well as legally, his battle would have likely ended prematurely. This is evidenced by the fact that most of his colleagues did not wish to sit out the entire battle and somewhere along the way accepted settlement offers by the brewery. In all likelihood he would have been forced to accept the offers made to him on several occasions during the proceedings. This would have meant that the ECJ's ruling would not have existed to make clear that Dutch implementation of workers' protections based on EU law in fact left the door open for companies to circumvent the Directive's stipulations. Even though previously the supervisor would have been willing to come to a settlement, after the increased tension and the realization that his case was in fact a chance to put a stop to the practices that undermined workers' rights, he refused to give up before a final judgment by the Dutch court:

> "After the ECJ ruling they wanted to reach a compromise. So I said, you can buy me out, but I want everything I am entitled to. If I get a dime from you, and it costs a euro, I'll be coming for that euro. So I wanted that final judgment. I want this to never be done again. And they offered large sums. But it's not about the money. It is of course important, but at some point it goes beyond that. I just wanted it to stop. And once that judgment is there, they can no longer do to anyone in the Netherlands what they did to us, then it's done."

Indeed, the ECJ's judgment and subsequent Supreme Court ruling effectively closed the door on devices that could circumvent the aim of the Directive. It did not address the ways in which the Directive and the ECJ's interpretation affects other constructions such as pay rolling, and clarification on this is likely to require new litigation.

5 A Collection of Interests

5.1 Introduction

The analysis in Chapter 4 has highlighted how the preliminary reference procedure is a unique legal procedure, with specific consequences for litigation dynamics. And while it is often an interesting experience for the lawyers concerned, it is usually difficult for the litigants to comprehend. Even if substantively individuals' interests can be served with a reference to the ECJ in a strict sense, when it comes to the duration, cost and uncertainty related to the procedure, a reference in itself does not always serve litigants' interests in a broader sense. Especially due to the extended duration of the procedure, there is therefore a tension between the structural consequences a reference may have (including sometimes full revision of national laws or policies) and the costs to the parties involved. The lack of explanatory value of cost-benefit considerations, as well as the detrimental impact of the procedures themselves in some cases, raises the question of how and why these cases reach the ECJ.

Due to their reference to the ECJ, individual cases may serve the interests of larger collectives beyond the individual litigant. This has made the procedure of particular significance to both interest groups seeking strategic litigation as well as scholars studying such a form of legal mobilisation. As such, individual cases may be the means by which collective interests are championed, both actively and more unwittingly. This, however, also has repercussions for litigation dynamics. When the 'nominal' and the 'real' litigant have different motives for participating in the same process, this could result in a different experience of the process of law and sense of justice; resulting in a discrepancy between the evaluation of the judicial process by lawyers and the valuation by the litigants. The procedure can thus at the same time be an opportunity for championing the rights of a larger collective, and a further burden on those seeking the application of those rights. This chapter will further address how individual litigation may be a 'front' for more hidden interests, as well as the tensions that may arise between different interested parties.

5.2 Real and Nominal Litigants

As we have established, the motivation of an individual litigant can be an important factor and take on various forms, from the resilient to the frivolous. However, another explanation for why some cases, in which at a first glance the possible individual benefits do not outweigh the costs of the proceedings, reach the ECJ lies in the fact that an individual may act merely as the 'nominal' litigant in the legal action. One aspect that is particularly hard to determine when investigating litigation based on court documents or statistics alone is the type of litigant behind the legal action, giving rise to the complicated question of the identity of the 'real' litigant. While there may be an individual name at the basis of legal action, other parties may be responsible for initiating and continuing litigation. In the following examples of firms and interest groups pushing legal action, the litigant may act only as a 'straw man', or as a 'nominal' litigant, where the 'real' litigant is the wider collective of similar individuals (like asylum seekers or transnational workers) or the interests behind litigation lie with different parties not directly apparent from the substance of the case.

A good example of what court documents, case files, and jurisprudence do not show is whether or not the case is a result of a real life dispute, or in fact a fabricated 'test case' aimed at setting a precedent or obtaining a judicial answer to a practical question. Harlow and Rawlings distinguish two types of test cases, or test case strategies.[1] The first type includes cases that are brought explicitly to test the meaning of the law in a given context. The second covers the class- lead- or representative action in which one case among many disputes is put forward to establish how the law affects all those cases. In its purest form, test cases are not only aimed at testing the meaning of the law, but the dispute is also actually created with the explicit purpose of testing a legal proposition before the courts. Instead of the legal question being part of a dispute, the question itself lies at the basis of the legal action and the cases themselves are set up to invoke a judicial decision.

European Support Schemes

An example of the first type distinguished by Harlow and Rawlings, *Lessee Entitlements* was a 'dispute' between a Dutch municipality and a farmer and lessee of municipal land, regarding the nature and extent of the obligations resulting from an agricultural lease. For a number of years the farmer had received, on the basis of two European Regulations,[2] compensatory payments under the supported scheme for producers, which was linked to the production of certain crops. Following the entry into force of a new EU Regulation[3] he was granted entitlement to payment as a producer based on the amount of land used. The question being litigated was whether EU law required a lessee, on the expiry of the lease, to deliver to the lessor the leased land along with the payment

1 Harlow & Rawlings 1992, 282-5.
2 Council Regulations 1765/92 and 1251/1999.
3 Council Regulation 1782/2003.

entitlements accumulated thereon or relating thereto, or to pay him compensation.

Judging merely from the court documents this was a case concerning a dispute between a lessee and the leasing party, regarding the nature and the extent of the obligations under the lease. In reality, both the lessor and the lessee were so-called dummies, and an association of lessors (including private as well as public landowners) in collaboration with the Dutch Federation of Agriculture and Horticulture (an entrepreneurial and employers' organization, from here: LTO), orchestrated the dispute. As the lawyer on the side of the lessee explains:

> "The association of landowners represented the lessors who chose a lawyer. On the farmers' side stood LTO, who also chose a lawyer and who came to me. And then both went looking for a 'guinea pig'. And that organization came up with a town, and a tenant of that municipality. I already knew him from something else, and he was willing to play along with the whole charade. And then we clearly agreed, remember, this is a test case, it should not lead to a real conflict."

The question arose as to whether these farmers were in fact the personal addressees of these entitlements and allowed to sell them, as they had been allowed with comparable entitlements in the past, particularly if they were in fact not the owner but merely a lessee of the land on which these entitlements were (partly) based. Such cases, that on paper entail a dispute between two parties – in this case a municipality as the lessor and a farmer as the lessee, and their respective legal counsel – in reality are initiated based on far greater interests than those of merely one of the two, or even both parties to the proceedings. As the aforementioned lawyer explains:

> "I think there is up to a billion euro of these entitlements distributed across the Netherlands. And then say a quarter of the land is leased. So then the recipient of the entitlement is not the owner of the land he uses, but someone else, for example an institutional investor. So suppose you have leased a quarter of a billion euro per year, that was what the dispute was actually about. On an individual level you're talking about maybe 1,000 euro. But all those people in the Netherlands added together, it was not about a triviality. An individual farmer who sells his entitlements and who loses a few euros, those are not amounts on which you're going to litigate. But if you add all farmers together, it runs in the millions."

The interest in resolving this question thus lay not with the individual lessee, for whom in fact the potential gain did not measure up to the cost of a judicial procedure, but with the lessors, who were the owners of significant amounts of land. The costs incurred for the legal proceedings were covered by, on the one hand, LTO championing the rights of individual lessees through collective action, and on the other the association of lessors. These organisations both represented the interests of large collectives and both collectives stood to gain considerably from a favourable judicial decision. Eventually this case was resolved in favour of the farmers.

Soft Drugs and Free Movement

A similar example of such a test case is the *Free Movement of Cannabis* case.[4] Here the Dutch Ministry of Justice collaborated with a municipality and a coffee shop owner to see whether municipal rules could refuse non-residents access to so-called 'coffee shops' in light of free movement and non-discrimination principles of EU law. The marketing of narcotic drugs is prohibited in the Netherlands as in all the Member States. However, the Netherlands applies a policy of tolerance with regard to cannabis, which may be sold and consumed in these coffee shops, subject to conditions set by the local authorities. To combat the phenomenon of 'drug tourism', a border town adopted a municipal regulation in December 2005 forbidding the proprietors of coffee shops from admitting persons not resident in the Netherlands from their establishments. What was not clear was whether or not the residence criterion introduced by the municipal regulation at issue was contrary to Union law.

This question was a pertinent one to both the Dutch authorities (local and national) and indeed the coffee shop owners in the border areas who stood to lose significant portions of their clientele. The litigant, and chairman of an Association of Official Coffee Shops (VOCM), explains how he became part of an effort to clear up the matter by means of a test case:

> "In 2006 the municipality was approached by the Minister of Justice, asking if we could start a test case to look if it is possible for us coffee shop owners to refuse non-residents access to the coffee shop. To this end the local ordinance was altered stating that a non-resident should be denied access to the coffee shop. In that period two supposed violations had been established in my business and an official report was made. Also, my establishment was supposedly closed for three months. However, this is not true. It was just a 'gentlemen's agreement' between the municipality and me. Until the time the court issued a ruling, the authorities would no longer enforce the ordinance. We started this process to see what exactly is possible under EU law."

This case shows how EU law becomes part of the practice of local governance, possibly restricting authorities' room for regulating local matters. Instead of the coffee shop owners invoking the principles of non-discrimination, free movement of goods and freedom to provide services in order to defend their interests,

4 For a review see Van Harten & Van Eijken 2011.

the parties on both sides agreed to 'test the water' as to the applicability of these principles to the Dutch software policy.

Both aforementioned cases involved organised interests employing a legal strategy when it came to the applicability and interpretation of EU law. In both cases the affair supposedly leading up to the legal proceedings was staged in agreement with the opposing side and never actually took place. In the first case this happened in the form of a letter from the farmer addressed to the municipality informing them of his intention to resell his entitlements and in the second case in the form of two fictional contested violations. In these cases both sides were thus in full agreement. What is interesting about such cases is that the ECJ had explicitly resisted "turning the [reference] procedure into a continuous deliberative assembly of lawyers, judges, and litigants"[5] with its (second) *Foglia* decision in the early 1980s.[6] In that decision, the Court considered its task in preliminary references to be "not that of delivering opinions on general or hypothetical questions but of assisting the administration of justice in the Member States".[7] In its judgment it insisted on a 'genuine dispute' and declined jurisdiction in replying to questions 'posed within the framework of procedural devices arranged by the parties'. In *Foglia* the Court indeed sniffed out the orchestrated nature of the dispute. The abovementioned cases, however, reveal that such vigilance for 'questions without a genuine dispute' is not failsafe.

5.3 Employing an Individual Case

One requirement for the orchestration of a test case is the collaboration between both parties. In many instances such collaboration lies beyond the possibilities, especially if one of the sides to a potential dispute does not have an interest in resolving the question. Since many questions about the interpretation of EU law are about national law or policy in light of certain EU law provisions, the state often has a vested interest in existing policy, and therefore collaborations between litigants and the government are not obvious. For those aiming to test the interpretation of the law within such a context, the setting up of a test case thus requires a genuine dispute. Such cases fall under what Harlow and Rawlings consider the class- lead- or representative action in which one case among many disputes is put forward to establish how the law affects all those cases.

5 Schepel & Blankenburg 2001, 39.
6 *Foglia* Case 244/80.
7 *Foglia* Case 244/80, point 18.

Tax Consultancy on a European Level

Two examples show how a third party can be responsible for initiating proceedings. These cases, aimed at clearing up a specific (practical) question, originated not with one of the parties involved but with their counsel or third parties. These cases both involved tax consultancy firms that used individual cases to address a practical question, in which one case among many was put forward to establish how the law affected all those cases.

The first example (*Concealed Foreign Savings*) revolved around a question regarding the statutory recovery period in the voluntary disclosure scheme for taxpayers with undisclosed foreign financial assets, which was litigated by a large consultancy firm. In the second case (*Self-Employed Tax Deductions*) a small regional tax consultancy firm used an individual case to address a question of cross-border taxation in light of non-discrimination principles in EU law. Both cases were actively selected from among the firms' clientele after the question was brought up among the firms' advisors. One of the consultants elaborates:

> "We had debated internally whether this constitutes discrimination based on nationality. In the sense that, a Dutch national who has a permanent establishment in Germany, to keep it simple, he may count his hours, but a German with a permanent establishment in the Netherlands cannot count the hours made in his German establishment for the Dutch self-employed deduction. The tax forms weren't even designed for this. You could not put that down. Since we had some German customers with a permanent establishment in the Netherlands, we said, well, let's look at how the tax office, and probably the court looks at this."

The individual case was thus selected from among their clientele, which allowed these firms, who for these principle cases often employed dedicated teams of advisors, to commit to one specific case while serving a larger group of clients. The individual case thus served as a vehicle:

> "This case was the first procedure that was turned down by the tax authorities. For that matter it could have been anyone else. But these clients supported the procedure. That is also important. They must agree that the proceedings are done on their behalf. We came to an agreement, for that price, we go all the way. They have to agree with the fact that you litigate on their behalf, because ultimately, the deduction value was fairly limited on an annual basis."

With this last remark the advisor pointed to the fact that in order to reach a principle judgment, and to be able to continue a case, the lawyers or advisors litigating on someone's behalf needed explicit consent and continued support, not least because their consecutive tax returns would be stayed for the duration of the proceedings. In this case the costs of the proceedings were divided between a number of clients in order to make the whole action possible, so that the advisors did not work for nothing and the amount of money paid individually made the effort worthwhile for the clients. While the one principle case was being decided, these other clients all had their cases stayed until a final judgment had been given. Both cases show how the actual initial motive for engaging in the judicial action lay not directly with the individual litigants but with the interests of the consultancy firms, which were informed by their commercial aim and service provision.

> "Yes, it really must have a certain added value for our office. In smaller offices it is perhaps the lawyer who is vain, but we as a firm want to present ourselves more as a brand. Because [this judgment] is now associated with [our office]. So that's why we do it too. We seek publicity when it turns out well for us. So that we as an office have something to gain from it."

The common thread in these test cases is that the initial effort did not come from the parties to the proceedings. The tax consultancy firms were able, through their clientele, to select cases based on which they sought an answer to the relevant questions. The ability to divide costs among different clients was an important advantage in such test case litigation. The motives for litigation thus also lay with actors other than these individuals, and were informed by interests beyond the individual litigant. The involvement of the litigants in these cases consequently differed substantially, and the role of the individuals on whose behalf these cases were litigated was marginal.

Test cases, in the strictest sense, concern cases that are set up explicitly to test a certain interpretation of the law. Such cases have a strong connection between the matter that is addressed in court and the original context of the (fictitious) dispute, thus there is little ambiguity when it comes to the interests of those litigants directly involved, who agreed to this set-up. The advantage of such a structured design is that there is no ambiguity for the parties, and thus it is easy to estimate costs and benefits. There will be no disagreement about the appropriate approach and no risk of anyone pulling out. Other examples show how an individual case may be employed to test a certain legal question, not by creating a dispute, but by latching a particular legal strategy onto an existing individual case.

A good example of the latter is the case against increases in fees for residence permits *(Case Study C)*. The individual case responsible for (eventually successfully) challenging the validity of the policy of increasing fees for residence permits initially was merely an appeal against the decision of non-consideration of the request for prolongation of the residence and worker's permit of a Turkish national, who was subsequently threatened with expulsion.

While the interest of the individual involved was obviously the retaining of his residence status, the question that was actually addressed before the ECJ was whether this policy of treating Turkish citizens differently from EU citizens in this respect was allowed in light of the 'standstill clause' in the Association Agreement between the EU and Turkey.[8] A Working Group made up of lawyers, academics and an interest group searched for a suitable case to serve as a procedural solution for the fact that previous attempts at addressing the same matter by means of a civil lawsuit had stranded in the Dutch Supreme Court on account of the inadmissibility of the interest organizations that had pressed the claim.

This case shows how the legal question that was addressed before the ECJ pre-existed before a case was initiated, and how individual cases may be co-opted for the purposes of addressing certain legal questions. The individual cases were used specifically for this purpose; however, references to the ECJ may in themselves turn otherwise unremarkable cases into cases with potentially greater impact. The next section will therefore focus on how along the way cases may turn into principle cases and how interests are transformed or augmented by the fact that a case is (potentially) referred to the ECJ.

5.4 The Transformation: How Individual Interests Become Collective

Because an ECJ judgment has a *de facto* impact beyond the individual case, since it resolves questions for all cases regarding similar situations, referral to the ECJ means a case increases its scope. As we have seen above, this transformation of a case due to a reference may occur apart from any deliberate effort on the part of either the litigant or the lawyer. The interests that are being promoted by a single case can thus transform from merely individual to including more collective interests. This combination of interests that come together in one case is a dynamic especially prevalent in this study in the cases concerning migrants and asylum seekers. Cases may thus evolve to become principle cases that have an impact beyond the individual dispute. This is rarely the explicit aim of the individual litigant. In fact, when asked directly about the possible, and often real political effects or collective interests, very few litigants themselves were, especially initially, interested in such broader impact, nor were they always aware of the further collective interests that were associated with their case. After a decision by the ECJ, litigants may become aware of the bigger impact their case can have, as one litigant recalls:

8 See *Case Study C* for a description of the standstill clauses in EU-Turkey Association law.

> "What I thought was very interesting at that time, when the judgment was there, was that at one point, I read that my case had consequences for Germans who bought a house in Mallorca. Only then did I realize what far-reaching consequences something like this can have."

It is then often the lawyers, and possible third parties, who employ a certain case in order to elicit a judgment on principle (for instance to challenge national policy). These cases are comparable to the test cases that were described before, but differ in that they were not explicitly set up as such and a real dispute lies at its origin. This last aspect has repercussions for the interests that are at stake, possibly leading to conflicts between individual interests and the more collective interests a case may serve. As described by Bruinsma, especially at the higher judicial levels motives behind litigation may change.[9] Here, individuals who are seeking justice without interest in the external effect of a judgment are faced with actors 'that are playing for the rules'. Even their own lawyers may fall within this category. With respect to litigation up to the higher judicial levels, starting motives are rarely a sufficient explanation. At this level, litigation is largely dependent upon the efforts of the lawyer in question or the other supporting parties involved. The motives for lawyers in doing so are, like those of litigants, very diverse, and the fervour with which they pursue this strategy differs; yet all are aimed at furthering some form of collective interest. The next section deals with lawyers that aim to employ cases to this end and the possible conflicting interests this may cause.

5.5 The Art of Soliciting a Reference

The cases that were studied show a large number of lawyers who are more or less unexpectedly confronted with a reference, which will be explored in more detail in Chapter 6. A small number of lawyers, however, actively aim to use the preliminary reference procedure as a means to an end, especially in areas where collective interests may be served. As discussed, the willingness of the national judge to refer forms an important obstacle to those aiming for a preliminary reference. In order to implore the national judge to refer a certain question, lawyers have to convince him or her of the salience of the question. Multiple studies point to a general reluctance among the national judiciary to refer questions to the ECJ.[10] The interviews with lawyers that aim to bring certain matters before the ECJ give insight into how 'the art of' soliciting a reference works in practice. It shows how practitioners go about pushing judges towards the decision to

9 Bruinsma 2010.

10 Chalmers 2000; Nowak et al. 2012.

refer a case. Some lawyers attest to systematically putting in a lot of work when trying to convince national judges of the necessity for a reference:

> "You obviously have to find a national court willing to submit such a case to the Court, which is a major obstacle. And you have to pay attention as a lawyer, which I always do consistently. If we find that this is a matter in which the court could have doubt, we always write a detailed justification in the case before the court, on paper, motivated, substantiated, why we would eventually like to have submitted a question to the Court of Justice. So, not only casually mentioning it to the Court during hearings, no, really supported by well-grounded arguments."

Part of such a strategy, being well aware of the reluctance of (especially lower) courts to refer cases, is taking as much work out of the hands of the judge as possible and presenting their case for the necessity of a referral, including formulating the questions. The lawyer continues:

> "What I always do is to formulate the questions in advance. I think judges do appreciate that, because otherwise they have to start from scratch themselves, and they still find it difficult I think. If you as a lawyer do the work for them, I think that helps a lot in convincing them."

Another lawyer adjusted his strategy from steering a case towards a question, with which he had experienced little success in convincing the judges, towards focusing on creating uncertainty as to the interpretation of certain EU legislation:

> "Ultimately the question is whether the judge is in doubt about the interpretation. And as a lawyer, you present your position as: This is how EU law is to be interpreted. And the mere fact that one party has a different interpretation of EU law than the other may cast doubt in the mind of the judge, so you can direct the judge towards doubt."

A tried-and-true method for some lawyers is using the inconsistency in national jurisprudence among courts to convince especially the highest courts of the necessity to create clarity. The developments in ECJ jurisprudence may also help in getting this point across, as explained by one tax lawyer:

> "I had a case before, exactly the same case as this one. And the Council of State rejected that one based on European law. But you also have to look at the case law of the European Court of Justice, which may give a different interpretation of European law. And by then there had been new decisions, and so I raised those in the proceedings. Because, what was the ruling then, could not apply anymore. And I

> was able to convince them that it changed a bit, and that it was unclear now. And so they asked the Court of Justice how it should be interpreted."

This lawyer was one of the few practitioners that actively followed and then used new ECJ jurisprudence in order to challenge national policies. This practice does not appear to be widespread among the practitioners interviewed for this study.

In such strategies, playing different national courts against each other may also prove effective. Lower courts may go against the prevailing doctrine and use the preliminary reference procedure to outflank the higher courts in pursuit of a different interpretation of the law.[11] In one of the cases in this study (*Double Nationality*), the lower court chose not to refer the question to the ECJ. Instead, it considered the matter an *acte clair*, clear enough to give its own ruling, and went against prevailing doctrine without consulting the ECJ. Following the appeal by the Dutch immigration authorities against this decision, the Council of State was in essence forced to ask these questions, where in an earlier judgment it had found no reason to do so. A judgment by a lower court that runs counter to such interpretation in effect puts pressure on a higher court because it underscores that there is indeed uncertainty as to the interpretation of relevant EU law. Attentive lawyers are able to respond to such inconsistencies by arguing that there 'apparently' exists uncertainty regarding the interpretation of EU law, and that therefore referral is necessary. Instead of conflicting explanations, the absence of jurisprudence at the supranational level can also be a fruitful argument:

> "We advocated that what some judges in the Netherlands had so far decided, under pressure of the Council of State, was wrong. That EU law must be interpreted otherwise. And if they did not agree, then they should just ask the Court of Justice, because they could not say on their own, we know it ourselves because the case law is clear, because it clearly was not. There was no jurisprudence yet."

These strategies only sporadically succeed and the lawyers interviewed, without exception, expressed their struggles. A related strategy for convincing especially the higher courts, that are responsible for ensuring legal uniformity, is to bring the same arguments in multiple cases before multiple courts. By serially stressing the need for referral, lawyers can emphasise the recurrent nature of the question and influence the national judges' inclinations:

> "Normally, if it is a decision I can follow, I will not try again with another case. You can jump high or low, but you don't give your clients hope if there is none. But in

11 Alter 1998; 2000; 2001; Burley & Mattli 1993: 64.

> that one case I thought, this is just not right. So, now this time I filed appeal, because they should at least refer to the Court of Justice. Of course they didn't. Well, I have more cases, and I'm just going to continue until these questions are asked. Maybe I am annoying them, because this is already the 20th case, well fine. But this simply is not right, and I think they realise that."

A higher occurrence rate of the same or similar claims may persuade the judges that the matter is salient enough to refer one or more cases to the ECJ, a 'numbers game' according to another lawyer:

> "Ultimately, I think that you can only win the debate by bringing forward a lot of cases, to bring the same kind of argument in big numbers. I mean, it really is a 'numbers game'. You can go and cry foul in one case, but that one case will not get it done."

Lawyers that recognise the opportunity or indeed the necessity to have a matter decided by the ECJ thus develop coping strategies to deal with the perceived and sometimes confirmed reluctance of national judges to refer cases to Luxembourg. Such forms of cause lawyering are especially prevalent in areas of EU law where the interests of a larger group of lawyers' clientele can be served by principle judgments by the ECJ.

5.6 Cause Lawyering and the Balancing of Interests

Sarat and Scheingold describe how cause lawyering differs from conventional conceptions of lawyering, according to which lawyers are expected to 'provide case-by-case, transaction-by-transaction service to particular clients' without a further focus on specific policy preferences. [12] However, these two ideal types of lawyering overlap in significant ways and cause lawyering in itself can be considered a moving target with individual lawyers crossing lines back and forth between conventional practice and cause lawyering. Boundaries between the two are therefore fluid, particularly if we look at the perspective of individual lawyers. We see this illustrated by cases that are referred to the ECJ, where lawyers may recognize the collective interests that such cases represent. Lawyers in such cases may cross the line between conventional lawyering for a particular client to advocating the interests of an entire group of clients.

The act of serving general interests through European proceedings is not always a preconceived plan. Lawyers who may have an inclination towards cause lawyering with a small 'c' may find themselves in the position of being intro-

12 Sarat & Scheingold 1998.

duced to the European stage merely by serving the interests of a nominal client (who at that point is still the *real* client as well). Since preliminary referrals prolong proceedings that in many cases have been going on for many years at the national stage anyway, there are cases that are continued even after the nominal client has in fact given up, when the lawyer in question has lost all contact or even when the client has passed away.[13] In these cases, it is the lawyer that continues the case because he or she recognises the general interest (and the interests of other clients) that is being served by adjudication on the matter at the European level. In such cases the personal dedication of a practitioner to a case is an essential factor.

References to the ECJ often carry in them the possibility of addressing legal questions that potentially benefit a larger group of individuals. Whether or not a reference was part of an active legal strategy, or came more or less as a surprise, for lawyers this provides the opportunity to serve the interests of not only their direct client but also those of a larger section of their clientele, or a larger collective more generally. For lawyers with such goals in mind, the so-called 'cause lawyers' an ECJ judgment can provide a way to correct purported wrong political choices by the government. As one migration lawyer explains:

> "I see the law, especially in these times of a truly different political climate, really as a safety valve. Seeing the judge in general is already a safety valve against outlandish policy, or illegal policy, that is of course one of the pillars of our rule of law. And in the Netherlands we do not have a constitutional court so there is no constitutional review. But there is the ECHR and EU law. So that's such an important guarantee. I think that preliminary questions, European Union law and the Court of Justice in Luxembourg are a good tool in order to make a legal correction for illegal policies."

The opportunity to influence jurisprudence allows lawyers to 'play for the rules' and serve a greater cause than the interests of their client alone. With a reference to the ECJ, the goals of a procedure can thus be transformed from winning the case in the interests of one client to serving the greater cause of legal protection for many. While a great opportunity, not all lawyers are particularly prepared to take on this role. As one social security lawyer explains:

> "At that moment you really can create jurisprudence, but you have to explain why a rule is different from how it is applied. Then it really becomes a question of general interest. That is very strange in such a preliminary procedure, because in fact, you have become a bit of a lawyer of the general interest. Formally, I really have to go

13 One example of this was in *Export of Benefits* regarding the export of social benefits, the interests of which were then transferred to the inheritors.

> for my client, so those interests have to be balanced. But pleading for the general interest, that takes some getting used to."

As stressed by Galanter, the differences between so-called repeat players and one-shotters not only exist between different types of litigants but also between litigants and legal professionals. The employment of a single client's case to further more general interests has repercussions for the way a case is dealt with. Tamanaha describes this as follows: "In ordinary cases, the lawyer is the instrument to advance the client's interests; in cause litigation, the named client is mainly an accoutrement to advance the lawyer's goals. In these cases, the *real* 'client' is the cause the lawyer aims to promote; sometimes this greater objective is inconsistent with what might be best for the named client, raising significant ethical concerns".[14] For a lawyer, this requires a balancing of (collective versus individual) interests, and it is not hard to imagine how this may put pressure on the relationship between lawyer and client. For a lawyer that recognizes the more collective interest in a potentially favourable judgment by the ECJ, this can be a dilemma, and result in tensions between lawyer and client, as one migration lawyer describes:

> "It will take a lot of time, that's always the first thing you have to explain to your client. At first, you have a good relationship with your client and they trust you as a lawyer. But a year further in, you'll get tensions. Then you will get phone calls, asking when I expect a judgment. And of course you cannot give a good indication. These are always tricky conversations. So at first if you say it's going to take a long time they are fine with it, then they do not really have a good idea. But if it lasts really long then those tensions will rise, and that's something you have to deal with as a lawyer."

Such tensions arise especially when the prolonged proceedings put people in a particularly dire situation. The risk of clients giving up and pulling their claim can be a dilemma:

> "It breaks people. And those people, and I can understand that, say listen, I cannot take it anymore, psychologically. Because, I cannot afford that my family is supported by only the work of my wife, or my children. Because, I'm sitting here alone all day, doing nothing. People suffer from it. And then I really have to take the lead. Like, let's continue, give me the power so to speak, the authorization to proceed with your case."

14 Tamanaha 2006, 157.

Sometimes, these lawyers thus choose to continue with cases even after the client has in fact given up and, for instance, returned to his or her country of origin. In one case, a lawyer recognising the potential impact of the ECJ judgment, went so far as to carry on the case although he had lost contact with his client altogether.

A difference in the individual interests and this legal reality may be further exacerbated by the different (e)valuation of lawyer and client of what is relevant to the dispute, as is clear from this next remark by one of the lawyers:

> "Personally, I hate client relations. Generally, the whole on-going debate is about a legal question, not whether someone is nice or not nice, a man or a woman, that does not matter, it is a completely legal issue and that's what I like best. And I think it's generally quite annoying when, especially in cases that have become so juridified, it is so abstract that the client really does not matter anymore, and then the client really only can become a hindrance of what you as a lawyer are trying to bring forward."

Not all lawyers who are put in a position to promote the interests of a larger collective feel as comfortable with this opportunity. One asylum lawyer stressed the stark contrast he noticed between the academic discussion about EU or international law and the practice of where and when that law was applied:

> "What puts me off in a lot of those human rights discussions. When you get in one of those meetings and there is a discussion of one of these judgments, with professors who find it all terribly interesting. Saying, ah, it's all terribly interesting what the Court is doing here and blah blah blah. And as such, I understand that, but when I have to explain it to my client, I think, this doesn't help him one iota. I mean, it is all very nice to have an academic discussion on a comma somewhere in a piece of legislation, but the client is the one it is ultimately about. And they do not understand it. And if they do understand, it becomes a kind of weird abstract discussion. 'Yes, very interesting. It's a beautiful judgment, but I am expelled.'"

This tension between the interests of a litigant as real and as nominal interests also has important ramifications for the ability to focus interests. Felstiner et al. point to this problem, that may arise particularly when a case involves individuals: "A party may change his objectives in two ways: what he seeks or is willing to concede and how much. Stakes go up or down as new information comes available, a party's needs change, rules are adjusted, and costs are incurred. Delay, frustration, and despair may produce a change in objectives".[15] Thus, having a truly interested party at the root of litigation provides its own challenges, and relies to a great extent on the resilience of litigants.

15 Felstiner, Abel & Sarat 1980, 638.

The significance of such personal characteristics is prominently illustrated in the aforementioned case of the catering employees against their (former) employer (*Case Study A*). Primarily, because in this case those affected were in the precarious situation of being in a dependent employment relationship with the opponent and the arduous task of fighting a former and current employer can easily dissuade one from taking legal action. Nonetheless, one employee took it upon himself to represent and fight for the interests of a larger group of affected employees all whilst still working at one of their former employer's sites. The transformation of their claim into a legal dispute could have been forestalled with successful settlement negotiations. And were it not for this one employee's personal tenacity in combating the brewery's policy the matter would likely have died a premature death, either because the employees would have been dissuaded from undertaking action at all, or because they would have accepted the proposed agreements or the later settlement agreements, which, eventually, many of his colleagues did.

The trajectory of the case and the fact that it reached the ECJ at all can in very large part be ascribed to this employee who was able to mobilise the relevant support and, moreover, to stay the course and not to be swayed by settlement proposals or deterred by personal attacks. Of course, all the employee's efforts would have been impossible, had he not found the willing support of the labour union that took care of the financial burden, which amounted to several hundreds of thousands of euros. Unlike the case of the pensioners (*Case Study B*) whose potential interested constituency consisted of several thousand affected pensioners living abroad, the catering employee's potential allies were, at least directly, only his small group of affected colleagues. This makes it very unlikely that he would have been able to solicit the necessary funds by collective contributions. Such dependence, however, works both ways, as the labour union for their part, in trying to serve the interests of their constituency via legal means, were dependent upon individuals like this employee who were willing to battle with their employers with possibly dire personal consequences. As the legal expert for the labour union states:@

"I have seen lots of cases fail, because that happens often. I see that a lot in my practice, when you have a principle matter, then you should often have to play it through an individual, you have to have something concrete to start a case. And when that starts to take off, then the company or employer or whatever, who have an interest in that it is not more widely known or that there won't be any more claims ... then someone is approached, made a proposal and a declaration of secrecy and you are gone. And we as a union are gone as well. And I do not blame those people, because I know very well, because I've been a lawyer, what you ask of people. However, for the general interest it is a pity sometimes."

From this perspective, not having a truly interested party at the root of the litigation may increase the chances of success since the litigation effort is not dependent upon the spurious nature of individual objectives and may provide a shield against opposition interference, particularly in the form of settlements.

5.7 Conclusion

While Chapter 4 has tempered the tendency in research to ascribe to litigants motivations and intentions absent in fact, this chapter on the other hand, has revealed that preliminary references may conceal more test cases, cause lawyering and overall strategic legal action than may be deduced from a glance at the legal documentation. As we have seen, a significant portion of the cases (over half) studied show actors other than the 'real' litigant involved in, or even responsible for the litigation. To the outside observer, individual cases may thus be hiding a third party initiative and the championing of collective interests. In some cases this third party initiative may be responsible for the legal action in the first place, for instance by setting up legal action as a test case. Yet, even cases that were not set up to serve as test cases, may transform into a case that serves a similar purpose. It is often the lawyers in such cases that are the drivers behind litigation, and therefore, when examining the motives of different actors behind litigation we have to take into account that different motives behind litigation may exist simultaneously, and may even contradict each other. However, such insights are also a mixed bag since cases that may end up championing collective interests do not always result from strategic action. They are thus a reminder for researchers to be attentive to the way superficial investigation of court proceedings could leave us with an incomplete picture, which clouds our understanding of who is able to profit from opportunities in legal structures. The significant share of cases where the litigation involves more than a mere client with (or even without) legal support directs our attention to the opportunities that are available, and recognised, by those with the resources and legal capital to pursue them, as well as underscores the cost of accessing this form of justice.

The challenges lawyers face in balancing the interests of their clients with the more collective interests, highlight the downside of individual rights-based litigation strategies. The combination of these insights with the characterisation of litigants as particularly persistent individuals, helps to further understand the pressure such prolonged legal contest puts on those affected. Considering that the EU legal system is dependent to a significant degree upon legal contestation and EU law mobilisation, an individual rights-based legal structure thus puts significant pressure on those affected by possible rights violations and non-compliance by Member States. Where no willing and able individual claimants are available to contest such violations, EU law mobilisation depends significantly upon the ability of those affected to mobilise collectively, or on those with the resources and legal capital to pursue such legal strategies for them.

Case Study B. Pensioners Abroad

B.1 Introduction: Between Social Rights and Free Movement

This case describes the story of Dutch pensioners living outside the Netherlands fighting changes in Dutch policies on health insurance by legal means all the way to the ECJ. Theirs is a story of European citizens using their right to free movement but becoming the subjects of the complex European efforts at coordinating social rights and benefits for people using that fundamental freedom. All European Union citizens, including those who have ended their working careers and have become entitled to an old age or other pension, enjoy the right to freedom of movement. Pensioners who have previously exercised their economic free movement rights may decide to remain in the former state of employment, to return to their Member State of origin or choose to live in another Member State. In addition, EU citizens may decide to move to another Member State only after their retirement. The group of pensioners residing abroad, often nationals of one of the 'northern' Member States who move to one of the southern Member States after their retirement, face many questions in the fields of social security and tax law. In which Member State do they have to pay income tax? Which social security rules apply to them? From which Member State(s) do they receive a statutory and/or supplementary pension? In which Member State are they entitled to health care and who bears the costs of treatment? In which Member State do they have to pay health insurance premiums?

Subsequently, this group is confronted with EU rules or national policy affected by those rules, since they are the embodiment of a 'transnational' group using their right of free movement. Because this group is disproportionally dependent on care, changes in this context can have a significant impact on their living situation. Their insurance situation is usually much more complex than the usual Dutch cases having to do not only with the Dutch health care legislation, but also complicated Treaty law and the legal rules of the country of residence. The contest for the group of pensioners central to this case study started when Dutch legislation was changed, effectively bringing their health care arrangements within the scope of European Regulations. The problems arising from the perspective of these pensioners can be ascribed to relevant European Regulations that only provide for a coordination regime.[1] Since they do not provide for harmonisation, it is inherent in such a scheme that cross-

1 Van de Mei 2011.

border movement may work out favourably or unfavourably for individuals or groups because such movement is not financially neutral. In the case of the pensioners, 'free movement' combined with a 'social Europe' did not have a positive outcome. This effectively created a situation in which pensioners had a 'right', the right to health care in their country of residence, that they did not actually want.

B.2 The Contested Policy

On January 1st 2006, a new Health Insurance Act was introduced in the Netherlands. This law replaced the previously applicable Health Care Act (*Ziekenfondswet*). Under the old rules, employees and pensioners with incomes below a certain threshold were publicly insured. Individuals who were not covered by this law due to their high income, at least as regards ordinary medical expenses, had to rely on private insurance. The Health Insurance Act, introduced in 2006, put an end to this distinction. The new law attracted early attention publicly and politically mainly because of the health care privatization it entailed in practice, and the abolishment of the fairly popular public option. Everyone who lived or worked in Netherlands was now legally required to take out private health care insurance. This change in Dutch legislation, however, also meant an expansion of the scope of EU Regulation 1408/71, a Regulation containing rules determining the social security systems to which people moving within the EU were subject, from which Member State(s) one could receive pension(s), where they could obtain health care and which Member State or institution was responsible for bearing the costs.

The expansion of the scope of this Regulation within the new Dutch law impacted in particular the group of old age pensioners who were long-term residents in another Member State and who, because of their income level had never – or only very long ago – been insured under the old public option scheme. This group had for a long time relied on private insurance. They were generally very satisfied with their private insurance contracts and the resulting quality of the covered health care services, which were often tailored to their needs and requirements.[2] By amending the Dutch legislation these people were, as far as their health care concerns, confronted with Regulation 1408/71 (as well as the new Regulation 883/2004), in particular the provisions relating to the right to care for persons residing in one Member State but receiving a

2 In some southern European countries, hospitals and other services appeared with the purpose of providing care specifically to this group of privately insured foreign pensioners. Gehring 2016.

pension from another Member State. These Regulations were meant to grant health care rights to people that made use of their right to freely move and reside within the EU. Based on these Regulations, individuals had a right to care in their state of residence similar to care they would have received in the pension paying Member State, had they lived in that state. Based on provisions contained in Regulation 1408/71, Article 69 of the new Dutch Health Care Insurance Act stated that people living abroad who fell within the scope of EU Regulations and were entitled to residence care in case of need, had to sign up as 'treaty entitled' (*verdragsgerechtigde*) with the Dutch Health Care Insurance Board (CVZ)[3] and with it became liable for contributions.[4] This had some profound financial implications for pensioners living abroad and registered as resident in another Member State. Instead of having a private insurance contract, these pensioners now had to pay contributions for general Dutch health insurance and contributions under the Emergency Medical Expenses Act (AWBZ), which were to be subtracted from their pensions and/or benefits. The Health Insurance Act thus expanded the statutory health insurance scheme to all residents of the Netherlands.

However, the provisions based on the EU Regulations meant that the retirees were suddenly, due to Regulation 1408/71, entitled to health care in their state of residence. The retirees did not appreciate this new right at all. This had to do with a provision in Regulation 1408/71 (Article 33), which meant that the Member State bearing the costs was entitled to collect health insurance premiums from their pensions and benefits. But the main reason for their opposition was that the Regulation entitled them to medical care under the law and standards of the state of residence, which in many cases was different from the care they had enjoyed previously, and often at considerably higher costs. They considered this a decline in rights because they were accustomed to care in accordance with the standards of their private insurance contracts.[5] The pensioners concerned did not wish to fall under the mandatory scheme and did

3 The CVZ (now *Het Zorginstituut*) is a quasi-autonomous non-governmental organisation that takes an independent position between the Ministry of Health, Welfare and Sport (VWS), health insurers, health care providers and patients (organizations). After the introduction of the ZVW in 2006 the CVZ was also responsible for the implementation of Article 69 of the Insurance Act and collecting contributions from people who fell under EU regulations, the so-called 'treaty entitled'.

4 Non-registration would be met with a fine of 130% of the contributions.

5 One of the contributors to an online discussion forum formulated it as if they received a letter stating: "Congratulations, you have won a prize (the right to care). Though, if you place your signature for acceptance, soon we will send you the bill for that prize." http://www.vngsint.com/ [last accessed 15 February 2016], the website is no longer available and has been replaced by https://vbngb.eu/ [last accessed 2 November 2017].

not want to pay these contributions. Their preference was to keep the private insurance they had had for years.

B.3 Consequences for Pensioners Living Abroad

Under the new health care system, formerly privately insured people living abroad became dependent on the legal system of health care in their country of residence.[6] In the new system, the hitherto privately insured lost the right to go to their own, local Dutch private physician or the fully equipped private clinics.[7] As of 2006, they were forced to go to the public hospitals within the national health insurance scheme. Many experienced this as an erosion of their insurance position because the quality of care in the country of residence, according to them, was significantly lower than in the (private) facilities to which they were previously entitled. For people who relied on health care (not uncommon among pensioners) this meant that they were forced to take out additional private insurance to extend their coverage back to the level they had previously enjoyed. Due to their age, however, premiums generally rose to several times the amount they had been paying before.

Additionally, these people were at the time either voluntarily insured, or in many cases not at all,[8] under the Exceptional Medical Expenses Act (AWBZ), which funded long-term home care and elderly care. With the new Act the AWBZ premium became obligatory and would also be deducted from their pension or benefits. However, due to differences in welfare state systems, in some countries this type of care was not available under the public health care system. An estimated thirty-five thousand people living abroad who received a Dutch pension or benefits, now had to pay premiums for care that was sometimes not available in their countries of residence. Nevertheless, the majority had significant cuts in their benefits/pension because of the required contributions based on the level of the health care in the Netherlands, even though the level of health care they would actually receive in their country of residence was lower or non-existent. They were essentially paying for care they did not receive.

6 Incidentally, the new regime had implications not only for Dutch nationals living in another European country, but also for Moroccans, Turks, Cape Verdeans, Tunisians and residents of the former Yugoslavia who received benefits or a state pension from the Netherlands.

7 For a discussion of additional practical problems, like the need for a translator when visiting a doctor in the public health care system, see Gehring 2016.

8 According to the chairman of the French wing of the Pensioners Association at the time approximately 2,000 out of 35,000 pensioners had chosen to insure additionally for exceptional medical expenses.

Figure III: Fictional Example of contribution to be paid by pensioners abroad

The contribution consists of:
a. A non-income-related contribution, equal to the average 'regular' non-income-related contribution to the Health Insurance Act, amounting in 2006 to € 1,106,- per year.
b. An income-related contribution equal to the 'regular' income-related contribution to the Health Insurance Act, which in 2006 for state pension recipients with an additional pension is equivalent to a premium of 6.5% over the statutory pension and 4.4% for the supplementary pension, to be calculated over a 'contribution income' up to € 30,000,-
c. An income-related contribution of 70% of the premium for the Exceptional Medical Expenses Act (AWBZ), amounting in 2006 to approximately 8.8% to be calculated over a 'premium income' up to € 30,000,-

For example: a retired Dutch couple living in Spain, both with a state pension of € 10,000, and both with a € 20,000,- supplementary pension from a pension fund (thereby enjoying a statutory pension from the Netherlands), and no additional income. Total income and assessed income for care allowance: € 60,000,- as far as they would be taxable in the Netherlands. Furthermore, suppose they have (Spanish) private health insurance for which they pay € 3,000,- premium per year to a package of their choice. They are not at present compulsory or optionally AWBZ insured.

Their yearly contribution to CVZ would be:
a) Annual nominal premium:
2*1,106 = € 2,200,-
b) Income-related HIA contribution:
2*6.5%*10,000 = € 1,300,- &
2*4,4%*20,000 = € 1,760,-
c) AWBZ-premium:
2*8.8%*30,000 = € 5,280,-
d) Health care benefits:
None
Total: **€ 10,540,-**
Amounting to over 17.5% of their total income and 350% of their former premium.

However, the issue was not only about the increasing financial burden but also about people who were in hospital and were suddenly no longer insured – people who were receiving medical treatment in the Netherlands were affected, since it had also been possible for them to receive treatment in the Netherlands while privately insured. The new rules meant that they now had to ask permission from their local public health insurance abroad whether or not the treatment was covered. With the introduction of the new Health Insurance Act, these people were effectively excluded from the regular Dutch health insurance system. Although they were legally included in the new Insurance Act, they experienced it as follows: They had throughout their life contributed to the Dutch solidarity based health care system (by paying taxes), but as of 2006, while still contributing an income-dependent premium, they could no longer benefit from this solidarity because the interpretation of EU Regulations effectively placed them outside the Dutch system.

B.4 Organizing Opposition

Immediately after the announcement of the new Health Insurance Act, unrest emerged among the large group of expatriate pensioners who were unsure of what this change would mean for their situation.[9] The real effect of the new law became clear when in response virtually all private health insurers unilaterally terminated the private insurance policies of people living abroad or replaced them with new policies with much higher premiums, leading to unrest among the pensioners. [10] The Dutch Health Care Insurance Board (CVZ), which had circulated more than 200,000 (different) information leaflets informing people of the upcoming changes, was flooded with phone calls and emails from angry pensioners.[11]

From this collective outrage grew the idea to unite with the aim of bringing the issue to court. The Association for Representation of Dutch Pensioners Abroad (the VBNGB, from here on: the Pensioners Association) "established to represent those groups of Dutch pensioners in combating the unlawful consequences of the introduction of the Health Insurance Act, including in legal cases against insurance companies and the Dutch government, insofar as they cannot be resolved by other means," became the umbrella organisation for a

9 Evidenced by a stream of questions and comments on the online discussion forum launched especially for people living abroad confronted with issues surrounding the new Insurance Act.
http://www.vngsint.com/ [last accessed 15 February 2016], the website is no longer available and has been replaced by https://vbngb.eu/ [last accessed 2 November 2017]. The original forum thread can be found on http://www.zorgwet.info/buitennl/ (the website is no longer updated) [last accessed 2 November 2017]

10 While some insurers changed existing premiums or offered new ones, some insurers cancelled existing contracts outright. However, after pressure from the media and parliament most insurers started to offer new insurance policies, often at significantly higher premiums. After the first summary process started by the Pensioners Association at the end of 2005 – at the direction of the judge – some of these premiums were lowered to more reasonable rates.

11 Even before the administration was well underway 50,000 letters and e-mails from concerned Dutch living abroad (especially retirees) were already waiting for a response from the CVZ. Two months after the entry into force of the law between 2,800 and 4,000 appeals were received, later rising to 5,000. The CVZ became overloaded and in tens of thousands of cases lagged behind with the timely processing of annual accounts. Rapport Ombudsman 2006/300, *Zorg(en) in het buitenland*, 22 and 30. Available at: https://www.nationaleombudsman.nl/onderzoeken/2006/300 [last accessed 2 November 2017].

collection of smaller groups from different countries.[12] However, the group of people affected by the change in the law was substantial and not everyone involved agreed on the most effective approach. Not only were there differences of opinion on whether the new law should be challenged by lobbying or through the courts, even after it was decided to proceed with legal action, there were different opinions on the arguments and strategy. Thus several localised organisations of pensioners arose, including the Pensioners Association and another group, aptly named 'Second Front'. The Pensioners Association demanded, firstly, a right of option to arrange an insurance policy in the country of residence or through a custom policy from a Dutch or local insurer, and secondly, the abolition of the compulsory AWBZ premium and restoration of the ability to insure voluntarily for AWBZ care. The Pensioners Association enlisted supporters, and collected money in order to be able to bring the matter to court. Supporters were asked to contribute 100 euro to the cause. Due to the size of the affected group as well as the general outrage and concern among the pensioners, the Pensioners Association was able to muster a significant amount of support and resources.

B.5 Extra-Legal Opposition

The pensioners were effectively fighting two battles. Firstly, they opposed the unilateral termination of their private insurance policies by the insurers and objected directly to these insurers. "We are trying to settle the matter amicably, but that has not paid off yet", the president of the Pensioners Association stated in an interview for a Dutch newspaper.[13] Some insurers did not respond to complaints by the pensioners at all. One insurer offered a transitional contract to continue the policy until the retiree was accepted into the local public health insurance scheme. Another offered to continue the insurance at a premium of 400 euro per month.[14] For a pensioner, however, that would have been in addition to the income-dependent contribution and nominal premiums of the compulsory basic insurance scheme. Financially, this was in no way a solution for the pensioners.

12 From the website of the Pensioners Association: http://www.vngsint.com/ [last accessed 15 February 2016], the website is no longer available and has been replaced by https:// vbngb.eu/ [last accessed 2 November 2017].

13 'Pensionados Dagen hun Zorgverzekeraars', *Het Financieele dagblad*, 13 December 2005.

14 Amounting to approximately three or four times the amount of the old premiums.

The insurers pointed to the new law to justify their actions, relying on the Implementing and Adjustment Act[15] of the new health care legislation that stated that as of January 1st 2006 all Dutch private insurance policies for people living abroad would become void. A spokesman for one of the insurance companies referred the pensioners to the legislator, considering that the rules had changed with the introduction of the new health care system: "It is very frustrating for the insured, but we do not feel we are a player here. And we think the judge will agree".[16] However, the lawyer for the Pensioners Association at that time believed that a lawsuit was more likely to succeed against the insurers than against the Ministry of Health. "[The Minister] is not a policyholder" and "he has no power over the insurers" he explained his belief that liability lay with those holding the pensioners' insurance policies. Therefore, with a lack of acceptable response from the insurers and no expected political intervention, a court case was deemed the only option.

The second fight was against (the effects of) the new legislation altogether, with a focus on two elements: first, the so-called 'treaty entitlement' that was responsible for the main changes in the pensioners' situation, and second, the mandatory premium for the AWBZ. Before and during the legal actions the Pensioners Association worked to lobby the political arena in order to repeal, delay or amend the new legislation. By putting pressure on both parliament and the ministry, they were able to solicit parliamentary questions to the Minister of Health by several MPs. However, the Minister provided few clear answers and left them none the wiser. He did not appear very willing to accommodate the pensioners' concerns. The Minister's apparent disinterest may in part have been a result of the negative image of the pensioners. In the public mind, they were generally considered rich retirees enjoying the sun in a country were life was cheaper, and therefore they had little right to complain. As the director of the Pensioners Association states:

> "We have a bad image in the Netherlands, people think we're calculating tax evaders. People who want to have it both ways. If reports are made here, you always see a shot of two old people in Benidorm and then a white villa and Cava drinking people on the edge of a pool. The image in Calvinist Netherlands is that we just want to take advantage of the system."[17]

---

15 Article 2.5.2 of the Implementing- and Adjustment Act.

16 Boom, H. 'Pensionados Slijpen de Messen', *Het Financieele dagblad*, 14 January 2006.

17 Pensioners living abroad had become known as 'Pensionados', a somewhat derogatory nickname for the group of people moving from one (typically Northern) Member State to live out their retirement in another (Southern) Member State while receiving statutory pensions from the former. Within the EU this includes an estimated 100,000 people.

The Pensioners Association, together with hundreds of individual complainants, brought the matter to the attention of the Dutch Ombudsman. After investigation into the implementation of the law, the Ombudsman established that the government had failed to foresee the impact the new legislation would have for, in particular, the group of formerly privately insured pensioners living abroad.[18] The report contained descriptions of some striking examples of difficult situations in which the pensioners found themselves as a result.[19]

B.6 Legal Contestation: From Pillar to Post

Part of the problem from the outset was the question of who to blame. Health insurers terminated private insurance policies but pointed to the new law. The responsible Minister had no control over private contracts. Pension funds and the Social Security Office (SVB)[20] were charged with collecting the contributions, yet pointed to the CVZ as the responsible agency.[21] The CVZ was overloaded with complaints due to late and imprecise information and was unable to cope with the myriad problems caused by the new Regulations. Because of the ambiguity of who was to be held accountable legally, the stream of litigation followed a somewhat staggered pattern. To be clear, the Pensioners Association was not the only one responsible for court cases. Multiple individual cases were started, and as discussed, apart from the Pensioners Association there was a second group of pensioners, the 'Second Front', who had a differ-

18 A conclusion that was later confirmed by an answer of the director of the CVZ to one of the complainants, confessing that due to their former focus on the group of people that were publicly insured, the CVZ had not been prepared for the problems that would occur with the privately insured. Letter published on the Pensioners Association online forum: http://www.vngsint.com/ [last accessed 15 February 2016], the website is no longer available and has been replaced by https://vbngb.eu/ [last accessed 2 November 2017].

19 Rapport Ombudsman 2006/300, *Zorg(en) in het buitenland*. Available at: https://www.nationaleombudsman.nl/onderzoeken/2006/300 [last accessed 2 November 2017].

20 The Social Insurance Bank (SVB) is an independent administrative body in the field of social security in the Netherlands. The SVB is responsible for the implementation of the state pension AOW, the survivors pension ANW, child benefits and other provisions.

21 An open letter (dated June 9th 2006) by several pension funds to Minister Hoogervorst is testament to the similar discontent with the chaotic state of affairs resulting from the new Act among these organizations that were effectively tasked with the implementation of the new legislation. Letter published on the Pensioners Association online forum: http://www. vngsint.com/ [last accessed 15 February 2016], the website is no longer available and has been replaced by https://vbngb.eu/ [last accessed 2 November 2017].

ent legal approach to the claims. The focus of this analysis is on the actions taken by the Pensioners Association, and where relevant I will mention the other litigants.

Pensioners v. Private Insurers

Even before the new law went into effect the first summary proceedings were started in December 2005 against the insurance companies' decision to unilaterally cancel existing insurance policies. On behalf of thousands of pensioners in Spain, Belgium, France, Germany, Ireland, Portugal, Malta and Cyprus, with the aim of continuing the current insurance, it was claimed that insurers could not unilaterally terminate private policies, and that it was unfair for the insurers to charge exorbitant new premiums while coverage remained the same. The relief judge ruled in favour of the insurers stating that because the new Insurance Act contained a provision which stipulated that all existing contracts had been terminated, the insurers' hands were in effect tied. However, the new premiums offered by the insurers were considered to be indeed exorbitant, and the judge instructed the insurers to offer more reasonable premiums.[22]

Pensioners v. Ministry of Health

Early in 2006, the Pensioners Association initiated summary proceedings against the state, represented by the Ministry of Health, with the aim of getting the new Health Insurance Act declared void. In order to achieve this aim, they hired two new lawyers, a former employee of the legal department of the European Commission and specialist in tax law and free movement, and a repeat player before the ECJ, a lawyer specialised in EU and Dutch competition law and EU law who had pleaded before the ECJ in over fifty preliminary reference procedure cases and over thirty direct actions.

They claimed firstly, a right of option to arrange an insurance policy in the country of residence or through a special policy from a Dutch insurer, and not the required registration with the CVZ and local public health system in the country of residence. Secondly, they demanded an exemption from AWBZ premiums because in a majority of countries no such AWBZ care existed. The Pensioners Association argued *inter alia* that Articles 18 and 39 of the EC Treaty (now 21 and 45 TFEU) on the freedom of movement of people and workers had been violated, by charging all pensioners residing outside the Netherlands a premium that did not in any way reflect the (lower) cost of

22 Rechtbank 's-Gravenhage 30 December 2005, ECLI:NL:RBSGR:2005:AU8874.

health care in the state of residence. This created a disparity between the contributions charged to the pensioners and the amounts to be paid by the Dutch State to the other Member States for the care provided.

On March 31st 2006, the relief judge of the District Court in The Hague gave a verdict.[23] Their first claim, the right of option to voluntary insurance, was rejected. However, according to the judge the general principle of equality in conjunction with Articles 18 and 39 EC had been violated with a 'high degree of likelihood'. Therefore, it was not justified to levy the same contributions from all Dutch pensioners resident abroad separate from the lump sums their resident countries charged the Netherlands. The law thus infringed the general principle of equality because different situations were treated equally.[24] With regard to the AWBZ, the court held that the contributions of the pensioners should not exceed what the Netherlands had to pay the country of residence. The judge instructed the Minister to change the implementation regulation accordingly. On April 27th 2006, the Minister informed parliament that the Act had been changed retroactively from January 1st 2006 onwards. The most important change was that the contribution was now based on the average cost of care for the social health insurance in the country of residence, in relation to the average health care costs of health insurance in the Netherlands. This was also known as the 'state of residence factor'.[25] This differentiation was introduced in the contribution. In general, this would mean that most of the insured would pay a lower contribution.[26] Since this judgment was only preliminary in that these were summary proceedings[27] one prerequisite the relief judge added to the judgment was that the Pensioners Association submit an application for court proceedings to be brought regarding the main action.

23 Rechtbank 's-Gravenhage 31 March 2006, ECLI:NL:RBSGR:2006:AV7778.

24 According to the Ministry's own calculations the amounts paid to different Member States differed considerably: Belgium € 3,450,- per person annually; France € 3,667,-; Latvia € 179,-; Luxembourg € 4,510,-; Spain € 2,586,-.

25 The Pensioners Association concurred with the principle of 'country of residence factor' but not the calculation method, which compared the average cost of care for the entire population in the country of residence to those costs in the Netherlands. According to the Pensioners Association the comparison should have been made for the group over sixty-five years of age.

26 The already overburdened CVZ was tasked with refunding the excessively charged contributions. The monitor reports of 12 and 30 June 2006 contain a detailed description of the problems that the CVZ received with respect to the deductions at the SVB, UWV and private pension funds.

27 Formally, a judgment in summary proceedings is only an interim order, for which the court has mainly considered the immediate interests of the parties and to a lesser degree the legal subtleties of the law at issue.

Pensioners v. CVZ

The Social Insurance Bank (SVB), charged with levying the contributions, began deducting them from state pensions in January 2006 and announced that any objections should be directed to the CVZ. The SVB itself received over 5,000 such objections. After several unsuccessful complaints to both the SVB and CVZ, two groups of plaintiffs ended up before the Council of State.[28] Apart from the Pensioners Association there was also the aforementioned 'Second Front'. As mentioned, the Pensioners Association and the Second Front had differing legal approaches. The former based its claim mainly on a violation of the basic principles of Community law (non-discrimination and freedom of movement), the latter particularly on the national texts underlying the levied contributions.

Following consultations between the lawyers, the CVZ and Council of State a number of cases were selected and test proceedings were initiated for the entire group. In a controversial ruling on April 25th 2007, the Council of State declared[29] that all concerns were understood as being directed towards a letter, sent in December of 2005, in which the CVZ had informed stakeholders that they had the right to care in accordance with European rules, that the Netherlands was liable for the costs and that the pensioners therefore had to pay contributions. The relevant provisions of Regulation 1408/71, according to the Council of State, were derived directly from the Regulation and therefore the letter from the CVZ had no legal effect. That meant that all (seven) cases were deemed inadmissible. Simply stated, they should have waited for the first payment claim in order to be able to appeal, an understandably frustrating result for the pensioners after six months of waiting.

In response to this judgment, the SVB sent letters to the pensioners stating, "your objection is unfounded because this is not a decision". New appeals were lodged, this time at the Amsterdam District Court. Contrary to the decision by the Council of State, this court ruled that these letters were in fact decisions with legal effect and that the appeals were grounded, therefore the SVB was ordered to make new decisions, which it did, stating that the pensioners had no right of option and that the new system was compulsory. As expected, new appeals were lodged against this decision.

---

28 Under the Health Insurance Act at that time, derogating from the General Administrative Law (AWB), appeal could only be lodged with the Administrative Jurisdiction Division of the Council of State.

29 Raad van State 25 April 2007, ECLI:NL:RVS:2007:BA3743.

The Road to the ECJ

By now, faith in the Dutch legal system had diminished significantly among the pensioners and the Pensioners Association chose to start administrative proceedings against the CVZ,[30] with the aim of possibly getting the case referred to the ECJ. As the chairman of the Pensioners Association concluded: "The Dutch administrative court is only there to give citizens the idea that they have access to justice, but in reality has to make sure that the government is always vindicated." The hope was that the ECJ would be less lenient towards the Dutch legislature and would give a more objective and therefore favourable judgment. The Pensioners Association, together with their lawyer, had selected several suitable cases on which to litigate. They chose appellants that most clearly showed what the consequences of the new law were in the various countries and who could serve as prototypes of how people had been affected.[31]

The claimants, all Dutch nationals resident in other EU Member States (Belgium, Spain, France and Malta), were entitled to either a pension under the state pension scheme or benefits under the Dutch Disability Insurance (WAO). Prior to January 1st 2006, they had insurance contracts with private insurance companies established in the Netherlands or in other Member States. On the same January 1st 2006, these contracts with providers in the Netherlands had been terminated in accordance with the New Insurance Act. Of those among them who had concluded such an agreement with a provider established in another Member State, however, the agreement remained intact. The appeal by the claimants was based on the argument that Articles 28 and 28bis of Regulation No 1408/71 did not contain binding rules for determining the applicable legislation on the basis of which they were automatically subject to the system of benefits of the Member State of residence. They considered, rather, that they could choose either to register with the competent institution of the state of residence, in order to receive benefits in that state, or, if they did not register with that institution, to take out private insurance. In the latter case, since the cost of the benefits had not been borne by an institution of that state, the Mem-

30 Because of the large number of complaints and appeals that were filed against the actions taken by the CVZ, the SVB and also by private pension funds (who were ordered by the CVZ to deduct the contributions from pensions and benefits) an amendment to the new legislation was made (August 2008) that formally considered all these actions a decision by the CVZ against which appeal was possible before the administrative courts. *Wijziging van de Zorgverzekeringswet in verband met de rechtsgang bij inhouding van de bijdrage van verdragsgerechtigden (rechtsgang bronheffing verdragsgerechtigden)*, *Kamerstukken* 2007/2008, 31377, 1-9.

31 The eventual reference to the ECJ would include other individual litigants that had filed a similar appeal.

ber State responsible for payment of the pension could not deduct a contribution under Article 33 of that Regulation. Three appellants had registered at the CVZ ('under protest' as one of them stated). The three others had refused to register. By decisions taken during 2006 and 2007, the CVZ nonetheless deducted contributions from their pensions. In judgments of January 31st and December 17th 2008, the Amsterdam District Court had dismissed the actions brought by the appellants. They appealed their case before the Central Appeals Tribunal (CRvB), which in late August 2009 (almost four years after the implementation of the new legislation) decided to refer two questions to the ECJ about the compatibility of the Dutch scheme with the European rules.[32] This was a welcome development for the Pensioners Association that had pressed for a referral, since they felt, after the many attempts and disappointments they had had up until then, that the Dutch system was not in their favour.

Substantively, the Court was asked to consider whether the new Dutch legislation was compatible with Regulation 1408/71 (on the application of social security schemes), the point stressed by the 'Second Front', and with Article 21 TFEU (freedom of movement and residence of EU citizens).[33] In its judgment of October 2010, the Court ruled that the European rules (Regulation 1408/71) must be interpreted as meaning that the Dutch legislation did not violate its terms. On Article 21 TFEU, the point stressed by the Pensioners Association, it decided, however, that it must it be interpreted as "precluding such national legislation in so far as it induces or provides for [...] an unjustified difference of treatment between residents and non-residents as regards ensuring the continuity of the overall protection against the risk of sickness enjoyed by them under insurance contracts concluded before the entry into force of that legislation". This unjustified difference in treatment was for the national court to establish. In its judgment, the ECJ instructed the CRvB on the relevant elements it had to take into account:

1. Were private insurance contracts by residents, on the basis of the law of 2006, also terminated?;
2. Has that termination had the same effect for residents and non-residents?;

32 The Pensioners Association argued for priority treatment given the vulnerability of the complainants due to their old age and, at the request of the CRvB, the Court decided to treat the matter as a priority case, which resulted in a relatively quick judgment in October 2010.

33 The argument brought forward by appellants, that their situation also fell within the scope of Article 45 TFEU on the freedom of movement for workers, was thrown out by the Court. It considered that since the appellants in question had migrated to another Member State after they had reached retirement age the freedom of movement for workers could not apply.

3. Were the insurance companies obligated to accept non-residents?;
4. Have the insurance companies undertaken actions, at the request of the Dutch government, to ensure that the overall coverage was maintained after 2006, and if so applied that commitment only to residents or also to non-residents?

Returning from the ECJ

Although the ECJ wasn't the competent court to give a final verdict on this matter, the pensioners and their lawyer considered it clear that the ECJ had concluded that they had been discriminated against. They were supported in their conviction by the fact that the representative of the Netherlands before the ECJ, in response to questions by the judges had admitted that "at no point had the Dutch government considered the consequences of the introduction of the new Dutch Health Insurance Act would have for the so-called 'treaty-entitled'". In anticipation of the CRvB's concurring conclusion, their lawyer had therefore already sent a letter holding the Minister accountable and thus liable for any damages the pensioners had suffered due to the introduction of the Health Insurance Act. An offer was made to reach a settlement. After a negative response by the Minister, the Dutch Ombudsman was requested to intervene in the matter. The Ombudsman subsequently, in a detailed letter to the Minister (March 4th 2011) once again reiterated his concern for the pensioners' problems and implored the Minister to consult with the Pensioners Association in order to resolve the matter.

The crux of the subsequent oral argument of the attorney before the CRvB was, therefore, that the discrimination was uncontested and that the only question remaining was the consequence of this determination for the contested decisions by the CVZ. The answer to this question was, according to the lawyer, that the contested decisions must be annulled, despite the fact that the Court had held that the deductions of contributions by the CVZ were in themselves not contrary to EU law. However, in its judgment of December 13th 2011, the CRvB decided that the alleged difference in treatment between residents and non-residents – constituting discrimination – did not exist. First, it established that under Dutch legislation no difference in treatment arose since both residents and non-residents retained minimum coverage. Neither did it see a demonstrable difference in treatment between residents and non-residents triggered by the Dutch government or, with its cooperation, by the Dutch-based insurance companies. In its judgment the CRvB included the phrase:

> "That in hindsight perhaps there has been a degree of administrative naivety, does not mean that the Court finds that it has been the deliberate intention of the Dutch

> government to treat residents and non-resident treaty beneficiaries (unjustifiably) different."

These final considerations in this, in the words of their lawyer, "inexplicable" verdict led to understandable agitation among the pensioners. According to the chairman of the Pensioners Association this left them feeling like:

> "Don Quichote fighting against the Dutch windmills. This means that if the Dutch state is doing something bad to its citizens, one can say, 'This has been naive and as long as you cannot prove that there was intent, they did not act against the law'."

After losing their battles, the Pensioners Association turned to the European Court of Human Rights, contesting the final decision by the CRvB and arguing *inter alia* that the termination of their insurance contracts in 2006 constituted a violation of their right to the peaceful enjoyment of their possessions under Article 1 Protocol Nr. 1 of the ECHR. The Court did not concur and, moreover, confirmed in part the conclusion by the CRvB that residents and non-residents were not in a similar situation and that therefore this was not a case of discrimination.[34]

B.7 Effects of the Legal Contest

After an extended struggle, numerous courts, and even after activation of the ECJ, the Dutch Ombudsman and the ECtHR, the endeavour left the pensioners with a bitter sense of injustice. As summarised in a fact sheet for their members entitled 'the lawsuit that could not be won':

> "The government's so-called naivety liberated the Netherlands from all those expensive retirees, and donated the tens of millions reserved for us on the balance sheets of the insurance companies to those same companies. [...] The court's judgment completely undermines confidence in administrative law that should give the citizen the opportunity to subject government wrongdoing to judicial scrutiny. In this way it translates into an institute that intends to convince the citizen that the state is always right."

One small success the pensioners did manage to obtain was the establishment, also through court interference, of the so-called 'country of residence factor'

34 ECHR Decision of 23 October 2012 in *Ramaer and van Willigen v the Netherlands*, Application Nr. 34880/12, at 80.

within the health insurance scheme. This led to premium reductions for most of the pensioners living abroad. The residence factor affects the basic monthly premium that is deducted in the Netherlands on the pensions paid. This adjustment is based on the care package that the pensioner is receiving in the public provision of care in his or her country of residence. A calculation by the Pensioners Association shows that over the period 2006 to 2013 individual savings were achieved for their constituents of up to 31,000 euro for the 'treaty entitled' with a maximum deduction and 9,000 euro in savings for the married retirement beneficiary. In addition, they obtained the so-called 'country of pension care' whereby 'treaty entitled' pensioners remained entitled at all times to access to the basic service of the Dutch health care system. Although these partial victories alleviated the financial burden, it did not change the fact that most pensioners were no longer able to enjoy the health care of their choice. They lost the ability to go to their own, local, Dutch private physician or the fully equipped private clinics and were forced to go to the local public hospitals.

Through its efforts fighting the new Dutch health care system, the Pensioners Association developed to become a central source of information, support and representation for pensioners living abroad. It established itself as a permanent interlocutor of the Care Institute Netherlands (formerly CVZ), and therefore acquired a permanent voice to advocate the interests of all its members at earlier stages of political development. Their legal efforts also continued against other Dutch policies that affected their members. In subsequent proceedings, the Pensioners Association was successful with litigation against the withholding of the purchasing power allowance (KOB), which included complaints to the European Commission resulting in infringement proceedings being lodged against the Netherlands. While the Netherlands appealed in national proceedings, it decided to reverse the decision when the European Commission announced infringement proceedings.[35] This resulted in a full refund, including interest of all withheld payments.[36]

B.8 Collective Mobilisation

The pensioners (unlike the group of migrants affected by the fees increase: *Case Study C*) were able to self-organise and raise the needed financial capital within their own group, although they did have the challenge of mobilising in

35 http://europa.eu/rapid/press-release_IP-13-140_en.htm [last accessed 2 November 2017].

36 As of February 2015 this compensation has been abolished altogether.

an *ad hoc* fashion. The effect of the amendment to the Dutch Insurance Act was directly and for all, and the consternation it brought about made the mobilisation and organization of the interests of this group of people easier by effectively creating a constituency around the issue. The size of the group supporting the legal battle meant that they had a substantial number of members with legal expertise and organizational skills, as well as considerable potential for financial support from their members. The large group of affected pensioners also meant that they had a pool of cases to select from and litigate on. Test cases were chosen on the basis of the best context. The group made use of the social and financial capital that existed among their members. In contrast to the migrants who were represented by the IOT, members of this group were generally more affluent, as evidenced by the amount of capital that they managed to collect and individuals with social capital who were present among this group; including a former Minister of Finance and former vice-president of the European Commission. This social capital helped them in mobilising other institutional actors like the European Commission and the Dutch Ombudsman. Among the members that got involved in the discussions on the Pensioners Association's online forum were trained lawyers, former tax advisors and notaries. This available capital contributed to their ability to organize opposition to the policy themselves.

However, the size of the group of affected pensioners also opened the door for dissenting opinions about the legal approach and splinter groups who took their own approach. These findings corroborate conclusions in legal mobilisation research that a larger constituency and mandate of any interest group increases the difficulty of reaching the necessary consensus over a relatively specific set of preferred policy outcomes for longer periods of time.[37] While mobilising the group around the issue was relatively easy, reaching consensus on the strategy to be followed proved to be more difficult, as was illustrated by the aforementioned 'Second Front', and some individuals who chose to litigate on their own.

B.9 Assigning Blame and Finding The Right Forum

The staggered nature of the trajectory of the pensioners' efforts to fight the new health care policies through the courts can be explained by the complex collection of applicable national and European rules and regulations. The situation was further complicated by the interposition of insurance companies and the problem of assigning blame. Insurers were effectively 'burdened' with

37 Bouwen & McCown 2007, 429.

the difficulties resulting from the implementation of the new Dutch health care law, and were therefore not very indulgent, invariably pointing to the government. The '*administrative naivety*' in the design and implementation of the new law meant that for a long time it remained unclear to whom the pensioners should turn with their grievances, both in terms of complaints and legal contestation. This resulted in a long line of failed litigation efforts, increasing the need for organisation. After the unsatisfactory trials within the Dutch legal system, the desire for review by the ECJ grew among the pensioners, with the expectation of a more independent, and therefore positive, judgment. Although the pensioners felt the ECJ judgment vindicated their claim, it left the real determination up to the Dutch court, which eventually left them empty-handed.

The long road and perseverance of the pensioners is illustrated by the fact that the Pensioners Association, after the disappointing ruling of the CRvB also undertook another attempt at the ECtHR, again without success. That the pensioners were earnest in their battle is also evident from their legal assistance. Despite the considerable 'in-house' expertise, for the legal part they chose the 'hired gun' and opted for the help of a well-regarded lawyer with significant experience in litigating before the ECJ. This did, of course, increase the costs incurred by the group since in this case it was not a matter of *pro bono* work. The total costs for the Pensioners Association was estimated to be up to 600,000 euro. All this taken together meant a steep hill and long contest for the pensioners, of whom many did not see the end of it. As one of the litigants involved concluded cynically: "Old people tend to die out."

6 Lawyering Eurolaw

6.1 Introduction

The European legal system, which combines both centralised enforcement by the vigilance and supervision of the European Commission with a decentralised form of enforcement through national courts, relies to a significant extent on the responsiveness of the European polity. The effective application of EU law cannot be ensured by the European Union and the ECJ alone. It depends strongly on domestic courts and citizens that initiate proceedings before these courts to enforce their rights. When it comes to signalling possible infringements and stimulating the application of EU rules and principles, a large part of this responsibility falls into the hands of legal practitioners that use and invoke these rules in assisting their clients in national legal proceedings. The previous chapters have given first indications of the characteristics that are inherent in preliminary references from the perspective of the litigant, and how individual cases may conceal more collective interests behind litigation. These observations give rise to further investigation into other actors involved in the mobilisation of EU law through preliminary references. Effective advocacy, an element that can 'make or break' a case is important for the application of law, especially in the creation of new jurisprudence. The perspective of legal practitioners in preliminary reference cases is therefore the focus of this chapter.

The litigants that fall within the 'individual' category are, with the exception of those acting as a 'straw man' for organised third parties, prototypical one-shotters. Galanter described the legal service provider as a possible remedy to the structurally disadvantaged position of the individual one-shotter: "The existence of a specialized bar on the one-shotter side should overcome the gap in expertise, allow some economies of scale, provide for bargaining commitment and personal familiarity. But," he adds, "this is short of overcoming the fundamental strategic advantages of repeat players – their capacity to structure the transaction, play the odds, and influence rule-development and enforcement policy."[1] Lawyers, themselves in many respects repeat players in the legal system, can compensate for the individual litigant's lack of legal capital and their presence in legal proceedings may influence judicial outcomes.[2] Lawyers with their professional experience and expertise can make up for the disadvantages one-shotters have, especially in having only episodic encounters with the legal system. By knowing their way around the court and court procedures, legal aid

1 Galanter 1974, 308.
2 McGuire 1995.

providers may provide a counterbalance to the structural disadvantage of one-shotters. As one of the advantages of lawyers as repeat players, McGuire has pointed to their closeness to the judiciary and their familiarity with the preferences and 'modus operandi' of courts and judges.[3] When we look at individuals in the European legal system, it is thus important to look at the extent to which their relatively disadvantaged position is offset by the presence of a lawyer or other form of legal support.

Based on interviews with lawyers that have assisted litigants in preliminary reference procedures, the next section focuses on the ways in which practitioners[4] deal with preliminary references and analyses the challenges of a procedure most of them encounter for the very first time. The aim of this chapter is to give insight into the context within which legal practitioners have to work on preliminary reference cases, the kinds of issues that arise from peculiarities of the procedure, the options lawyers have for dealing with these matters and the considerations that play a role in this respect. Where Chapter 5 focused on lawyers actively aiming to employ preliminary references, the following paragraphs will zoom in specifically on the preliminary references from the perspective of practitioners who were not pushing for, but instead were confronted with a reference to the ECJ.

6.2 Lawyers and References: Allocating Effects in Eurolaw Expertise

From a judicial review perspective, the preliminary reference procedure can have far-reaching consequences for legal dynamics both nationally and in the EU. However, as we have seen in the previous chapters, the fact that such influence is being exerted strategically and with the deliberate aim of changing policies is not self-evident. In a significant portion of the cases, a reference to the ECJ comes as a surprise, regardless of whether or not EU law arguments have been used. Earlier research has focused on familiarity with and experience of the procedure among national judges, with differing but overall not all too promising results. National judges seem to lack the necessary knowledge of EU law or they appear simply unwilling to refer.[5] This study provides the opportunity to see how this plays out among lawyers and their clients.

As concluded in Chapter 4, when it comes to preliminary references, there is an important distinction to be made between proactive and reactive litigation. In over 60% of the cases studied, the parties made no active effort to push for a

3 McGuire 1995.

4 The practitioners that are discussed in this chapter include both lawyers and non-lawyers, like tax advisors; therefore I use the term practitioner to cover both groups.

5 Jaremba 2013; European Parliament 2007b.

reference. This is in itself an important observation about the (non-)purposefulness behind references to the ECJ, but it also has important repercussions for the way legal practitioners (can) work a case once it is referred. When the decision to refer cannot be ascribed to pressure from the litigating party, it is less likely that the lawyer in question has any particular expertise in either EU law or preliminary references. Legal practitioners that have worked on a case that has reached the ECJ through a preliminary reference belong to a very select group. When considering that judges in the Netherlands – a country with a total caseload in the tens of thousands and one of the Member States with the highest number of references to the ECJ every year[6] – still only make some thirty references annually,[7] participating in this procedure is a rare experience.[8] For many it will happen only once in their entire career. By the very nature of preliminary ruling proceedings, the uncertainty of referrals and the multiplicity of subjects and legal disciplines, the collection of legal practitioners in the cases at hand can therefore hardly be considered homogeneous. In many respects these practitioners share only the fact that they have participated in these proceedings. The practitioners interviewed thus include both lawyers from larger legal firms (especially in tax law) as well as many one-man offices. The one striking general characteristic among them is that the vast majority is not specialised in EU law.

Some lawyers do advertise their experience with litigating before the ECJ, but for most this is a form of *post hoc* advertisement of broadened expertise after they have had one case before the Court, rather than actually profiling themselves as experienced 'Eurolawyers'. The main exceptions are law firms that specifically profile themselves as Eurolawyers, even for individual claimants, specifically targeting their services at certain societal groups or professions with distinct (usually cross-border) characteristics. Such groups are likely to come into contact with EU law in ways that might lead to judicial procedures, e.g. cross-border workers or migrating pensioners. Of the lawyers directly assisting clients in preliminary references, only one had a record of acting before the ECJ. This particular lawyer had acted, among others, on behalf of larger associations of farmers, but mainly on behalf of government agencies[9] in over fifty prelimi-

6 See *Appendix B* for numbers of references according to Member State.

7 On average twenty-eight references were made annually by the Dutch judiciary in the period between 2003-2012. Statistics available at: http://curia.europa.eu/jcms/upload/docs/application/pdf/2013-04/192685_2012_6020_cdj_ra_2012_en_proof_01.pdf. [last accessed 10 September 2017].

8 According to statistics from the Dutch Bar Association, the Netherlands has over 17,000 active lawyers. This number does not include the legal practitioners like tax advisors (over 11,000) who may also act as counsel in preliminary reference cases.

9 In particular de *Sociale Verzekeringsbank* (the agency responsible for national insurance schemes in the Netherlands).

nary reference procedure cases and over thirty direct actions (of which over ten were appealed before the ECJ) over the course of twenty-five years.

The majority of lawyers in this study admitted to having no previous experience in EU law beyond a general familiarity, before their case was referred to the ECJ. This included all cases where the referral was not the aim of the litigants or their counsel; but even in cases where lawyers were pressing for a reference some of them underlined their relative inexperience going in. On the micro level, an unexpected referral to the ECJ can create different challenges for lawyers, especially since they are not prepared for a reference, nor do they generally possess the expertise or experience to work a case at the level of the ECJ. The next sections deal with the practical aspects of a reference that may hamper practitioners in their effective advocacy.

6.3 Allocating Resources

One of the major challenges for lawyers related to preliminary references is the extra time that is involved when working a case after reference to the ECJ. The amount of time spent by a lawyer on the reference part of any single case varies considerably, ranging from no additional work done up to many work days. The extra hours involved in preparation of a reference does not fall within a lawyer's regular day-to-day practice. Initially, the time consumption can increase by the simple fact that the procedure is different from what they are used to. Apart from the substantive legal work, a reference comes with its own timeline, its own rules of procedure and requirements. Even before dealing with the intricacies of EU law, these practitioners are thus confronted with procedural requirements with which they are unfamiliar. One lawyer specialised in social security describes the extra time involved in the minutiae related to a reference case:

> "Whether it's all really efficient working hours, I don't know. The procedural documents, with the gathering of attachments on a Sunday afternoon, and copying six-fold so that it can be at the Court in time. And then discover that formal deadline is on Monday and then think, shit, I need someone today that makes sure it's there tomorrow. Well, and then you are here all day. Coming in the office early in the morning and leaving in the evening at about eight or nine. Simply because, you don't know it, it's all new, a new kind of stress. It all just takes more time."

If part of their network, lawyers turn to colleagues with previous experience with preliminary references for help. However, with the scarcity of references this is not a large pool from which to choose. Some, being unfamiliar with the preliminary reference procedure, unaware of the way such cases are dealt with and without help from their network decide to simply await the answers by the ECJ:

> "At the time we wondered whether anyone in our office had litigated before the ECJ. Well, that was not the case. So we did not know how that works. And so, if you do not know, we do know how to go to the Supreme Court, in tax cases. Where the Supreme Court just considers whether the Appeals Court erred in law. And if so, then it'll be referred back. And if not so then you're finished. And now we have questions that go to the ECJ. So we did, not knowing how to react, decide to act as if we went to the Supreme Court. So in that sense to do nothing and wait for how the Court would answer the questions."

The difference in the amount of time lawyers spend on references is in large part dependent upon the complexity of the case as well as the nature of the questions that are referred to the ECJ. The preliminary questions can be the result of arguments presented in the national court that cast doubt on the interpretation of certain EU legislation. The substantive argumentation that is built before the national court then in large part coincides with the way in which a case is advocated before the ECJ. In these cases, practitioners choose to do little more than adjust their main written arguments to the format of the ECJ, and possibly expand on certain arguments brought forward in national proceedings. In other cases, the central questions that lie at the basis of a referral involve much more complex combinations of national rules, EU legislation, ECJ jurisprudence, as well as written observations by the European Commission and possibly multiple Member States. In such a case, a lawyer may wish to respond to these observations during the oral stage of a case. This can require a whole new line of arguments aimed at taking a position on the specific matter dealt with in the reference, which may be a significant side-track from the arguments brought forth in the main proceedings. In such cases lawyers spend several full working weeks merely preparing the written part of the proceedings, and more hours on the remainder of the procedure. Especially for the one-man offices that do not have as much flexibility in allocating their resources this creates a challenge. As one lawyer states:

> "You don't want to know how many hours I put into this case, it really is a lot. [...] Especially on appeal, I have spent a lot of time. It really became a matter of principle. That's when I really wanted the case to go on. I think I've put 700 hours into in. Do I exaggerate? If you look at the whole process, definitely not."

A preliminary reference thus adds an element of complexity that forces practitioners to spend more time on a case than they in many instances had anticipated. Since most clients in the individual cases are not financially capable of paying such an increase in cost, the extra time lawyers put into it often occurs essentially *pro bono*. Litigants in that respect are significantly dependent upon the goodwill of their lawyer for pleading their case before the ECJ. And due to the limited financial resources of most litigants, soliciting expertise from a lawyer specialised in EU law and experienced in pleading before the ECJ is not an option.

There is only one exception, which in many respects proves the rule that for most litigants switching to specialised counsel after referral to the ECJ is largely financially unfeasible. A specialist, with twenty-five years of experience in litigating before the ECJ (as described above), was hired by the association that acted on behalf of a large group of pensioners that opposed a change in the Dutch health insurance regime (*Case Study B*). The association was able to mobilise significant support and financial contributions from their members, which made it possible for them to cover the accompanying costs of specialised counsel. The majority of litigants did not enjoy such an advantage and were therefore not in a position to consider switching counsel or hiring experts.

6.4 Going to Luxembourg

All preliminary cases include a written stage, in which parties to the proceedings, as well as privileged actors like the European Commission and Member States, may submit their written observations. Within the written procedure there is no opportunity to respond to the observations filed by other parties. The only opportunity for parties to react to these positions is during the oral proceedings, requiring the counsellors to make a trip to Luxembourg.[10] The extra costs involved in a preliminary procedure thus includes both the additional work that goes into the reference part of the proceedings, as well as the cost involved with a trip to Luxembourg if the parties choose to participate in the oral proceedings. Participation in the oral proceedings as such thus becomes a financial consideration. In a regular private practice the financial burden of the added hours, and additional expenses, will be charged to the client. These cases involve individual litigants, and unless third parties financially back them, such additional costs are not easily covered. In such cases, lawyers have to come to an agreement with their client about the amount they will charge. This generally results in two possible outcomes. Either the decision is made to stick with the written observations

10 Not every case includes an oral stage. The rules of procedure of the ECJ allow the oral procedure to be dispensed with unless one of the litigants or, an interested party taking part in the procedure has lodged a request for a hearing to be held, giving the reasons for which that litigant or interested party wishes to be heard. Article 59 of the Statute of the Court of Justice of the European Union.

and forego the possibility of participating in the oral proceedings, or the lawyers charge only a minor amount or even none of the costs related to the trip to Luxembourg and pick up the bill themselves. In only one instance the client insisted on going to Luxembourg and was willing and/or able to pay the additional costs.[11] Where these costs are considered too high, clients and their counsel may choose to forego their chance to plead their case before the ECJ, and with it the chance to respond to the observations of both the opposing party as well as other intervening parties.

A similar dilemma occurred for one litigant who had chosen to represent himself in court. Due to procedural rules he would have required a lawyer in order to be able to plead his case in Luxembourg:

> "As a citizen you can basically do tax cases by yourself, so you don't have to have a lawyer. [But] if you want to plead before the Supreme Court, to plead orally, you need a lawyer. You are not allowed to do that yourself. European law says that when it comes to pleading the treatment in the European Court always depends on how it is regulated in the Netherlands. So when you need a lawyer at the Supreme Court, you also need a lawyer to plead before the European Court. I thought that was also very frustrating and unfortunate."

The frustration was such that he reconsidered hiring a lawyer. However, after consulting a law firm on the estimated cost of getting someone up to speed on the details of his case and the additional costs of the trip to Luxembourg ran in the tens of thousands of euros, he abandoned the idea, foregoing the possibility of pleading his case in Luxembourg.

When individuals are backed by third parties with more financial means this is, of course, less of an obstacle. As the selection for this study included only individual litigants, a large number of them were eligible for subsidized legal aid. In cases financed through legal aid, similar but also different financial considerations play a role. The next section deals with the importance as well as difficulties of legal aid schemes with respect to preliminary references.

6.5 Legal Aid and References

A large portion of the legal practitioners, especially those working in the areas of asylum, migration and social security, practice so-called social advocacy, assisting people who cannot afford a lawyer. They help clients who receive sup-

11 In other cases, where clients insisted on attending the hearing, third parties, like a union or an interest group, covered the costs and the individuals themselves did thus not incur additional costs.

port from the government for financing their legal actions, the so-called subsidized legal aid. The importance of legal aid increases when one's case is referred to the ECJ. References in general mean more work than planned. And as previously discussed, the relative complexity of such cases in comparison to practitioners' day-to-day practice provides lawyers with a substantial amount of extra hours to charge. Without the possibility of legal aid, the costs would be difficult for low-income individuals to cover. As most lawyers in the areas of asylum and migration law confirm:

> "Imagine that this would be settled on the basis of the hourly rate, then it really is not funny anymore. Look, the stakes for a client are huge. But for someone to do it on the basis of the hourly rate, it really is an impossible investment."

Subsidized legal aid thus for the most part relieves litigants of such a burden. The Dutch system is based on the granting of an amount of 'points' for providing legal aid at a certain stage in the procedure. One point equals 106 euro and reflects approximately one hour of work. [12] However, since subsidized legal aid only provides for a fixed fee based on the stage of proceedings, there is a limit to the number of hours of work for which a lawyer can be reimbursed:

> "The procedure before the Court of Justice was equivalent to eleven points. That is 1,100 euro or thereabouts. And you'll just have to manage with that. And then write twenty-five pages, and do all the research. So yeah, it was a little like volunteer work. Those proceedings before the Court, that is not in proportion to the hours we put into it."

In very complicated and thus time-consuming cases, officially called 'laborious cases', a lawyer can request reimbursement of extra hours on top of the compensation granted by the fixed fee system. Every hour above the fixed fee is compensated with one point, that is, if the request (including a budget estimating the hours needed) is authorised by the Legal Aid Board in advance.[13] The Board can accept the request and award additional remuneration when there is substantial

12 Previously this hourly wage was indexed every year. However, because of government budget cuts, this amount has been reduced several times in recent years. Since 2012, the hourly wage is around € 106. Even with subsidized legal aid, clients have to contribute an income dependent contribution varying from € 143 to € 823. Article 3 Remuneration Legal Aid Decree 2000 (*Besluit vergoedingen rechtsbijstand 2000*). Available at: http://maxius.nl/besluit-vergoedingen-rechtsbijstand-2000/hoofdstuk1 [last accessed 2 November 2017].

13 Article 5a (6) Remuneration Legal Aid Decree 2000.

factual complexity that is legally relevant or when the case is legally complex.[14] However, even when considering the extra remuneration, there is no compensation for the expenses of the trip to Luxembourg. And even when the extra hours are granted it may still not completely cover the effective time put into such a case:

> "When the case was referred to Luxembourg I asked the legal aid board for extra hours. Because it was in fact a legally complex case and I made more than three times the required number of points in hours. An appeal is five points, and then they say three times, so if you've spent more than fifteen hours, then you may request additional hours. I do not even know exactly how many hours I wrote. I finally got something like seventy extra hours. Well, I think I've worked a multitude of that."

It is up to the lawyer to decide whether or not he or she is willing to bear this additional expenditure. Advocating the client's interests in these cases thus depends to a large extent on his or her lawyer's personal investment in a case. As explained by one lawyer specialised in migration law:

> "We have a bit of a strange profession in the social advocacy. We just get a fixed amount for a case, and it does not pay to actually do your job too well. That sounds really weird, and I will not say that my work is by definition not done well. But you know, you get paid eight hours. And cases like these just take a lot more time, but the chances that you will get paid more is simply extremely small. So when you come to about twenty hours, then you start thinking how far you are willing to dive in it. And that means that sometimes you cannot get everything out of it, because it simply is not commercially viable."

Preliminary references put an added strain on the legal aid provided by these lawyers. Where it is the explicit aim of the lawyer to get a judgment on principle (either specifically from the ECJ or the national High Court), these considerations can of course be made beforehand, and some form of agreement can be reached with the client or several interested parties, as we have seen in the test cases. In the case of multiple interested clients, or other parties like interest groups and unions, these costs can more easily be covered. For individual clients such options are not available, and financial aspects thus impact individual litigants to a greater extent.

14 Legal Aid Board's Complex Cases Guide (*Leidraad Bewerkelijke Zaken*). Available at: https://www.recht.nl/doc/kst31753-3-bijlage.pdf. [last accessed 2 November 2017].

6.6 Lawyers' Motivation

Regardless of the costs involved with references, many lawyers choose to invest in these cases and make the trip to Luxembourg anyway. Lawyers give several (non-exclusionary) motivations for their decision to do so. The motivation for such a trip often comes from both personal interest and professional ethics with regard to representing the interests of one's client. Some consider the opportunity to plead a case before the ECJ an honour or feel it is their professional duty to work a case to the fullest of their ability:

> "If you look at the hours and time, and the research as well, then it is totally disproportionate. I think I haven't even claimed expenses for that case. I just do not want to dig through that entire file and figure out all those hours, because you get so little compensation for it. If you consider the time and energy you put in such a case, then it's really absurd what you would get from the legal aid board. But you do it for the substantive legal side, and the honour of it."

Cases like these are, due to their legal complexity as well as the possibility of creating a precedent at the ECJ level, appealing to work on. The professional interest of lawyers plays a role. As one migration lawyer clarifies his own motivations:

> "This whole case, the appeal and the Court of Justice, is done with [subsidized legal aid]. And if you really look at the hours and time, and the studying as well, yes, that really far outweighs compensation. But when you see it legally is an interesting case. Really a matter of principle, with interesting jurisprudence, and you see the difficult financial situation of those people, you do not want to lose such a case. Then you won't say, I will not do it based on [subsidized legal aid], find another lawyer. No, you want to do it yourself."

Part of that motivation and interest is usually also of a more personal nature in it simply being a once in a lifetime opportunity to plead a case before the highest court in the EU. As explained by a lawyer working in the area of social security:

> "I have explicitly requested a hearing in Luxembourg. Because, as a lawyer, it is firstly important that you really grab every opportunity, and that you should never abandon a hearing beforehand. The moment you do that, you know that there is a judgment coming on which you have had no influence. So if you have the opportunity then at least keep your options open. At the last minute you can always say, look I've motivated enough and then you can say yes, I won't go. But I would never say that with the European Court because when you can make it, it is a fantastic experience."

Professional consideration and a personal interest in the 'Luxembourg experience' are not mutually exclusive. When it comes to representing the interests of one's client, even when neither the client nor subsidised legal aid covers the costs, professional ethics implore lawyers to at least try to make the most of what for some is a significant investment. However, not all lawyers are willing to do so. This becomes clear from cases that are joined (either by the referring court or by the ECJ) and where lawyers testify to the lack of involvement (either written or at the ECJ hearing, or both) from lawyers of one of the other parties. One of the lawyers comments on the other party's counsel's lack of involvement:

> "The third party did not submit anything. Look, regardless of whether you do this because you like it as a lawyer, and that's how it is for me. I found it exciting and also nice to have experienced this in my law career, you've been there and have done your thing, that's a lot of fun. But regardless of your own ambitions and whether you like it or not, and whether you feel like putting in the extra time. I do find it troubling when you as a lawyer assist someone, but not at that stage, that you then still proceed with representing your client. Like one of those other lawyers, no observations, did not do anything at all. Then I think you are lacking as a lawyer. I think that's bad, almost worthy of complaint."

This lack of involvement could be due to the fact that this lawyer was aware that a team of academics was assisting the lawyer quoted above, and thus chose to leave it to them. The same lawyer discusses the actions of the lawyer in the other of the two cases that were joined with his before reference to the ECJ:

> "One of the other lawyers did submit observations. Which was mainly bashing the Council of State, and further reference to my observations. And that was while my piece was not even ready yet [laughs]. I was in contact with them, and they knew in which direction my observations went."

As we have seen, however, in some cases, counsel refrain from filing any observations based on their general unfamiliarity (and possible misunderstanding) of the nature of these proceedings.

Lawyers can thus play a key role in the dynamics of these cases and in balancing collective and individual interests, taking on cases that in and of themselves, from a commercial point of view, are not viable. This especially applies to cases pertaining to migrants and asylum seekers. Asylum and migration law are areas of law where practitioners can be found to have a certain professional engagement specific to these types of legal action, which is directly related to the stakes in these cases. One lawyer describes his personal and professional motivations:

> "That's a big difference with, for example, the legal issues businesses have. I must say that it really motivates me as a lawyer to act for these people. Because it is not just a sum of 10,000 euro. It really is about people's lives. Like in criminal law, immigration law has a real impact on the course of people's lives. You really make a difference. And that's what matters, I think."

There is a general professional interest among the lawyers in the 'Luxembourg experience', which is seen as a once in a lifetime opportunity, even by those who do not consider the hearings of any practical use in their legal strategy. Lawyers are forced to make decisions on the amount of (over) time they are willing to spend on a case, which will thus effectively be truly *pro bono*. Moreover, since these lawyers have no certainty as to the chances of a case actually being referred to the ECJ – as we have seen in several cases it came as a complete surprise – they have no way of preparing for this additional expenditure and thus have to make *ad hoc* decisions on whether or not they are willing to spend additional time, and/or if the client can be asked to cover those costs.

6.7 Eurolaw Expertise

The 'Language' of EU law

Apart from structural obstacles, like time and financial considerations, there is also the added challenge of a general lack of expertise in working cases within the context of EU law, supranational jurisprudence and possible conflicts between EU and national law. EU law has its own structure and logic and ECJ jurisprudence its own language. Scholars and lawyers that deal with EU law regularly are very much familiar with its logic, and have been acculturated into this language. They share the *argot* of EU law and are familiar with the legal grammar of both EU principles as well as the reasoning style in ECJ jurisprudence.[15] Regular practitioners, who only occasionally deal with EU law, let alone have their case referred to the ECJ, do not share this trait. Once a case gets referred to the ECJ, both the venue and the context of the case change, which means lawyers have to adapt both their 'language' and strategy accordingly. Practitioners are thus confronted with a situation where they have to argue a

15 ECJ jurisprudence is particularly structured along very specific, almost syntax-like, lines due to the need for uniformity. As analyzed by Lasser, who states "ECJ decisions are rather short, terse, and magisterial decisions that offer condensed factual descriptions, impersonally clipped and collegial legal reasoning, and ritualized stylistic forms." Lasser 2004, 16.

matter within the framework of an unfamiliar legal sphere, in a different language so to speak, that of European law and ECJ jurisprudence.

Suggesting that their actual knowledge of EU law was not adequate for immigration and asylum lawyers to work with in any meaningful way in their daily practice, one asylum lawyer states:

> "I do think the majority [of lawyers] know what's in those directives. Most can recite what is in Article 33 or whatever. But I feel we really lack knowledge about how the principles of effectiveness, proportionality, defence, how you work with those kinds of principles."

Many lawyers are not in any way experts in the field of Euro-litigation, at least not beyond the point of bringing up possible infringements of EU law in national proceedings. Only six of the twenty-three lawyers interviewed in the case selection for this research claimed to have more than a basic knowledge of the jurisprudence of the ECJ relevant to their case. Moreover, the expertise lawyers did claim to have was usually *post hoc*, gained while working on 'that one particular case':

> "I have learned a lot from this one case, and really internalised it. What was really important in this one case was the 'effect utile'. That's what you learn when you start to think in a European way, you always have to say: if you do it like this, that will go against the effect utile."

Depending on the complexity of the questions referred to the court, references are something outside of the daily expertise of many lawyers. The following quote is an illustration of how many lawyers feel ill-equipped to work on the complexities in EU law, and also hints at a lack of knowledge of EU law among legal practitioners in general, including national judges:

> "That's when you realise that many of those fundamentals and how they are enshrined in European law, that those are really unknown with those who have to work with them. I did not know either. [...] I've uttered more than once that there should be a course on EU law principles for immigration lawyers, in which you think about how the principle of effectiveness in, let's say, the Definition Directive, how that principle works with that directive, or how you can work with it in your practice. I think everyone knows a bit about the effectiveness principle, but no one has really mastered it, to really work with it. That's basically what has to happen, because the judges do not understand either. [Laughs]"

This lack of knowledge and expertise in the field of EU law influences practitioners' capacity for effective advocacy at different stages in the preliminary reference proceedings, from the formulation of the questions that are referred to the ECJ, the writing of observations as well as participating effectively in the oral stage before the ECJ.

The Significance of the Hearing

The technical legal nature of procedures before the ECJ leads some lawyers to conclude that the oral proceedings do not matter a great deal to the outcome of a case. And even among insiders the idea is that the hearing is more a sign of goodwill from the judges, of which the practical importance for the conclusion of a case is seen as auxiliary to the written proceedings. The idea of its relatively diminished usefulness can play a role in practitioners' decision not to attend the hearing in Luxembourg. As one lawyer specialised in social security and labour law concludes:

> "The hearing, with all due respect to everyone who participates in it, is nothing more than a ritual, I think. All documents have been filed; the opinion of the Advocate General is already there.[16] You also only get twenty minutes. With a little goodwill can you double it to forty minutes. But it would be very bad, showing poor quality as a lawyer, if you in that brief plea bring things forward that were not put in the written observation. That would be bad. [Laughs]"

However, the oral stage of the proceedings provides parties with the only possibility to respond to observations filed by both the European Commission and intervening Member States. And there are a number of examples that show that these proceedings can and do matter, and that the parties involved have an interest in pleading their case both in the written and in the oral stage of the proceedings.

Firstly, the fact that Member States choose to intervene and provide their view on the matter at hand shows that they acknowledge the importance of pleading a case before the ECJ. Secondly, the Advocate General's opinion[17] is formulated after the written and (if applicable) oral proceedings, giving him or her the chance to ask questions that may help in formulating a stance. Thus, written and oral observations and the possibility of answering questions on the matter may influence the Advocate General's stance. And thirdly, an advocate has the opportunity at a hearing especially to provide and clarify 'pure facts or

16 This erroneous conclusion about the Advocate General's opinion, which in fact is completed after the hearing takes place, is indicative of some of the misunderstandings practitioners may have about the course of action before the ECJ.

17 The Court may choose to deal with cases without an opinion of the appointed Advocate General.

aspects of national law'.[18] Broberg and Fenger describe how "[o]ften the judges or the Advocate General will ask more argumentative questions in order to test the strength of a legal argument".[19] The questions asked by the Advocate General and the judges can play an important role in the framing of the issue before the ECJ and allow for elaboration on the way national policies work out in practice, details that may matter greatly for the conclusion of the case.

As Edward states: "The court relies heavily on the Commission, to fill in the factual and legal background".[20] Cases are examined by the Court on the basis of the observations by the parties, and being present gives an opportunity to fill in and clarify certain points, as well as respond to the representation of the facts by the other parties. Member States, where they have an interest in a certain outcome of a case, intervene in order to provide their viewpoint. The fact that the Court relies on these pleadings for its judgment, and thus the significance of providing one's viewpoint, is confirmed by lawyers who attended the hearing and claim this was crucial in their case:

> R: "Well, you don't have to go. But I really think we won our case there.
> I: What makes you think that?
> R: Well look, they have only limited insight in how Dutch law works out in practise within the national context. And in this case my colleague, who is very up to date on both social security and the association agreement [with Turkey]. And I am not specialised in immigration law so even when I read all the jurisprudence, that is probably the same when you read it, then you have a lack in your capability to convert that into arguments. You know what it says but you miss all the nuances. [...] And at one point you just felt the penny drop. And that had to do with the fact that [the representative for the Netherlands] said that these people were able to come back, that that was according to the law. But one of the oldest [ECJ] jurisprudence issues related to that was actually a case my colleague had done, which had a contrary conclusion. And that, no matter how good you are, I had not been able to make that connection right then and there."

We find another example in *Self-Employed Tax Deductions* where we see a significant moment in the hearing actually return in the opinion of the Advocate General. In his opinion, Advocate General Colomer considered that the matter addressed in the preliminary questions boiled down to whether the discrimination was justified on the grounds that the non-resident taxpayer could have opted voluntarily for the residents' tax regime. The Advocate General considered that this question was not just a matter of the 'legal fiction' of an option, but that it

18 Edward 1995, 545. See also Vaughan & Grey 2007.
19 Broberg & Fenger 2010, 382.
20 Edward 1995.

mattered whether or not this option posed a practical barrier, which could be taken as a difference in treatment, thus violating the freedom of establishment. Therefore the language in which one was able to file his or her tax return might create an obstacle. One of the lawyers in the case specifically remembered when this subject was brought up in the hearing and describes it as follows:

> "That's quite an unusual story. That hearing was fun. Because the point was, if you want to opt in as a resident taxpayer, that of course brings a lot of red tape with it. You must fill in a tax return in Dutch for example. So the Advocate General said: I have a question for the representative of the Dutch government. Okay, well if he files his taxes, can he call the tax authorities in German. So the Dutch agent responds: yes, yes, absolutely, simply in German, everyone speaks German. And he can also fill his declaration in German? Yes he can! [laughs] So, that is an example of, I think, well, that is borderline dishonest. And then he also said, I would also like to have the opinion of the party concerned. And my colleague answered: Well, I have been a tax advisor for more than fifteen years and that which is being stated here, I've never seen that. Then the Advocate General said: Yeah, thought so, I have no further questions. [laughs]"

In his opinion, the Advocate General came to the conclusion that this practical difference had as a result that a taxpayer who did not live in the Netherlands was not in the same situation as someone who paid taxes and resided in that state. In footnote 29 of his opinion Advocate General Colomer describes how he came to his conclusion on the matter:

> "On the subject of language, the agent of the Netherlands Government acknowledged at the hearing that the Dutch tax authority will accept documents and communications in 'commonly used languages' other than Dutch, albeit on an informal basis and without any legal guarantee. In that connection, the agent did not provide any details about the actual situation of someone who needs to deal with the Netherlands authorities in a language other than Dutch. However, [the lawyers] told the Court that, in the Netherlands, anyone who contacts the tax authorities must do so in the official language of the State, which, to my mind, is more plausible."

Choosing to plead one's case before the ECJ may thus prove to be worthwhile. The example provided above underscores how important such advocacy can be in providing the ECJ judges with the necessary facts and context to a case. The general lack of experience in this arena diminishes lawyers' effectiveness once their case is brought before the ECJ, where they find themselves up against (often several) representatives of Member States who litigate before the ECJ on a regular basis. Thus, the 'distance' to the Court and the rarity of having hands-on experience can significantly reduce this type of advantage in preliminary reference procedure cases. Especially when compared to the legal professionals that represent the genuine repeat players before the ECJ – i.e. the representatives of Member States and the European Commission, who work on ECJ cases on a daily basis and are able to build up significant familiarity with the Court's *modus operandi* and culture – this can be an important disadvantage.

The Language of the Court

Language and translation play an immense part in the day-to-day practice of the ECJ. Almost 1,000 posts and over 45% of the ECJ's staff consist of language and translation related services. These include over 600 lawyer linguists and over seventy interpreters that translate all the work done at the ECJ into the twenty-four official languages in 552 language combinations, and over one million pages are translated each year.[21] The multi-linguistic nature of the EU also plays an important role during the oral proceedings. While the written observations are meticulously translated, and often discussed in detail in the judgment itself, the oral observations are subject to simultaneous interpretation, with the consequent risk of communication problems, translation mistakes and failure of judges to understand immediately the points that a party is trying to get across. Lawyers are therefore implored to speak slowly and clearly, and where possible, provide their plea notes beforehand to the relevant interpreters.

When it comes to pleading one's case before the Court, language also matters in a different sense. Lawyers acting more often before the ECJ know how to address the Court. Repeat players, and this is certainly the case for the European Commission's representatives and the agents of the Member States, and also for specialised lawyers that are hired to appear before the ECJ, know its 'language' and style. Where most Member States have an experienced array of lawyers at their disposal who attend hearings and deal with cases before the ECJ on a regular basis, the average litigant does not have such representation at his or her disposal. This applies to his or her knowledge of EU law, and also to the knowledge of procedural requirements, accurate knowledge of the possibilities and importance of the written and oral stages in the proceedings as well as to the 'ways of the Court'. As a long-standing member of the ECJ bench has said, "[t]he basic rules of advocacy apply as much in pleading before the European Court of Justice as before any court or tribunal […]: know your court; know your procedure; and know what you are trying to achieve".[22] One of the interviewed lawyers, who appears before the Court on a regular basis, discussed how experience with the Court's ways may help one make his case, and possibly

21 The Court of Justice in figures: http://curia.europa.eu/jcms/jcms/P_80908/en/ [last accessed 2 November 2017].

22 Edward 1998, 28.

influence the Court's decision. To the question whether it was worth attending the hearing, he answers:

> "In my experience, I once had the feeling that it was decided in advance, so I could have said anything. But there are other occasions where you can make the difference. So you have to prepare. You should know your judge, Google him or her and try and go through the case law of that judge. It can help you to avoid major gaffes. Don't criticise case law written by a certain judge. So, you better know the case law. The hearing can make a huge difference. The solution of a case is not the difficult part, it's the reasoning, and the hearing can influence this a lot."

This respondent (who was not among the lawyers in the case selection for this research) belongs to a small group of lawyers that represent (corporate) clients with cases before the ECJ on a regular basis. The bulk of his work is concentrated in the areas of antitrust, cartels, merger control and state aid control, in which large economic interests are at stake. Such lawyers, together with the representatives of the Member States and the European Commission, make up the inner circle of the Court. Their amount of experience in litigating before the ECJ contrasts enormously with the one-shot lawyer who only occasionally, or most often just once, has a case referred. In this respect, lawyers of one-shotters are unable to counteract the differences in arms that exist between litigating parties before the courts, since in the case of a referral to the ECJ lawyers are themselves in many respects one-shotters.

The inexperience of these one-shot lawyers starts simply with the proceedings and a general unfamiliarity with the Court's ways. Like this lawyer who left the Grand Chamber of the Court quite disappointed with the amount of help he received once at the ECJ:

> "I was not happy with the guidance. No one could tell me where the lawyers' chambers were. And I still had to prepare. The best information I got from the interpreter, who came up to me to ask whether I had plead notes, so he could prepare in advance. But at the hearing there were, for instance, controls for translation, which were not explained to me. During the session I found out that if you pressed a button you could hear what was said in Dutch. Well, luckily the discussion was only in English and French, which I can understand. And where did you have to leave your coat? I just placed it against the wall."

Of course, such practicalities will not fundamentally make or break a case, but they serve as an illustration of the unfamiliarity of lawyers with a court, and proceedings they see for the first time. This extends to the question of how to argue their case before a Court with which they are unfamiliar, as a criminal law lawyer explains:

> R: "At some point they said, this case is going to Luxembourg. Then I thought, I really have no business there. I mean what the hell am I going to do there? But then the case was referred to the Grand Chamber, and then I thought, yeah, you know, I may have another sixty years as a lawyer, but the chances that I'm going to go before the Grand Chamber ever again are so negligible that I have to go.
> I: And you also pleaded?
> R: Yeah, of course. If you go, then you have to plead... Totally pointless! [Laughs].
> I: What was that like?
> R: Yeah, well, 'nice to be here, I want to say hello to my mother', something like that. [Laughing]"

Apart from preparing the way one will address the Court, it also proves useful to be aware of the way proceedings are conducted, as well as the preferences of the judges. Discussing the second round, in which one is permitted to speak and respond to arguments put forward by other parties, the experienced 'Euro-lawyer' explains how it helped to understand the judges' preferences:

> "What they call 'reply and rejoinder' is a bit false; it's more a conclusion. You have the time to respond to questions but you also have to come to a conclusion. Judges hate repetitions, and they will cut you off."

For the inexperienced lawyer such preferences and unwritten rules may result in a frustrating experience, especially in contrast to national proceedings where there is generally much more time for a back and forth between sides, and ample opportunity to make one's case:

> "In general, I have experienced that hearing as something very strange. You get fifteen minutes to hurry through your plea and then you have to respond to those Member States in the second term. And then you're insulted by the president with the comment that I should focus on the questions and come to conclusion. But yeah, that Member State said all kinds of nonsense; I simply want to straighten that out. I was really quite flabbergasted. So, you pick yourself up as best you can and respond a little, and then you sit down again. And if nobody wants to respond then, well, session closed, and then you walk out again. And I was like, huh? Was this it? Wait ... what!?"

Lawyers try to make the best of the opportunity but are generally not very optimistic about the room the hearing provides for making one's case and especially in responding to the observations by other parties, including the opposing party, the European Commission as well as other Member States:

> "Well, you try, but that is very difficult. You have fifteen minutes time for your position at the hearing, or what you think is necessary to touch upon. What took thirty pages to write. But you cannot respond to all of these seven countries, that in

> part say the same thing, but in nuances have very different positions. So you cannot respond well to that, in my opinion."

Lawyers who only occasionally appear before the Court will be in a sense addressing the Court in another language, in another *argot*. He or she may be very blunt in making certain points or simply speaking in the legal language of their national jurisdiction, possibly causing difficulty in communication. It is then for the Court to find out whether the one-shotter really has a good point, even though he or she is not as capable of making this point *à la communautaire*. At times however, this may require the Court to go beyond the arguments that are presented to it. It remains an open question to what extent the judges and Advocate General of the ECJ are willing to do so, and therefore how effective these lawyers can be.

6.8 Coping Strategies

The aforementioned lack of experience and expertise among lawyers confronted with a reference to the ECJ prompts many of them to seek outside assistance. Turning to experts, usually EU law scholars, helps them work their case at the ECJ level. On the question of whether one of the lawyers saw a lack of expertise as influencing the course and result of a case, he answers:

> "It all depends on how active you are. And if you seek help, which you should definitely do, because it is very theoretical and you're on new ground. You can try to think up everything yourself, but that is just unfeasible. You have to realize that you can just not do it alone."

For many lawyers, the first time they are called on to deal with matters beyond their daily practice is the moment a national judge decides to refer questions to the ECJ. The questions that the national judge will ask the ECJ are sometimes formulated in cooperation with the parties to the proceedings and usually provided to them for comments, revision or reformulation. Debating the formulation of questions with the aim of steering them in a desired direction again requires at least some expertise in the field of EU law. On this issue, one lawyer states the following:

> "Well look, at some point the cogs start turning, and then there are three parties who formulate those questions. The court just said, and now we will all think of questions together. Well, who am I? That's hilarious of course, because the matter is ridiculously complicated. And well, I have other things to do in my life, so I cannot spend an indefinite amount of time studying on this."

Since the opposing party called in the help of experts to make sure the questions were formulated to their satisfaction, like most lawyers, he too decided to seek the help of experts. The natural source of expertise came from local scholars commenting on the draft questions:

> "When the court suggested they were going to refer questions to the Court of Justice, I sat down with a professor of criminal law from the university here. [...] When I called him, and said, you know, they are saying all kinds of clever things, so I also need some smart feedback. [...] So I visited him a few times, simply to spar with him and exchange views. And he explained what direction it went in and what I should say. And that is all very enlightening and helpful."

The formulation of the questions that are referred to the ECJ can have an important bearing on not only the focus of what will be discussed before the Court but also on the scope of the eventual judgment. Where questions are formulated very narrowly and focused on very specific circumstances, the impact of the ECJ's answers will potentially be smaller than when the questions are formulated more broadly. The understanding of these nuances as well as signalling possible opportunities and suggesting other formulations to the national court also requires expertise.

After the questions are referred to the ECJ, the parties are requested to send in their observations and formulate their stance on how the questions are supposed to be answered. This is the next stage where lawyers may feel under-equipped to be effective. Over half of the lawyers interviewed decided to reach out to experts in academic circles for help, as this asylum lawyer did:

> "The questions were referred and I was like, oh god. It cannot be true that I am now going to discuss this difficult matter at the highest stage of Europe. I still find it really shocking. But it suddenly becomes very big and you have never done that before and you're really just not sure how to proceed, how it all works there. So I sent out emails to a whole host of people like, help me. Because, I do not know. And of the about twenty I had sent, ultimately a small group remained, a core of four, five people. My former colleague, who is now writing a dissertation, wrote a substantial part of the introduction. And she could just recite all the relevant jurisprudence, which was really fantastic. That's when you see the difference between scholars and practitioners like me. Because, as a practitioner you sort of know what the law is, but how it is worded exactly and where to find it you don't know. And that alone will take you three days just to work out."

His reaction to his own lack of expertise, and soliciting help from external experts, not only underscores a general lack of expertise among those 'confronted' with a reference, it also reveals where the expertise is to be found. Academia is the obvious choice for most lawyers when seeking help with working on the complexities of EU law questions. Experts with a good understanding of particular fields of EU law, with knowledge of the relevant ECJ jurisprudence are usually found among scholars. While their expertise helps lawyers formulate their arguments and include relevant case law, their knowledge of the practice of ECJ proceedings is usually also limited. Therefore the amount of help they can provide in this area is limited.

6.9 Macro Effects of the Allocation of Eurolaw Expertise

The previous paragraphs have laid out a general lack of experience and expertise among lawyers that are confronted with a reference to the ECJ. The unpredictability of preliminary references is an important aspect to these procedures and the related possibility for litigants to solicit expert services. In comparison, in direct actions before the ECJ the dispute clearly unfolds within the sphere of EU law since it is addressed at one of the EU institutions. In the preliminary reference procedure, however, a dispute may in the course of proceedings gradually turn into a matter of EU law, which makes it unlikely that litigants have EU law expertise at their disposal then and there. The unpredictability of a reference thus forms an inherent obstacle to the efficient advocacy of preliminary cases at the ECJ level.

Given the inherent obstacles to hiring expertise, when looking at the lawyers involved in these proceedings it is all the more striking to see some names occurring more than once. Considering that only a few dozen references are made each year, as well as the fact that the case selection in this study only spans a period of five years, being involved in more than one case suggests something more than coincidence. This could lead to the conclusion that these lawyers must have some form of expertise in EU law and are actively approached by parties (litigants or other interested actors involved in litigation) because of that. However, this could only be confirmed in four cases. Only in two cases however did the litigant or litigants themselves hire them before their case was referred to the ECJ. In the other cases, others were responsible for involving these lawyers in the proceedings. In two cases, lawyers were approached by colleagues to assist in a preliminary reference case based on their (albeit single) previous experience with the procedure. Another lawyer, who had no significant expertise in EU law, considered it a complete coincidence that he had participated in two preliminary reference cases, especially given the fact that the two cases he had were in two completely unrelated fields of law. These lawyers, although they have some repeated experiences with the ECJ cannot be considered true repeat players.

There are, however small in number, repeat players before the ECJ among lawyers in individuals' cases. Of all the legal counsel in the total of selected cases that could be identified a small minority was specialized in EU law specifically. Among them, professors of (European) fiscal law, lawyers with a specialisation in the Association Agreement between the EU and Turkey, and lawyers working in the area of labour law and social security specifically for cross-border workers. It can easily be reasoned that the individual one-shotter will not be among those able to solicit the services of these professionals with extensive Euro-litigation expertise. This is why in preliminary reference procedure cases, experienced Euro-lawyers show up mainly in support of larger (repeat) players, both private and (semi)public. His acting on behalf of individual claimants can be explained by the fact that these individuals had mobilised collectively. As described in depth in *Case Study B*, the group of pensioners was able to accrue enough funds from among their members. The total number of procedures, of which this particular case was only one, are said to have cost the Pensioners Association over half a million euro. Funded by the contributions, they were thus able to afford a specialist in order to increase their chances of success at the ECJ level.[23]

This is a striking example of what Galanter called the 'allocating effects' of lawyer expertise, meaning that some lawyers may specialize and build up experience with Euro-litigation, but that we can expect these lawyers to take up positions litigating on behalf of the more affluent parties, i.e. the larger companies, Member States and institutions, NGOs, interest groups, etc. As we have seen, this is also why these 'Euro-litigation one-shotters' – litigants as well as lawyers – often reach out to academics with expertise in the field of EU law, who subsequently act *pro bono* in support of these parties. For these one-shotters soliciting the expertise of scholars who are willing to lend their services free of charge may be the only option of getting help.

6.10 Conclusion

This chapter set out to give insight into the context in which legal practitioners have to work on preliminary reference cases, the kinds of issues that arise from peculiarities of the procedure, the options lawyers have for dealing with these matters and the considerations that play a role in this respect. I have identified several aspects of the preliminary procedure that significantly diminish the effectiveness of lawyers in working a case at the ECJ level.

23 Ultimately without success, see *Case Study B*.

Due to the highly infrequent nature of referrals, the more general build-up of expertise of lawyers in this area becomes less likely. For a practitioner, having a case referred to the ECJ is a very unlikely event and often a once in a lifetime experience. For most lawyers therefore the ECJ remains an improbable destination, both in result as well as in objectives. This makes it difficult to find and solicit lawyers specialized in Euro-litigation. For the bulk of the individual litigants in these cases, hiring specialized Eurolaw experts does not always prove to be an option, considering the fact that these lawyers will usually be more expensive as compared to any generalist practitioner. Therefore, cost considerations often fall on the lawyers themselves who have to decide how much unpaid extra work they are willing to put into a case. Furthermore, in the case of the ECJ and preliminary references, it is well-nigh impossible for a lawyer with a general practice to build up any significant amount of experience with Euro-litigation and thus with the European judiciary. Therefore the ability of lawyers to mitigate a disadvantaged position in Euro-litigation based on closeness to the judiciary is significantly limited, especially when compared to the legal services Member States' governments are able to solicit. On the macro level, this means that these references do not automatically fall into the hands of the lawyers best equipped to work such a case. Furthermore, the additional cost involved in hiring experts after referral makes it unlikely that the litigants will decide to switch lawyers or hire additional experts. This causes practitioners, who consider themselves unapt to effectively advocate a case at the ECJ level, to seek help among experts willing to assist free of charge. Usually these are sought and found among academics. Effective advocacy at the ECJ level then becomes dependent to a large degree on the willingness of lawyers to put in unpaid overtime, and on the availability of expert legal support that is willing to act *pro bono*.

Galanter saw lawyers as repeat players in themselves, able to offset some of the disadvantages of their one-shotter clients. In the case of Euro-litigation, however, the extent to which practitioners can perform this function decreases significantly. The insights presented in this chapter show how the preliminary reference procedure in itself undermines the capacity of lawyers to make up for the disadvantage of the one-shotters, and diminishes lawyers' effectiveness when it comes to advocacy at the ECJ level. This raises questions about the effectiveness of legal protection at the individual level and the effectiveness of the review function of the preliminary procedure at the macro level. Where a preliminary question fulfils the latter function, the differences in legal representation between different parties are striking and important. The sporadic activation of the procedure and its often unexpected character means that private parties and their counsel are generally at a disadvantage when it comes to the expertise that is brought before the ECJ, as compared to the better equipped Member State that is usually the opposition. A reference to the ECJ may thus not only provide an obstacle to inexperienced lawyers, but may also actually exacerbate the differences between individual litigants as one-shotters and Member States as repeat players at the supranational level.

Case Study C. Fees in Migration Law

C.1 Introduction: Championing the Rights of Migrants

Where some preliminary references may be the result of national judges seeking clarification on certain EU legislation without the explicit wish of the litigating parties, others may be part of strategic efforts by political actors seeking to utilise EU law in order to put pressure on national policy. As part of wider political action preliminary references may prove to be a useful tool in the hands of those that seek to effect political change. This case study illustrates how actors may mobilise EU law in order to contest national policy, and by extension contribute to the enforcement of EU law, with transnational consequences. In this case, the combination of allying with the Commission and concerted legal efforts by a small group of lawyers, academics and interest groups was successful in forcing compliance by the Dutch government. EU law offered the framework within which to question the legality of national increases in fees for residence permits at the European level. It became an obvious step after the fight was lost at the national level. This case provides a particularly effective example of a well-organised group of actors proactively employing EU law in order to change national policy. Analysing the actors and their litigation strategies, as well as the conditions for success in employing the channels offered by the EU legal system, shows the role of private actors in contesting national policy by employing EU law. This case study provides us with a number of important elements that help us to understand the dynamics behind such litigation efforts, and adds to an understanding of how local conflicts are channelled through the courts and how local private interests serve to enforce EU policy at the national level.

C.2 The Contested Policy

In 2002, by means of ministerial decree, the administrative fees for the application for or the renewal of residence permits were increased. As of 1965 and up until 1994, there had been no additional fees payable on an application for the grant or renewal of a residence permit. An earlier attempt by the Dutch government to increase these fees in 1994 had resulted in significant, and successful, opposition. An amendment to the Aliens Act of 1993 applied an additional fee for the application for a residence permit. For example 1,000 guilders for the application for a residence permit for migrant workers (employed and self-employed), compared to Dutch passport costs of 35 guilders. This change in policy was met with swift opposition by large companies. Representing the interests of their workers, these companies challenged the additional fees because in many cases it was the employers who paid these costs. This opposition resulted in a retroactive withdrawal within months and refunds of the fees charged in excess.[1] As of 2002 and again in 2003 similar amendments were made, with fee increases ranging from 290% to 1150% in some cases.

Figure IV: Changes in fees before and after 2003 (in euros)

	Before	1/5/02	1/1/03	Increase
Application and/or change temporary residence permit	56.72	258	430	**660%**
Application and/or change temporary residence permit (12 years and younger)	22.69	169	285	**1150%**
Permanent residence permit	226,89	539	890	**290%**
Extension temporary residence permit	0	169	285	-

The numbers in Figure IV show the dramatic increase in costs for a request or renewal of a residence permit. A calculation example (Figure V) sets out the costs for a family with three children when applying for residence permits over the course of five years. Moreover, an amendment to the ministerial decree stated that non-payment of these additional fees would mean that the application would not be processed.[2] Given that a substantial number of migrant families belonged to the lower classes of society, and had a net minimum annual income of 12,324 euro at the time, these fees had significant financial impact on migrant families and the threat of non-consideration, and thus the risk of losing one's residence permit, left migrants little choice but to pay.

1 Groenendijk & Kortmann 2003.
2 Article 24(2) Vw 2000.

Figure V: Calculation example residence permits of a family with three children (in euros)[3]

	Application temporary residence permit	2nd year Extension	3rd year Extension	4th year Extension	Application regular residence permit	Total
Father	430	285	285	285	890	2,175
Mother	430	285	285	285	890	2,175
Child 10 yr.	285	285	285	285	890	2,030
Child 12 yr.	430	285	285	285	890	2,175
Child 14 yr.	430	285	285	285	890	2,175
						10,730

Although the officially stated reason for these increases was to make the processing of residence applications cost-effective, these measures arguably had another dual purpose: Firstly, it raised the budget of the Ministry of Justice[4] (by an approximate amount of twenty million euro annually).[5] The increases were justified with reference to an increased financial target, which had been imposed on the Immigration and Naturalisation Service (IND), the Dutch government agency responsible for handling the applications, by the ministry.[6] Secondly, the strong suspicion arose that the Dutch government was using the fees as an intended brake on the influx of immigrants.[7] Although it was never officially confirmed, one remark by then Minister Nawijn seemed to confirm these suspicions. Questioned on the financial impact of these increases on migrant families he answered: "If we want to allow foreigners in more restrictively, we should have stricter entry requirements. This is one of the groups that we can allow less, simply because there are loads coming in".[8] However, this statement was never

3 Inspraak Orgaan Turken in Nederland, *Jaarverslag 2007*, 2007, 7. Retrieved from: http:// www.iot.nl/?page=sayfa&sayfa_id=43 [last accessed 2 November 2017]. Further costs: Legalization and verification of documents (€ 136.13 per document), DNA test (€ 199.66), Provisional residence permit (€ 50 p/p), Integration courses (€ 6.000 p/p) and examination (€ 350). The first years after immigration are very costly.

4 Additionally, the Immigration and Naturalisation Service (IND) grew more and more dependent upon the revenues of these fees; from 2.4% in 2001, and 15.4% in 2005 to 20.4% of its total budget in 2010. These budgetary shifts seem to explain at least in part the reluctant attitude of the ministers in their willingness to give in to social, political and legal opposition.

5 *Kamerstukken II* 2002-2003, 28 600 VI, nr. 2, p. 39.

6 See Groenendijk & Kortmann 2003.

7 These suspicions were voiced by several political parties in deliberations on the budget statement of the Ministry of Justice in 2004. See *Verslag schriftelijk overleg vaste commissie voor Justitie* 13 december 2004 (29 800 VI).

8 *Kamerstukken II* 2002-2003, 28 600 VI, nr. 18, p. 39.

seized upon by other MPs and it remained unclear whether this was a slip of the tongue, or whether the Minister spoke in a personal capacity. Yet, this policy was one among more changes in Dutch politics in a trend towards more restrictive migration politics since the turn of the century.[9]

As before in 1994, these policy changes in 2003 met opposition, this time in the form of (among other organized actions) legal proceedings, several of which reached the ECJ.[10] The next section will cover how these legal proceedings emerged and the ways in which opposition was organized.

C.3 Organizing Opposition: Introducing the IOT

The central actor that mobilised opposition to this policy was the Consultative Council of Turkish Migrants in the Netherlands (*Stichting Inspraak Orgaan Turken in Nederland*, from here on: IOT).[11] The IOT was founded in 1985 by four existing Turkish organizations. Its aim is to represent the interests of the Turkish community in the Netherlands and is committed to improving its position in society. Its operations have long been part of the National Advisory and Consultative Structure for Minorities (*Landelijk Advies en Overlegstructuur voor Minderheden*, LAO), which was established in 1984. As part of this structure the IOT, as well as seven other consultative bodies, was funded by a grant from the Ministry of Internal Affairs. In 1997, this structure was reinforced by the adaptation of the Minority Policy Consultation Act (*Wet Overleg Minderheden*, WOM[12]) which stipulated that these bodies had consultations with Ministers or Secretaries at least three times a year to discuss policy regarding the integration of minorities and developments of interest to minorities within the context of integration. As an organization the IOT has a small office – consisting only of a director, a policy officer, secretarial support and one or more trainees – but a large and active body of supporters, the Turkish migrants. Its monthly newsletter *Sözhakki* is sent out on paper to 3,000, digitally to 4,000 addresses and its website was visited more than a million times in 2012. At the time of writing, nearly 300 local organizations operate under its aegis.[13]

9 Bonjour 2011, 100.

10 Total number of cases concerning administrative fees in the Dutch legal system. From 1990-1999: 1, after 2002: 450+ national judgments on fees. As found through a search in the Dutch online judgment database *rechtspraak.nl*, search term: *leges*.

11 Dutch universities also contested the policy, with some success. The increase in fees for students was postponed for a year.

12 On June 18th 2013 this law was repealed; consequently as of 1st January 2015 all funding for these organizations has stopped.

13 www.iot.nl.

C.4 Extra-Legal Opposition to the Policy

For a long time, legal actions were not a specific part of the IOT's strategy.[14] Before the decision was made to employ legal proceedings in the matter, the IOT had already employed all kinds of lobbying activities and deliberations with other actors and organizations. Before initiating a civil suit and other legal proceedings, the IOT tried to raise the matters, on which these later proceedings were conducted, in the political arena by attempting to mobilise politicians,[15] and other societal actors.[16] They organized consultations with political bodies, deliberations with other interest groups and they obtained expert advice from outsiders.

Prior to the implementation of the contested policy, the IOT repeatedly but unsuccessfully tried to negotiate with the responsible Minister. Various organizations protested the announcement of the policy to parliament and after the implementation successively to Minister Nawijn (LPF: Fortuynist/populist party) and his successor Verdonk (VVD: Conservative liberals). Also, several complaints had been brought to the attention of members of parliament who put the matter on the agenda for parliamentary debate.[17] With its large backing, the IOT was able to mobilise its supporters for demonstrations and other actions. Among others, the IOT mobilised its supporters to sign a petition against the fee increase that was launched after its implementation in 2003, resulting in over 30,000 signatures that were presented to members of the Standing Committee for Security and Justice (*Vaste Kamercommissie voor Veiligheid en Justitie*) of the House of Representatives.

Despite all these efforts they had no success in the political arena. The repeated protests revealed that this issue yielded hardly any parliamentary attention or mobilisation. The lack of political response against the high fees finally stimulated the IOT to set up ongoing consultations of IOT insiders and outsiders in a working group, specifically dedicated to attacking this policy in early 2003 – the Working Group Against the Increases of the Fees for Residence Permits

14 For a good overview of the evolution of the IOT's political and legal strategies see Groenendijk, Rondhuis & Strik 2015.

15 Some of which in periodic consultations that the IOT held with Ministers lawfully prescribed under the aforementioned WOM.

16 Among other things, deliberations with the VSNU (Association of Universities in the Netherlands), since international students are also among those impacted by the policy.

17 Before the policy was implemented a letter was sent [5 November 2002] to members of the Permanent Parliamentary Committee on Justice urging them 'to do everything in your power to stop this disastrous increase'. After its implementation a letter [2 February 2003] was sent to Minister Nawijn in which multiple organizations, based on the arguments from the article by Groenendijk and Kortmann (2003, footnote 17), opposed the increases of January 1st 2003.

(*Werkgroep tegen de legesverhoging,* from here on: Working Group).[18] The core of the Working Group included lawyers, representatives of various social organizations and academics.[19] This course of action was a tried method for the IOT that had encountered a similar situation a few years earlier when protesting the reduction in the export of supplementary disability benefits, which impacted Turkish beneficiaries who had moved back to Turkey.[20] The previous Working Group Social Security – consisting of IOT staffers, the labour union, social workers, lawyers and academics – had been established to take (legal) action against the policy.[21] Several members of this Working Group also featured in the Working Group against the fees policy, most notably one lawyer (from here on: the leading lawyer) who would become responsible for most of the legal work in multiple court proceedings.

During the legal proceedings that followed, the Working Group remained active in the political realm. The interim court rulings in the various procedures, and the complaints and negotiations with the European Commission were structurally linked back to the Minister, by means of the mobilisation of MPs, in order to keep up the pressure. On several occasions, MPs were implored to raise these matters during deliberations in parliament. During their first meeting in early 2003, the Working Group also discussed a media strategy, planning the peak of their publicity around the announcement of their legal action. Members of the European Parliament were mobilised; two Dutch Members of the European Parliament submitted written questions to then Commissioner Vitorino to question whether the legal fees for residence permits constituted a new restriction within the meaning of the Association Agreement between the EEC and Turkey.[22] This question on the possible violation of the so-called 'standstill clause'[23] in the Association Agreement, would become a central legal question.

18 The declared aim of the *Werkgroep tegen de Legesverhogingen* was 'to achieve by political and/or legal means that the government reduces the excessive fees for applying for residence permits to a reasonable amount'.
From http://www.inlia.nl/werkgroepleges.html. [last accessed 8 November 2017].

19 Including, but not limited to, representatives of the Dutch Council for Refugees (*Vereniging Vluchtelingenwerk Nederland*) and the Association of Moroccan-Dutch in the Netherlands (*Samenwerkingsverband van Marokkanen in Nederland: SMN*).

20 The Export Restrictions on Benefits Act (*Wet Beperking Export Uitkeringen*).

21 The Working Group featured different lawyers and other external experts at different times during the course of its activity, all of whom acted *pro bono public*, save for its chairman and central lawyer.

22 Written question E-2752/03, PB C 65 E of 13/03/2004, 207-8.

23 As part of the Association Agreement between the EU and Turkey Decision No 1/80 EEC-Turkey Association Council stipulates the measures 'for the revitalization and development of the Association between the Community and Turkey'. The standstill clauses in Association law between the EU and Turkey intend to freeze in time existing restrictions (if any) and ban the introduction of new restrictions that hamper the economic →

C.5 The Decision to Take Legal Action

In 2003, after the policy had come into effect, the Working Group decided – after repeated, unsuccessful attempts to mobilise the responsible Minister, and because of a lack of meaningful alternatives – to attack the policy by legal means. Choosing this legal path was motivated in large part by an article in a leading law journal by Groenendijk and Kortman[24] (two law professors specialized in (European) migration law and constitutional law respectively) on the unlawfulness of the fee increases, of which the former had been involved in the Working Group Social Security and would become an important consultant for this Working Group during the subsequent legal actions. In letters addressing possible co-claimants and financial supporters the Working Group cited a list of further reasons for legal action:

- By litigating with a large number of organizations counter pressure could be mobilised;
- It was made clear that organizations of ethnic minorities did not simply accept anything;
- Further increases, which were planned by the Ministry of Justice, would be counteracted;
- It was not fair to ask an individual migrant to act in person, because he or she would be deported;
- Based on the article by Groenendijk and Kortmann the chances of success seemed reasonably high.

Additionally, an evaluation of the parliament's attitude, and explanation for its inactivity was given:

> "Members of Parliament realize perfectly well that these increases are objectionable, but the House of Parliament so far yields to the argument that the Ministry of Justice needs the money to pay for the IND's budget. The House will probably use the result of the [legal] procedure [of the Working Group] to move Verdonk [the responsible Minister at the time] towards more reasonable rates."

---

activities of EU- and Turkish nationals. The Association contains two such clauses: one for Turkish nationals who want to take up self-employment (Article 41(1) of the Additional Protocol) and one for Turkish workers (Article 13 of Decision 1/80 of the EU-Turkey Association Council). They entered into force in 1973, respectively 1980, for the nine oldest Member States and for the other EU Member States upon the date of their accession to the EU. In addition, the Working Group focused on diplomatic representation and appeal to other countries by, for example, mobilising contacts within the Turkish embassy, in order to apply pressure from multiple angles.

24 Groenendijk & Kortmann 2003.

Due to the restrictive political climate towards migration at the time, further political mobilisation was not expected, therefore at this point legal action was deemed the only viable way forward. The Working Group chose to employ several legal strategies simultaneously. Firstly, a civil suit was initiated on behalf of twenty-five different migrant organizations. Secondly, the administrative law route was employed to contest the policy on an individual case basis. And thirdly, the European Commission was mobilised through complaints addressing the Netherlands' failure to comply with EU law. In the next section these cases will be discussed successively and in more detail.

C.6 Legal Contestations

The Civil Lawsuit

In 2003, a civil suit was initiated on behalf of twenty-five different migrant organizations.[25] This group included a diverse range of organizations that championed the interests of certain societal (migrant) groups, including Turks, Moroccans, Tunisians and southern Europeans, and also organizations that supported more general migration-related causes like the legal aid foundations for asylum seekers, the Dutch Council for Refugees (*Vereniging Vluchtelingenwerk Nederland*) and supporting associations for foreigners in general.[26] The inclusion of multiple parties in the case served to make the endeavour financially feasible by spreading the cost over a significant number of collaborators as well as spreading the bets with regard to the standing of the different organizations in court. Additionally, it helped to increase the societal impact and raise awareness of the matter. The civil proceedings started in 2003 with the aim of getting the ministerial regulation declared non-binding because it was inconsistent with Dutch (constitutional) laws and several international Treaties.[27]

25 Rechtbank 's-Gravenhage 16 February 2005, ECLI:NL:RBSGR:2005:AS7584.

26 Several more organizations, which were not a party to the proceedings, did provide financial or other more general support. For example the group got endorsements from the Netherlands America Commission for Educational Exchange (NACEE, as of 2004 the Fulbright Center) serving the interests of students from the USA. and also more general human rights NGOs like the Netherlands Helsinki Committee (NHC).

27 The EU law argument on which the matter would ultimately be decided by the ECJ – the violation of the standstill clause of the Association Agreement – was only one of the arguments put forward. Following in large part the article by Groenendijk & Kortmann, the policy was also argued to be in violation of Art. 104 the Dutch Constitution, Art. 8 and Art. 14 of the European Convention on Human Rights, Art. 26 of the International Covenant on Civil and Political Rights, the European Social Charter and the European Convention on Establishment. At a later stage, in second instance, the Family Reunification →

The legal strategy included bringing forward multiple legal challenges to the policy based on different national and international laws. As the lawyer in the case confirmed, this was firstly a matter of spreading your bets and "trying to collect as many arguments as possible", however this strategy also made sure that the interests of different societal groups were covered, in order to tie the different migrant organizations to the cause. For instance, the argument of a conflict with the provisions in the Association Agreement applied only to Turks, for other groups other arguments were needed. For Moroccans for instance: Constitution and Article 26 ICCPR (anti-discrimination), and for refugees: Article 8 ECHR (right to family life). The argument thus had to be built differently for the different groups represented in the civil proceedings.

One of the two main problems that had to be overcome was the standing of the plaintiffs, who had to have a demonstrable interest in the disputed legislation. The second issue was the question of whether or not the civil suit would be deemed justified by the judges, based on the prerequisite of having no remedy under administrative law.[28] In the first two instances, most of the migrant organizations were ruled to be inadmissible based on the aforementioned requirement of demonstrable interest, and all legal arguments were rejected except for the arguments based on the Association Agreement and a possible infringement of Article 8 ECHR.[29] Both the plaintiffs and the state appealed the decision in second instance and finally the case was brought before the Supreme Court of the Netherlands (*Hoge Raad*, the highest Dutch court in civil, criminal and tax law). As a result, the Working Group had to increase their already significant fundraising efforts, because this procedure meant that they had to hire a qualified cassation attorney. Despite the fact that this lawyer submitted a pleading of 118 points spread over forty pages, which was incidentally also reviewed by the academic involved, the case was dismissed in its entirety. All the plaintiffs were

Directive 2003/86, which had entered into force in 2005, was also included by the Working Group.

28 Under Dutch established case law one requirement for civil redress against a public body is that no remedy exists under administrative law.

29 During the legal proceedings contact was also made with members or committees of the parliament. The Parliamentary Committee on Justice was moved to ask parliamentary questions, especially in order to get a response to the court ruling, with some success: As a result of the first judgment in the civil proceedings and the resulting debate in the House, Art. 3.34f *Voorschrift Vreemdelingen 2000* was introduced into Dutch law, which grants exemption from charges if "the foreigner makes justified use of Article 8 ECHR and proves not to have the means to meet the obligatory fees." At least in one case, of a Moroccan father who could not pay the total fee of EUR 2,290 for his four children, this claim was brought to court. On which the professor states critically: "The fact that the Dutch government left it to the courts to decide the matter, is illustrative for the adamant stance of the current Minister and the IND. Respect for human rights has to be enforced through the courts."

deemed inadmissible because of their lack of demonstrable personal interest. Moreover, as was initially feared, and following the position of the Dutch government in the case, the Supreme Court ruled the claim to be a matter that could be appealed before the administrative courts and therefore inadmissible in the civil courts.[30] The court upheld the argument of the Dutch State that the administrative courts provided sufficient safeguards for individual residence permit applicants. Thus, after seven years and three instances the case was dismissed and left the Working Group empty-handed, save for a total bill of over 57,000 euro. Moreover, they were ordered to bear the additional costs of around 10,000 euro incurred by the state. The resulting expenses thus amounted to approximately 70,000 euro.

Administrative Law

As a second strategy, simultaneously with the civil suit, cases were being sought among possible individual claimants whose situation would lend itself to being litigated upon in order to attack the policy through administrative law. The argument for employing this strategy was put forward in one of the earlier meetings of the Working Group by the lawyer in the case (and coincidentally the lawyer in the civil suit as well) that civil judges might argue that the administrative remedy had not been pursued – an assessment that, as we have seen, would later prove to be correct. He initially advocated starting administrative procedures by letting people file for refunds of the excessive fees. In order to do this, a sample request was drawn up and used by the IOT and associated lawyers to provide to members and lawyers' clients. Several cases were brought to the courts this way by the IOT for some of their Turkish followers, and also by affiliated lawyers on behalf of other groups such as Polish and Romanian clients. However, the case that would later end up at the ECJ, landed on the lawyer's desk fortuitously through his general practice.

The client, a Turkish national who had obtained a residence permit in the Netherlands to live with his Dutch wife, applied for an extension of his permit. Due to the fact that he was too late paying the administrative fee for this application (which amounted to 169 euro) his application was not considered, and the client received notification ordering him to leave the country. In 2003, the lawyer filed a complaint on his behalf against the refusal and the case was eventually brought before the court in Rotterdam in 2004. As it turned out, this case lent itself perfectly to the Working Group's intended goal. The lawyer, who was the leading lawyer in the Working Group, explains that he largely used the same

30 Rechtbank 's-Gravenhage 16 February 2005, ECLI:NL:RBSGR:2005:AS7584.

arguments in the administrative law case as were formulated for the purpose of the civil suit.

> "We were looking for individual cases to fight the battle on two fronts. They came to me mainly because their request for a permit was denied. However, the case of my client allowed us to address the issue by means of administrative law as well."

In May 2005, the court in Rotterdam, like the courts in the first two instances of the civil suit, judged in favour of his client and confirmed that the standstill clause in the Association Agreement prohibited the introduction of new restrictions on the conditions of access for Turkish nationals.[31] The introduced increase in fees was indeed considered a 'new restriction' as prohibited by the provision and thus in breach of the standstill clause. The state appealed this decision before the Council of State, which in May 2006, referred several questions to the Court of Justice regarding the legality of the Dutch policy in light of the Association Agreement.

After over three years, in September 2009, the ECJ confirmed the implications of the standstill clause in Article 13 of Decision No 1/80, pointing out that this Article had direct effect. The Article thus prohibited Member States from introducing new restrictions on the conditions of access to employment applicable to Turkish workers and members of their families who had fulfilled the legal requirements. The Court held that Member States could introduce new restrictions on Turkish citizens where these same restrictions also applied to Community nationals; however, Member States could not subject Turkish nationals to new obligations which were disproportionate compared with those established for Community nationals. It was thus considered to be disproportionate to charge Turkish nationals administrative expenses amounting to 169 euro on submission of their application for a residence permit (or extension thereof), when this charge was only thirty euro for Community nationals.[32] Six months later, in March 2010, the Council of State followed the ECJ's judgment and declared the increase in administrative fees to be in violation of the standstill clause, and so the appeal was upheld. It was an individual victory for the client who was granted his application, yet only a partial victory from the perspective of the Working Group, whose aim was to challenge the legality of the

31 The court referred to the earlier judgment by the District Court of The Hague, which had decided on the matter in the civil suit, and adopted its reasoning.

32 Who also receive residence permits with a longer period of validity, so that they do not have to apply for the renewal of residence permits as often. In this respect raising the fees for all applicants, including Community nationals, would have made the increase legally sound. However, the political backlash from such a decision could have been much greater.

fees policy in its entirety, irrespective of the origin of the applicant, and not only for Turkish nationals.

Complaints to the European Commission

A third strategy employed by the Working Group entailed complaining to the European Commission. One of the lawyers involved in the Working Group pleaded for such a strategy in order to provoke infringement proceedings against the Netherlands for not complying with EU law. This lawyer, himself specialized in the Association Agreement, filed the complaint on behalf of his Turkish partner, who was personally confronted with the increased administrative fees while filing for a renewal of her permit. The IOT had previous experience with complaints to the Commission. The earlier 'Working Group Social Security' had also applied this strategy. In that instance, however, the Commission did not start proceedings against the Netherlands, and urged the IOT to try and elicit preliminary questions in a court case.[33] In the case of the administrative fees, the Commission turned out to be more willing and started the informal phase of the infringement procedure in early 2005, informing the Netherlands that it considered the administrative fees system to be in violation of the standstill clause in the Association Agreement. In 2007, after an unsuccessful informal phase, (and significantly after the preliminary reference by the Dutch Council of State) the Commission started infringement proceedings against the Netherlands.[34] The ECJ stayed these proceedings in expectation of its own judgment in the preliminary reference case that had been on the docket since 2006. In its final judgment, in April 2010, the Court confirmed its conclusions in that case, stating that the Netherlands had indeed failed to fulfil its obligations based on Article 9 of the Association Agreement, Article 41 of the Additional Protocol and Articles 10(1) and 13 of Decision No 1/80.

C.7 Effects of the Various Cases for Dutch Policy

Taken together, these proceedings show that the Working Group was quite successful in mobilising strong opposition and putting pressure on the Dutch government from multiple angles to get it to change its policy. As a direct result of the ECJ judgment, fees for the applications (extension or permanent) by Turks were reduced to the fees paid by EU citizens – from 200 euro or 400 euro re-

33 Groenendijk, Rondhuis & Strik 2015.
34 C-92/07 *European Commission v Kingdom of the Netherlands.*

spectively to forty euro.[35] Similarly, as a result of the infringement proceedings, fees for the applications by Turkish nationals for residence with their (working) partner were lowered to sixty euro.[36] The combination of these two ECJ judgments thus resulted in helping to bring down the fees for Turkish applicants to the level of the fees for EU citizens.

However, the impact of these judgments was not limited to these consequences but had significant follow-up effects. The wording of the two judgments was later also codified in a new EU Directive on the permits of migrant workers, stating that the fee for the permit must be proportionate.[37] Furthermore, the judgment in the infringement proceedings played an important role in subsequent proceedings on the legality of the integration requirement for Turkish citizens.[38] Additionally, these judgments also sparked discussion about the legality of the high fees for residence permits that were granted under the Family Reunification Directive 2003/86/EC and Directive 2003/109/EC on the status of third-country nationals who are long-term residents. At the beginning of the legal action, negotiations on these two relevant new Directives had just been completed. It was clear that about two years later (when they came into force) the rules in the Directives could also be used as arguments. The duration of the cases in the Netherlands meant that the substantive law changed along with the relevant actors. Where opportunities at supranational level were at first limited to the Association Agreement, these Directives provided more opportunities and other actors became involved, including the European Commission, the European Parliament and eventually the ECJ. These arguments were brought forward in second instance in the civil suit as well as in the administrative law case. However, since that preliminary reference was decided with regard to Turkish nationals only and the arguments in the civil suit were thrown out altogether, a complaint to the Commission was chosen as an alternative, again resulting in infringement proceedings in 2010.[39]

The judgment in the infringement case initially led to a reduction in the fees for the residence permit for long-term resident third country nationals from 400 euro to 130 euro. The latter amount was increased shortly afterwards to 152 euro, but since then also applies to long-term resident third country nationals

35 Estimated cost Dutch treasury: € 250,000 for the purpose of restitution, four million loss on an annual basis. *Kamerstukken II* 20092010, 30 573, nr. 48.

36 Estimated cost Dutch treasury: € 140,000 for the purpose of restitution, two million loss on an annual basis. *Kamerstukken II* 2009-2010, 30 573, nr. 56.

37 Council Directive 2011/98/EU, Article 10.

38 The EC declared, in a reaction arising from subsequent complaints about the integration policy, that they saw the judgments on the fees as a support for critical monitoring of the Dutch policy on other issues. Groenendijk, Rondhuis & Strik 2015.

39 C-508/10, *European Commission v Kingdom of the Netherlands*.

from another Member State (as a student, as family and as a working or economically inactive person) in the Netherlands.[40] A few months later, the Dutch Council of State declared that the ECJ's judgment also applied to the fees for family reunification. These fees were subsequently reduced from 1,250 euro plus 250 euro per accompanying family member to 225 euro per family member. Furthermore, the Council of State decided in mid-2014, again citing the judgment of the ECJ that the amount for large families could lead to an obstruction to integration. The fees for minors were therefore reduced to fifty-two euro per child. After the judgment of the Council of State on the analogous application of that judgment to family reunification, the Department of Justice also halved the fees for students and researchers from 600 euro to 300 euro.[41]

We can conclude that the effects of the Working Group's efforts via the courts, including the ECJ judgments, were significant. The reduction in fees increasingly applied not only to Turkish citizens but also to all third country nationals, regardless of nationality. They were thus quite successful in contesting Dutch policy by invoking EU law and soliciting ECJ judgments. Moreover, the outcome of these cases also had beneficial effects for Turkish citizens and third country nationals living in other countries.[42] Following the judgments of the Court of Justice in both infringement proceedings on the fees, new EU Directives for all other groups of third country nationals (including workers and students) included the rule that the fees could not be 'disproportionate or excessive'.[43] These judgments by the Court on this point, therefore, were also meaningful for large groups of immigrants from countries outside the EU in all Member States.[44] The judgments of the Court of Justice about the fees were also a major incentive for lawyers to litigate against other measures in migration law, because they were a strong argument that new restrictive policies were probably also at odds with the standstill clause. Furthermore, the European Commission considered the rulings on the fees a support in its debate with the Dutch gov-

40 These people had to pay between € 430 and € 830 before the judgment.

41 At the time of writing the high fees for labour migrants are still under litigation.

42 Shortly after Bart De Wever of the New Flemish Alliance (N-VA) was elected in 2013 as mayor of Antwerp, the City Council decided to charge a fee of € 250 for the registration of any "new residents of foreign origin". That decision was overruled by the Governor of the Province of Antwerp with reference to the decisions of the ECJ. The German Federal Administrative Court also stated that the fees for residence permits of Turkish citizens and long-term residents, considering all three judgments of the ECJ on the Dutch fees, should be the same as for EU citizens. Schaap 2014, 432.

43 The Single Permit Directive 2011/98 Article 10, the Seasonal Workers Directive 2014/36 Article 19, the Intra-Corporate Transferees Directive 2014/66 Article 16 and the proposed formulation of Article 31 of the revision of the Visa Directive 2004/114.

44 With the exception of the UK, Ireland and Denmark, who had opted out of Directives 2003/86 and 2003/109.

ernment on other immigration measures. The judgments thus had, as a side effect, the mobilisation of other actors: Turks complaining to the IOT about rejected refunds (which eventually resulted through the mobilisation of the IOT in new lawsuits and a follow-up complaint to the EC), lawyers who brought cases based on the judgments, as well as the European Commission which felt supported by the ECJ in its debate with the Dutch government on other immigration measures.

C.8 Deductions From a Long Contest: Credentials of the Working Group

The Working Group consisted of an informal collaboration of people who already knew each other from previous endeavours. Of course it was not a random group of individuals. The collective expertise was significant and in addition a number of those involved had previous experience with legal mobilisation strategies. It was a small club with sufficient relevant expertise in many different areas, including EU law, procedural and national rules, a network of strategic partners and the activation of the grassroots of the IOT. The group, that was on occasion accompanied by other lawyers and representatives from other interest groups, in all those years, came together approximately only ten times as most contact was via email. Outside this limited organization, this also emphasised that long-term commitment to the group was needed. As the IOT coordinator stressed: “What you mainly need is perseverance and a lot of patience”.

The trajectory of the IOT cases did not come about coincidentally but was the result of a thoroughly planned strategy (albeit of course with significant uncertainties and contingencies) by some key expert players. The support (financial or otherwise) of certain experts was an important element in the decision to litigate as well as the potential success of legal action. Apart from the fact that the initial legal strategy was in large part inspired by the article on the unlawfulness of the fee increases,[45] the expertise of one of the authors, a European migration law professor was also of great value during the proceedings. His role, not only in close cooperation with the leading IOT lawyer (commenting on all draft documents) but also in activating his own network by passing on information strategically to other possible key players, had been significant. For example, the documentation shows the professor sending information to a befriended official in the European Commission and to the Advisory Committee on Migration Affairs (ACVZ).[46] Additionally, the Working Group chairman (along with the

45 Groenendijk & Kortmann 2003.

46 The ACVZ was at that time working on a report on the fees for the Ministry, which was later used in court cases as supporting evidence.

professor) was a member of the Standing Committee of Experts on International Immigration, Refugee and Criminal Law (*Commissie Meijers*), a group of professors, judges, attorneys and academics in Europe who "systematically assess European legislative proposals in the areas of criminal law, migration law, privacy, and discrimination on their conformity with the requirements of a democratic constitutional state" and with close connection to the (inter)national political arena "informing both houses of the Netherlands parliament about significant developments in negotiations between the Member States on directives and regulations".[47] The Working Group of the IOT thus featured some heavyweights in the field of EU law as well as European civil society, joining forces with several other lawyers with their own relevant specialization who all (except for the leading lawyer) acted *pro bono*. Incidentally, this also points to the vulnerability of such organized advocacy; being very much dependent upon the expertise and willingness of a small group of people. A significant Achilles' heel when compared to the ability to employ specialists, the so-called 'hired guns', by the more affluent actors.

C.9 The ECJ as an Unintended Target

Importantly, despite the organised efforts behind litigation in this case, and despite the far-reaching consequences of the different ECJ judgments, it was never the explicit aim of the Working Group to reach the ECJ. The fact that in first and second instances the Working Group's claims based on the Association Agreement had been vindicated showed the potential for success based on EU law at the national level. Bringing the cases to the ECJ via preliminary questions was never an explicit part of their strategy. In fact, in internal communications to the leading lawyer on the strategy before the Council of State, the academic involved, well aware of the ECJ's production time, closed with:

> "Incidentally, I fear, however, that the Council of State will have the tendency to refer the case to the Court of Justice. And then we will be in the waiting room for two years. Therefore, don't mention it and present everything as clear and already decided by the Court."

Next to general concerns of a prolonged process, since their case involved an actual individual litigant, the interests of the client were considered as well. As the lawyer explained, for the individual involved, it is not a most welcome development when their case gets extended by, in *Case Study C*, another three and

47 http://www.commissie-meijers.nl/en [last accessed 10 November 2017].

a half years, due to a reference to the ECJ. Therefore the preference was for a national judgment with the same effect. In this respect, it is striking that the outcome of the final judgment of the ECJ on conflict with the Association Agreement had been confirmed both in first instance in the administrative law case and in the civil proceedings by successively the Court and the Court of Appeal. The ECJ arguably served as a supreme court in finalizing this interpretation.

Although the ECJ judgment served as a vindication of the Working Group's efforts, their success was thus already evident at earlier stages. As the professor explains:

> "The importance of that court ruling, the first judgment on the administrative fees is that they had said that a) it is in breach of the standstill provision, and b) in circumstances can also lead to conflict with Art. 8 ECHR. That judgement supported the action and legitimized it to the group itself and to the outside. So, towards lawyers and other relevant people it showed we had a point. And at the same time it delegitimised the government and the policy. So the Ministry of Justice from that moment on was on the defensive. I think that court ruling was ten times if not 100 times more important than that of the Supreme Court. The first blow is actually half the battle in this case."

Part of the effort was convincing other lawyers to file similar claims. As the leading lawyer describes:

> "For me, the administrative fees had become somewhat of a private hobby. I have asked other lawyers, why do you never bring up those fees in court? And when they reply, well my clients never asked me to. Of course, that was rare for me as well. Because people came to you because their application has been refused."

The eventual Supreme Court ruling in the civil suit was disappointing to the Working Group, but meanwhile, the administrative procedure was already well on its way and the earlier case and judgment had already had their effect. Such lower rulings thus can have a major impact. Why it eventually had to be fought all the way to the ECJ can largely be attributed to the attitude of the Dutch government.

C.10 Government Stance as Push Factor

The uncompromising stance of the Dutch government served as a push factor in the direction of legal action, essentially channelling all opposition through the courts. The Working Group's decision to litigate came after political lobbying yielded little result. Illustrative in this respect, next to the unsuccessful attempts for political pressure by the IOT in the early stages, is the way the administration dealt with restitution claims subsequent to the ECJ ruling. The then Secretary of State Albayrak herself explicitly showed the IOT the way to court. In early 2010, in consultation with the State Secretary on the refund of previously unlawfully levied fees, the IOT was told that the initiated legal process would be completed and that no restitution would be made on the basis of the ECJ judgment. 'If you believe that the arrangements made by the government are in conflict with European law, then you should submit your claim to the court' she added.[48] Moreover, with the delay in the court proceedings the costs could be passed on to a new administration. The number of court cases related to the fees illustrates the active legal opposition to the policy and also the rigidity of the national system. The prolonged duration of all the different court cases with distinct but limited effects served the Dutch government in that in the meantime it was able to rely on the continued income from the higher fees for other categories of migrants that had yet to be contested successfully.[49]

Relatedly, as previously hinted at by Broberg and Fenger, the stance of the authorities (or other opposing party in the case of civil proceedings) plays an important part as well, and persistence thus goes for both the individuals as well as their opposition. In this respect, multiple (migration and social security) lawyers point to the tendency on the part of the Dutch government to keep litigating, regardless of context or expected outcome. For such cases to reach the ECJ, then, depends in large part on the willingness of litigants to go up against the state. On the consequences of their efforts against the Dutch policy the leading lawyer concludes:

> "Because the legal battle over the fees has taken so long, the Dutch government has been able to continue for a long time to unlawfully levy these fees. In the case of Turkish nationals, a refund scheme existed for some time, although the disclosure of this arrangement also immediately meant the end of it.[50] Thus, a large number of Turkish nationals have never been able to make use of this so-called transitional arrangement."

48 Inspraak Orgaan Turken in Nederland, *Jaarverslag 2010*, 2010, 9. Retrieved from: http://www.iot.nl/?page=sayfa&sayfa_id=43 [last Accessed 2 November 2017].

49 In the end, the Ministry paid a refund to only a very small proportion of the Turkish citizens who had paid the unlawfully high fees since 2003. A ruling by the Council of State in September 2011 stated that the government was required to refund the overpayment only to Turkish citizens who opposed the fees from the outset, even when those procedures were then hopeless in a national legal context. Restitution requests cost up to € 300,- per person, therefore the number of people actually applying would be slim, and for the state the restitution of these few complaints would still be significantly lower than any collective scheme.

50 ABRvS 2 September 2011, ECLI:NL:RVS:2011:BR6949.

The unlawfulness of the Dutch policy has thus gone largely unpunished and unlawfully levied fees, adding up to millions of euros of additional income for the ministry on an annual basis, have been largely retained.[51]

C.11 Advantages of Organised Opposition

The IOT was able to serve the interests of a large and relatively homogeneous group with similar interests, which, next to resources and lack of success in the political sphere, served as an explanation for their choice to litigate. The Working Group effectively created a constituency around the issue of the new Dutch administrative fees policy. The direct constituency of the IOT, Turks living in the Netherlands, was additionally, though separately, protected by the Association Agreement EEC/Turkey. However, this case shows how the development of a precedent can subsequently also result in legal developments that affect other groups. The strategy of the Working Group was exactly this, as explained by the lawyer:

> "The scope of this case did not go beyond the Turks. But when the judge in the administrative proceedings ruled that the fees are an additional restriction given the Association Agreement, a lot was gained. If this falls, everything falls was the idea."

This strategy, extending beyond the single case and for the interests of multiple stakeholders, indicates explicitly repeat player behaviour in the sense of 'playing for the rules'. Although well organised, the effort saw its fair share of obstacles, among which were the eventual costs of around 70,000 euro in total. From the broader perspective, this amount was a relatively small investment when compared to the many millions the state would lose as a result, and how much expenditure the immigrants would save. Nevertheless, it was an amount that was not easily brought up, even for a well-organised group like this one. In the end they were unable to cover the total amount from the contributions of the various supporting organizations. As the academic involved recalled: "We had misjudged a bit how expensive of a hobby it would turn out to be". Eventually, it was thanks to one private donor and a test cases fund that the Working Group was able to cover all the expenses.

51 See *Case Study C* paragraph 7.

Part III

7 Challenges and Opportunities

7.1 Introduction

Social movement scholarship has documented a general increase over the past decades in social movements' tendency to turn to the law and pursue litigation strategies in their efforts to bring about social change.[1] In the study of European integration the role of social movement activists in mobilising EU law and activating the preliminary reference mechanism, and with it feeding integration dynamics, has been an important focus of research.[2] Several studies have revealed the involvement and at times significant successes of interest groups and strategic litigation in different areas of EU law.[3] While the European system has been described as a particularly viable opportunity for politicised litigation, with the opportunity of using EU law and the preliminary reference procedure to put pressure on national policy, social movement and legal activism scholarship has yet to engage fully with the European legal system as a potentially rich area for inquiry.[4] On the other hand, European integration scholarship has hardly ventured beyond reiterating classic examples of the use of EU law and the ECJ for political ends in the past,[5] and has paid little attention to analysing what legal mobilisation in an EU law context entails, when it occurs and under what conditions it can be an effective avenue for social change. Where neofunctionalist literature hypothesizes that litigants will draw on EU law to promote their interests whenever there is a potential benefit to doing so,[6] others have concluded that, despite the numerous situations in which a litigation strategy could have been profitably employed, EU law litigation strategies are used relatively infrequently.[7] Empirical analysis of strategic EU law mobilisation is as yet sparse and inconclusive.

Where the previous chapters mainly showed how the reference procedure can be an obstacle to those who are confronted with it, this chapter focuses on

1 McCammon & McGrath 2015.

2 Alter & Meunier-Aitsahalia 1994; Alter & Vargas 2000; Börzel 2006; Cichowski 1998 and 2006; Conant 2002 and 2003; Kelemen 2006.

3 Alter & Vargas 2000; Börzel 2006; Cichowski 1998 and 2006; Conant 2002 and 2003; Harlow & Rawlings 1992; Kelemen 2006; Micklitz 2005; Micklitz & Reich 1996.

4 Scholars point to a more general gap between social movement research and sociolegal studies, see McCann 2006; Rubin 2001.

5 As described in more detail in Chapter 2 a few 'token cases' play an important part in the discourses on empowerment-through-law and participation-through-law-enforcement.

6 Such reasoning can be found in Burley & Mattli 1993; Mattli & Slaughter 1998; Stone Sweet & Brunell 1998.

7 Alter & Vargas 2000.

the question of who is most likely to make use of the opportunities in EU law and which legal strategies are effective. We have seen how practitioners play an integral part in preliminary reference cases when it comes to effective advocacy, when references to the ECJ more or less come as a surprise. Other references are the result (at least in part) of parties and especially their counsel 'pushing for' a reference, or strategic players may interpose in a case after reference to the ECJ. The forms of EU law mobilisation and the activation of the preliminary reference procedure are thus manifold, and by no means always a manifestation of a supranational legal strategy, or a 'demand for integration' as some have defined it.[8] The question of successful mobilisation of EU law is a pertinent one since strategic litigation is one of the ways in which both supranational as well as domestic legal and political developments are shaped. The reverse question, when and why EU law is not mobilised, may be important, since this may reveal structural obstacles and inequalities inherent in the European legal system. In this chapter, I will therefore focus on the mobilisation of EU law and the activation of the preliminary reference procedure as part of strategic litigation, analyse obstacles to using the procedure as a legal tool, as well as the coping strategies strategic actors have developed to navigate the European legal system.

7.2 Opportunities in EU Law

Litigation has long been recognised among political scientists, as one of the methods employed by interest groups in fighting for political change. In 1992, Harlow and Rawlings published their extensive work on the strategic use of courts and the legal system by pressure groups in the United Kingdom.[9] Their book is an exposé on what they bring under the general header of 'pressure through law', or "the use of law and legal techniques as an instrument for obtaining wider collective objectives".[10] They set out to analyse the use of law by organised interests or 'pressure groups' and 'cause groups' in terms of collective interest representation and cause lawyering in both a historic as well as contemporary perspective. Harlow and Rawlings show how, by looking at the case of the UK, the use of courts for political ends is not exclusively an American phenomenon[11] and can be identified as a practice in the UK as far back as the 18th

8 Wind, Martinsen & Potger 2013; Broberg & Fenger 2013; Carrubba and Murrah 2005; Golub 1996.

9 Harlow & Rawlings 1992.

10 Harlow & Rawlings 1992, 1.

11 This (typically American, as Vauchez (2008a, 449) argues) political science perspective may be in part responsible for the focus on 'pressure through EU law' by political scientists when approaching the EU legal system.

century. They point to a fairly recent shift towards litigation as a method of campaigning by British interest organisations that saw their chances of gaining entry by lobbying diminish due to changes in governmental attitudes in the 1980s. They furthermore cite the rise of the EU together with increasingly legalistic frameworks in governmental systems as creating new 'windows of opportunity' for pressure through law.[12] It has generally been understood that litigation, a court's resolution of societal questions or disputes, can lead to the clarification and expansion of existing laws and to the construction of new rules, and in that sense provides opportunities for strategic actors.[13] Here, I use the term *strategic litigation* as a generic denotation of all forms of the use of law and legal techniques as an instrument for obtaining wider collective objectives. With the term *cause lawyers* I mean those practitioners who are disposed to the usage of law for the promotion of social change, especially in order to empower the weaker members of society.

The idea that the legal system can be a potent tool for political influence is hardly novel, yet EU law mobilisation differs from traditional litigation strategies, in that it provides a unique way for groups to influence national policy. The EU legal system, which includes private parties as subjects, has changed the field opportunities for such forms of 'pressure through law'.[14] As Chalmers & Chaves conclude, "as a preliminary ruling resettles the legal settlement it attracts those who litigate to change the law to meet ideological preferences. Litigation offers high returns here, as it does not require litigants to negotiate with other constituencies. Judgments of the Court of Justice are almost never overturned, and, in terms of profile for the litigants and entrenching particular belief-systems, rulings govern a large territory of nearly half a billion people".[15]

Using EU law has advantages that a domestic legal strategy does not offer. In its most influential form, the preliminary reference procedure serves as a form of judicial review of domestic legislation by invoking (higher order) EU law. Alter and Vargas describe the effect the European legal system has had on politics within the Member States, by providing domestic groups with a tool that can be used to impose new costs on their government.[16] They posit that the possibility of mobilising EU law has transformed previously weak organizations with little leverage in domestic politics into veritable political players capable of directly influencing national policy. The EU legal system creates the means to circumvent the domestic system, allowing a litigation strategy to succeed with

12 Cf. Kelemen 2011.
13 Shapiro 1981.
14 Kelemen 2011.
15 Chalmers & Chaves 2012, 35.
16 Alter & Vargas 2000.

the support of only a few (lower level) members of the national judiciary. Furthermore, a change in policy based on EU law is much harder for national governments to reverse than a legal victory based on domestic law, because such a reversal would require legislating at the European level.

From a rule of law perspective – the idea that law, the legal system and especially judicial review provide the means for the public to call their government to account – EU law and the preliminary reference procedure provide means of review of government acts that were previously unavailable. The mobilisation of EU law in the national courtroom thus provides the public with new means of addressing possible government trespasses as well as bypassing the domestic system by invoking the powers of the ECJ. While the vast majority of EU law claims are still dealt with within the national courtrooms, the preliminary reference procedure provides a form of supranational judicial review, and judgments on principle by the ECJ have the capacity to halt certain national policies and set precedents that have an effect beyond the nation-state. In this sense, the shield and sword analogy, as borrowed from Dworkin, has been used to describe the use of EU law and preliminary reference procedure as a strategic tool in the hands of litigants and civil society.[17]

7.3 The EU Legal System Reviewed

Before going further it is useful to characterise the preliminary reference system, and scrutinise this idea of EU law and the preliminary reference procedure as a potential tool in the hands of domestic groups aiming to influence national policy. Although the idea of the legal system as a potent tool for influencing national policy is not new, the EU legal system has a distinct nature compared to more traditional forms of litigation strategies. A useful way of assessing the opportunity structure in legal systems focuses on the nature of legal opportunities and amount of access available to actors who aim to use the law as a strategic tool. In this respect, Harlow and Rawlings distinguish between three ideal types of judicial review. The first of these models, the 'drainpipe', is described as 'a narrow tube barred at intervals by valves'. This inflexible system is thus characterised by significant procedural barriers at different stages of legal action. Only when the threshold requirements of one of these stages have been met, is a case deemed eligible for a next stage in the pathway to judicial review. Access to courts in such a system is very limited. At the opposite end of the spectrum we find what they call the 'freeway' model. This ideal type of a system of judicial review is characterised by permeability at every stage of the action. "While the

17 European Parliament 2007a.

drainpipe treats judicial review largely as a mechanism for the protection of individual and private rights and is therefore relatively difficult for non-parties to permeate, the freeway is especially favourable to permeation by non-parties, including groups." Finally, Harlow and Rawlings provide a third model, 'the funnel', which takes a compromise position between the other two. [18] For the purposes of clarifying the EU preliminary reference system, the two models at the extremes serve as a benchmark.

Looking at the setup of the EU legal system it is not hard to discount the 'freeway' model as an apt description for the nature of the judicial review by the ECJ. For private parties, direct access to the ECJ is limited to contesting the validity of measures adopted by EU institutions. Furthermore, the strict interpretation of standing rules by the ECJ means that such EU measures can only be contested if and when they directly affect a party. In practice, this means that only a very small minority of private parties may be eligible to access the ECJ via this route and access is arguably even more restricted if not impossible for pressure groups that are unlikely to fulfil these standing requirements. Furthermore, the opportunity for third party interventions in ECJ cases in general is as of yet very limited.[19] The remaining access points to the ECJ are characterised by limited control over whether or not one is able to reach the Court. Private parties thus have no direct way of challenging Member States' policies for non-compliance with EU law before the ECJ. The EU system, that combines both centralised and decentralised EU law enforcement, provides private parties with two alternatives for reaching the ECJ. The first is the possibility of petitioning the European Commission to start infringement proceedings against a Member State by lodging a complaint. From the perspective of strategic actors, this avenue, although in effect a potent legal measure against Member States, does not give any control over whether or not a case is brought, or over the substance of the subsequent legal action. Because of their judicial review character and their high impact, potential preliminary references are therefore the theoretically most auspicious option.[20]

Legal strategies are influenced to a great extent by the procedural context of the legal action, and this EU law avenue comes with its own peculiarities that shape the ways in which strategic legal action may be practised. Legal strategies that aim to invoke EU law and the authority of the ECJ have to navigate a procedural context that is unique to the European legal system. Alter and Vargas have used the case of the British Equal Opportunities Commission – which was

18 Harlow & Rawlings 1992, 310.

19 Carrera & Petkova 2013.

20 See Rasmussen 1986, who shows how, in its early days, the Court made efforts to channel questions of judicial review through the preliminary reference procedure.

successful in shifting the domestic balance of power through Euro-litigation and the creation of ECJ jurisprudence – to identify the structural factors that contribute to successful use of EU law litigation strategies.[21] They discern four separate steps in EU litigation strategies that determine whether EU law can successfully be invoked. The first is the precondition of the existence of relevant EU legislation, and the ECJ's interpretation of this law, on which domestic actors can draw. Second, is the active usage of EU legal arguments in national court cases. Third, is the requirement of support of the national judiciary by reference to the ECJ through the preliminary reference procedure or by applying ECJ jurisprudence instead of conflicting national legislation. And the fourth and final step is the active follow-up of a legal victory by drawing on or creating more legal precedents to increase political and material costs for government non-compliance.

Alter and Vargas stress that, with the exception of the first, all these steps require significant actor agency. The notion of agency plays a significant part in legal proceedings in general, but is essential when considering law as a strategic tool. Similarly, recent studies on EU law mobilisation in the area of environmental protection have directed our attention to the significant role, next to structural and contextual factors, played by the actors involved in strategic legal action. Vanhala, who studied the mobilisation of EU law and strategic litigation among environmental groups, concludes, "there is not one overarching theoretical branch that can account for legal mobilization dynamics both across and within countries", and she directs future research towards the development of a more synthetic theoretical framework "that takes both contextual factors and agent-level characteristics seriously and explores the interaction between them".[22]

Before strategic action of any sort is channelled through the courts, the issue has to be framed and a legal opportunity has to be identified. As is evident from the different case studies presented throughout this book, the decision to proceed by legal means is often the result of a complex combination of factors. For such legal action to be framed as a matter of EU law, it is necessary for the parties to identify an opportunity in existing legislation or jurisprudence. After an opportunity in EU law has been identified, there is a need for a case based on which a litigation strategy can be employed. Once a case has been brought before a national court, the parties need to convince the national judge of the need for a referral to the ECJ. And depending on the aims of the legal strategy, there is a need for further action. In some cases, an ECJ judgment is decisive for the intended aim; in others further (legal) action is needed. The setup of the EU legal system significantly discourages the strategic use of EU law and the preliminary

21 Alter & Vargas 2000.
22 Vanhala 2017, 34.

references system. Yet, strategic litigation is not completely absent among cases that reach the ECJ. The next paragraphs will first focus on the requirements for strategic action, and subsequently on how strategic actors cope within this context.

7.4 Awareness, Opportunity and the Litigability of EU Rules

Scholarship on the interplay between social movements and the legal system has distilled some of the strategies that are employed by social movements that employ litigation as a means to an end. The main strategies that are discerned are the strategic choosing of legal areas as well as particular cases, the strategic legal framing and the mobilisation of networks of support.[23] While the first two strategies are aimed particularly at making the most effective use of opportunity structures in the legal system as well as trying to steer legal developments discursively, the last strategy deals more with the broader mobilisation of support and media attention for certain cases in order to put additional pressure on government agents. Litigation activism in many respects lacks full control over choices regarding issue areas and specific cases and legal strategies are to a large extent determined by the legal opportunity structures that are available. The EU legal system presents its own opportunities and constraints, and making use of the preliminary references system as a means to an end presents its own puzzles for those who aim to use it.

Where in general a legal strategy entails the subsequent steps for identifying the issue, finding the right narrative and filing the claim, using EU law and preliminary references as part of a legal strategy is a decidedly more arduous task. For example, in the case of direct actions at the ECJ level, legal action entails the challenging of a decision by an EU institution. Such legal action is relatively straightforward, to the extent that it is clear from the outset what the target is, both in terms of the contested act, and the relevant EU legislation, as well as the intended court (the ECJ) that will deal with the case. In contrast, using the preliminary reference procedure to challenge national policy based on EU law is less straightforward and implies identifying in the national legal system an EU principle on which to build an EU law case. This can be relatively more straightforward when a national measure flows directly from EU rules. In that case, one identifies the EU provision underlying the national measure and challenges the national interpretation of that provision. It becomes especially challenging when it entails invoking more general principles of EU law, which requires legal expertise and craft to identify and frame the issue.

23 Vanhala 2012.

Needless to say, EU law does not affect all policy areas equally,[24] and not all aspects of European law can be invoked in national courts. In order for EU law and the ECJ to become part of a litigation strategy, there has to be an EU law or principle on which parties can rely. Whether this is the case is determined by the context within which an issue is situated.[25] Additionally, opportunities for mobilising EU law and the ECJ exist in areas where the interpretation of EU legislation is still open-ended. Especially where new EU legislation enters into force, the interpretation and application of new EU rules in specific contexts and circumstances is often still quite unclear, and new legislation can provide strategic actors with new ammunition to take on national policy. As discussed, the relatively high number of references in the areas of migration and asylum law can at least partly be attributed to the more recent entry into force of EU Directives in these particular areas, providing new potential 'points of contact' between EU law and national policy and legislation. In other instances, existing EU legislation can become a relevant source of legal contestation when national policies change in a way that encroaches on (administrative) boundaries set by EU law. We find a prime example of this in *Case Study C* in which the decades old standstill clause in the Association Agreement with Turkey was successfully invoked to roll back the new Dutch policy that increased administrative fees for residence permits.

Whether a legal strategy entails invoking new ECJ jurisprudence, focusing on more open-ended interpretations of EU law or using existing EU legislation and jurisprudence against new national policies, all require an awareness of legislative and jurisprudential developments at the EU level as well as the know-how to signal possible discrepancies between EU law or jurisprudence and national policy. Such awareness is an important part of what Galanter refers to as 'legal competence' – "the capacity for optimal use of the legal process to pursue one's interests, which includes information, access, judgment, psychic readiness and so on".[26] Apart from a general form of agency, such competence also in-

24 Research by the Asser Institute in 2007 shows that the size of the Europeanisation of national law varies considerably by sector. On environmental protection, for instance, the researchers conclude that 66% of all legislation is influenced by the EU. With regard to education this amounts to only 6%. Asser Institute, *Pilot-Monitor EU Invloed*, 2007. https://www.recht.nl/exit.html?id=59078&url=http%3A%2F%2Fwww.asser.nl%2Feurlaw%2Fdocuments%2Fcms_eurlaw_id52_1_EINDRAPPORT%2520dd%2520061206%2520def.pdf [last accessed 9 November 2017].

25 Alter & Vargas 2000, show in this respect how the existence of EU law in the area of gender equality, the direct effect and supremacy of these laws in the national context, as well as the favourable interpretations of these laws by the ECJ, granting more protection than existing British legislation, were all important preconditions for domestic groups using an EU law litigation strategy to challenge national policy.

26 Galanter 1976. See also Carlin & Howard 1965 and Nonet 1969.

cludes a specific form of 'legal consciousness'. Not to be confused with the more anthropological use of the term, I use the term 'legal consciousness' as it relates to the legal profession, as described by Kennedy: "The main peculiarity of this consciousness is that it contains a vast number of legal rules, arguments, and theories, a great deal of information about the institutional workings of the legal process, and the constellation of ideals and goals current in the profession at a given moment."[27] With respect to Euro-litigation strategies, such consciousness thus includes attention to EU rules, ECJ jurisprudence and a general knowledge of the European legal process.

As discussed in Chapter 6, among practitioners and legal advisors such expertise for signalling opportunities in EU law is not widespread. Differences not only occur based on the existence or absence of EU law specialization of any lawyer or legal office, but looking at the lawyers in the cases studied reveals there is also a clear differentiation among lawyers in different areas of law. Where lawyers working in the area of agricultural law, as one of the oldest areas of law subject to EU legislation, show more general awareness of EU law, other areas of law, where the existence of relevant EU law is still more embryonic, show substantially less attention to possible European aspects of legislation and ECJ jurisprudence development. Similarly, the relative complexity of the EU legal framework, and the related possibilities for using EU law arguments against policy or legislation have a bearing on the ease with which such claims are brought forward. Among tax consultants, for instance, the applicable EU law provides a relatively clear framework for assessing the legality of new national measures. In particular, the prohibition of discriminatory restrictions on the freedom of persons, services and goods provides an important restriction on new national tax policies. As one tax advisor, employed by one of the larger tax firms explains:

> "Nowadays, the nature of EU law is such that every change in national legislation automatically raises the question of whether there is a difference in treatment based on nationality. Well then, the legislature of course says, it's fine. And we often say, it's not fine. And that is what the Court then has to decide."

Similarly, the standstill clauses in the Association Agreement between the EU and Turkey and the Association Council's decision 1/80, both responsible for a significant number of preliminary references,[28] provided a clear and simple limit

27 Kennedy 1980, 27.

28 Since its first judgment in the *Demirel* case in 1987, the ECJ has handed down over sixty-five judgments on EU-Turkey association law. The standstill clauses require that, in the event that a Turkish citizen seeks to enter an EU country to make use of his or her economic rights, the regulation that applies is the most lenient regulation passed since the →

to the measures that were allowed with respect to the rights of Turkish nationals. As one of the academics involved in references to the ECJ regarding the Agreement states:

> "The advantage of the standstill clause was that it is a relatively clear rule. Other legal rules are often far more ambiguous, and one judge may interpret it different from another. But the standstill clause simply stipulates that there may be 'no new restriction', and that that was the case here was obvious."

The 'litigability', an EU rule's suitability for being used in litigation strategies, is thus an important factor in whether or not parties will choose to invoke EU law in opposition to national policy. Some rules, such as the mentioned standstill clause allow for a fairly straightforward challenge to, in this case, new and stricter migration policies in the Netherlands. The litigability of the standstill clause has over the years resulted in a significant portion of cases being brought before the ECJ in order to shed light on its applicability to various national policies, most notably in the Netherlands and Germany.[29]

In other areas, the signalling of opportunities in EU law requires more complex expertise, both in the sense of awareness as well as in putting such claims into practice. Especially, when it comes to signalling the aforementioned conflicts between national and EU law, which requires intricate knowledge of both. EU law awareness and expertise is not particularly widespread among legal practitioners and may be reserved for a minority of legal professionals. Even among those who were successful in employing an EU law strategy, such awareness was considered limited. For example, the trade union legal expert assisting the catering employees (*Case Study A*) who successfully invoked protections for employees as laid down in the Transfer of Undertakings Directive in court,[30] describes the difficulty in identifying such opportunities:

> "I think that a lot of opportunities in EU law simply go unseen. We are simply stuck thinking in a national framework. And I really think still that there are many cases where you can denounce certain issues or policy using an EU directive or whatever. Look, whether or not you will be able to make it work practically is another thing. But you've got to come up with it first."

Additional Protocol came into effect and the Association Council's decision was passed. Groenendijk 2015.

29 In the five-year selection period of Dutch references for this study, six out of forty cases including individual litigants dealt with Association law, of which three directly with the standstill clauses therein.

30 Council Directive 2001/23/EC.

The focus on the domestic legal system in the day-to-day practice of legal professionals might thus result in a neglect of opportunities in EU legislation and ECJ jurisprudence.

7.5 Standing Rules and Strategically Choosing Cases

The mere existence of legislation and opportunities in law, and legal consciousness among litigants and lawyers alone are unlikely to single-handedly produce strategic legal action. Law is not self-executing and needs mobilisation by individuals or groups. Apart from the prerequisite of existing legislation on which a claim can be built, the using of EU law arguments in national courts obviously requires a court case in which to invoke such arguments. National standing rules matter significantly in this respect, and can have a limiting effect on legal opportunities. Unless generous standing rules are available to interest groups, issues have to be addressed based on a party affected by the contested national policy, which requires access to potential litigants. As discussed in Chapter 2, EU law channels many interests through individual rights language, and therefore legal strategies are steered towards employing individual cases.

Finding such a suitable case is not always as straightforward as one may wish, especially when there is the need for cooperation by an individual for whom a prolonged legal battle, as described in Chapter 3, can have a significant negative personal impact. As explained by the lawyer in *Case Study D* on pre-entry integration requirements, after the Dutch government had prevented the ECJ judgment by providing a residence permit, he sought another case in which he could address the same issue:

> "When it comes to preliminary questions, you are talking about three to four years that you are completely engaged. And you never know what the outcome is. I can say I have strong arguments, but you do not know what the Court is going to say. There are strong indications that the Dutch system is not lawful, but there are no guarantees. I cannot give my client any certainty. Well, if you tell them that it will take five years and I do not know what the outcome will be, then my clients will opt out."

The tensions that arise between the interests of the individual litigant and the collective interests that may be served by a single referral to the ECJ, as described at the end of Chapter 3, thus have a limiting effect on the pursuit of such a strategy. Even if it is fairly certain what the procedural outcome is going to be, because no interpretation exists yet on the subject and therefore in all likelihood a case will be sent to the ECJ, lawyers have to cope with the tension between the wider interests that may be served with a case and the direct interests of the client that may be better served by other means. The outcome is, of course, always uncertain, so it is an investment that few people are willing to make, unless they have no other options.[31] As described for instance in *Case Study C* regarding the legality of integration tests as a requirement for entry into the Netherlands, it is simply cheaper as well as faster for applicants to try and pass the test, instead of taking on the entire national policy in court.

Strategic actors like interest groups may aim to use the law and legal techniques as an instrument for obtaining wider collective objectives through soliciting a judgment on principle that sets a favourable precedent. In order to maximise the impact of one case, in both nationally focused litigation strategies as well as strategic litigation aimed at the ECJ, the aim is to provide a case with the best 'fit' for the purpose of the action.[32] Having a case with the right context and relevant characteristics can significantly increase one's chances of steering the final ECJ decision in a desirable direction. The opposite is also true; when the wrong case is referred within the context of the same principle matter, this may lead to undesirable outcomes.[33] Trying to get the right case referred is therefore an important part of strategic litigation. For this reason, strategic actors employ the strategy of selecting cases based on their specific characteristics and contextual facts, for if a case is void of any circumstances that may 'cloud' a decision or result in an unclear ruling due to too many circumstantial facts, it may not result in the intended objective. As one tax consultant explained, finding someone willing to be the subject of a litigation strategy is further complicated by the fact that such a subject also has to have a case with the right context:

> "We can only litigate based on someone's tax returns, so someone must be found willing. With this case we really had to search for someone who wanted to do that, who also had a good case. You should always find a clean case, without a lot of noise. And that is difficult."

Of course, the fact that these cases reach the Court by way of preliminary questions, formulated by national judges, further narrows down the applicable area

31 Going back to the *Defrenne* cases as described in Chapter 2, cause lawyer Vogel-Polsky too had trouble in finding an individual willing to lend their case to her goals. Although her aim was clear, to revive Article 119, it took Vogel-Polsky a long time to find a case on which to apply her strategy, underscoring one of the main difficulties in gaining strategic access to the ECJ in practice. Havinga & Hoevenaars 2015.

32 Harlow & Rawlings (1992, 10 and 307) also use the notion of a 'good fit', but do so in a more general sense of pressure through law campaigns having a good (or bad) fit with the legal process based on subject matter, means and objectives.

33 Member States may apply opposite strategies, in the sense of preventing the wrong case from reaching the ECJ. Unlike private parties, the Member State government in most situations does have some 'bottom-up docked control'. See Chapter 8.

of law to which the judgment will be applicable.[34] As discussed in Chapter 6, the framing of preliminary questions can significantly broaden or narrow the scope of the eventual ECJ judgment. When actors aim at using a case to address a principle question, the strategic need for a case with a 'good fit', devoid of any complicating characteristics, is augmented. A lawyer from a large tax firm explained their wish in *Foreign Savings* for an 'honest client' who had voluntarily disclosed foreign funds, in order for them to test the legality of an extended recovery period for foreign savings. The question was whether the tax authorities would be allowed, under EU rules, to use a different recovery period for people with foreign assets than the period used for all domestic assets:

> "This was a question our office really wanted to litigate. So we were kind of looking for a victim. Usually it's the other way around. Typically someone comes to us with a problem. But here we were actively looking for a case, because this is a matter that is not lucrative enough for any one client to litigate on. And there were enough clients who wanted to cooperate. But we specifically wanted someone who had voluntarily disclosed his funds, because that worked better for the question."

The 'good fit' of a case does not necessarily have to revolve around the substantive or factual characteristics of a case but can also lie in its context. As illustrated in *Case Study D* the individual case in many respects was perfectly suited for the aim of attacking the legality of the Dutch policy on requiring prospective immigrants to pass an integration test abroad. The circumstances were clearly making it in every respect impossible for her to meet the requirements for passing the examination. Apart from her illiteracy and the fact that she only spoke Pashtu, that her eight children were separated from their mother (who had raised them for the past seven years) and were staying with their father (whom they had not seen for the same period of time) added a layer of both poignancy and urgency. As the lawyer in that case explained:

> "The awkward part is, you hope bad things happen with your client because you get a better case. Child protective services became involved and began to threaten with [state guardianship] and other such things. So it was very easy to make the case for those kids. Because I can say the children are not doing well, the children are pitiable. But at the moment the Council for Child Protection says it; that weighs very heavy before a court."

34 The fact notwithstanding that the judges at the ECJ on occasion reformulate the preliminary questions, sometimes significantly narrowing down or broadening the context to which the eventual judgment will be applicable.

This reasoning, and the search for a good case with as little 'static' as possible, is comparable to considerations in test cases, as discussed in Chapter 3, with the significant difference that in some of these test cases the 'conflict' underlying the legal action is in fact orchestrated, allowing for more control over the 'fit' of the chosen case. With 'noise' respondents refer to case-specific circumstances that may unnecessarily complicate the context of a case and thus may result in a too specific judgment, a judgment that focuses on the wrong aspects, or an all-out negative judgment. In the latter case, this could actually run counter to the aims because such a negative judgment may definitively 'close the door' on a certain question.

The uncertainty of referrals thus makes strategic use of the procedure more problematic. Due to the nature of the preliminary reference procedure, even when a suitable case has been found (or created in some instances) litigating parties have only limited influence on whether or not, as well as which case is referred to the ECJ. This uncertainty of the preliminary reference system makes what can best be described as a form of 'bottom-up docket control' decidedly more difficult.[35] In that sense this setup is closer to a 'drainpipe model' as described by Harlow and Rawlings, with the reference to the ECJ constituting an important 'valve'. Strategies that focus on getting one specific case referred to the ECJ, may find their investment nullified by being unable to find a national judge willing to refer the case. Therefore, when strategic litigation efforts aim to have one specific case referred to the ECJ, convincing the national judge to refer the case is a decisive step that can make or break a legal strategy.

7.6 The National Court: Before and After Referral

Apart from forming a barrier, by being the sole competent actor to decide whether or not a case is referred, national courts can play another important role in strategic action. While ECJ judgments in themselves can have important ramifications in the legal sphere, by creating a precedent, and in the political sphere, by delimiting the room national governments have in stipulating certain policies, the use of the preliminary reference to this end has an important drawback. Since the ECJ only deals with matters of interpretation of EU law, and does not deal with the legality of national rules and policies, the direct effects of ECJ rulings depend significantly on what transpires after an ECJ judgment and after a referred case returns to the national court. After the ECJ has given its judgment on the interpretation of EU law, it is still up to the national judge to apply

35 Not unlike the US Supreme Court system, although there it is the Court itself that has control over which cases are adjudicated.

the conclusions of the Court in the case at hand. National courts can have an important impact on the effective strategic use of preliminary references. Firstly, the formulation of the questions that are referred to the ECJ can greatly determine the scope of the subsequent ECJ judgment. While strategic actors may wish to address the legality of a certain national law or entire policy, the questions referred to the ECJ often revolve around the interpretation of EU law in very specific contexts. A narrower formulation of the referred questions, essentially narrowing down the applicability of the answers to very specific conditions, can thus limit the impact of an ECJ judgment, potentially leaving the broader policy intact. Secondly, after a case returns from the ECJ to the national setting, the national court has to give effect to the judgment and apply it to the case at hand. The ECJ does not always give a straightforward conclusion as to how its judgment is to be applied in the case at hand, as the judgment is often related to the way in which the preliminary questions have been formulated. The subsequent interpretation of the ECJ judgment by the referring court may then turn out to temper (in the case of a broadly formulated judgment), or even be a complete reversal, of a perceived win at the ECJ (especially where the ECJ leaves some questions for the national court to answer: for instance in *Case Study B* on the pensioners). Thirdly, especially if an ECJ judgment has repercussions for existing national law or policy, the effect of its judgment requires government response. As Greer & Iniesta have reminded us, such a response does not always occur automatically, and Member States may move to contain an ECJ judgment and "balance the costs of knowledge and compliance against the risks of ignorance and lost cases".[36] Subsequent (non-)action by national bureaucracies can limit the impact of the ECJ judgment and thus enhance the need for follow-up action. It goes without saying that not every actor is capable of applying subsequent pressure, and strategic action thus requires the resources to follow up on litigation.

7.7 Lessons from the Netherlands: Recipes for Getting Access

The aforementioned structural characteristics of the preliminary reference system, the indirect access to the Court necessitating an individual case to work with, the need to convince a national court to refer (the right) questions to the ECJ as well as the potential of using preliminary references as part of a wider strategy, together form the opportunity structure within which strategic actors may employ their litigation strategies. The cases studied for this research allow for a focus on how strategic actors have dealt with this structure and have used

36 Greer & Martín de Almagro Iniesta 2014, 22.

EU law and the preliminary reference as part of a litigation strategy. The next section deals with how strategic actors have made use of the legal system for the purpose of wider political objectives. Discussing several cases as examples, the next sections outline the different strategies that are employed and analyses them in light of the opportunity structures in EU law.

The cases selected for this research reveal a significant portion of Dutch reference cases in the area of migration and asylum law. As mentioned, this relatively high number of references in this particular area can be explained in part by new EU legislation in the wake of the efforts to develop a common immigration policy for Europe.[37] However, the in-depth study of these cases and interviews with those active behind the scenes reveal instances of EU law scholars teaming up with lawyers and interest groups in order to work cases at the ECJ level. Therefore, this chapter focuses for the most part on cases that in one way or another were part of more strategic efforts at legal mobilisation predominantly in the areas of migration and asylum. With few exceptions, other cases will largely be left aside.

Post Hoc strategies

The potential high impact of reference cases before the ECJ expectedly attracts the interest of third parties that seek to challenge certain national policies. However, while the involvement of interest groups in direct litigation before the Court of Justice of the EU may not be very surprising – similar to lawsuits challenging government actions in national court cases – the involvement of these groups in the preliminary reference procedure is not as self-evident. Due to the differences in procedure – a *direct* access to the ECJ versus *indirect* access through a national court – the involvement of interest groups, similarly to that of expert lawyers, in cases that reach the ECJ indirectly is impeded by the fact that there is no assurance of actually reaching the ECJ due to dependence on the national judge.

From a strategic litigation perspective, working a case to serve a particular strategic goal from the outset significantly increases one's options to frame the dispute in the right terms and anticipate a favourable interpretation of the matter at hand. This is why test cases are a tried method for pressure groups aiming to use the legal system to serve a general interest. As discussed, in the case of references to the ECJ this is a more problematic strategy. Due to the uncertainty of referral, third parties often get involved only after the national court has decided

37 Among others the Family Reunification Directive (2003/86) and the Directive on the Status of Third-Country Nationals Who are Long-Term Residents (2003/109), which went into force in 2005.

to refer the case to the ECJ, or has expressed an intention to do so. Usually this occurs at the request of the lawyer involved. As described in Chapter 6, lawyers, in response to an unexpected referral, set out to find either formal or informal help from others with more expertise in the area of both preliminary references and EU law. Usually these are sought, and found, in academic circles. In over half of the cases studied, the parties and/or their lawyers chose to consult or hire academic experts before a reference to the ECJ, after indications by the national judge of his or her intention to refer, or after a reference was made, allowing for more strategic players to get involved.

Some references to the ECJ can contain questions that may require clearing up, which scholars have identified as a relevant matter even before it is referred to the ECJ. In the case of more activist academics, the moment such questions are referred to the ECJ may provide the opportunity to influence the way in which this question is then addressed, albeit in an *ad hoc* fashion. As an example, one of the first and quite famous preliminary reference cases in the area of asylum law (*Subsidiary protection*) revolved around two Iraqi nationals whose request for asylum in the Netherlands was denied. In Iraq, they had received a threatening letter after militia had killed their uncle. The couple had found a note on their door in late 2006, which read "*Death to Collaborators!*". They had made their way to the Netherlands, where they applied for a temporary residence permit based on the dangers they faced from indiscriminate violence in Iraq. The Dutch immigration authorities rejected their application, and a series of appeals brought their case to the Dutch Council of State, which referred the case to the ECJ seeking an interpretation of the new EU Qualification Directive on asylum, in particular on Article 15c, stipulating the qualification for subsidiary protection in cases of "serious and individual threat to a civilian's life or person by reason of indiscriminate violence in situations of international or internal armed conflict".[38] The Council of State asked the question whether, especially in comparison with Article 3 of the European Convention on Human Rights, this provision offered supplementary or other protection. This referral potentially broadened the scope of the protection asylum seekers enjoyed under EU law, and was therefore an interesting target for champions of the rights of asylum seekers.

After the referral, the couple's lawyer, inexperienced in litigating at the European level and for whom the referral came unexpectedly, solicited the help of three EU (migration) law scholars, a representative of UNHCR and a representative of Amnesty International. Together this group worked on the case, arguing for an interpretation of Article 15c that gave additional protection under Article 3 ECHR to asylum seekers. In 2009, the ECJ ruled, as the group had argued, that proof of indiscriminate violence could warrant asylum under EU law. The ECJ

38 Council Directive 2004/83/EC.

effectively created a 'sliding scale test' for national authorities to assess individual applications in order to determine whether or not one qualified for protection. According to this test, the more an applicant is able to show that he or she is specifically affected by reason of factors particular to his or her personal circumstances, the lower the level of indiscriminate violence required.

However, the explanation by the ECJ was formulated broadly enough for the Dutch Council of State to give its own interpretation. The lawyer explains:

> "I found the ECJ's answer way too vague. And, of course I can interpret it to my advantage, but the IND can unfortunately do that too, so we draw the short straw because the Council of State usually sides with the IND."

Indeed, in his letter to parliament regarding the ECJ judgment, the Dutch Secretary of Justice stated: "I am of the opinion that the wording of the judgment shows that this will involve a very limited number of situations."[39] The sliding scale test leaves it to national determining authorities and appellate bodies to assess whether the degree of indiscriminate violence is sufficiently high to pose a risk to the individual. The Court did not explain how intense the indiscriminate violence must be to reach the threshold of a 'real risk', or how to assess the level of indiscriminate violence.[40] In a report on the consequences of the ECJ judgment on the practice in the Netherlands, UNHCR concluded: "Both the case law and government policy of the Netherlands reflect the view that Article 15 (c) Qualification Directive applies only to 'exceptional situations' of indiscriminate violence and, therefore, Article 15 (c) will rarely be applied."[41]

When compared to practitioners in general, third parties with more expertise can have a decidedly more accurate idea of the possible impact of an ECJ judgment, and thus awareness of the opportunities in EU law, as well as the capacity to apply legal argumentation that might steer the ECJ in a desired direction. Actors like UNHCR, with considerable resources as well as structural access to the national and international political arena, are, moreover, capable of subse-

39 Letter from the Ministry of Justice to the Speaker of the Lower House of the Netherlands Parliament, of 17 March 2009, regarding the judgment of the European Court of Justice of the European Communities in respect of the Qualification Directive. Available at: https://www.tweedekamer.nl/downloads/document?id=e282df00-c48c-49bd-8ee6-6237af d605b 6&title=Engelstalige%20brief%20over%20het%20arrest.pdf [last accessed 9 November 2017].

40 A complicating factor in this case was that meanwhile the European Court of Human Rights had given a judgment that significantly broadened the scope of Article 3 of the ECHR making the argued protection under Article 15c largely superfluous. The lawyer subsequently set out to try and get a judgment on the additional protection of Article 15c but was unable to find a suitable case. This underscores the difficulties in addressing certain issues strategically and the associated problem of finding a suitable case.

41 UNHCR 2011, 33.

quently using such judgments to put further pressure on Member States and the European legislature, or indeed providing the ECJ with the impetus for revisiting the question.[42] However, when their involvement comes only after a referral, they have neither influence on the context of the case, nor on the argumentation that has led to the national judge referring the case. As such, single case strategies and legal framing are an issue when it comes to strategically using preliminary references. Even where questions of interpretation of new EU legislation are expected, the uncertainty of referral to the ECJ means that third party actors aiming to influence ECJ case law are often forced to 'make do' with a case after it is referred or after a national judge has expressed the intention to refer. Depending on the complexity of the matter being addressed, this form of *post hoc* third party involvement limits the potential of issue framing in a case to serve a strategic purpose.

Strategically Employing an Individual Case

In other instances, more coordinated legal strategies included the employment of a particular case for the purposes of a pre-designed legal strategy. A prime example is *Case Study C* where an individual case was used to attack a Dutch policy increasing the administrative fees for residence permits. This case included the efforts by a select group of lawyers, legal scholars and members of a Dutch interest group representing the interest of Turks in the Netherlands (IOT) who devised a Working Group that set out the attack (by both a political campaign as well as legal means). The Working Group consisted of an informal collaboration of people that already knew each other from past collaborations. It was a small club, of scholars, legal experts, lawyers and political actors with sufficient expertise in many relevant areas, including EU law, procedural and national rules, political networks and the activation of strategic partners as well as the IOT for grassroots mobilisation. With this combination of skills and networks (and, of course, the necessary financial support), the group was able to devise a long-term strategy for challenging the Dutch increase in administrative fees. The strategy included, next to political lobbying and publicity campaigns both a civil suit and an administrative case based on an individual's rejected application for a residence permit. The group also successfully mobilised the European Commission by filing complaints that eventually resulted in infringement proceedings against the Netherlands.

42 In its report on the indiscriminate violence, UNHCR concluded in its recommendations that "[i]t seems clear that more guidance will be needed from the ECJ on the relevance of individual factors and circumstances in the interpretation of Article 15 (c), and the meaning of the term 'exceptional' as used by that Court". UNHCR 2011, 102.

This case is the most elaborate form of organised litigation to be found in the selection for this research. Although the inner circle of the Working Group was a small club of people, they were able to cover the multiple aspects needed for a successful strategy, as explained by the migration law professor who was one of the central figures in the thirteen-year strategy:

> "You have to know your stuff in different areas. I did, of course, know the European legal area, our lawyer was the man of procedural law, who knew the national rules. Another one of us checked at every stage whether political action could be useful. The political channel was obviously constantly closed. And then there was the IOT, which had close contact with the Turkish constituency, both through administrative contacts and through its newspaper and website."

Several of these actors had been involved in similar strategic actions before, challenging the Dutch policies on limits to the export of benefits. Among them was the aforementioned migration law professor, who had played an important part in many of the migration related references from the Netherlands. Such 'legal insiders' can be essential to intricate legal strategies. Especially when it comes to the signalling of opportunities in EU law the expertise of some players is crucial in the strategic mobilisation of EU law. McCammon and McRath state in this respect, "[p]ursuing social change via the courts typically means relying on legal experts, lawyers who themselves may identify as activists and prioritize the movement's reform goals, and, yet, who are also insiders to the legal profession and thus possess the necessary legal knowledge and litigation expertise".[43] Where possibilities exist in the *effet utile* of EU Directives, where implementation by the Netherlands may be incorrect, or where the implications of new regulations for existing or new national policies are not immediately apparent, this requires a focus of litigants, practitioners and/or supporting actors on the European level. One should thus be attentive to Dutch implementation as well as the underlying regulations. As we have seen, this focus is often lacking in the 'average' practitioner, and it is especially the academics who have the expertise, speak the 'language' of EU law and are able to signal opportunities in EU rules. Their help is indispensable in such strategic actions, not only by providing the needed expertise but also in informing and mobilising important stakeholders.

The support (financially solicited or otherwise) of certain experts is an important element in the decision to litigate as well as the potential success of strategic legal action. In that sense, it is impossible to overestimate the centrality of figures like the migration law professor. He is not only the 'go to' expert for lawyers in the areas of EU migration and asylum law as well as the Association

43 McCammon & McGrath 2015, 128.

Agreement with Turkey, when the possibility of a preliminary reference arises, but also in generally showing organised interest organisations the 'way to the Court', by providing EU law arguments and imploring them to focus on EU rights for migrants and asylum seekers and actively employing legal strategies, thus pushing stakeholders towards adopting strategies of pressure through law focusing on the rights of migrants in EU law. In the case of the pre-entry integration requirements *(Case Study D)*, the migration law professor was personally responsible for getting the Dutch Refugee Council to focus their efforts on helping asylum seekers not just with general support (like providing language courses) and legal counsel, but to also invest their efforts in advocating the rights of refugees. This signals the fact that for interest groups, who by all accounts may be very well equipped to undertake such strategic legal action, the path to the court, and in particular the ECJ, may simply not be a natural proclivity.[44] Additionally, the professor thus not only had a role in providing legal expertise, but also fulfilled a role in activating stakeholders and imploring them to focus on the possible broader social impact of preliminary reference cases; something that did not prove to be self-evident. He explains:

> "In one case, an extremely important case in hindsight, I really had to put in an effort to get that lawyer to go [to Luxembourg], he thought it was all just a bunch of nonsense. It was all too much trouble, and of course, on the commercial side it did not make him any money. So if I had not called him and put him under moral pressure, it's unjustifiable towards your client, but also in light of more general interests [...] The general interest is not always obvious to lawyers."

These strategic collaborations thus feature heavyweights in the field of EU law as well as European civil society, joining forces with several other lawyers with their own relevant specialization, most of whom act *pro bono*. Incidentally, this also points to the vulnerability of such organized advocacy, being very much dependent upon the expertise and willingness of a small group of people. This is a significant Achilles' heel when compared to the ability of more affluent actors to employ specialists, the so-called 'hired guns', although the personal investment of these cause lawyers may counterbalance this disparity to some extent.

44 In fact, interest groups, unless they have legal action as a distinct part of their modus operandi, rarely in and of themselves initiate such collaborations. As stated by Vauchez: "Legal expertise (lawyers' specialized networks, amount of legal training in the field...) are indeed considered as an essential factor in terms of interest groups' proclivity to take on the judicial route." See also Vanhala 2017.

The Preliminary Reference as a Threat

The aforementioned strategies either use a preliminary reference in a *post hoc* sense, with the interposing of strategic experts after referral, or employ a single case as part of wider legal and political actions. However, the impact of preliminary references is not always limited to its direct effect in that one case. As concluded by Alter & Vargas: "[P]rivate litigants may reveal to groups the potential of EC law, and create legal precedent that is later picked up by groups to promote changes in national policy. But the issue of follow-through is crucial if legal decisions are to lead to policy change, and one cannot assume that there will be follow-through on legal victories, especially for cases raised by individuals".[45] ECJ cases may, for example, serve as a signal to the Dutch government that further restrictions on entry would likely be struck down by the ECJ's interpretation of EU legislation. As we will see in *Case Study D,* which features a reference to the ECJ but no judgment, preliminary references can have an impact with or without an ECJ judgment. When strategic actors mobilise to challenge certain laws or policies, the possibility of a reference can be used as a source of leverage in itself, regardless of whether or not such strategy actually results in a judgment. While a legal strategy aimed at employing the restrictive qualities of EU law to curtail certain national policy may fail, an encompassing strategy, combining legal and political campaigns, using both the courts as well as lobbying the legislator, can be successful nonetheless. Such success thus doesn't necessarily rely on the potential in EU law alone. The threat of EU law, especially where the outcome of litigation is less certain and thus the risk for Member States is greater, can serve as a deterring force.[46] Similarly, new ECJ jurisprudence may serve as beacons or provide new arguments for practitioners, opening up new avenues for legal reasoning and possibly individual protection. However, such spin-off effects do not occur in a path-dependent fashion. Practitioners still have to actively adopt these new arguments. A judgment by the ECJ may help to mobilise lawyers to start using certain legal arguments they were reluctant to use before. One of the EU law experts involved in more strategic

45 Alter & Vargas 2000.

46 Similarly, even the 'Sunday traders', repeat players with almost unlimited resources, were not successful in having part of the British Shops Act, forbidding Sunday trading, declared incompatible with EU rules prohibiting quantitative restrictions on imports. The various references that were sent to the ECJ did not result in a favourable judgment to that part of the traders' cause. However, they were quite successful in their political campaign for a reform of said Sunday trading legislation, managing the support of unions, the British Labour Party, consumers as well as previous opponents, resulting eventually in a new Sunday Trading Act in 1994. As Micklitz (2005) describes: "Sunday traders succeeded due to their flexibility in shifting the issue back and forth between law and politics and to some extent also between the national and the European levels."

litigation describes his experience trying to convince lawyers of the relevance of EU law:

> "Whether you win or lose, judgments make your point visible, and you can use it in further litigation. It is also important for judges and lawyers, because they will only take an EU Directive seriously when there are judgments on it. One of the things I learned from these actions, as well as my teaching, is how unassertive lawyers can be. They will always have all sorts of reasons not to apply Union law. So you first need judgments to convince them of the relevance."

ECJ judgments can create a circular effect after being brought to the attention of interlocutors that are able to respond to, use and reify, or attack its results. In this case these interlocutors are practitioners that employ certain legal reasoning in new cases, and legal commentators and practitioners that use these arguments in publications, commentary, court proceedings as well as in imploring other actors to focus on them. With new ECJ (or national) judgments highlighting the importance of EU legislation, more lawyers may be inclined to use certain EU law arguments in cases they bring before national judges and with that facilitate the dissemination of certain interpretations of EU law, making national courts aware of the issues and possibly eliciting further references to the ECJ.

7.8 Networks and Alliances: A Learning Curve?

The case studies in the area of migration and asylum law show how strategic litigation within the context of EU law takes on various forms; from the more *post hoc* forms of cause litigation, by the interposing of strategic players at a later stage after a more unexpected referral (*Subsidiary Protection*), via setting out to challenge national policy by using EU law within a strategy worked out in advance (*Fees in Migration Law*), to the more structural organisation of lawyers, experts and organisation (*Integration Abroad*). Yet, they also show significant similarities. All these initiatives greatly rely on the input from (academic) experts in the field of EU (migration) law as well as different forms of support. Financial support is especially relevant when devising long-term strategies and when expertise and input is not available on a *pro bono* basis. Organisations like the Dutch Council for Refugees and the IOT thus played an important role in both providing the financial means and organizing capacity for such strategic efforts. Unless civil law action is possible, an individual case is needed. Cases are not always readily available; therefore the cooperation between lawyers, academics and interest organisations helps to connect case potential with expertise and strategic organisation. Networking, the deliberate exchange and bundling of skills, information and resources are important determining factors in the success of these legal strategies. Practitioners usually use the activation of networks as a coping strategy to deal with their lack of experience and expertise, while in other instances, networking is employed proactively. Bringing together scholars, lawyers and organisations helps to cover several bases of strategic legal action.

The experience from these past examples has pressed some of these actors to organise more structurally to cope with the systemic obstacles to their legal strategies. Learning especially from their experience in the case on the legality of integration tests, the Dutch Council for Refugees, several asylum lawyers and EU legal scholars have joined forces in the Strategic Litigation Committee (CSP) in order to more systematically and strategically litigate and bring principle matters before the ECJ. The strategy employed by the Committee is to formulate issues of EU and international law and to actively look for cases suitable for bringing before the European courts: the ECJ as well as the European Court of Human Rights. Such initiatives actively try to employ EU law and litigation as one of their modes of contesting national policies, by bringing together scholars and practitioners. Such efforts use networks of experts and practitioners to try and solve the misfit in that the (often less equipped) practitioners are the ones who potentially have cases, and scholars usually have the expertise. One way in which the CSP tackles the problem of finding a suitable case is by making use of the network provided by the Dutch Council for Refugees. The organisation has for a long time provided assistance to associated practitioners by means of a consultation service. This way they are able to respond to the needs of asylum lawyers by providing them with specialised legal expertise. One important additional advantage of this practice is that the Committee can tap into most of the available cases that are brought before the courts and select those that are most suitable for the legal strategy they have devised beforehand. Additionally, this system allows for putting out a general call to practitioners imploring them to bring cases that may suit one of the devised strategies. When trying to litigate on principle matters, this signalling of EU law opportunities is an important aspect. A vantage point on multiple cases provides the opportunity to tap into the case law potential.[47]

47 Cf. Harlow & Rawlings who discuss the availability of lawyers and legal advice as an important factor in determining success, the essential link with what they call 'control' being that "in-house lawyers are able to take control of potentially good cases at an early stage". Harlow & Rawlings 1992, 303.

7.9 Conclusion

Strategic litigation efforts can be important drivers of legal change through influencing jurisprudential development by bringing certain legal arguments and specific strategically chosen or framed cases. While most matters of EU law are dealt with by national judges, and references to the ECJ are a relatively infrequent phenomenon, the path to the ECJ may provide strategic actors with the possibility of outflanking a domestic system in deadlock. This chapter dealt with the question of strategic mobilisation of EU law and the preliminary reference procedure, and aimed to analyse who is most likely to make use of the opportunities in EU law and which legal strategies are effective. It identified characteristics specific to the preliminary reference system that provide the opportunity structure within which strategic actors may employ EU law. Within the context of EU law and the preliminary reference system, the uncertain nature of the preliminary references constitutes the most significant barrier to such coordinated action, since strategic actors lack control over when and how cases are brought before the ECJ. While the 'shield and sword' terminology, used by some to describe the potential of EU law and the preliminary reference procedure, may be adequate when speaking of the invoking of EU law in the national courtroom,[48] it is a rather optimistic characterisation when we look at the nature of the reference procedure and the practical way in which strategic actors are able to use it. From a strategic perspective the preliminary reference system is by no means an easy 'sword' to harness. Parties have limited control over whether or not their case actually gets a referral. This uncertainty of actually seizing the ECJ makes this type of strategic action more challenging. One has little control over which case is referred to the ECJ, with which legal and factual context. So the uncertainty accompanying 'going all in' on one case is multiplied by the fact that a national court may decide to refer a different case with different representation. One is left to approach those parties and offer one's expertise and support. This obviously takes away the possibility of 'building' a case from the ground up. Having a case with the right context and relevant characteristics can significantly increase one's chances of steering the final ECJ decision in a desirable direction. The opposite is also true; when the wrong case is referred within the context of the same principle matter this may lead to undesirable outcomes.

Due to the more general requirements of financial capital, organisational capacity, expertise and economies of scale, strategies that aim to include a reference to the ECJ are likely to be reserved for a select collection of interest groups and specialized lawyers. Moreover, given such obstacles, using EU law for po-

48 See for instance Tridimas & Tridimas 2004, 128.

litical ends in many cases may not be the most accessible avenue. However, given the more stringent migration policy and associated national judicial deadlock, for some underprivileged and politically underrepresented groups it may be one of the few options for truly benefiting from the rights provided by EU law. The existence of EU rights, the availability of resources, experts and organisational capacity as well as alliances with other actors like the European Commission provide the context within which EU law can be mobilised effectively. From this we can also infer the opposite; those with a limited capacity to (collectively) mobilise their interests will be less likely to (successfully) mobilise their rights.

Case Study D. Integration Abroad

D.1 Introduction: Investigating an Invisible Case

One of the salient aspects of preliminary references is the fact they may threaten to undermine national policies whenever questions sent to the ECJ are meant to address the legality of national policy in light of provisions in EU law. Member States are confronted with this function of the preliminary reference procedure and may choose to contain or even ignore detrimental ECJ judgments.[1] However, Member States may also choose to move strategically in order to prevent certain judgments by the ECJ that could threaten certain national policy. This case study discusses such an event. The case under study in the following chapter is a striking, yet fairly invisible preliminary reference case. As part of a string of ECJ cases on Dutch migration related policies, this case is well-known among scholars in the field of Dutch asylum and migration law, yet absent in the ECJ's official jurisprudence. The story of this case illustrates how national court cases can, through their referral to the ECJ, become a threat to existing national policy by subjecting it to supranational judicial review. Here, the referral was the result of collaboration between academia and a Dutch NGO that champions the rights of asylum seekers. It also reveals the ways in which national governments may respond to such a threat and can move to thwart a possible detrimental ECJ judgment. In this case study, an ECJ judgment that would have undermined Dutch policy on the requirement to pass a pre-entry integration test for people seeking asylum in the Netherlands was successfully prevented by the Dutch administration. The following case description provides an overview of the origins of the case, the way the Dutch government responded, as well as the subsequent attempts by the protagonists to attack Dutch policy by exerting more pressure through the courts.

D.2 The Contested Policy

In the post-2000 period, the Dutch government introduced a series of measures with the stated aim of better integrating its migrant population. These policies were adopted during a period of heightened public concern about the impact that migrant communities had on social cohesion. The two key measures were integration tests – one administered in the Netherlands that most foreign residents had to take, and another that had to be passed by prospective family migrants

1 Greer & Martín de Almagro Iniesta 2014.

from specific countries[2] before they could join spouses or family members in the Netherlands. The Civic Integration Abroad Act (*Wet Inburgering Buitenland*, from here on: WIB) came into effect on 15 March 2006. The WIB required a foreign national to complete a civic integration examination abroad if he or she was at least eighteen years old, before receiving a provisional residence permit (mvv) and being allowed entry into the Netherlands. An official self-study pack was developed, to help applicants prepare for the test, which included the requisite educational material to enable the applicant to speak, understand and read Dutch at the required level. It also included the material one needed to prepare for the 'Knowledge of Dutch Society' test; a controversial part of the test that was meant to assess one's basic knowledge of Dutch society.[3] The Netherlands was the first country in the EU to introduce such requirements.

The WIB was in line with a shift in Dutch politics towards more restrictive migration policies, and a focus on the integration of migrants into society, starting with the Law on the Integration of Newcomers in 1998. The tougher integration policies increasingly became a tool for restricting immigration. The legislation introduced in the early 2000s by then Minister Verdonk was controversial. It was changed by order of the Dutch Council of State several times, the last time even after its adoption by the House, after the Council of State concluded that immigrants with a Dutch passport were not to be discriminated against compared to natives with a Dutch passport. This decreased the number of people that eventually had to integrate to a total of 250,000. The WIB, as part of the larger policy on integration, was a precarious policy issue for the minority government that was backed by the right-wing PVV of Geert Wilders, which strongly focused on issues concerning immigrants.

D.3 Organizing Opposition

The case, which posed a challenge to the WIB, ended up at the ECJ in an interesting way. Digging into the context of the case reveals a story very similar to that of *Case Study C*. The migration law professor, who has been described as a central figure in the actions against the increases in administrative fees for residence permits, also takes centre stage in this story. Here, he was personally responsible for convincing the Dutch Council for Refugees (*Vereniging Vluchtelingenwerk Nederland,* from here on: the Refugee Council), a Dutch independ-

2 Citizens of European Union (EU) and European Economic Area (EEA) states and Switzerland, Australia, Canada, Japan, New Zealand, South Korea, and the United States (US) are not required to take the test.

3 Van Oers 2013.

ent, non-governmental organization that champions the interests of asylum seekers, to focus their efforts on helping asylum seekers not just with general personal support (like providing language courses) and legal counsel, but to also invest their efforts in actually fighting for the rights of refugees. He explains:

> "The case started because I was angry at the Refugee Council that they never showed some teeth. The board had asked me if I wanted to give a presentation about how I saw the development of refugee law and policy in the Netherlands, and the role of the Refugee Council therein. I then gave a presentation in which I said that they were too much focused on the integration of admitted refugees. And that their key task is to ensure that people receive protection, because no one else does that. So they asked me, how can we do that. Well, if you have a good case, then preliminary questions should be asked whether the Integration test complies with EU law. I told them, if you bring me a good case, I will help guide it."

As an important part of their activities the Refugee Council has, for a long time, been in constant contact with associated asylum lawyers, providing them assistance by means of a consultation service. In this way, they are able to respond to the needs of asylum lawyers by providing them with specialized legal expertise. One important additional advantage of this practice is that the Council can keep tabs on most of the cases that are brought before the courts and have an idea of what types of problems occur both inside and outside the courtroom. As a result, before long the appeal by the professor to come forward with a case got a response. The Refugee Council contacted the professor informing him that they had a possible candidate for addressing the legality of the Dutch WIB. Apart from facilitating the collaboration between the professor and an associated lawyer, the Refugee Council also filed a complaint with the European Commission, and implored the Dutch Ombudsman to look into the matter, which resulted in a damning report about the excessively strict application of the integration requirements by the Dutch administration.

D.4 Legal Contestation

A Dream Case

The husband of the client in this case, who had fled from Afghanistan in 2000, after initially being refused asylum, obtained a residence permit for the Netherlands through a general pardon in 2007. Meanwhile, he worked hard in the Netherlands to meet the income requirements, on the basis of which his family would be allowed entry under family reunification rules, and after that to support all eight of his children. After nine years, in 2009, he was finally reunited with his children, who had lived with their mother in a refugee camp in Pakistan. The application for a provisional residence permit for his wife, however, who had travelled with her children to the Dutch embassy in New Delhi, was refused. Her application was subject to the (new) Dutch rules under the WIB, which required her to first pass the civic integration test in Pakistan before she would be allowed to travel to the Netherlands. The client, however, only spoke Pashtu and was also illiterate. No textbook for preparing for said test in Pashtu existed, nor was assistance to the illiterate available at the time. This meant that she was expected to learn another language before being able to take the test. Generally, it was almost impossible to learn the necessary level of Dutch in Pakistan, let alone for someone who was illiterate. Although the Dutch government claimed that the test was also designed for people who were illiterate, her chances of passing the examination were virtually non-existent. To further complicate the situation, it was at the time not possible to take the examination in Afghanistan or Pakistan.[4] So, she would again have had to travel from Pakistan to the Dutch Embassy in New Delhi, India. A local branch of the Refugee Council that was assisting the husband of the client brought the case to the attention of one of the asylum and migration lawyers associated with the organisation. After the case was refused a second time in the objection stage it was brought before the District Court in Zwolle. At this stage the national office of the Refugee Council contacted the lawyer to inquire whether he would object to the involvement of the aforementioned professor. The lawyer, familiar with the professor's résumé, unsurprisingly responded favourably:

> "When he had heard of the case, the national office of the Refugee Council offered up his assistance in the case. Well, then thank you god on your bare knees, because that saved me an incredible amount of time. And what is much more important, look, I can do two things. I can take up what he writes neatly in my appeal and pretend I invented it myself. But I consciously chose to write briefly on what he had concluded, and then to refer to an annex of his opinion. Because let's face it, even with a court it is not only important what you say, but it's also very important who's talking."

The case in many respects was perfectly suited for the aim of attacking the legality of the Dutch policy on integration abroad, both at the national level, and as we will see later on, at the ECJ level as well. The circumstances of the client were clearly making it in every respect impossible for her to meet the require-

4 The Dutch embassy in Afghanistan had been closed for some time and the closest alternative Dutch embassy in Islamabad at the time only dealt with minor administrative tasks due to threats to the embassy, following the release of the controversial anti-Islam film 'Fitna' by Dutch right-wing MP Geert Wilders.

ments for passing the integration examination. Apart from her illiteracy and the fact that she only spoke Pashtu, the fact that her eight children were now separated from their mother (who had raised them for the past seven years) and were now staying with their father (whom they had not seen for the same period of time) added a layer of both poignancy and urgency. The lawyer had already hinted at a conflict with European law in the initial objection stage; however since this stage was only dealing with the Immigration and Naturalization Service (IND), the focus then lay in getting the authorities to make an exception based on humanitarian grounds. Once the case was brought before the court, the emphasis was put on the incompatibility of the WIB with the Directive on Family Reunification and on soliciting a reference to the ECJ.

The Road to the ECJ

Among other new EU legislation in the post-2000 period, Directive 2003/86 on the right to family reunification (from here on: the Family Reunification Directive) was an important potential source for attacking Dutch restrictive migration policies. The case focused on the compatibility of the WIB with especially Article 7(2) in the Family Reunification Directive. Although the Directive does stipulate in said Article that Member States are allowed to require third country nationals' family members to comply with integration measures before being granted family reunification, the ECJ had, in 2010, already concluded that family reunification was the general rule and that any condition to that rule had to be interpreted strictly.[5] The question of whether it was allowed to require family members to pass a pre-entry test before being allowed into the country was still an unanswered one. The professor proceeded to write the opinion for the lawyer, arguing that the pre-entry test was indeed problematic in light of the Family Reunification Directive:

> "It was just before the summer holidays, so on vacation in a cottage I wrote a note of I think eight pages. To explain why the integration test was incompatible with the Family Reunification Directive, on which points, and that the court should refer questions to the ECJ. So I suggested the questions, because I think that if you want to convince a judge to go as far as referring a question you must provide him all the arguments. And then you write it in a way that the lawyer can present it to the court."

5 C-578/08 *Rhimou Chakroun v Minister van Buitenlandse Zaken*.

With this expert opinion[6] in hand, the lawyer then started pushing for a preliminary reference. At the time, the possibility to refer questions to the ECJ was fairly new for lower courts dealing with asylum and migration matters,[7] and even more so given the recent implementation of the Family Reunification Directive.

Because the case involved eight children who were separated from their mother and under the supervision of child protective services, the court put in a request for the case to be dealt with under the urgent procedure (PPU).[8] The ECJ granted this request, which meant that the timeline in Luxembourg would be drastically shortened. Additionally, the PPU means that only the parties to the national proceedings, the Member State of the court making the reference and the EC institutions may submit written observations. Significantly, other Member States are not allowed to intervene in the written stage of PPU cases, preventing them from filing written observations. The time for filing written observations to the Court of Justice is fixed and significantly shorter than in usual reference cases.[9] While in other cases those involved may complain about the lengthy proceedings before the ECJ, in this case the shorter time frame was perceived as a challenge. The lawyer recalls:

> "Yes, the hearing date was really quick. It really is very fast. In my opinion it was really impossibly soon. It was only because [the professor] had practically written the observations that it was doable. But in terms of the amount of work, I found it unworkable."

6 The professor had also sent the note to Dutch online database Migratieweb.nl in order for other lawyers to use it to their advantage.

7 Since 1 December 2009, the reference procedure has been open to all courts and tribunals. Former Article 68 EC limited then Article 234 EC so that references in relation to the areas of freedom, justice and security (which included asylum) could only be made by national courts "against whose decision there is no judicial remedy under national law". However, there was a great deal of criticism of this limitation, given it fragmented the reference scheme, was detrimental to the rule of law and could lead to a vital area of Community or EU law being left outside supervision by the ECJ. See Broberg & Fenger 2014, 99.

8 The Protocol on the Statute of the Court of Justice was amended in 2008 to allow for the possibility of an urgent procedure in the areas covered by Title VI of the EU Treaty and Title IV of the EC Treaty (freedom, security and justice). The referring national court may request that the urgent procedure be applied or the Court of Justice may decide to apply it of its own motion in exceptional cases.

9 On average the duration of the written procedure in cases dealt with under the urgent preliminary ruling procedure is around seventeen days. See report on the use of the urgent preliminary ruling procedure, available at: https://curia.europa.eu/jcms/upload/docs/application/pdf/2012-07/en_rapport.pdf [last accessed 10 November 2017].

This 'true pressure cooker', as described by ECJ judge Prechal,[10] puts all of those involved under additional pressure, not just the parties, but also the other participants in the proceedings, most notably in this case the Dutch representation in Luxembourg.

D.5 Government Intervention

As per regular procedure, the case was brought to the attention of the agents of the Dutch government to inform them of the pending case and allow them time to prepare an observation. Agents of a national government at such a moment have the task, on the one hand, of analysing a case and preparing the legal arguments, but on the other hand, also to make assessments of the political salience and possible (legal) consequences of an ECJ judgment.[11] On the political sensitivity of the subject the then Dutch agent states:

> "The integration policy, as initiated by the Minister of Immigration and Integration and at the time of the case under responsibility of then Minister of the Interior and Kingdom Relations Donner, was politically very sensitive. It was quite clear that the policy regarding the WIB had to remain intact."

It became clear to the Dutch agents that the context in which the WIB was now put under scrutiny with this reference, did not bode well for the Dutch position. Additionally, the fact that a case with such high political salience was dealt with as an urgent procedure before the ECJ further complicated the matter. Instead of the regular two months, now the deadline for filing written observations was reduced to a maximum of three weeks. In the words of a then Dutch agent for the Netherlands:

> "The fact that it was a PPU was entirely justified, because it concerned so many children. But the case was not only highly sensitive from a political perspective, it represented a complex matter from a legal point of view. It is almost impossible in such a short time frame to address all factual and legal aspects of the case, the objectives of the WIB. For the Dutch government this was simply not a good case to be addressed as PPU."

From the perspective of the Dutch government, and the fact that the integration policies were an important part of a shift towards more stringent and restrictive

10 During a conference call presentation at a meeting for Dutch asylum lawyers in 2015.

11 Cf. Granger 2001, on the way (Dutch) representation before the ECJ deals with new references and the role they play in assessing the possible consequences of a judgment.

immigration policies, this preliminary reference was rather problematic. The context of the client's situation was such that it was by all means a case that qualified for an exception to the rule; a possibility the WIB provided for by means of a hardship clause, giving the Minister the authority to make exceptions in cases with exceptional circumstances. Nowhere in the development of this case, however, was a decision made to apply the clause.[12] By the time the case was brought before the ECJ it had turned into a threat to the policy as a whole, by providing a showcase for the extremely stringent way in which the policy was applied in the Netherlands.[13] The Dutch agents who reviewed the case did realise the severity of the situation and the possible consequences of having the ECJ assess the legality of the policy based on a case with such an inconvenient factual context:

> "We realised that the particular circumstances of the case would make the integration requirements of the WIB look extremely harsh and wondered whether it would be possible to explain to the Court the background, objective and all the nuances of the legislative system. It became clear to us that this would be very difficult in such a pressure cooker procedure. We were worried that the question would be answered by the Court based on the context of a case with rather extreme facts. This posed a real risk to the future of the WIB."

In the role of both legal representative of as well as advisor to the government of possible consequences of specific cases, the agent then informed the ministry of the imminent threat to the Dutch policy were this case to be decided upon by the ECJ. The assessment was that a similar question would eventually be raised again and would inevitably end up before the ECJ. The Dutch representation saw no way that the Netherlands would be able to win the case. The agent was invited to the ministry to personally clarify the consequences of the case.

> "Your role is to occasionally just to stand back and assess what is happening here and what the consequences may be. You should at least inform the Ministers in order for them to make an informed decision."

12 In reality, the clause was almost never applied, as concluded by the Dutch Ombudsman. Nationale Ombudsman, *Rapport Inburgeren in het Buitenland*, 2011/135, 2011, 36.

13 The report by the Dutch Ombudsman (at the insistence of the Refugee Council) dealing with whether exemption from the civic integration requirement is granted when this requirement in view of all the circumstances in a specific situation is not proportional, it was concluded on the application of the law by the IND: "[I]nstead of reviewing of all the relevant circumstances in their interrelationship, the Immigration and Naturalization Service in its daily practice assesses all circumstances separately and concludes - without any real exception - that none of these circumstances justify an exception." Nationale Ombudsman, *Rapport Inburgeren in het Buitenland*, 2011/135, 2011, 37.

The ministry, for the first time since the existence of the law, subsequently made an exception.[14] As is apparent from the official order of the ECJ, the Dutch ministry moved very quickly to inform the Court that a permit had been granted and that therefore the decision against which the appeal in the proceedings was directed had become inoperative. After consulting the referring national court as to the status of the case, the ECJ concluded that the main proceedings no longer had a purpose and that it was no longer necessary to give a ruling on the request for a preliminary ruling. Although the national court indicated that the parties were considering filing for damages, the ECJ reasoned this to be merely hypothetical. To the disappointment of the lawyer, the professor and the Refugee Council, the possibility of having the ECJ shine its light on the WIB was therefore successfully thwarted. In the end the lawyer did file for damages, which was resolved, at the insistence of the court, through mediation, with a settlement as a result.[15]

D.6 The Aftermath

The assessment of the Dutch agent in Luxembourg, that the questions regarding the Dutch policy would inevitably be raised again since 'it had now been discovered by lawyers', was accurate; however, it took longer than one might have expected. The lawyer, who was of course keen to bring the matter before the Court again, had trouble finding a new suitable case. He recalls:

> "After the first case, of course I had quite a lot of people who came to me, saying: I do not want to do my civic integration examination either. But it is then very practical, I just said to most clients, how much time and how much money do you have? Because that's what it comes down to. And my experience is that it's quicker to just do the test, and it is also cheaper than to litigate against it. And so, I only had one case where someone was willing to litigate it. Most people figured that someone else should go litigate and spend the money, and choose the safest way and just do the test. And that is the reason that despite the questions by [the court in Zwolle] it still took so very long before new questions are on the table."

The individual interest of applicants in receiving a provisional residence permit, effectively making passing the examination the preferable option to litigating for several years at increased costs, thus worked as a brake on possible cases to

14 The Ombudsman's report mentions one previous case; however that case was dealt with at a bureaucratic level due to its urgent nature, and was therefore not coordinated with central staff. Nationale Ombudsman, *Rapport Inburgeren in het Buitenland*, 2011/135, 2011, 29.

15 The settlement included a non-disclosure agreement as to the terms of the settlement.

bring the matter to a court's attention again. But finally, after two years, the lawyer found the case of a woman from Azerbaijan, who had to pass the integration examination abroad before she could join her husband in the Netherlands, willing to litigate on the matter. In that case, the court in Den Bosch concluded in first instance that passing an integration examination as a condition for family reunification was contrary to the Family Reunification Directive.[16] The court, controversially, based its judgment on the European Commission's position in the preliminary proceedings that never made it and the ECJ's judgment. It had been put forward by the lawyer in the proceedings, a point to which I will return later. He had also pressed again for a preliminary reference, proposing to reapply the questions posed in the earlier case; however the Dutch court concluded *ex officio* that, although Member States were allowed to require certain measures of integration, the requirement of passing the civics test abroad was incompatible with the Directive. It thus ruled that the Minister should grant his client a temporary residence permit. With this highly debated judgment, the court in Den Bosch effectively put the Council of State on the spot, since the court's conclusion on the incompatibility of the requirement of passing the test with the Directive forced the Council of State in onward appeal to either agree with the court or, if disagreeing or unsure, bring the matter before the ECJ. After a full seventeen months, joining this case with one other similar case,[17] the Council of State chose the latter. At this point the lawyer was assisted in drafting his observations for the ECJ by the so-called Migration Law Clinic of the Vrije Universiteit Amsterdam in which law students, under the supervision of EU migration law scholars, write custom-tailored legal advice for practising lawyers, non-governmental organisations and other actors in the field of migration law. In the time between the two cases, arguably due to the dust stirred up by the first, some of the context surrounding the subject of integration tests had changed. The Commission's Green Paper on the right to family reunification of third country nationals living in the European Union that was published in the course of the national proceedings in the second case especially had an impact on the direction of the ECJ's judgment.[18] Postdating the Commission's written observations in the first case, which were very critical towards the Dutch policy, the Green Paper indicated that the Commission did not consider the pre-entry test to be contrary to Article 7(2) of the Directive in every case.

16 Rechtbank 's-Gravenhage 23 November 2012, ECLI:NL:RBSGR:2012:BY4171.

17 Actors on both sides of the isle speculated on why the Counsel chose to combine two cases. While the professor speculated whether the Counsel wanted to prevent the Ministry from repeating what it did in the first case, the Dutch agent argued that the aim was to provide the ECJ with more context by adding a second case with a different factual background, allowing for a more balanced judgment.

18 European Commission 2011.

In July 2015, the ECJ held that the Directive, in particular Article 7(2) permitted a Member State to require a third country national to pass a civics test abroad before granting him or her permission to enter and reside on its territory under family reunification.[19] In addition, the Court concluded that the integration requirement for the exercise of the right to family reunification should not be impossible or excessively difficult and the principle of proportionality required that the integration requirement did not go beyond what was necessary to achieve the objective pursued. Ultimately, the ECJ thus concluded that the tests were, although with certain reservations, allowed because they were of a basic nature. The professor, however, pointed out that in the meantime the nature of the test in the Netherlands had changed:

> "It is clear that they now have made the test so difficult that even 60% of those with higher education do not pass the examination. But, even there we have formally lost the battle. And it was so unfortunate that the first judgment about the integration test abroad was not based on that first case."

D.7 The Traveling Commission Opinion

Although the first case never made it to a conclusion at ECJ level, it stirred up a significant response from different actors and can be placed in a complex dynamic of contestations of both Dutch and German integration policies. Even though the case was averted from being adjudicated by the ECJ, because of the accelerated procedure of the PPU the European Commission had already formulated and filed an opinion on the matter. This document showed a clear stance that the Dutch policy of structurally rejecting a provisional residence permit whenever the applicant had not passed the civic integration examination abroad undermined the aim (to promote family reunification) and the *effect utile* of the Directive. The European Commission concluded that Article 7(2) of the Directive did not permit a Member State to refuse the spouse or minor child of a lawfully resident citizen of a third country entry and residence 'solely on the ground that the family member has not passed the integration examination abroad prescribed by the law of that State'.

The stance by the Commission was a clear indication of the tenability of the WIB, or at least its application in practice, and it went on to play an important role in the wake of the thwarted preliminary reference. Even though it was not an official public statement but a court document that is generally not available to the public, the Commission's opinion found its way into the public arena.

19 C-153/14, *Minister van Buitenlandse Zaken v K and A*, para. 49 and 53.

After the case was concluded as described above, the opinion was published on *Migratieweb.nl*, a Dutch online knowledge database for migration related issues, focused especially on practitioners in the field of migration and asylum law. The Commission's opinion led to parliamentary questions.[20] In October 2011, the opinion also surfaced in Germany after which the *Bundesverwaltungsgericht*, going back to one of its own judgments of 2010, concluded that it had wrongfully neglected to refer questions to the ECJ on the compatibility of the German language test with Article 7(2) of the Family Reunification Directive. In its earlier judgment the court had effectively considered the matter an *acte clair*.[21] Two years later, on March 19th 2013, the Berlin *Verwaltungsgericht* referred questions to the ECJ about the compatibility of the language test with the Directive, resulting in the *Dogan* judgment of July 10th 2014.[22] *Dogan* was however not the first; the *Ayalti* case referred to the ECJ by the Berlin *Verwaltungsgericht* at the end of 2012 was meant to deal with the legality of integration tests in Germany.[23] However, similar to the dynamics described in this case study, this case was stricken from the ECJ's registry after a visa was granted to the applicant.

The Commission's Green Paper, published on November 15th 2011, revealed that the Netherlands had pressed for a change in the Directive, but as it turned out no other Member States felt this was a necessary step to take. In 2012, the European Commission started the informal phase of infringement proceedings against both Germany and the Netherlands for non-compliance with the Directive. In April 2013, the Dutch Deputy Minister of Security and Justice announced a loosening of the policy on family reunification of asylum seekers and accepted amendments proposed by parliament to simplify the policy for granting a residence permit to asylum seekers' family members.[24]

D.8 Deductions from an Invisible Case

Although the eventual success of the efforts in challenging the legality of the Dutch policy on integration tests was limited, this case is an exposé of how strategic actors may employ individual cases to attack national policies by invoking EU law. Especially important in this respect is the role of the professor in imploring an interest group like the Refugee Council to focus its efforts on the

20 *Aanh. Hand. TK* 2010-2011, nr. 3334.
21 BVerwG 25 March 2010, ECLI:DE:BVerwG:2008:160608B3B9.08.0.
22 C-138/13 *Naime Dogan v Bundesrepublik Deutschland.*
23 C-513/12 *Aslihan Nazli Ayalti v Bundesrepublik Deutschland.*
24 https://www.eerstekamer.nl/wetsvoorstel/33293_herschikken_gronden_voor [last accessed 10 November 2017].

rights and legal protection of their constituents as laid down in EU law. The Refugee Council, furthermore, had a tactical position in being able to bring together the expertise of the professor with a case that lent itself perfectly to the strategy of legally challenging Dutch policies. The organisation has for a long time provided assistance to associated practitioners by means of a consultation service. In this way they are able to respond to the needs of asylum lawyers by providing them with specialised legal expertise. One important additional advantage of this practice is that the Committee can tap into most of the available cases that are brought before the courts and select those that are most suitable for the legal strategy they have devised beforehand. Additionally, this system allows for putting out a general call to practitioners imploring them to bring cases that may suit one of the devised strategies. When trying to litigate on principle matters, this signalling of EU law opportunities is an important aspect. A vantage point on multiple cases provides the opportunity to tap into the case law potential.[25]

D.9 Changing Context, Same Questions?

The limited effect of the efforts of the professor and the Refugee Council are in large part explained by the fact that the preliminary reference was cut short before an ECJ judgment, which allowed for further developments that would drastically diminish the chances of success in subsequent cases. Political developments during the period between the first and the second round of preliminary questions resulted in a change in context, which arguably lessened the potential effect of the legal strategy. The interpretation of the relevant EU legislation at the time of the first case, as evidenced by the Commission's observations in that case, changed into a more generous reading, which allowed Member States more leeway in applying 'integration measures'. These developments also found their way into the questions that were put before the ECJ. In the first case the questions directly challenged the legality of the Dutch policy in light of the Reunification Directive, with the Dutch court asking:

> "Does Article 7(2) of the Family Reunification Directive allow a Member State to refuse entry and residence to a family member, as referred to in Article 4 of that directive, of a third country national lawfully residing in that Member State, exclusive-

25 Cf. Harlow & Rawlings who discuss the availability of lawyers and legal advice as an important factor in determining success, the essential link with what they call 'control' being that "in-house lawyers are able to take control of potentially good cases at an early stage". Harlow & Rawlings 1992, 303.

> ly on the ground that that family member has not passed the civic integration examination abroad as prescribed in the legislation of that Member State?"

After two years and with the intermediate publication of the Commission's Green Paper, the questions asked in the second case were much more detailed in nature, and in its questions the Dutch Council of State explicitly referred to the Commission's Green Paper. The Green Paper indicated that the Commission did not consider the requirement of a pre-entry test to be contrary to Article 7(2) of the Directive in every case. In this respect it might also be relevant that initially the questions came from a lower court, which might have been less concerned with the legal and political consequences of a question as compared to the Council of State that went into much more detail in its reference, thereby anticipating the possible impact of the ECJ judgment. Of these questions the lawyer states:

> "When you see these questions from the Council of State and the considerations of how they come to them, that really raises some eyebrows here and there. They gave us the question for review, but then we got the interim ruling and then we saw the considerations, and then you think, huh? They actually decide things in advance when there is a real possibility that the Court thinks otherwise, so that's really weird. One of the very important points, and that played in the first case as well, is whether there is a translation error in the Dutch version of the Directive. The Council of State has already decided that it did not think that there is a translation error. Well, that's very strange because in his conclusion, the Advocate General does conclude there is a translation error. I don't understand why they would run the risk of embarrassing themselves."

Even though in the Netherlands it is quite common practice for the court to provide the preliminary questions to the parties for review, the parties are limited in the amount of influence they have over the framing and scope of the questions. Especially in light of the way in which the ECJ is relatively limited in its handling of cases by the framework as provided by the referring court, this can be an opportunity or present itself as an obstacle to strategic actors. However, it must also be emphasized that the ECJ itself does sometimes reformulate the questions, or goes beyond the scope of the questions as formulated by the referring national court.[26]

26 Broberg & Fenger 2010, 349.

D.10 The Withdrawal of References

The most interesting element in the developments in this case, the actions by the Dutch government, illustrate the power of Member States' administrations to influence the types of cases the ECJ gets to pass judgment on. In the case of residence permits, the possibility of preventing a reference or a judgment are relatively straightforward, since the provision of a residence permit generally takes away the standing of litigants. In this case, the Dutch government acted very quickly and informed the ECJ of the permit that was provided. The Dutch government was very fast in its actions, and on the client's side the response was not fast enough. Filing for damages in this case would have retained her legal interest in a resolution of the questions referred to the ECJ. However, developments happened so quickly that the request by the ECJ to the referring court inquiring whether or not its intention was to continue their request came before the lawyer was able to officially file for damages. At that stage the ECJ decided that the intention to bring an action for damages was merely hypothetical. This consideration by the ECJ contrasts with the Court's own decision in *Siemens AG Österreich* where admissibility was considered acceptable, since the Court could not exclude the possibility that an answer to the question could still be of interest to the resolution of the dispute in the main proceedings.[27]

Generally, if a party withdraws or the government concerned grants a residence permit, or something similar, to the asylum applicant and a settlement is thereby reached in the main proceedings then the referring court or tribunal is expected to withdraw the reference on its own initiative in order to save the ECJ time and expense. In this case the ECJ decided, after being informed by the Dutch government of the granting of a permit and asking the Dutch referring court about its intention, not to answer the questions. However, the fact that the government gives some kind of residence permit is not necessarily a reason for the national court to withdraw the reference. In other cases the ECJ has taken a different stance. In *Baumbast* the Court noted that the permits had been granted under national law and so the question of the rights conferred under EU law on the persons concerned had therefore not been resolved.[28] In *Bernini* one of the reasons the referring court decided to maintain the reference was that the questions were also relevant to other pending cases. [29] Therefore, although the Court could have decided one way or the other, the Dutch administration was successful in preventing a likely disastrous decision by the ECJ with regard to its policy on integration tests. The examples of similar cases in Germany suggest that such

27 See Broberg & Fenger 2010, 165-6.

28 C-413/99 *Baumbast and R v Secretary of State for the Home Department*, paras. 29-38.

29 C-3/90 *M.J.E. Bernini v Minister van Onderwijs en Wetenschappen.*

a strategy may be more common than is visible to the outside observer and illustrates Member States' ability to 'play the Eurolaw game' by attempting to control the ECJ's docket.

8 Preliminary Reference as a Multiplier of Interests

8.1 Introduction

Previous chapters have illustrated how a reference to the ECJ may transform a single court case into a possible jurisprudential precedent in which both national and EU governance is fought out, with opportunities for strategic actors to challenge national policy and influence the course of European integration. One peculiar aspect of the EU legal system is that at the ECJ level the legal arena is opened up to other interested parties. After referral to the ECJ, both individual litigants and strategic actors with considerably more organisational capacity and legal agency may then find themselves in the company of other actors with their own agendas. A conventional view of law and litigation relies heavily on an adversarial view of disputes, with two parties, supported by their lawyer advocates, advancing their own interests by pleading their case against that of their adversaries. When it comes to the preliminary reference procedure, it is important to distinguish between different adversaries (or allies for that matter). Even if one considers the reference part of a case as a formalistic procedure and not an actual part of the dispute *per se*, the fact that questions are asked in order to enable a judgment at the national level makes these procedures essential moments in any case.

Therefore, it is important to consider the changing dynamics in the case of a referral to the ECJ. References to the ECJ can, and often do, transform a case from a localised dispute into a matter of significance for interests that may exist at other levels. The reference by a national court to the ECJ means that, because it breaks out of the confines of the national legal system, the context changes and the possible effects of a case become supranational. At that point a host of other potentially interested actors may be mobilised. Most prominently among them are the European Commission and (other) Member States – who have direct access to the proceedings before the ECJ. Theoretically, the European Parliament, the European Council, (and the European Central Bank for that matter) also have privileged access to ECJ proceedings and third parties may be introduced into proceedings by the ECJ itself. In this analysis, I exclude these other actors. On the one hand, because they are simply absent in all of the cases studied, and on the other hand, because they have a limited stake when it comes to the type of 'game' that is played with regard to the type of preliminary references central to this study.[1] This chapter will focus on the relationship between the litigating parties with these two most prominent actors and on the role that

1 Stein 1981, 8.

they play in the dynamics of a case before and after referral.[2] The first section addresses the European Commission and its role in the enforcement of EU law before analysing some of the ways in which private parties may encounter the European Commission during litigation. The second section zooms in on the position of the Member States and the structural and practical advantages they enjoy as a repeat player, compared to private parties.

8.2 The European Commission: Repeat Player *Par Excellence*

The European Commission is a key player when it comes to ECJ adjudication. As a privileged actor it has structural access to the ECJ and acts as an *amicus* to the Court by systemic participation in every case brought before it, both in direct actions and preliminary reference cases. As an institutional actor the Commission provides legal expertise and policy guidance as well as contextual information in specific court proceedings, and as a central institutional player in policy development and the drafting of legislation it plays an important part outside the Court as well. As an *amicus* of the Court the Commission has been credited with successfully pushing towards more legal integration in close alliance with the Court, as well as essentially fashioning the legal arguments that led to the constitutionalisation of European law. The Commission is thus involved in most instances of decision-making by the ECJ and is in that way the European repeat player *par excellence*.

Empirical studies on the outcome of proceedings before the Court of Justice have repeatedly demonstrated a high rate of success for the Commission.[3] Börzel finds that between 1978 and 1999, the European Commission won 95% of the infringement cases that were adjudicated by the Court.[4] In the case of preliminary references the Commission appears to have a similarly positive record. Stone Sweet and Brunell show how in situations where the Commission and Member States have opposed one another before the ECJ, the ECJ has ruled in favour of the position taken by the Commission in a majority of the cases.[5] For those seeking enforcement of their EU rights, the European Commission may thus be a powerful ally, given its institutionalised position as one of the

2 Third parties are only scarcely employed by the ECJ. See Carrera & Petkova (2013, 245-246) on the role and the potential for future involvement of civil society in third party interventions before the European Courts.

3 Conant 2007, 53.

4 Börzel 2006, 33. Schepel and Blankenburg have commented that, in the case of infringement proceedings "its success rate is so high as to make the ECJ look like a kangaroo court – being the baby in the pouch of the mother, it has to follow wherever the Commission goes". Schepel & Blankenburg 2001, 18.

5 Stone Sweet 2010; Stone Sweet & Brunell 2012, 212.

privileged players at the ECJ. Conversely, from the perspective of the Commission, individuals seeking justice are part of the institutional setup designed to foster EU law enforcement and by extension Member States' compliance with EU law. The next section deals with both the theoretical and practical *consociation* between individual claimants and the Commission.

8.3 The Commission as Guardian of the Treaties

Traditionally, it has been the formal role of the Commission to safeguard the effectiveness of EU rules and rights. Within the EU, the Commission is charged with the active protection and promotion of the interests of the Union and, in tandem with the ECJ, is responsible for ensuring that EU law is properly applied in all the Member States. In its 2001 White Paper on European governance, the Commission reiterated that the primary responsibility for the implementation of Union law lies with national administrations and the Member States' courts.[6] However, as so-called *guardian of the treaties* the European Commission has the formal task of safeguarding the timely implementation of new EU legislation and the effective application of EU law, including the rights that individuals may derive from them.

Whenever Member States are suspected of not fulfilling their obligations under EU law, the Commission can move to ensure compliance. Formally the Commission has several different instruments at its disposal in order to do this. The Commission enjoys powers of investigation (securing any information and carrying out any checks required for the performance of its duties), prevention (by informal meetings, opinions, recommendations or binding acts), sanction (to be imposed on Member States and on companies, especially in the case of competition law) and authorisation (allowing for the temporary suspension of the application of EU law). The Treaties confer powers upon the Commission to institute proceedings before the Court of Justice if it considers that a Member State has failed to fulfil an obligation under a Treaty.[7] If the Commission notes such failure, the state concerned is asked to submit its observations. If the Member State is then still considered to be in violation, the Commission delivers a reasoned opinion, with which the state must comply within the time limit laid down therein. If the state in question does not comply, the Commission may bring the matter before the Court of Justice by means of infringement proceedings. The continual supply of new legislation means that the Commission is in a

6 European Commission 2001.
7 Article 258 TFEU.

virtually constant dialogue with Member States in order to ensure timely and effective EU law implementation.

To perform its task, the Commission has the discretion to choose the instrument it considers most effective, expedient and appropriate in different situations of implementation and application deficiency.[8] The Commission summarizes its own role as stimulating the Member States to comply with Union law as quickly as possible, for which it ultimately has the infringement procedure at its disposal. In order to keep tabs on the implementation of EU legislation at the national level, the Commission may start an investigation on its own initiative or respond to complaints or requests by other parties. Due to its limited investigative means, the Commission is very much dependent upon signals it receives from within Members States and information provided by national administrations whenever it investigates a possible breach of EU law. The Commission therefore emphasizes the significant role played by the complaints it receives from the public, businesses and NGOs in signalling possible breaches of Union law. The Commission receives between 3,000 and 4,000 such complaints annually.[9]

The Commission has, in both practice and policy, shown a preference for more cost-effective, non-litigious rule enforcement through informal resolution.[10] Although informal pre-litigation actions are frequent, the Commission brings alleged infringements before the Court in only a minority of those cases. By compiling the total number of Article 258 infringement procedures since 1978, Börzel shows that the Commission made ample use of its compliance powers, opening more than 20,000 proceedings against Member States.[11] Yet, only a fraction of these cases resulted in judgments by the ECJ. In practice, both the Commission and Member States make efforts to resolve allegations without Court proceedings. Between 1978 and 1999, two-thirds of the nearly 17,000 procedures were settled after the informal (and confidential) phase and before the procedure entered the formal phase. In fact, even during the formal part of the procedures, discussions between the Commission and Member States continued. A further two-thirds of the remaining cases were settled subsequent to the reasoned opinion issued by the Commission, and of the 1,619 referrals to the

8 It is important to point out that the Commission should by no means be considered a monolith in its policies and actions and many decisions are made on a case-by-case basis and approaches may differ considerably between different policy fields and between or even within the different Directorates-General. While acknowledging this nuance, for brevity, I will stick to denoting all actions as performed by *the Commission*.

9 Additionally, petitions by citizens to the European Parliament as well as questions from Members of Parliament can raise perceived deficiencies in the way Member States apply EU law. See European Commission 2013, 6.

10 Weatherill 2014, 86.

11 Börzel 2003.

ECJ only 972 actually resulted in a Court ruling. This trend of pre-litigation resolution continues to this day: in 2014 only thirty-eight infringement cases were resolved through a Court judgment.[12]

Looking further at the statistics of the ECJ (Figure VI) we can see that the number of infringement cases brought before the ECJ has, since peaking in 2007, been declining steadily to below 100 annually in recent years.

Figure VI: New cases brought before the Court of Justice

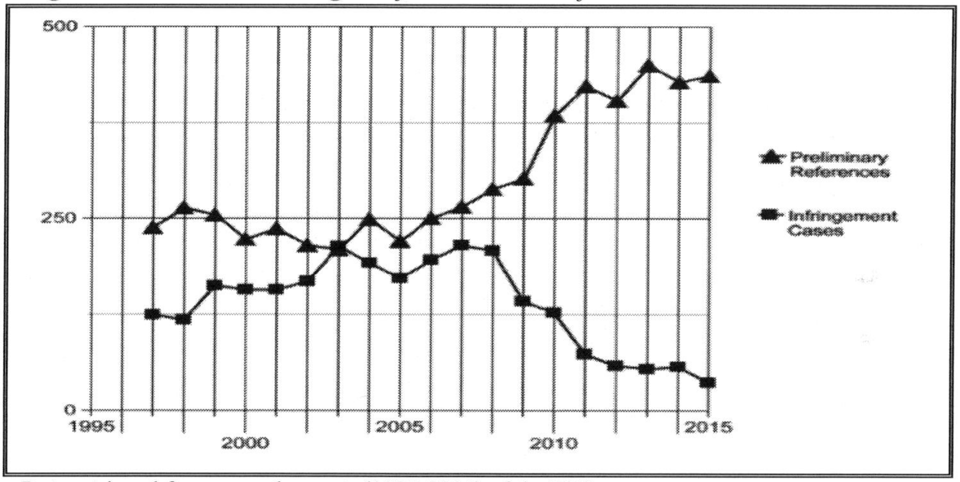

Data retrieved from annual reports (1997-2015) of the ECJ. www.curia.europa.eu.

Although on average the number of complaints remained constant or even increased slightly in the period after 2010,[13] the number of letters of formal notice fell by approximately half between 2011 and 2012 and the number of cases brought before the Court declined at an ever higher rate; from 216 in 2007 to only thirty-seven in 2015. This downward trend follows some major revisions to the Commission's infringement management after 2007.[14] The Commission set out to improve its operations in the areas of prevention (by increased attention to implementation throughout the policy cycle), efficient and effective response

12 In 2014, a total of 797 infringement cases were closed by the Commission before Court proceedings, either after the initial letter of formal notice (580 cases), after the issuing of a reasoned opinion by the Commission (190 cases) or the cases were withdrawn from the Court after being filed (11 cases). In addition, the Commission withdrew sixteen cases from the Court before it handed down its ruling. European Commission 2014, 15.

13 With the lowest number of complaints at 3,115 in 2011 to the highest number of 3715 in 2014. http://ec.europa.eu/atwork/applying-eu-law/docs/annual_report_32/com_2015_329_en.pdf [last accessed 10 November 2017].

14 European Commission 2007.

(by improving the exchange of information and problem-solving), improving its working methods (by prioritising and accelerating infringements management) and enhancing dialogue and transparency (between the European institutions and improving information for the public).

One important new measure in this respect was the introduction of 'EU Pilot', a Commission initiative, supported by an online database and communication tool, aimed at 'providing quicker and better answers to questions raised by citizens or businesses and solutions to those problems arising in the application of EU law'.[15] Through the structured dialogue in the EU Pilot programme, the Commission and Member States are expected to solve problems more quickly and expedite the achievement of compliance with EU law obligations without having to resort to infringement proceedings. The new system was introduced in a number of volunteer Member States in 2008 and currently all twenty-eight Member States are participating in it. The new system is considered to be responsible in significant part for a reduction in the number of infringement procedures[16] and eventual court cases by an increase in early resolution. According to the Commission: "The structured dialogue via EU Pilot has proven effective in the early resolution of potential infringements, to the benefit of citizens and business alike."[17] In addition to the reported success of the EU Pilot programme, according to the Commission resulting in more pre-litigation resolutions, structural factors may have also contributed to this trend. Among them is a decrease in new Directives that were introduced in the period 2008-2012, leading to a related decrease in possible late transposition infringements, which take up, on average, about a third of the infringement procedures.[18]

8.4 Preliminary References as Alternative Enforcement

The structured nature of the dialogue between the Commission and Member States creates the impression that the enforcement actions of the Commission are systemic and automatic. However, the Commission has full discretion to choose the way in which it acts on suspected infringements. In addition to the structural factors that largely account for the downward trend in infringement

15 European Commission 2010a, 8.

16 The term 'infringement procedure' denotes the formal infringement phase where (at least) a letter of formal notice has been sent to the Member State, in most cases after informal bilateral discussion between the Commission and the Member State. This does not yet mean that the case has been brought before the ECJ but does mean that the Commission (after the informal phase) considers that there has been a violation of EU law obligations.

17 European Commission 2013, 16.

18 European Commission 2012, 2.

proceedings, there is another related development that illustrates the Commission's freedom to choose the instruments it employs. Looking at the trend in the number of cases brought before the Court in its totality, we see that conversely to the decrease in infringement cases there has been a significant increase in the number of preliminary references that have been brought before the Court since 2008. Apart from more structural factors that may explain the converse trends in preliminary references and infringement actions (more pre-litigation resolution for infringement actions and an increase in the total number of Member States referring preliminary cases to the ECJ since 2004), there is reason to believe that the Commission views the preliminary reference procedure as a viable alternative to its own efforts – either on its own initiative or based on complaints – to force Member States' compliance.[19] In its own analysis, the Commission linked the two trends:

> "The overall decrease of the number of infringement procedures can be put in relation to the important increase of preliminary rulings under Article 267 TFEU since 2010. [...] Whilst preliminary rulings are distinct from infringement judgments, this gives the Commission an additional opportunity to ensure in a more systematic manner that violations of Union law deriving from national legislation or its application are remedied."[20]

According to the Commission's own reporting, conformity issues of national laws in regard to EU legislation took up about half of the ECJ's judgments in preliminary reference cases in the period 2010-2014. This confirms the idea that for the Commission, from the perspective of ensuring Member States' compliance, preliminary reference cases form an alternative to the initiation of infringement proceedings. Even when counting only preliminary references concerning conformity issues (approximately half), preliminary reference cases have outnumbered infringement proceedings by approximately five-to-one on average over the past five years.[21] The increase in references may thus be a welcome development for the Commission; reducing significantly the time and resources that it would otherwise have to spend in the run-up to infringement proceedings. The more EU law violations are brought before the ECJ through national courts, the more the Commission can focus its resources elsewhere.[22] Preliminary reference cases provide the Commission with the ability to repri-

19 Hoffmann 2016.

20 European Commission 2013, 16.

21 This difference grows even larger when excluding the 25-35% late transposition infringement cases.

22 A lack of resources, of both Commission and national competition authorities, was explicitly named by the Commission as one of the advantages of private enforcement when it comes to competition rules and actions for damages. European Commission 2005.

mand a Member State while consolidating European integration through the Court, without having to initiate infringement proceedings. These developments fit with an emerging picture of general shifts in modes of regulation, towards a greater emphasis on private enforcement.[23]

8.5 Two Pathways to Allying with the Ultimate Repeat Player

Changing our perspective from that of the Commission to those seeking to have their EU rights enforced, the Commission is an attractive actor to have on one's side. Once court proceedings are initiated, the Commission enjoys a privileged position before the Court. In infringement proceedings the Commission acts essentially as the prosecutor, bringing a Member State to Court, and in the case of preliminary references the Commission is always among those informed of new references and effectively acts as an *amicus* of the ECJ. The Commission is therefore potentially a powerful ally for private parties seeking to address possible violations of their EU rights by Member States, or in other ways furthering their interests through EU law.

From the perspective of private actors that seek the Commission's support in having their EU rights enforced, there are two pathways to doing so. Firstly, individuals may choose to file a complaint in order to inform the Commission of a possible infringement of EU law obligations and violation of their rights in the hope of moving it towards using its enforcement powers to ensure compliance by the Member State. And secondly, private parties may take their grievance to national courts and invoke a reference to the ECJ where they may find the Commission as one of the privileged parties that participate in the proceedings. From the perspective of strategic actors aiming for an ECJ judgment on a matter, both pathways essentially provide access points. Both preliminary references and complaints to the European Commission can end in an ECJ judgment; however, from the perspective of individuals there are a number of important differences between these two 'pathways to compliance'.

Complaining to the Commission has some significant drawbacks. Firstly, the most important issue is the uncertainty related to whether or not the Commission will decide to start procedures. The Commission's discretion gives no guarantee as to whether one's complaint yields a follow-up. Secondly, assuming the Commission does decide to act on a complaint (and assuming it acts without delay) the procedure from the first informal contact between Commission and Member State to a potential referral to the ECJ takes around four years on aver-

23 In environmental law: Hofmann 2016; competition law: Wigger & Nölke 2007; and consumer protection: Kelemen 2011.

age.[24] The eventual court case will add several months to years to the total duration. Although presented as a success by the Commission itself, the long pre-litigation process of the EU Pilot Programme has been criticized for potentially extending the duration of the process further and undermining the claim that compliance through the threat of prosecution always results in a swift end to non-compliance. This conclusion by the Commission should be considered with further reservation, as there is no real way of ascertaining whether or not such cases were actually resolved and thus lead to compliance or whether they have a different result.[25] Furthermore, as argued by Smith, it allows Member States to comply at the last possible opportunity in order to reap any financial or political benefits that could have been gained through non-compliance for the longest time possible. We have seen an example of this in *Case Study C* where the Dutch government managed to play out the contestation of the amount of administrative fees it charged for residence permits for the longest possible time. The legal battle over the increase in fees continued well after the ECJ judgment found that the Netherlands was in violation of the standstill clause in the Association Agreement with Turkey. Subsequent claims for restitution of the unlawfully levied fees resulted in a declaration by the Dutch Council of State that there was a refund scheme only for Turkish nationals, although the announcement of this scheme also immediately meant the end of it.[26] Many Turkish nationals therefore were never able to reclaim the fees through these 'transitional arrangements', and the Dutch government was able to retain millions of euros of unlawfully charged fees.

During such a prolonged process, the individual complainant receives no interim relief for his or her grievance. As the Commission itself acknowledges: "Only a national tribunal can apply remedies like injunctions to the administrations, cancellation of national decisions, damages etc."[27] The Commission does not have the power to apply these kinds of measures of judicial protection. Thirdly, in infringement actions the complainant is not a party to the proceedings and has little input compared to preliminary references, where parties have the ability to participate in the proceedings and provide their own legal argumentation. This is, of course, especially relevant for strategic actors aiming not only for the enforcement of a specific right but for a judgment on principle by

24 Most procedures initiated by the Commission never reach the Court and will be resolved in the preceding phases. Smith 2010, 557.

25 For example, the Commission has powers of authorisation and may allow for the temporary suspension of the application of EU law. Which would not resolve the right claim of the complaining individual.

26 Raad van State 2 September 2011, ECLI:NL:RVS:2011:BR6949. For a review see Schaap 2014, 432.

27 European Commission 2007, 8.

the ECJ on a broader issue. And finally, even after the procedure has been completed and a Member State has been deemed in violation of its obligations, compliance is not always effectively ensured. At the end of 2013, the Commission considered that 113 judgments passed under Article 258 TFEU had still not been fully complied with by the Member States concerned.[28]

The next section deals with the relationship between the Commission and litigating parties and illustrates the ways in which parties may (or may not) ally themselves with the Commission, both inside and outside the courtroom. The cases in the selection for this study are used to reveal several instances where the Commission has played a role in the development of a case, both where the parties have made efforts to mobilise the Commission, as well as cases where the Commission has acted on its own initiative and intervened.

8.6 Mobilising the Commission

From the perspective of the litigating parties the Commission can be a powerful ally to have on their side, and thus an attractive actor to mobilise. The case of the Working Group together with the interest group IOT (*Case Study C*), and their experience with organized litigation as well as filing complaints to the Commission, reveals several ways in which the Commission may respond to complaints. The group of lawyers, academics and the IOT, previous to their efforts against the Dutch fees policy, had built up some experience with organised litigation and strategic action at the supranational level.[29] The very first complaint this group filed to the Commission was with regard to the Dutch *Export Restrictions on Benefits Act*. In that effort, contact with the Commission played a vital role. In response to their complaint, the Commission communicated that it would not proceed with infringement proceedings, because the matter was deemed too politically sensitive.[30] Officials of the Directorate of Social Affairs subsequently suggested that the IOT lawyer should try to solicit a preliminary reference in the national courtroom. "The Commission's opinion will be certainly much more definite and pronounced. And of course I will also be willing to provide informal assistance," they informed the lawyer.[31] The Commission was in this instance not ready to risk the political backlash of starting infringement procedures on such a sensitive issue. Instead, they showed the IOT the way through the national courts.

28 European Commission 2013.
29 For an extensive overview of the supranational efforts of the IOT, see Groenendijk, Rondhuis & Strik 2015.
30 Groenendijk, Rondhuis & Strik 2015, 28.
31 Groenendijk, Rondhuis & Strik 2015, 28.

At the request of the IOT's lawyer, the Commission did write a letter that included its position that Article 6 (1) of Decision 3/80, which prohibits restricting the export of benefits, had direct effect and could thus be used directly in the national courtroom. That letter was subsequently presented by the lawyer to the Dutch courts, of which the Amsterdam Court followed the Commission's interpretation on the direct effect of Article 6. After appeal, the Council of State referred that case to the ECJ. This led to the judgment in *Export of Benefits* that had far-reaching consequences for the interpretation of the Association Agreement, in line with what the IOT's initial complaint had intended to accomplish.[32] The ECJ judgment meant that export of benefits under various Dutch laws couldn't be limited or discontinued. Having built up experience with these proceedings, the IOT and the Working Group subsequently sought to use the complaints procedure to implore the Commission to use its enforcement action against the Netherlands on several different issues.[33] It became a natural step for the group to include a complaint to the Commission in their litigation strategies. The IOT eventually chose the path of the national courtroom on several occasions, as we have seen, sometimes on explicit advice from the Commission, after it decided not to proceed with infringement proceedings.

From the perspective of the litigating parties, making use of the Commission and infringement action can be an important signal to both national administrations as well as to one's constituency and the public at large. The mere fact that the European Commission is actively engaged in investigating a possible infringement by a Member State helps to legitimise one's claim and further mobilise one's constituency. Court judgments in infringement actions can subsequently be used to apply further pressure on Member States' administrations. From the perspective of the Commission, such actions (the letter provided to the IOT lawyer) could be considered somewhat of a non-formalized 'cousin' to the formalised mechanism that was set out in Article 15(1) of Regulation 1/2003, pursuant to which courts of the Member States may contact the Commission and ask it to give its opinion on questions concerning the application of EU competi-

32 Apart from the explicit advice of the Commission to the IOT to pursue a preliminary reference, in two other cases complaints by the IOT were deemed unfounded by the Commission, yet later PRP cases resulted in ECJ judgments to the same effect: C-578/08 *Rhimou Chakroun v Minister van Buitenlandse Zaken* and C-7/10 *Staatssecretaris van Justitie v Tayfun Kahveci and Osman Inan*. Both lawyers in the latter case were also involved in the IOT Working Group described in *Case Study C*. One of them was responsible for the initial complaint to the European Commission that led to case C-92/07 *European Commission v Netherlands*.

33 Including restrictions on the export of benefits, income requirement for family reunification, dual nationality, administrative fees for permits, and later on the limited restitution for the unlawfully levied fees, integration requirements, and the country of residence principle. Groenendijk, Rondhuis & Strik 2015.

tion rules – albeit in this case on the initiative of one of the parties instead of the national judge. In a sense this goes against the Commission's own reservations about its role in national proceedings. As it ensures with regard to its neutrality and objectivity in the case of such an *amicus* intervention in proceedings before the national courts:

> "Indeed, the Commission's assistance to national courts is part of its duty to defend the public interest. It has therefore no intention to serve the private interests of the parties involved in the case pending before the national court. As a consequence, the Commission will not hear any of the parties about its assistance to the national court. In case the Commission has been contacted by any of the parties in the case pending before the court on issues which are raised before the national court, it will inform the national court thereof, independent of whether these contacts took place before or after the national court's request for co-operation."[34]

This general stance by the Commission was confirmed by a Commission official stating that it did not wish to 'transform into an investigator for the benefit of national litigation at the request of national courts'.[35] Ostensibly, the Commission is cautious in its aid to private parties, for the interests of those parties often go against the interests of the Member States. The open support by the Commission for certain private interests is therefore a politically sensitive issue. However, these private party interests may coincide with those of the Commission, and private enforcement allows for a reinforcement of the Commission's own efforts. When private interests align with its priorities, preliminary reference cases provide the Commission with an opportunity to fulfil its enforcement mandate. The Commission thus on occasion can be seen to interpret this principle of fulfilling the role of *amicus* of national courts, but explicitly not of serving private interests, somewhat more freely than it portrays publicly. This means encouraging developments outside the courtroom as well, directly or indirectly lending a helping hand to private parties.

In the example given above, the Commission's actions outside the courtroom occur as a response to attempts at mobilisation of the Commission by private parties. However, the Commission is not only reactive in its efforts to use preliminary references as an alternative enforcement instrument. The next section deals with examples where the Commission influences developments outside the courtroom, even without an explicit request by the parties involved.

34 European Commission 2004, para. 19.
35 As reported in Komninos 2003, xxx.

8.7 Unsolicited Alliances: The Commission Behind the Scenes

Although actively trying to mobilise the Commission can be a viable strategy, the Commission can also become an ally in an unsolicited way. This is, of course, the case when one's claim in court is backed by the Commission's interpretation of EU law before the ECJ after referral. But the Commission also has its own policy objectives and on occasion also plays a role that is less visible to the outside observer. Several of the cases studied reveal instances where the Commission was active both in front of as well as behind the scenes. A case in point is the *Self-Employed Tax Deductions* case discussed in Chapter 5. This case involved a small accountancy firm in a border region of the Netherlands. In order to serve their clients, many of whom engaged in cross-border activities, the firm set out to get a judgment on principle on the question of whether or not tax deductions for the self-employed should apply to anyone regardless of whether or not they opted for treatment as a resident taxpayer.[36] The firm took the difference in treatment of resident versus non-resident entrepreneurs to be a possible case of discrimination within the context of the right to freedom of establishment, and started a test case. The goal and expectation in this test case was to get a ruling from the Dutch Supreme Court, not a reference to Luxembourg. After the Supreme Court unexpectedly decided to refer the case to Luxembourg, the accountancy firm decided, since no one in the office had any experience with preliminary references, to await the answers by the ECJ without any active participation in the proceedings before the Court. With this referral to the ECJ, the context of the case changed from an internal question to one of compliance with EU tax regulations by the Dutch government, opening it up to additional interested parties.

Since this case revolved around this central matter in the 'European plan' (uniform application of EU law, negative integration and a fundamental European principle; non-discrimination based on nationality) once these questions were on the table, the Commission seized the opportunity, not only by providing a

36 To make the income tax 'EU proof', the Netherlands had introduced the so-called option scheme in the 2001 Income Tax Act. Non-resident taxpayers could choose to be charged as residents, even if less than 90% of their total income came from the Netherlands. This way they were entitled to tax credits, personal deductions and deductions of mortgage interest for a private property located abroad. Up until the change in Dutch tax law in 2001 non-Dutch companies with a permanent establishment in the Netherlands were excluded from entrepreneurial deduction, among which was a tax deduction for the self-employed. In order to be eligible for this deduction, entrepreneurs had to meet an annual criterion of 1225 hours worked. Any entrepreneur could count the hours he worked for his company in order to be eligible for the self-employed deduction. However, entrepreneurs with a permanent establishment in another Member State were not allowed to count the hours worked across the border.

'more definite and pronounced' opinion in their role as an *amicus* of the Court, but also by intervening on the side of the parties. After the Dutch Supreme Court made the referral, an official of the Commission contacted the tax firm to inquire into their intended course of action. After revealing that they had no intention of providing any additional argumentation to the ECJ than had already been included in the national proceedings, the tax advisor was asked whether or not he would object to the Commission soliciting the help of experts. Two EU tax law specialists and legal scholars, one of whom had written on the subject of a right of option and the foreign tax liability,[37] were approached and asked to take on the case on a *pro bono* basis. Eventually, the resulting ECJ judgment made it clear that the Dutch choice scheme did not neutralize discrimination against non-residents.[38] Direct recourse to freedom of establishment (Article 49 TFEU) was possible without opting for domestic tax obligation. This judgment eventually contributed to the recall of the choice scheme by January 1st, 2015 in the Dutch *Income Tax Act*.

The rationale behind the Commission's intervention in this case seems to have been that after reviewing the case files it was concluded that on the part of the individual better EU law input was required than had been shown up until then. As concluded by Granger, the access to the Court or the 'direct voice' in the proceedings was restricted to the parties in the case before the national court, leading to a 'variation in the quality of persons [sic] allowed in the Luxembourg courtroom depending on the national standing rules'.[39] Although no official account of the Commission's actions has been found, we can deduce the reasoning behind it from the subject matter of the case. The way this case fits into a pattern of ECJ tax law cases over the past decade reveals that it aligned with the Commission's enforcement priorities; breaches of EU law 'concerning the application of Treaty principles and main elements of framework regulations and directives'.[40] The Commission set out to prevent an interpretation of non-discrimination that would allow Member States to circumvent the prohibitive function of then Article 43 EC, by introducing the possibility of choice for for-

37 Engelen & Pötgens 2001. A book that according to its own summary "provides a clear and complete source of information for anyone who comes across situations in practice where foreign taxation is central".

38 The *Schumacker* doctrine included two requirements for a non-resident to be eligible for tax deductions in the state of employment. It required first that a worker 'obtains his income entirely or almost exclusively from the work performed in the first State', and secondly that he or she 'does not receive in the second State sufficient income to be subject to taxation there in a manner enabling his personal and family circumstances to be taken into account'. Thus, the wording of the operative part in C-279/93 *Finanzamt Köln-Altstadt v Roland Schumacker*.

39 Granger 2001, 238-9.

40 European Commission 2007, 9.

eign taxable persons. To be clear, there is no indication that the Commission actually provided legal arguments or other assistance to the parties, however, the choice for certain representation was of course not random, and the two scholars who were put on the case were expected to strengthen the Commission's own arguments presented before the ECJ. Arguably, the Commission sought to even the playing field before the Court by making sure that the party to the proceedings was well equipped to argue a preferred interpretation of EU law. By soliciting the services of two EU tax law experts, they made sure that the Commission would not be the only party arguing against the Member States, four of whom (apart from the Netherlands) joined in the proceedings. Although there is no way of quantifying the times that the Commission takes this course of action, it shows how the Commission on occasion actively tries to influence the manner in which a case is argued before the ECJ, and that it considers it important how the case is presented by the parties.

8.8 The Weight of Commission Involvement

A key player like the Commission, or more specifically its stance on interpretation of EU law in specific instances, can be used as well without its active and deliberate involvement. Developments in both Germany and the Netherlands as a result of the Commission's 'leaked' written observation in *Case Study D* are testament to this fact. In this case, the Dutch government prevented an ECJ decision after the Dutch court referred the case, by pre-emptively providing a provisional residence permit. As described in *Case Study D,* the position taken by the Commission in that case played a role in prompting German courts to refer questions to the ECJ about the compatibility of the language test with the Directive, resulting in the *Dogan* judgment.[41] Congruently, in his quest to get questions referred to the ECJ in a second instance, the lawyer in *Case Study D* also brought the Commission's position forward in a subsequent national procedure. The Dutch Council of State indeed referred that case to the ECJ, questioning the Dutch policy on integration test requirements for a second time, leading to the ECJ's judgment.[42] Similarly, in *Export of Benefits* (as described above) the lawyer was able to obtain an officially formulated position of the Commission on the direct effect of the prohibition on restricting the export of benefits in Decision 3/80,[43] which he subsequently used in national proceedings in support of his clients.

41 C-138/13 *Naime Dogan v Bundesrepublik Deutschland.*

42 C-153/14 *Minister van Buitenlandse Zaken v K and A.*

43 Groenendijk, Rondhuis & Strik 2015, 32.

These cases illustrate how, because of its authoritative institutionalized position, the Commission's stance (in written form) helps proliferate certain interpretations of EU legislation that can be used by strategic actors to further a certain legal narrative for specific aims outside of the ECJ as well. By soliciting judgments and responses from institutionalized actors, as well as on occasion public attention, that narrative is strengthened, and further actors may be mobilised by it. The Commission's interpretation of EU law can be an important signal to national judges of the need for a reference to the ECJ or may push them to divert from existing national doctrine, and it helps to legitimise one's claim and further mobilise one's constituency. By eliciting judgments that include such arguments, or their relevant elements, strategic actors may thus use the Commission's stance to contribute to dynamics beyond their own efforts alone.

8.9 The Commission as an Additional Opponent

The abovementioned could create the impression that the European Commission is always an important ally for individual claimants that plead their case before the ECJ. However, this depends greatly on whether or not one's interests align with the priorities and position of the Commission. Since the Commission generally has a vested interest – even a Treaty-given obligation – to ensure the correct and uniform application of EU legislation and thus in essence to 'defend' EU policy, in the many cases where EU law is pitted against national policy, the Commission is indeed generally on the side of the litigant. While, with respect to EU rights claims, the Commission is in that sense an expected ally at the supranational level, not all cases before the ECJ revolve around EU rights claims with those characteristics. Where these cases do not necessarily revolve around an individual rights claim – or where the claims themselves may be at odds with the application or enforcement of EU law in the way the Commission intends – the Commission can turn out to be an additional powerful opponent.[44] Since its mandate is to further the correct application of EU legislation, not every individual rights claim is necessarily in line with the Commission's priorities and/or position.

Given the nature of legislation in this area, effectively conveying various obligations and practical restrictions on farmers as entrepreneurs, especially with regard to animal welfare regulations, the area of agriculture is a case in point. In addition to being subject to restrictive regulations, many farmers receive EU

44 This is especially true when private parties bring claims challenging the legality of European acts using Article 23 TFEU, and proceedings or actions for damages (Article 340 TFEU). However, these cases have not been included in this research.

subsidies in one form or another, effectively making them an addressee of obligations and requirements tied to those subsidies and opening them up to potential sanctions. This results in a situation where farmers' subsidies may be cut when they do not comply with relevant regulations. Individual agricultural cases therefore often revolve around individual litigants reactively defending themselves against such sanctions based on obligations flowing from EU legislation. The key point is that here EU law does not offer these litigants additional protection against national policy or government action, but the farmers' business operations are subject in large part to legislation originating from the EU. The nature of these cases from the perspective of litigants is therefore very different from cases in many of the other areas of law. This distinct nature of the cases also has implications for the position taken by the European Commission before the ECJ. In these agricultural cases, the litigant is more likely to find the Commission as an opponent, defending EU (animal welfare) policy.

There are thus also situations where a private litigant invokes EU law against a national rule, while the Commission disagrees. It may think the litigant's interpretation goes too far, or it is in some other way misaligned with the Commission's priorities and position. In the example of the case of the pensioners (*Case Study B*), at the ECJ they found no support from the European Commission for their interpretation of the relevant EU legislation. They were, furthermore, confronted with Finland, Luxembourg, France and the Czech Republic who all took a position supporting the Dutch interpretation of EU law. Taking on a Member State's policy by using EU law thus does not always ensure support by the Commission. There are other examples of this in citizenship case law, where litigants challenged the discretion of national authorities to subject movement rights to particular conditions. Hofmann describes how, in these cases, "somewhat surprisingly, the Commission did not always support an expansive stance where individual litigants challenged the limitations secondary law had placed on the exercise of their movement rights".[45] The European Commission may thus not always be on the individual litigant's side; however, in the cases studied for this research (where possible to determine) this applied in a small minority of cases.

8.10 The European Commission: Concluding Remarks

Private litigants with EU rights claims are in a clear *consociation* with the European Commission, thanks to the logic inherent in the EU's enforcement system, which is dependent in large part on private claims. With respect to the applica-

45 Hofmann 2013, 21.

tion of EU law and the effective enforcement of EU rights, the Commission is a key actor that works in a privileged field of opportunities.[46] The Commission is able to respond well to these opportunities because it is presented with all cases in due time, making it possible to assess certain opportunities provided – or risks posed – by a case. This is also because the Commission is generally well informed of local developments relating to EU law and non-compliance by Member States, as opposed to the ECJ judges who are otherwise very much dependent upon the information provided by both the referring judge and the Member States' representatives. The Commission can, therefore, be an important *amicus* to the Court, providing the necessary context to a case.

This strategic position of the Commission makes it an attractive actor for private parties to partner with, both in efforts at the national level as well as once their case has been referred to the ECJ. The examples presented in this chapter show the ways in which such alliances might develop and the usefulness of this course of action in particular cases. On paper, individuals seeking to protect the rights they derive from EU law have a direct way of trying to activate the centralized enforcement mechanism embodied by the complaint and infringement procedure of the European Commission. However, complaining to the Commission brings with it a high degree of uncertainty, particularly with respect to whether and when the Commission starts infraction proceedings. On the practical shortcomings of this system from the perspective of claimants, the Commission itself has concluded, with respect to the effectiveness of injunctions in 'policing the markets', that "their impact is projected more towards the future rather than being useful for correcting past damage".[47] Nevertheless, the Commission can be a powerful actor to have on your side and the examples in this chapter also show various other ways in which actors may strategically activate the Commission to pursue their goals via different avenues. A complaint may result in an alliance with the Commission that may favour one's chances of success, especially when these complaints are employed in conjunction with national court cases and preliminary references. However, this type of concerted effort is reserved for a particular kind of organised, strategic actor, and follow-up by the Commission is never guaranteed. The Commission aims to ensure effective application and enforcement of EU law, and sometimes employs strategies of 'aiding' private interests, yet with the explicit goal of championing a specific interpretation of EU legislation. Successfully allying with the Commission,

46 Kelemen 2011.

47 Report from the Commission to the European Parliament and the Council Concerning the Application of Directive 2009/22/EC on injunctions for the protection of consumers' interest. Available at: http://ec.europa.eu/consumers/enforcement/docs/report_inj_2012_en.pdf [last accessed 10 November 2017].

therefore, requires private claims to align with the general interests of the EU law or provision on which they are based.[48] Whether or not one will profit from this *consociation* between individual claimants and the Commission is, therefore, largely dependent on whether or not one's interests align with the priorities of the Commission.

8.11 Member States as Repeat Players Before the ECJ

In the previous section, I have discussed the position of the European Commission that can be considered the truest of repeat players, thanks to its privileged access to court proceedings as well as its role as *guardian of the treaties*, and thus part-time *prosecutor*. Member States, although on the receiving end of the prosecution in infringement cases, enjoy the privilege of having access to most of the ECJ's proceedings. Due to this fact, Member States enjoy many, if not all, of the advantages Galanter identifies for recurrent organizational players.[49]

Although there are significant differences among Member States in their engagement with ECJ proceedings,[50] the designation of Member States as repeat players before the ECJ is an obvious one. Not only do Member States enjoy privileged access to the Court's proceedings in most cases, most Member States have dedicated departments populated by EU law specialists, including permanent agents that plead cases before the Court and thus have low start-up costs, have ample opportunity to develop facilitative informal relationships with institutional incumbents as well as representatives of other Member States, they have a privileged and established voice in the Court, and last but not least the Member States are, of course, themselves (at least partly) responsible for the rules that are litigated before the Court. Taking examples from this study's case selection, the next section will analyse these advantages and the role that Member States play in the trajectory of ECJ cases, both upstream, by intervening in court procedures, and downstream, in dealing with the consequences of ECJ rulings. Further attention is paid to how administrations are able, as a form of 'bottom-up docket control', to influence the way in which matters are brought, and, more importantly, are not brought before the ECJ. Although certain characteristics as

48 From an individual perspective we can speculate about the fact that a reference to the ECJ could also have the opposite effect of what one is trying to achieve. One can imagine that within the 'confines' of the national legal system individual interests could find more room to be expressed. In other words, once a question is referred to the ECJ, the matter is simplified, or narrowed down to a question of principle of EU law, and is narrowed to the interpretation of EU law more generally instead of the specific application in an individual case.

49 Galanter 1976.

50 Granger 2001.

well as strategies of Member States can differ significantly, the findings in the analysis give important insight into Member States' structural opportunities across the board.

8.12 The Netherlands Before the ECJ

The role of Member States in dynamics at the supranational level has long been a central issue in studies on European integration. As a response to the more institutionalist analyses, constructivist approaches to the position and behaviour of Member States in the EU system have focused on forms of representation, advocacy and participation at national and European level.[51] Granger shows how Member States have very different approaches in their participation in proceedings before the ECJ, with highly variable usage of their 'participatory right' – their privilege to participate in proceedings before the ECJ. The Dutch government, she shows, follows a policy of 'careful selection'.[52] As one of the earliest Member States, and a state with a traditionally high number of references,[53] the Netherlands has built up significant experience with the ECJ's adjudication process. In the 1980s, Dutch participation in preliminary reference proceedings was considered necessary when the 'defence of existing legislation or existing national situations' was at stake or where questions were raised 'which were of direct relevance to the elaboration of the Community legal order'.[54] In recent years, the criteria for participation in defence of Dutch interests have been broadened significantly to include cases where the ruling may have consequences for Dutch legislation (or proposed legislation), for Dutch policies or implementation practices (or proposed policies and practices), for the discretion of Dutch authorities in politically sensitive areas, in cases involving general principles or doctrines of EC law, in cases where European transparency policy is involved, or to encourage the further development of EC law.[55] This policy shift towards more involvement is mirrored in the number of observations submitted annually by the Dutch government, which increased significantly from around twenty in the early 1990s to around fifty at the turn of the century, outpacing the growth in the total number of references.[56]

---

51 Granger 2001.

52 Granger 2001, 406.

53 In the period 1952-2014 the Court dealt with a total of 909 preliminary references from Dutch courts. Wind, Martinsen and Rotger (2009: 66) put the Netherlands in third place (behind Luxembourg and Belgium) when looking at preliminary references per capita. See also *Appendix B*.

54 Granger 2001, 406.

55 Granger 2001, 406.

56 Granger 2001, 426.

Since 1997, the Netherlands has had a dedicated department populated by EU law specialists, including permanent agents that plead cases before the Court. Dutch expertise in the area of EU law is brought together under the joint chair of the Ministries of Foreign Affairs and Justice in the Interdepartmental Committee on European Law (ICER). The ICER was set up to 'ensure that there will be, in a systematic and coordinated manner, attention paid to the impact of European legal developments for our national Justice system'.[57] The Committee is responsible for the interdepartmental coordination of the preparation for and implementation of European law in the Netherlands and for a more effective and efficient use of European law expertise by the various departments.[58] The ICER provides advice, manuals and checklists on a variety of topics to multiple national institutional players, including ministries, municipalities and other governmental bodies. The ICER includes three permanent working groups that are responsible for, respectively, implementation, notification and court procedures.

The ICER-H, an inter-ministerial committee and one of the three subgroups of the ICER, is in charge of the court proceedings. All departments are represented in the ICER-H, and they discuss biweekly whether or not the Netherlands intervenes in new cases brought before the ECJ. The committee is composed of representatives of all ministries in order to deal with the possibility of conflicting interests between two or more ministries in one case. The relevant Ministers are systematically informed of the course of action. After an ECJ decision, legal experts from the ICER also analyse and inform on the legal implications. Permanent agents of the Ministry of Foreign Affairs conduct procedures on behalf of the Dutch government in the EU courts. The Netherlands deploys a total of seven legal agents to the ECJ. The Dutch parliament is not involved systemically; however, adopted positions or outcomes may become the topic of debate between parliament and government. These debates will, however, rarely be started by the government and are usually initiated by a mobilised opposition, especially when ECJ judgments require adjustments to existing policies or legislation.

8.13 Preliminary References: Raising the Stakes

The number of instances where the Netherlands sees it has an interest in participation in proceedings before the ECJ underscores the potential far-reaching impact of ECJ decisions. Preliminary references not only provide an attractive

57 ICER 2007, 3, *my translation*.

58 Since late 2013, the ICER has met under the umbrella of the IOWJZ (Interdepartmental Consultation and Managements of Legislation and Legal Affairs).

tool for strategic players aiming to set a precedent, it is specifically this aspect of preliminary references that raises the stakes for Member States as well. A reference to the ECJ essentially upgrades a case from one decision among many at the national level to a (potentially) high stake supranational precedent before the ECJ. Whereas, theoretically, repeat players are interested in maximizing gain over a longer period of time and are relatively unconcerned about the outcome of one single case, preliminary references can upgrade a single case into a case of high interest by the mere fact that one decision by the ECJ can have far-reaching consequences. This is, of course, especially the case where preliminary questions carry in them the potential of having consequences for national legislation and policy or for the discretion of national authorities in politically sensitive areas. Member States thus have an interest in participating in the ECJ proceedings, and as repeat players we can expect them to adjust their strategies to this context. We therefore see Member States employing specialized legal services, like that of the Netherlands, to represent their interests in these proceedings.[59]

From the perspective of Member States' interests, arguably of the highest significance in ECJ cases (in both infringement proceedings and preliminary references) are questions of compliance with EU law. These ECJ cases embody a potential threat to the practices of national governments and, if lost, may force Member States to adjust their policy or legislation, due to non-compliance with rules stipulated by EU law. Falkner, Hartlapp and Treib discerned four different reasons for Member States' non-compliance with EU law: administrative incompetence, misinterpretations, linking the implementation to a national development and a deliberate choice by the government. To what extent Member States tend to implement European legislation that is inconsistent with national policy needs varies, according to Falkner et al, in part based on the political culture in a Member State. They distinguished three categories of political culture: the culture in which compliance is more important than national political preferences, the culture in which European legislation is ignored (especially as a result of administrative inaction and unilateral orientation) and the culture in which a Member State in any implementation requirement makes a cost-benefit analysis.[60] In 2008, Falkner and Treib added a fourth category: the 'world of dead letters'.[61] These include the Member States that neatly transpose a Di-

59 For an overview of the approaches by different Member States see Granger 2001.

60 Falkner, Hartlapp & Treib 2007. The culture of a 'world of law observance', according to the authors, exists in Denmark, Finland and Sweden; the culture of a 'world of transposition neglect' in France, Greece, Luxembourg and Portugal; the culture of a 'world of domestic politics' was observed in Austria, Belgium, Germany, the Netherlands, Spain and the United Kingdom.

61 Falkner & Treib 2010.

rective into legislation, but then proceed to not apply it. This practice is possible only in states where internal pressures to comply fail, due to overburdened courts or otherwise ineffective supervision and weak civil society. In Member States that conform to the third category, making cost-benefit calculations, a conflict between EU obligations and national political interests will more frequently lead to non-compliance. The researchers put the Netherlands (as well as Germany) in this category. Subsequently, the Netherlands is a Member State that finds itself before the ECJ defending its domestic policies on a regular basis.[62] Accordingly, the Netherlands is among the Member States with a long history of intervention in ECJ proceedings and Dutch expertise on EU law is well established and highly organised.

8.14 Member State Advantages Before the Court

Member States enjoy privileged access to the Court's proceedings, which allows them to submit their observations in any request for a preliminary ruling and they can intervene in any direct action without having to show that they have a legitimate interest in the case. By setting up specialised departments that are responsible for working the case law of the court, Member States are able to deploy single-case strategies and assign the relevant expertise to cases, as well as have long-term strategies by assessing the possible impact of cases on ECJ jurisprudence and its impact on national interests. Apart from these structural advantages for Member States, there are aspects of the preliminary reference system as well as the Court's procedures that provide relative advantages for Member States' representation in practice. Bulterman and Wissels give some important insight into the practice of Member States' representation before the court.[63] As former agents of the Dutch government, they identify structures of intra and interstate collaboration and techniques that Member States employ in order to influence the judicial decision-making both upstream, by intervening in court procedures, and downstream, in dealing with the consequences of ECJ rulings. The authors reveal that "[w]hile no formal structures have been established to coordinate the position of the Member States before the ECJ, there is

62 In the period 1952-2014 the Netherlands was brought before the Court in actions for failure to fulfil its obligations a total of 146 times, and the Court dealt with a total of 909 preliminary references from Dutch courts during the same period. To be clear, all of these references are of course not necessarily about non-compliance with EU law, however, according to the Commission's own reporting, compliance issues of national laws in regard to EU legislation takes up about half of the ECJ's judgments in preliminary reference cases in recent years.

63 Bulterman & Wissels 2013.

frequent contact between the agents of the different Member States".[64] The Netherlands has been the initiator of an informal network of national agents before the ECJ, organizing annual meetings to 'share experiences and discuss issues of mutual interests'. Although Bulterman and Wissels maintain that these issues pertain to the technical and procedural aspects of litigation, not substantive subjects, they state later that "[i]nformation of new cases before the ECJ, for example, is frequently shared via email to inform other agents of the importance of a specific case, or to inquire whether other Member States are considering intervening in a specific case. More substantive coordination as to the position adopted in specific cases takes place on a bilateral basis."[65] Where Member States have shared interests, the national agents are able to exchange views and align positions.[66] In addition to these formal cooperation structures, informal networks exist between national experts, who encounter each other before the Court on a regular basis. Member States are thus able to work together and coordinate their efforts and align their views in informal networks of their agents before the ECJ, in an attempt to convey their views, position and interests to the Court more effectively. For instance, if the Dutch authorities are aware that another state will submit observations along the same lines as its own, this could be a reason to submit observations too, in order to show the Court the political importance of a particular case.[67]

8.15 Private Parties Versus Member States

In the vast majority of cases in this study, the Dutch government took a position before the ECJ that was contrary to that of the individual party.[68] This is not

64 Bulterman & Wissels 2013, 269.

65 Bulterman & Wissels 2013, 269.

66 Bulterman and Wissels give gambling, taxation and transparency as examples of areas where the Netherlands has cooperated in the past with likeminded Member States with shared interests.

67 The coordination of Member States with regard to the arguments put forward in the oral stage of the proceedings are not only due to Members States strategically playing the 'Eurolaw game', but are in fact encouraged by the Court. In order to streamline proceedings, the Court implores Member States' representation not to superfluously repeat similar arguments and therefore encourages counsel to take the initiative themselves, and coordinate their oral submissions in order to limit the duration of the oral procedure. Broberg & Fenger 2010, 381. See also the ECJ's own 'Notes for the guidance of counsel', available at: https://curia.europa.eu/jcms/upload/docs/application/pdf/2008-09/txt9_2008-09-25_17-37-52_275.pdf [last accessed 9 November 2017].

68 The position taken by the Dutch government in these cases was deduced from the ICER-H's own yearly reporting. Available at:

→

surprising since, in the vast majority, Dutch public bodies were the opposing party in the national proceedings. Only two cases show an exception to this rule; the case of the catering employees (*Case Study A*), the one case where both sides of the dispute were in fact private parties. In this case, the interest of the government was in making sure that, in the end, the transposition of the Directive was not deemed incorrect. This would have shifted the financial burden from the employers to the legislator and would have made the government liable for the damages suffered by the catering employees. In the second case (*Lessee Entitlements*), a dispute between an individual and a public authority, however, the question was not one of administrative law. This case revolved around the question of whether EU law requires a lessee, on the expiry of the lease, to deliver to the lessor the leased land along with the payment entitlements accumulated thereon, or to pay him compensation. And although the opposing party was in fact a municipality, it was only part of the proceedings as lessor of a number of parcels of agricultural land, and not as a public authority *per se*. The position taken by the Dutch government before the ECJ in this test case was not contrary to the interests of the claimant.

The position of the Member States before the ECJ stands in stark contrast to that of the parties that, in all likelihood, will present their case before the Court for the very first time. We have already seen in Chapter 6 the difficulties practitioners face more generally when having to plead a case unexpectedly before an unknown court. In contrast to one-shot lawyers and litigants, representatives of the Netherlands are obviously well versed in both EU law and the language of the Court. Additionally, the practice of coordination of arguments between Member States puts the representatives of the parties to the proceedings at a further disadvantage. The oral proceedings offer the only opportunity for parties to respond to the other parties' arguments (either put forward in written observations or during the hearing), yet after all the parties have had a brief opportunity to expand on their position, each party is allotted only twenty minutes to respond to the comments of all the other parties. This is where Member States, when forming alliances, can exploit their privileged position. They can coordinate and jointly put forward several arguments, and also divide their time between them to effectively refute the party's (or other actors') positions. On the other hand, the individual party has just twenty minutes to discuss the arguments put forward by several Member States, and thus has significantly less time to go into detail on all the different points brought forward. As one social security lawyer explains his experience at the ECJ hearing:

---

http://www.minbuza.nl/ecer/hof-van-justitie/jaarverslagen-procesvoering-nederland.html [last accessed 9 November 2017].

> "They had divided their speech into say ten pieces or so, and they had coordinated it. Every Member State will receive twenty minutes of talking time. So you have the first Member State that expands on one argument first, and then the second on another. It's a long story, so they have not twenty but two hundred minutes. And we only had twenty minutes of our own. And so you have to respond to every argument in only twenty minutes, so that's done very cleverly."

While in this case the lawyer found most of the Member States present at the hearing taking on a position opposed to theirs, this doesn't mean all Member States are necessarily always on the same side of the argument. However, as concluded by Granger, Member States try to avoid risking good relations by challenging each other's interests in court.[69] It is therefore more likely for Member States that choose to intervene in the court proceedings to have similar interests.

The collaboration between Member States is especially relevant in light of findings like those of Kilroy, who shows how the "expression of a position by a simple majority, a blocking minority, or even a smaller coalition of states has a statistically significant effect on the probability of a particular type of ECJ ruling".[70] She found that the probability of the ECJ upholding a national rule was only 23% when no state made an observation, but increased by 73% to 96% when a simple majority of states articulated support for a national rule and 56% in the case of support from a blocking minority. Such findings support the hypothesis that the ECJ is unlikely to rule against majority preferences, and that Member States that coordinate their efforts have a significant advantage in trying to steer the Court in one direction or the other.[71]

Another way of coordination that allows Member States room to expand on their points is the fact that, in the case of a reference from their own jurisdiction, Member States often act before the Court in a double capacity. As an intervening party they are present to submit observations, but they are often also represented as one of the parties to the original proceedings. Especially in cases where national legislation or policies are under scrutiny, one of the parties to the proceedings is usually a public body. In these cases, government agents coordinate a position with these parties in order to ensure representation of both the interests of that body, as well as the more general interests of the Dutch government. A former agent of the Netherlands before the ECJ explains:

69 Based on an internal hand-out provided by a Dutch agent before the ECJ, Granger concludes on the approach by the Dutch government to participation in ECJ proceedings: "Submissions should also be avoided where there is a risk of harming good relations with other Member States or where there are politically sensitive issues outside the Netherlands (e.g. euthanasia, coffee shops)." Granger 2001, 407.

70 Kilroy 1999, 405-6.

71 See also Conant 2007, 51.

> R: "You obviously have the governing body at a lower level, which has an interest, because it of course has a dispute at the national level. And the Dutch Government, the state has an interest insofar that we want to protect that body, we want to support it."
> I: "Is it possible that you do not tell the same story?"
> R: "That you do not agree at all, well. That you should avoid. The governing body may plead themselves. But in such a case we make every effort to ensure that they do not have to do that. So they do come along and provide input, but you come up with one and the same story."

In some cases, it is opportune to have a representative of the governing body plead, again in order to divide the labour. The former representative of the Netherlands gave the example of a case revolving around the question of whether or not EU law was applicable to the Dutch soft drugs policy. The risk for the Dutch government in this case was that if the Court had decided that EU law was applicable the government would have been limited in the way it formulated its own drugs policy. She explains:

> "The mayor was the governing body. In that case, during the whole procedure, there was a lot of coordination with Justice, the Mayor, the lawyer and us, Foreign Affairs. We worked together very closely. And in that case they did plead. And we divided it up. So we say, if you guys provide the local context, we will do national policy."

The division of labour allowed them to cover both the specific context of the case at hand, as well as put an argument forward in protection of national policy. Moreover, the coordination allowed them to align these two stories.

Although the oral proceedings are generally considered of less importance than the written stage,[72] explaining the context of a case can be crucial. As explained by Broberg and Fenger: "the judge coming from the member state of the referring court does not sit on the case. Thus to some extent it might fall to the lawyers for the parties to the main proceedings to provide details on points of substantive law or procedure pertaining to the relevant national legal system which are necessary to a full understanding of the case". Depending on the complexities of a case, ECJ judges rely on the representation of the parties to clarify facts and arguments during the oral stage of the proceedings. This is particularly evident when it comes to the interpretation of national legislation and especially the implementation of legislation in policies. A tax lawyer explains:

72 Broberg & Fenger 2010, 384.

> "[In this case] you also saw that the Member States, there were ten or so, were all against us. And they had coordinated their arguments in advance with one another. They know each other well. And so, they coordinate to go fully against you. And with no holds barred, not even lying a bit to the Court, proclaiming half-truths, caricatures, etc."

Whether this is an example of lack of particular knowledge of the Dutch representatives or (as the representative of the claimant saw it) strategic insincerity, is up for debate. However, it illustrates the fact that the Court is in need of a context in order to get a grip on the facts of the case. Neutral experts are usually not available and therefore the judges and the Advocate General are largely dependent upon the information provided by the parties, intervening Member States and the European Commission. With regard to the details of national policies, the expertise of the lawyers of the respective states is, understandably, sought; however, this does create one more opportunity for those on this side of the argument to frame the context of a case in a more favourable way. In addition, it must also be taken into account that, as Broberg and Fenger describe, "all judges may not have studied equally thoroughly those parts of the written observations that are not summarised in the Report for the Hearing".[73] This underscores the significance of clarification during the oral proceedings.

Although Member States thus have significant advantages when it comes to long-term strategies before the ECJ, their agents may, due to their focus on EU law, be less knowledgeable when it comes to the details of national legislation or policy. As one migration lawyer described events during the hearing in his case:

> "There was someone from the IND and a lawyer of the Ministry of Foreign Affairs. And she was regularly asked: Ma'am, what about such and such. And she went back and forth deliberating with the person from the IND, until they got a scolding at one point. With the chair saying: You could have authorized someone, but you chose not to, and now you are going to answer the questions yourself!"

This speaks to the fact that Member States are, of course, not in a position of complete control. They too can be confronted unexpectedly with a reference. And they too can struggle with the combination of required EU law expertise and specific knowledge of the different national contexts they have to deal with before the Court.

73 Broberg & Fenger 2010, 382.

8.16 Member States' Control of the ECJ Docket

Case Study D provides a telling example of the largely invisible hand a Member State can have in influencing the ECJ's docket. In this case, the Dutch government anticipated a detrimental ECJ ruling on the policy of pre-entry integration requirements and was able to prevent the case from continuing after it had already been brought before the ECJ, by providing the litigant with a permit after all. After agents of the Dutch ICER-H had studied the case that was brought before the ECJ as an urgent procedure, they informed the Minister of the possible consequences of the case for the Dutch policy on integration requirements. Recognising the threat to the policy, the Minister saw fit to revise the earlier decision and provide a permit, thus forestalling a potentially detrimental ECJ judgment. This is likely an exceptional case, in the sense that it was cut short only at this late stage. The interviews with lawyers indicated that the Dutch administration makes calculations with regard to the risk of a preliminary reference, and may intervene at earlier stages during national proceedings more regularly. As one migration lawyer recalls:

> "Really just a few weeks ago, I received a note from the court that they were planning to ask questions. And asked what my view was. And what does the IND do? Suddenly, out of nowhere they repeal the contested decision. [...] Purely and simply, to ensure that the preliminary questions aren't asked. That is their only objective, because there are at least two or three hundred cases like this. It is not a coincidence that these questions are on the table."

By taking away the litigant's standing, the government thus essentially prevents requests for preliminary rulings from being made to the ECJ, in order to avert a judgement on principle that may undermine its policy. Although the frequency with which these strategies are employed are difficult to determine, this strategic action by the Dutch government is not limited to the field of migration and asylum law. Tax lawyers indicated similar events:

> "In some cases they do give in suddenly. And I think that's when they make an assessment that they really, really think they are going to lose. And they are willing to allow tax inspectors to handle the case outside of court. [...] In one case the inspector, pending the hearing, suddenly came with the offer to just give in. And why? To prevent a ruling by the Court of Justice. Because, it was obvious at the hearing that the court tended strongly towards asking preliminary questions. You could tell because they asked: If we want to ask questions, what would be your view? They gave a shot across the bow of the possibility of a reference."

The following quote illustrates that this strategy is not always employed, even in cases where it may have been expected. This lawyer evaluated his case between an individual and the IND regarding a negative decision on an application for a residence permit:

> "I think that if you have the same conversation with a supervisor at the IND, he will say it should have been dealt with differently from the side of the IND. [...] With this one case, they put the entire family definition at stake, and I think if you are going to make a cost/benefit analysis and will also delve into European law that yes, the IND should have come to the conclusion: the risk is too great that we'll lose this, we'll give this lady a permit. That is impossible once the Court has been asked questions. [...] Once the questions are asked it is a train that is unstoppable. And the IND should have come to their senses sooner."

This illustrates that the administrative vigilance in this respect is not fool-proof. However, as we learned from *Case Study D,* the assertion of this respondent, that once the questions are asked there is no way back, is not completely accurate. In that case, again, no assessment of possible consequences of preliminary reference was made during the national proceedings. It was only after the Dutch representation before the court raised the alarm about the possible consequences of an ECJ judgment, that action was taken to prevent a ruling. However, this decision did result in some political backlash, with members of parliament asking questions about the grounds for this revised decision. Vigilance at earlier stages in such proceedings is thus a preferable situation with less risk of a critical backlash. Moreover, the recurrent application of such strategies could result in critical investigation at the supranational level as well, as such actions could be considered detrimental to the integrity of the EU legal system as a whole.

These are examples of how sometimes the government gives in once a court indicates that it intends to refer questions to the ECJ. They illustrate that a consideration is made on the part of the administration on the basis of the likelihood that the case has an unfavourable result and could have far-reaching consequences through the creation of a precedent or the unfavourable interpretation of certain EU principles or doctrines. This constitutes a significant difference in power between individual or even organised litigants and the state. Because in such cases the litigation effort is thwarted, in many cases a complaint to the Commission is one of the few options left. From the individual's perspective, however, the uncertainty of follow-up on a complaint combined with the lack of interim measures makes this avenue a less attractive one, especially when one's situation is particularly dire. One other option for the parties is to try their luck by starting civil proceedings against the state; however, as we have seen in *Case Study C*, civil proceedings, due to their formal requirement for a lawyer, are particularly costly, and this is not a path that is often taken. Especially considering that from the perspective of the individual whose case is being litigated, usually the decision by the government to give in, implies that his or her goal has been achieved. For the litigants, it means that their taxes are reduced, their residence permit is granted, or they otherwise get what they were litigating for.[74] This is an especially pertinent problem for those organised litigation efforts pursuing more collective interests, as discussed in more detail in Chapter 7.

8.17 The Member States: Concluding Remarks

Over the past decades, research in the field of compliance has focused on how and why Member States deal with complying with EU law obligations. Enforcement of EU law through the courts forms an integral part of the fabric of the EU implementation system. Although governments actively negotiate new European legislation (to be adopted by Council and Parliament), their influence at that stage and the eventual agreement does not always guarantee compliance. And so, preliminary references form an important mechanism for signalling instances of non-compliance and, for private parties that enjoy EU law rights, enforcing compliance.

Access to a higher court such as the ECJ is unquestionably an important element in order for any form of judicial review to be meaningful. However, in the practice of the preliminary reference procedure this is not without complications. In a lot of cases, when review is deemed inconvenient from the perspective of the Member State, there is an opportunity for the state to block the proceedings. By striking a deal or by thwarting a judgment through taking away one's standing in the national proceedings, and therefore before the ECJ, the state is able to exert some control over which questions are adjudicated by the ECJ. The examples of the state 'giving in' in certain cases reflect a conscious strategy and shows that late or incorrect implementation is not necessarily linked to the complexity of the adjustment of national rules, and that Member States can be strategic in the extent to which they comply with EU legislation by 'playing the Eurolaw game'.[75] Member States are able to play this game on multiple levels and have a privileged position in several respects. Also, open-ended wording of European legislation is an often chosen solution for different interests, and fosters different interpretations and applications.[76] Although not always due to calculating behaviour or unwillingness, Member States choose the most desirable interpretation, that is, an interpretation that is most consistent with the

74 In some cases, for instance in tax cases, while successful for one or several tax returns, such a decision does not set a precedent. Therefore a new tax return will offer up the same question.

75 Cf. Mastenbroek & Van Keulen 2006.

76 According to Falkner, Hartlapp & Treib 2007 this is especially the case in decisions requiring unanimity.

existing national rules.[77] The Netherlands, in such a twilight zone, also often puts preference for their political interests above strict compliance.[78] Infringement proceedings or preliminary references are then necessary to arrive at uniform interpretation and implementation.[79] Having some control over the cases that reach the ECJ gives Member States the room to extend their non-compliance and proceed with conflicting policies. In cases where these policies have a clear financial incentive, as in *Case Study C* regarding administrative fees, or in particular tax matters, this is an obvious advantage. In other cases, such as certain migration and integration policies, such as the civic integration tests in *Case Study D*, this may be more due to political sensitivity. The possibility of governments to make cost-benefit calculations in essence allows for a form of docket control of the cases on which the ECJ gives its judgments. As such, this is part of what Falkner, Hartlapp and Treib have called the 'world of domestic politics', with political considerations not being limited to the political arena but extending into the national courtroom.[80] Individuals who challenge such measures through the courts, and manage to have their case referred to the ECJ, thus become (purposefully or unwittingly) the focal point of political interests at the highest level.

8.18 Conclusion

Analysing the arena litigating parties enter when their case is referred to the ECJ, this chapter highlighted their relative position in relation to two of the main actors that operate before the Court, whom litigation parties are likely to encounter. Both the European Commission and the Member States are in a particularly advantageous position that allows them to play 'the Eurolaw game' skilfully. Litigating parties, with rare exceptions, are in a clearly disadvantaged position when litigating before the ECJ. The examples presented in this chapter show that the Dutch government is strategic in its responses to litigation. In some cases it may even count on litigation, or expect no successful opposition. Since the vast majority of cases involving individual litigants directly or more indirectly concern questions of compatibility of national laws or policy with certain EU legislation, litigants often find themselves up against well-organised and experienced litigators defending the interests of the state and the integrity of national policy. Conversely, the European Commission may be a welcome ally in a litigant's quest for justice or for strategic players attacking national policy.

77 Falkner, Hartlapp & Treib 2007, 405.
78 Mastenbroek 2007, 159.
79 Falkner et al. 2005, 463.
80 Falkner, Hartlapp & Treib 2007, 405.

The Commission, tasked with safeguarding the effective implementation of EU rules and rights, can often be found arguing on the side of the litigants whenever a reference concerns the compatibility of national legislation with EU law. Examples provided in this chapter also revealed that the Commission on occasion goes beyond mere advocacy in the courtroom in attempts to utilise preliminary references as part of its political strategy and efforts to enforce compliance. The advantage litigants may gain from allying with the Commission is, however, fully dependent upon the alignment of their interests with the goals and priorities of the Commission. The analysis in this chapter has thus shown how these privileged players are able to influence the Court's case law both in court as well as in ways that are not directly visible to the outside observer. The resulting picture of the Eurolaw game is, therefore, one that is played on a non-level playing field.

Part IV

9 Conclusions

9.1 Euro-litigation Empowering EU Citizens?

The role of litigation before the ECJ in European integration dynamics has been described extensively in academic literature. In this literature, the role of litigants has, however, been described in largely passive terms, with assumptions about when and why litigants may have an interest in invoking EU law and using references to the ECJ as part of their litigation strategy. With the focus on the emancipatory effects of having a supranational system of review, capable of challenging national laws that contravene EU law, emphasis has been put predominantly on the opportunities that arise for those with access to these legal structures. This study critically approached resulting hypotheses of 'empowerment-through-law' and 'participation-through-law-enforcement' by looking in depth at the practice of Euro-litigation through preliminary references. This study therefore started out by asking the most basic questions: Who goes to court in Europe, and why? When and why do individuals invoke EU law and push for litigation before the ECJ? And to what extent can such litigation be considered empowering? By looking at litigation before the ECJ through the preliminary reference procedure from the ground up, this study aimed to offer a better understanding of the relationship between local interests, litigation and judicial politics from a relatively unstudied perspective, namely the micro and local level, connecting the EU and its legal system to its constituents.

This final chapter reflects on the analyses in this book, which have been essentially two-pronged. In Part II (Chapters 4, 5 and 6), this study focused on the ground level practice of the preliminary reference procedure by employing a broad explorative methodology to litigation before the ECJ. Two actors featured prominently at first: the individuals that were involved in litigation through preliminary references, as well as the practitioners that had to 'work a reference' to the ECJ. Part III of the book (Chapters 7 and 8) probed deeper into the so-called 'Eurolaw game', building on insights from the first section to lay out the playing field of Euro-litigation and the preliminary reference procedure. Here, other actors came into view, and the aim was to provide an estimation of who was (most) likely to use EU law and who was in the best position and had the most opportunity to do so. By looking at preliminary references from this perspective, I aimed to demonstrate that this playing field was not a level one, and that a multiplicity of interests could be at stake. I will recap the findings as presented in Chapters 4 to 8 and reflect on them in light of the central research question: *To what extent can EU law in general and specifically the preliminary reference procedure be considered an opportunity for empowerment and who is (most) likely to use it?* After that I will discuss some of the open questions that remain, as well as provide suggestions for a future research agenda.

9.2 Understanding Individual Litigation before the ECJ

As a first step in looking at Euro-litigation from the bottom-up, this study zoomed in on the motives of the individual litigants in order to determine the *how* and *why* of cases that reach the ECJ through preliminary references. This approach allowed for a critical examination of the purported 'use' of the procedure from the perspective of litigants. In this regard, the first important observation was the relative lack of intent behind references to the ECJ on the part of the litigating parties. In roughly two-thirds of the cases studied, it was neither the aim nor the wish of the litigants or their counsel to have their case referred to the ECJ. On the whole then, it was only in a minority of the cases that the litigating parties had an explicit aim to reach the ECJ and a reference was perceived as a goal that would help serve their interests. In these cases of 'proactive' Euro-litigation, either from the outset or developed during national proceedings, the parties had their express wish and aim to have their case adjudicated by the ECJ, and implored the national court(s) to refer their case. The reasons behind this aim varied considerably, and preliminary references were thus a mixed bag of a host of different types of litigation. Some cases simply revolved around a question of EU law for which there was no clear precedent in either national or ECJ jurisprudence and, therefore, the road to the ECJ was an expected and logical one. In other cases, the wish to reach the ECJ was indeed informed by a deadlock in national doctrine, making the road to the ECJ a particularly viable opportunity to 'outflank' the national system. But for most, whether or not EU law was part of the litigation strategy, the ECJ was not the intended target at all. Such findings should make us aware of the disparate nature of motives behind litigation that may end up before the ECJ.

The sectoral concentration of references in certain areas of law (predominantly agriculture, migration and social policy) revealed which types of individual litigants were most likely to appear before the ECJ. The predominance of migrants, workers and farmers among the litigants reflected a distribution of the types of EU legislation that might be part of challenges in the national courtrooms, including the four freedoms of EU law and rights derived by Turkish migrants from the Association Agreement between Turkey and the EU. The differentiation between areas of law, however, also revealed how the notion of references embodying challenges to national law by employing EU rules captured all types of references that were brought before the ECJ. The area of agriculture especially included almost exclusively cases brought by individual farmers challenging administrative decisions based directly on EU legislation. In these cases, the challenge was thus not to national legislation by employing rights derived from EU law, but to obligations flowing from EU law itself. These cases contrasted significantly in character, as well as in litigation motives, with cases relating to migration law that conformed much more to the idea of EU law as an emancipatory source for challenges, to national policy. It should thus be clear from the presented analyses that speaking about Euro-litigation in any generalizing terms was particularly difficult. There were considerable differences in actions, strategies and responses on the part of the parties, depending on their ultimate aims with litigation, aims that moreover might change and evolve according to developments both within and outside the confines of the legal proceedings.

Such findings highlight the difficulties of constructing any type of cross-European or Euro-profile of litigation. These difficulties are further exacerbated by the great diversity of sources from which cases come before the ECJ through preliminary references, and the great variation in types of litigants and types of referrals. This stresses the importance of differentiation when approaching the procedure as a legal and political mechanism. Lacking such detail runs the risk of oversimplification and misrepresentation. This constitutes a challenge to political scientists trying to deduce political dynamics from court decisions, and is a consideration that undermines the positivist tendency in European integration studies trying to establish strong causal links between actors' actions and outcomes. In this sense, correlation does not prove causation, and as Alter and Vargas conclude: "Even if litigants highlight a connection to transnational activities (to the four freedoms) to strengthen their legal case, this does not mean that transnational activity or a desire to capture the benefits of increased trade is the dominant factor mobilizing them to raise EC legal cases".[1]

9.3 Participation-Through-Law and the Assumption of Interest

Generally speaking, Euro-litigation through preliminary references to the ECJ is a consequence of the uncertainty of the law. References to the ECJ are meant to resolve possible conflicts in law between the supranational and the national level and ensure uniform application of EU law across Member States. Famously, this uncertainty allows for challenges in the courts to national laws that appear to contravene EU law, and in the study of European integration, the preliminary reference procedure often takes centre stage as the principal legal avenue through which European integration has been fostered. Given the role the proce-

1 Alter & Vargas 2000, 478.

dure has in the enforcement of EU law, and by extension the furthering of European integration, understanding the way the preliminary reference procedure is activated in practice is a central focus of inquiry. On the one hand, the attention generally goes towards the national judges and courts that are the principal decision-makers when it comes to references to the ECJ. On the other hand, when discussing the role of private litigants in activating the procedure, the emphasis generally lies on how private parties 'employ' the procedure in pursuit of their interests.

In neofunctionalist literature, which argues that private interests that turn to the EU realm contribute to European integration, there is an implicit assumption that people invoke EU law and EU rights before a judge whenever it serves their interests. There is a related tendency to consider cases that end up at the ECJ as the result of someone actively invoking EU law, and, moreover, that the interest in a case can be deduced from the subject matter and end result. In that respect, Harlow describes how the preliminary reference procedure is the 'principal avenue by which individuals use their rights'.[2] Granger even speaks in this regard of individuals as 'active crusaders for the enforcement of [EU] law'.[3] These ideas about the self-interested motives of private parties in the procedure are, apart from the occasional case study, largely based on speculation, often generalised, as in the case of the behaviour of national judges, from an ontologically rationalist perspective.

This study has revealed that litigation before the ECJ has the capacity to carry in it a multiplicity of interests, narratives and even results, depending on which, or whose, perspective is adopted. We have seen how litigation rates at the surface can be understood to reflect the influence of structural factors like the amount of EU legislation available in a certain sector, the emergence of newly applicable EU legislation or changes in national policy prompting resistance. This study has also shown that litigation before the ECJ through the preliminary reference procedure cannot be understood fully without taking into consideration behavioural aspects of litigating parties, government administrations and national judges, and factors such as agency, expertise, organisational capacity and networks, as well as the political context in which litigation occurs. Understanding litigation, therefore, requires awareness of all these aspects and inquiry that fails to take them into account is bound to over-emphasise the relative explanatory or predictive weight of certain aspects, possibly to the detriment of others.

The results from this research show how difficult it is to determine 'interests' and makes us aware that it becomes problematic when such interests are

2 Harlow 1992, 215.
3 Granger 2001, 238.

assumed, and when the behaviour of people and groups is implicitly or explicitly thought of in ontologically rationalist terms. The analyses in Chapter 5 reveal for instance that it is not always evident that individual litigants are the interested and/or active parties in the proceedings let alone the main actor behind the litigation. In a significant number of cases, the actual financial gains that were expected when 'winning' cases in Luxembourg (insofar as reaching the ECJ was their actual aim) did not weigh up to the costs of the extended litigating effort needed to complete the whole procedure. Furthermore, preliminary references, and the legal questions as well as the supranational relevance they contain, may or may not be aligned with the aims and interests of the 'real' litigant or the original dispute. Especially if we consider the augmented importance of some cases after they are sent to the ECJ, with more potentially interested parties, references can be, or become, an intersection of interests, legal questions and political strife. And so the interests that are served with a reference, a judgment or even a question may be refractions of the original interest and can, therefore, hardly be used to determine the 'original' meaning of litigative actions.

A striking observation in that respect was the relatively large share of test cases among the preliminary reference cases selected for this study. These included orchestrated disputes meant to 'test the waters' of national and EU law as well as strategic actors employing EU law as 'shield and sword', but they also included national judges seeking to resolve a recurrent question due to uncertainty in the interpretation of EU rules. Test cases by definition involve matters for which there exists no clear legal interpretation. Where a matter involves questions as to the application or interpretation of EU law, the chances that the case will be referred to the ECJ increase. The preliminary reference procedure thus has the structural characteristic of 'selecting' test cases, those cases that aim to answer questions of interpretation regarding EU law. In that sense, preliminary references can be seen as principle questions *by definition*. With EU law creating legal uncertainty at the domestic level, a relatively large portion of these cases is likely to set a precedent of sorts. The nature of the preliminary reference, as solving principle questions of interpretation and compliance, serves as an explanation for this relatively large number of cases that can be designated as test cases, as well as the presence of parties like interest groups and unions. This should not, however, lead to the automatic conclusion that these litigants are all actively engaging in supranational legal strategies. Many cases took on such a characteristic *as a result of* the reference, and third party actors became involved only after cases were referred to the ECJ.

The aforementioned disconnect between results and consequences of litigation on the one hand, and the aims of the litigants on the other, highlights the need for researchers that study the role of Euro-litigation in shaping domestic and European political and legal dynamics to be wary of assumptions and wide generalisations about the motives behind legal action. This study does not refute claims made by neofunctionalist scholars that suggest that Euro-litigation plays an important role in the integration of Europe or the possibility of empowering dynamics through litigation. The findings in this study partly mirror earlier conclusions like those of Conant, who summarises that "studies of the sectoral concentration of references and citations to ECJ case law demonstrate that commercial enterprises, societal interest organizations and public enforcement agencies are most likely to gain access to courts to enforce EU legal norms because they are most likely to possess the knowledge and financing necessary for litigation". However, such observations should not lead to the conclusion that litigation before the ECJ automatically reflects such organised interests or this type of legal challenge. The limited understanding of litigation that results from a top-down perspective could misjudge 'both' ways: On the one hand, it can assume a level of intent and strategy on the part of the litigating parties which is, in fact, absent, ascribing to litigants certain goals and gambits based on the resulting legal developments. And on the other hand, it may overlook strategic action behind the proverbial straw man, where organised actors (including institutional actors like the European Commission) are actively pushing for certain legal or political change by employing individual court cases.

Although we have seen in Chapter 7 that there is an important link between the expertise and financial capacity necessary for strategic EU law mobilisation, these do not play as much of a role when it comes to gaining access to the ECJ in general, because of the simple fact that references in numerous instances are not the result of parties pushing for an ECJ judgment. This suggests that the extent to which litigation before the ECJ occurs on the express wish of the parties to the national proceedings, and can thus be considered a form of 'societal mobilisation' or even 'demand for integration', is therefore more limited than studies on litigation and judicial politics in the EU suggest. In other words, even where litigation before the ECJ is concentrated in a certain area of law, this should not automatically lead to the conclusion that there is societal mobilisation behind the increase in references. Although legal mobilisation and other factors, like changes in domestic policy, may go hand in hand, assuming the one based on the other thus appears unsatisfactory. Taking on the perspective of the 'users' of EU law has revealed the ways in which interests can be diffuse, contradictory and even change over time. As stated by Alter, "[e]ven assuming rational behavior, no human error, and full information – unsustainable assumptions to be sure – where EU law influences national policy depends on the wording of the EU law, on ECJ legal doctrine and ECJ decision making, on private litigant mobilization, on national court support, and on follow-through".[4]

4 Alter 2000, 518.

In part, the failure to account for behavioural factors in understanding litigation before the ECJ can be explained by the predominantly supranational perspective in the study of Euro-litigation, implicitly assuming interest in supranational dynamics on the part of the litigating parties. As discussed, such interest and purposefulness is less self-evident than has been suggested. References to the ECJ can have a multitude of driving actors and motives that are moreover not mutually exclusive. Therefore, instead of approaching litigation from a supranational perspective, it appears far more fruitful to shift our focus from the supranational to the local and domestic level. Not only to the domestic political context in which litigation arises, but also to national structures that influence opportunities in pursuing legal strategies. Such national structures, like standing rules, rules on class actions and legal aid schemes, not only influence the decision-making process of national actors but also influence the ways in which disputes find their way through the legal system. For instance, a multitude of asylum claim cases brought before domestic courts by lawyers supported by state aid schemes will increase the number of cases possibly eligible for reference. Such domestic structures and behavioural aspects are interrelated, and a more localised and domestic focus on analysis should, therefore, be able to more accurately capture the ways in which EU law is effectively invoked and to what end. In other words, when we keep emphasising the supranational aspect of Euro-litigation, we are bound to miss the localised interests at stake, and consequently the local significance of legal dynamics. In fact, going forward the question should be: how 'Euro' is Euro-litigation? This shift in focus would also do justice to the localised aims of the litigating parties and thus the litigation itself.

9.4 The Multifarious Functions of the Preliminary Reference Procedure

The last part of Chapter 4 focused on the subjective experiences of individuals with having their case referred to the ECJ and their perceptions and expectations of the Court. Only a minority of litigants could be considered active in their pursuit of justice (not leaving their case completely in the hands of their lawyer). Among this small group, the perceptions of the Court and the way their case was handled differed considerably. While for many the referral to the ECJ felt like an improvement in their chances, perceiving the Court as a form of extended appeal beyond the national courts, physically attending the proceedings before the Court did not always serve to strengthen their belief in equitable treatment. The actual role for the individual in the procedure before the ECJ is very limited. And although only a minority of litigants actually expressed an interest in attending the Court's proceedings, this raises questions about the nature of the procedure and the possible impact of this experience on the perceived (procedural) justice of the parties. Although the Court itself presents these proceedings clearly as a form of 'judicial cooperation', it can be questioned how the procedure impacts the original dispute from the perspective of the litigant. The technical nature of the proceedings, with little to no role for the individual litigant, left some with the feeling of being a spectator to their own dispute. Relatedly, only rarely did litigants, whether they had travelled to Luxembourg or not, have a good understanding of the reason for, and function of referral of their case to the ECJ for a preliminary ruling. The perceived obscurity of these proceedings resulted in some remarkable misunderstandings, most notably about the intervening parties, the European Commission and other Member States. In the most extreme examples, this resulted in the perception by litigants that there had been evident foul play.

When looking at the preliminary reference procedure from an 'institutional perspective',[5] and thus focusing on the functions law has to perform in order to harmonise social life, there thus appears to be a discrepancy between the actual function of the procedure – the interpretation of EU legislation in order for EU law to be uniformly applied in all Member States – and the occasion on or form in which this function is performed, namely in the dispute resolution of an actual dispute. This discrepancy could be a partial explanation for a mismatch in perception of the ECJ's practice and the experiences and aspirations of the litigants. Since with EU law and the preliminary reference procedure the dispute in question gets transformed into a dispute at supranational level, thus transcending the confines of national interests (of both the state as well as the national judicial system), the ECJ may actually function as a more neutral arbitrator. This is an expectation voiced by many litigants. Since the ECJ is assumed to have no stake in looking after the interests of Member States as such, and is supposed to ensure uniform application of EU law throughout the Union, it can be argued that the ECJ is a possible ally for individuals in disputes against national governments whenever EU law provides them more protection than national laws or policy.

However, it is precisely because this task of interpretation and subsequent implementation (by the Member States) of these political compromises (EU legislation) is bestowed upon the ECJ that it could also be argued that once these disputes reach the ECJ they are transformed from a legal dispute between two parties into a political question. In this regard, the Court may very well act considerably differently from traditional national high courts that may take into account the national political, administrative and budgetary consequences of their judgments. This is tentatively confirmed by the fact that Member States are able to intervene in the proceedings and give their opinion as to the preferred

5 As distinguished by Evan 1962.

interpretation, and regularly do so. In this sense, the preliminary reference plays more roles than one and has the capacity to carry in it multiple interests, narratives and even results. It can simultaneously be a check on governments' trespasses of EU law by individuals or interest groups, it can temporarily extend the stay of otherwise undocumented immigrants or be an unwanted extension of an already precarious situation, it can be an alternative means of EU law enforcement for the European Commission, it can be an opportunity for extended negotiations of new EU legislation by Member States, it can signal the unwanted consequences of EU legislation for Member States and prompt renegotiations, and it can be the mechanism through which Europeanisation extends further and further into domestic politics. Including in this list the perspective of litigants may also lead to the conclusion that the preliminary reference may simultaneously be a check on government trespasses of EU law as well as an increased and sometimes insurmountable burden on the individual litigant.

9.5 The Enforcement Role of Litigation

Where the enforcement of EU law, in the absence of centralised enforcement mechanisms, relies heavily on the 'vigilance' of the polity and on claims brought before national courts, the burden of enforcement falls on individuals and organisations signalling Member States' trespasses. In practice, however, the larger part of this responsibility lies with the legal profession. This mechanism of enforcement presupposes the ability by the profession to effectively monitor Member States' implementation of rules stipulated by EU law and to be alert to possible infringements. The findings presented in Chapter 6 give an indication of how EU law and norms have (or have not) become integrated into the 'legal consciousness' of practitioners. It revealed differences in both the 'litigability' of certain legal principles in EU law, as well as the practical knowledge among practitioners when it comes to applying EU law in a meaningful way. In many instances, a reference to the ECJ comes unexpectedly and for many lawyers EU law in general, and the procedures before the ECJ in particular, is unknown territory and thus presents them with new challenges and dilemmas. There are evidently differences between different areas of law, with areas like agriculture with a longstanding history of EU legislation and, conversely, areas like migration and asylum law where EU law has only fairly recently become relevant. The self-reported domestic focus and lack of EU law expertise of legal practitioners (of lawyers as well as national judges[6]) could result in structural neglect of implementation errors and potential breaches of

6 See Jaremba 2013; Blom et al. 1995.

EU law by Member States. Given that compliance by Member States is not self-evident (due to administrative incompetence, misinterpretations, the linking of implementation to a national development or deliberate choice by the government), domestic pressure is needed in order to ensure compliance with EU law. When such pressure is effectively channelled through the courts, effective advocacy becomes especially salient.

When it comes to preliminary references taking on the character of judicial review of national policy and compliance with EU law, the fact that such cases do not necessarily fall into the hands of the practitioners best equipped to argue such claims can, on a macro scale, further undermine the effectiveness of the system. Although it is not in every case that ardent advocacy is needed for the ECJ to find a Member State in breach of EU law, the examples presented in Chapters 4 and 8, illustrate that the Court is highly dependent upon the (intervening) parties to the proceedings to provide the national context. Effectively arguing non-compliance by Member States in light of EU law provisions requires significant expertise in both the domestic policy context and national law and EU law. In this respect, the quality of advocacy thus plays a significant role, especially in Member States (including the Netherlands), which falls within Falkner, Hartlapp and Treib's 'world of domestic politics', where compliance with EU law is filtered through administrative cultures, implementation measures are based on a cost-benefit analysis and where 'playing the Eurolaw game' is part of governmental strategy. The existence of well-organised civil society groups with the necessary legal expertise at their disposal is then an important and sometimes necessary counter force.

9.6 Cause Lawyering and Pressure Through EU Law

The final sections of Chapter 5 zoomed in on lawyers that proactively aim to exploit opportunities in EU law and solicit references to the ECJ as part of their legal strategies. Such intentions often go beyond the direct interests of their clients and are aimed at serving the interests of larger collectives. Domestic doctrinal deadlock provides an important incentive for these cause lawyers to focus their efforts on getting a case referred to the ECJ in order to play out the matter at the supranational level. In these cases, the national judge especially forms an important barrier to strategic legal action. Although individual cases may serve as vehicles for change, by invoking judicial review of national policy, these lawyers do have to deal with the dilemma of serving collective interests by utilising one individual's case. Especially in areas of law where the stakes are high for the individual, and the impact of the procedure in itself can be detrimental, lawyers have to balance the interests of their client with that of the collective they are aiming to serve. EU law thus provides the means for collective legal protection, but where the interests of the individual oppose those defending domestic policy, the resulting dispute is augmented and often prolonged. The collective interests associated with this kind of judicial review are, therefore, sometimes contrary to the direct personal interests of the individual client. In that sense, the individual may become an unwitting (and not always willing) champion for collective interests. Examples of lawyers continuing cases after their client has given up his or her struggle for a residence permit and returned to his or her country of origin, underline this tension between individual and collective interests. Such tensions may also have a detrimental influence on the effective enforcement of EU law through the courts. Where domestic doctrinal deadlock may increase the need for judicial review by the ECJ, the extended duration of such complex legal strategies can serve as a deterrent for potential claimants. Examples of lawyers' difficulties finding willing clients in order to address certain perceived breaches of EU law attest to this fact.

Building on the insights into strategic use of EU law by lawyers, Chapter 7 focused on the preliminary reference procedure from the perspective of other strategic actors and analysed who were the actors most likely to signal opportunities in EU law, and what strategies were most likely to succeed in applying EU law litigation strategies. The case studies in this research underscore that when and how legal strategies, including the mobilisation of EU law, can be successful, is greatly dependent upon the ways in which parties are able to combine legal and extra-legal strategies and can pursue long-term strategies. In such long-term strategies, expertise and financial and organisational capital become increasingly important. The findings highlight the role of EU law experts, not only in signalling opportunities in EU law, but also in activating potential stakeholders to pursue legal strategies. The presented examples show that using EU law as part of activist strategies by interest groups is not widespread. This may be due to the high uncertainty that is associated with the use of the legal arena. However, the success of some of the actions also shows that it could simply be a matter of a lack of expertise in this area. Therefore, the role of activist lawyers and academics with the necessary expertise and the ability to mobilise is amplified.

I have shown how the most important structural problem such strategies have to overcome is the bringing together of expertise and court cases. The lack of direct access to the ECJ (as well as to the national courts in many cases) forces strategic actors to employ individual cases in order to address issues, i.e. Member States' non-compliance. In practice, this often means that the initiative of employing experts comes from lawyers who are confronted with a reference to the ECJ in one of their client's cases. Therefore, much of the expert advocacy is added to a legal strategy in a *post hoc* manner, sometimes undermining the effectiveness of such a strategy. As such, certain organisations able to bridge the gap between the experts and the legal practitioners who have a pool of cases from which to select are best situated to organise legal opposition to government practices. Alter and Vargas pointed out, based on examples in the United Kingdom, that in order for actors aiming to create pressure in the national system for doctrinal change, all it takes is one sympathetic judge located anywhere in the national legal system.[7] The examples discussed confirm some of the elements of pressure through law in the European context identified by Harlow and Rawlings, who conclude: "If the best use is to be made of pressure through international and [EU] law, new networks and new techniques are essential. Sharp issue focus, plaintiff stacking, forum shopping, political and legal campaigns in tandem are essential elements in transnational campaigns".[8] In that sense, forum shopping would help to find sympathetic members of the judiciary. However, the cases presented in Chapter 7, also reveal the drawbacks of such strategies. For example, given the observed general 'reluctance amongst the judiciary, and other adjudicators, to give effect to Community law principles'[9], increases the costs associated with efforts that fail to find such sympathetic judges. Such costs and uncertainty can certainly discourage would-be applicants from bringing cases, and make it that much harder for strategic actors to utilise this legal strategy. In practice, as expected, we see strategic actors acting in a more *post hoc* fashion by joining in legal action after a case is referred to the ECJ. This often occurs after requests for help by the lawyers in that case, but sometimes through offering assistance on their own initiative.

The analysis in Chapter 7 thus underscores how the possibilities in preliminary references are hampered by high uncertainty and, therefore, present a more problematic cost-benefit calculation. The recent emergence of initiatives by asylum and migration lawyers, academics and interest groups collaborating to more effectively employ EU law strategies, show how actors in the field of migration and asylum law try to cope with these structural aspects, and have the potential to build expertise in such supranational legal strategies. Such collaborations between practitioners, organised interest groups and EU law experts therefore provide a most fruitful way of gaining access to the ECJ and tapping into the possibilities of EU law and supranational review.

7 Alter & Vargas 2000, 475.
8 Harlow & Rawlings 1992, 289.
9 Blom et al. 1995: 35.

9.7 Reviewing the Dual Logic of Private Enforcement

Neofunctionalist accounts of European integration have stressed the circular reinforcement in litigation before the ECJ, and the mutual pursuit of 'instrumental self-interest' by private litigants, national judges and the ECJ as constitutive elements of Europeanisation dynamics. In this approach to legal and political dynamics in Europe, the private enforcement of EU rules before the national courts and especially the ECJ has been a central feature in the transformation of Europe. From an enforcement perspective of EU law too, private litigants have an important role to play by addressing in court possible infringements by Member States. In that respect, the 'dual vigilance', of both the public and the European Commission is one of the central mechanisms of the European legal and political organisation. With regard to this enforcement function of EU law, it is important to recognise that until recent years almost half the cases dealt with by the Court have been direct actions, a significant portion of which have been Member States being taken to court by the Commission for a failure to comply with EU law. As described in Chapter 8, these infringement actions and the preliminary reference procedure can be considered two sides of the same coin, and from the enforcement perspective of the European Commission can be part of one and the same effort to force compliance by Member States. Understanding the dynamics of European integration and the role of the legal arena therefore requires both avenues to be considered in tandem, and it underscores the enforcement function of private litigation.

Chapter 8 juxtaposed the advantageous position that both the European Commission as well as the Member States occupy in the supranational legal arena with those of the generally one-shotter litigants that appear before the ECJ. When it comes to enforcing one's rights at this level, the individual litigant may thus find him/herself in the presence of powerful supranational repeat players with interests that may or may not align with his or her personal stakes. In many respects, these players are much better positioned to make cost-benefit calculations, to be strategic in their actions and play the 'long game' in Eurolaw. Individuals, as well as more strategic players accompanying them, thus find themselves part of a game in which they do not hold all the cards. However, from the perspective of EU law enforcement, they play an important role nonetheless. In the case of the EU legal system, the effectiveness of some EU rules can be achieved almost exclusively when private parties assert their subjective rights before national courts.[10] This *dual logic* of private enforcement dates all

10 One way in which this is expressed by the Court is in the 'general interest function' of private enforcement, the reasoning behind which is that the existence of a right for private parties to pursue their private interest contributes at the same time to the protection →

the way back to the early years of the Court when it posited the enforcement by rights claims as part of the 'dual vigilance' within the legal system. In this respect, Wilman concludes that "[it] follows that the relevant case law and the EU legislation on private enforcement seek to ensure that the private parties concerned can effectively enforce their rights vested in EU law before national courts both as a means to safeguard the effective judicial protection of those parties and as a way to ensure that EU law is effectively applied and enforced at national level. This duality in effect constitutes the *very essence* of the concept of private enforcement as it exists in the EU legal order".[11] Individual litigants, then, are essential agents of enforcement when bringing EU law claims before national courts. When their case is referred to the ECJ, they may find themselves up against the interests of Member States with specialised representation. On the other hand, they may find in the European Commission a powerful ally, assuming that one's interests are aligned with the Commission's interpretation of EU law, its preferred policy outcomes and its enforcement priorities. The latter is in large part subject to political dynamics, and the Commission's position and priority may be influenced by considerations of a potential political backlash. This is why the Commission seems to prefer to tackle potential Member States' infringements by fostering private enforcement though national courts and preliminary references.[12]

From an enforcement perspective, the mechanism of private parties pursuing their own interests and in doing so simultaneously furthering the enforcement of EU law is obviously attractive. In this respect, Wilman invokes Adam Smith's notion of the 'invisible hand', the unintended result of an individual's pursuit of justice. However, this perspective does not necessarily include the practical perspective of these individual claimants. More often than not, the interests of individual claimants will be assumed to be relatively clear-cut, and, moreover, to be deduced from whichever matter is dealt with by the ECJ. Especially with regard to cases of compensation for a failure to comply with EU law, private claims serve to ensure the effective enforcement of EU legislation, and the protection of the public at large, by attaching a cost and discouragement to possible infringers: the Member States. The question is whether such a system of private enforcement is as effective where individual rights have a different character, where individual gains are less clear-cut and where the costs for private parties pursuing their interests may outweigh the possible benefits, as is often the case

of the public interest by discouraging practices that constitute infringements of EU rules. In practice the ECJ can be seen to link both expressions of effectiveness and treats them as 'two sides of the same coin'. In fact, they often not only coincide but also effectively reinforce each other. Wilman 2015, 457-8.

11 Wilman 2015, 463.

12 Cf. Hofmann 2016.

for individual litigants. Newly emerging areas where the influence of EU law is expanding, including areas that significantly impact citizens' lives, raise questions about the practical functionality of this dual logic. For instance, situations where the enforcement of a subjective right can be at odds with the effectiveness of public enforcement of EU rules and in situations where private parties may be persuaded to settle out of court, resulting in persistent non-compliance by Member States.

The deterrent effects of private enforcement serve the enforcement of EU law by providing a 'genuine incentive to compliance',[13] but, on an individual level, may not be of direct interest to private parties seeking to enforce their rights. The reluctance of national judges to decide on conflicts between EU law and national law *ex officio*, while also referring to the ECJ sporadically and selectively, increases the burden of litigation. The deterrent effect of such a system will, therefore, more likely fall on private parties, who are effectively dissuaded from litigation, than on the trespassing Member States. The obstacles individual litigants encounter as well as the selective nature inherent in preliminary references thus greatly undermines the enforcement function of the reference procedure. One such obstruction to this function of the preliminary reference procedure, and possibly the most problematic obstacle from a public power perspective, is the fact that the Member States have the opportunity to prevent judgments from the ECJ, as discussed in Chapter 8. Since references frequently deal with questions of the legality of national legislation or policy in light of EU legislation, a judgment by the ECJ may threaten national policy. From the perspective of the national government, references can, therefore, be very unwelcome, and the state will attempt to prevent a reference or a judgment. The findings presented of lawyers signaling thwarted efforts at getting cases referred to the ECJ suggest that it is not unusual for the government to curtail possible negative judgments in this way.

The results of this study thus illustrate how, depending on the potential impact of an individual claim, individual cases are played out in a multi-level political, administrative and legal arena that involves multiple interests. With their claim, parties may thus find themselves not only in opposition to a government body, but also the responsible ministries and, later in the procedure, face possible opposition from other Member States and even the European Commission all of whom have their own interest in the decision. Long-term strategies by national governments may be to the detriment of the individual party's interests.

13 As expressed by the European Commission 1990, 12-13. On later occasions the Commission has considered private enforcement to be a 'successful tool for policing markets' and 'a governance tool [which] can be used as a deterrent'. European Commission 2012, 7.

Member States are in a position to make risk assessments and, in cases that provoke a potentially unwelcome interpretation of EU law, move to contain the case by giving in; thus 'losing a battle to win the war'. Although in some cases such calculations may result in a win on the individual front, in the end this results in non-compliance by a Member State. Those that do decide to battle to the end are in for the long haul, and many can be expected to be dissuaded from litigation. As one respondent, who handled his case in full himself, summed it up: "It really is David against Goliath". The reliance on private enforcement of EU law, and the resulting unsystematic and selective address of enforcement deficits, in this sense has significant drawbacks and may require some critical reconsideration.

9.8 Re-Positioning the Individual in the European Legal System

This study gives impetus for a 're-positioning' of the individual in the legal system of Europe as a field of opportunities. The insights in part confirm the idea of the European legal system, and specifically the preliminary reference procedure, as a powerful mechanism, both in providing opportunities for those claiming rights in court as well as in transforming governance in Europe. However, the extent to which EU law and preliminary reference can be harnessed by those who wish to attack national policies and try to steer both domestic and supranational legal and political developments, is significantly limited. The purported 'emancipatory functionalism' of EU law, as a legitimizing rhetoric, creates high expectations for European citizens by offering individual empowerment and "liberating civil society from the shackles of parliamentary democracies".[14] However, one critical aspect to this individual rights rhetoric is the truism that the mere proclamation of rights does not necessarily mean actual social change. On what he famously called 'the myth of rights', Scheingold stated in this respect:

> "The assumption is that litigation can evoke a declaration of rights from courts; that it can, further, be used to assure the realization of these rights; and, finally, that realization is tantamount to meaningful change. The myth of rights is, in other words, premised on a direct linking of litigation, rights and remedies with social change."[15]

The legal approach to the subjects of rights, remedies, social change and litigation from an EU law perspective encourages a focus on judicial decisions and

14 Schepel 2004, 2.
15 Scheingold 1974, 5.

their implementation. Hence, the extensive literature on the ECJ's track record. The findings presented in this study critically examine the assumptions of macro-approaches to the preliminary reference procedure as a legal opportunity and an expression of 'demands for integration'. They shed light on the practicality of the use of EU law and the preliminary reference procedure as a so-called 'shield' and 'sword', empirically challenging the rights rhetoric and the narrative of empowerment by showing the constraints on the use of this procedure as a means to an end.

It has often been stressed that the distinct nature of the EU legal system, with the preliminary reference procedure as its most important instrument, makes for an enhanced opportunity to circumvent the domestic legal system. That same nature, however, makes deliberately aiming for the ECJ via this route a highly uncertain endeavour. The ability to make use of this procedure for underprivileged parties is, next to structural barriers, greatly hampered by an unequal distribution in (legal) agency and largely contingent on the ability to employ experts. Although the development of the European legal system has provided new avenues for individuals to seek justice, and the ECJ has been an ally for certain specific private interests and judicial politics in past decades, the empowerment rhetoric surrounding this should thus be considered a significant overstatement of the actual empowering effects of EU law for individual litigants. In practice, this is more about macro-legal developments and a form of extended political negotiation than about access to a meaningful form of justice. On the one hand, it does provide new possibilities for 'trumping' the domestic legal system whenever the supranational legislation provides opportunities against national policy or legislation; on the other hand, as a form of remedy the preliminary reference procedure remains a difficult 'sword' to harness and individual claimants are often better off with (swifter) adjudication within the national system. The effective use of it is largely reserved for organisations and 'strategy entrepreneurs'[16] with the necessary credentials, means and expertise.[17]

As concluded by Kelemen: "Consumers, airline passengers, shareholders, environmental nongovernmental organizations, victims of discrimination, and firms do not sue for Europe. They sue for themselves. Yet in doing so, they serve as the eyes, ears, and long arm of Brussels, providing strength to an otherwise weak state."[18] Individual litigants often unwittingly, and sometimes unwillingly, performing this task should not lead them to be co-opted uncritically into theories of integration as the beneficiaries thereof. Treating these litigants as such foregoes the inherent tensions that exist in legal practice. It ascribes to

16 Cf. Vanhala 2017.
17 Vauchez 2008a, 450.
18 Kelemen 2006, 121.

them motivations and intentions absent in fact. It, moreover, may overlook differences in agency among those that participate in the supranational political game. Rather than assuming pro-integrationist aims, or even sentiments, among those participating in the dynamics of integration-through-law, this can only be determined on a case-by-case basis. Therefore, the important enforcement role of the procedure notwithstanding, we should be wary of considering the preliminary reference procedure as a veritable form of access to justice from a litigant's perspective.

9.9 Methodological Reflections

The broad exploration of Euro-litigation and the resulting findings in this book direct attention to a broad range of mechanisms and 'forgotten narratives' in aggregated analyses of the European legal system in general and litigation in particular. The findings provide ample suggestion for further research in certain fields of law or in specific parts of the (European) legal field. The inductive approach of this study into an underexplored subject has provided new perspectives on largely uncharted territory. It provides a broad range of new insights and new narratives, but also presents us with particular challenges. Many of the political science approaches I have critically evaluated make use of econometric methods by reducing certain aspects of Euro-litigation (origin of reference, subject matter, etc.) to numerical units. This allows for complex model analysis based on functionally simplified representations of reality. Although I have identified several pitfalls, these approaches do allow for a high degree of control over one's research data. The methodology utilised in this study bears no such advantages. The dependence on the availability of respondents, the high uncertainty over the comprehensiveness of observation, the significant reliance upon the respondents' perspectives, as well as the great diversity in legal subjects, types of actors, interests and trajectories of cases has provided – apart from a rich body of data – a daunting challenge of distilling relevant perspectives and generalizable characteristics.

The methodological aim of this study – casting a wide net, without prejudging cases based on their doctrinal significance – has also had some repercussions for the depth with which issues that presented themselves inductively could be pursued. To capture fully the impact certain cases have on a local, national and supranational level requires a significant research effort with a selective focus on certain cases, and indeed certain areas of law or policy. The design of this research did not always allow for such an extensive archaeology of legal and political developments leading up to, and in the wake of certain cases. There is, therefore, a need to revalue the explanatory power of the case study. The recent work by Nicola and Davies is an example of such reappraisal of 'thick' descriptions, contextual histories and critical narratives by engaging with the personalities involved behind the scenes of as selection of some of the Court's *Grands arrêts*. The book convincingly shows how well-known ECJ cases can be retold through different contextual narratives, and thereby challenges the pervasive hegemony of legal reasoning in studies of Euro-litigation. However, by focusing exclusively on cases that have featured prominently in exactly that legal perspective on ECJ case law, it moves away from such perspective only in part. As concluded by Conant earlier, "scholars should try to look beyond an exclusive focus on ECJ decisions and references in order to explore how the majority of EU law is actually adjudicated, avoiding the blind spots associated with a disproportionate focus on a central high court and its 'constitutional' judgements".[19] This study has partly been able to overcome this focus on ECJ decisions by looking beyond 'constitutional' judgments and not selecting cases based on their salience, but it has not – due to its focus on actual preliminary references and not on 'non-litigation' or failed efforts at Euro-litigation – completely moved away from a focus on the ECJ in its study of EU law mobilisation. Indeed, the overwhelming majority of national court decisions on EU law do not involve a reference to the ECJ and are independent decisions.[20] The non-purposeful portion of references from the perspective of litigants as well as the number of cases where EU law was mobilised without the aim of reaching the ECJ, underscores the need for future research to 'domesticate' in empirical focus on EU judicial politics. This study did not overcome the obvious limitation that preliminary references to the ECJ constitute only the tip of the iceberg when it comes to the degree to which EU law is litigated in national courts. As such this study has its own blind spots. What this study can only infer from certain illustrative findings leaves room for speculation, but also gives indications of what future research might focus on to fill the knowledge gap.

9.10 Remaining Questions and Future Research Agenda

Member States in Comparison

An obvious remaining question is how the findings in this study compare to a similar analysis in other Member States. To what extent does national legal culture, described by Blankenburg[21] as the interrelationship of law, institutional

19 Conant 2007a, 57.
20 Conant 2002, 81-2.
21 Blankenburg 1997.

structures and behavioural patterns, play a role in determining active EU law mobilisation? As we have seen, the 'EU law consciousness' varies considerably among practitioners, litigants, judges, and between areas of law, and appears limited overall. Therefore, a difference in legal culture could have significant influence on the manner in which EU law is mobilised in different national contexts. The structure of law matters for the outcome of the so-called 'dialogue' between the courts and the application of EU law. The national cultures of judicial review as well as national standing rules and more general structures of access to justice are decisive elements for this dialogue as well. The existence or absence of a national culture of judicial review, and the existence or absence of a constitutional court, may influence the perception of the ECJ as a possible partner in this dialogue. This is the case for national judges and their proclivity to send cases to the ECJ as it is for national litigation cultures that may or may not focus on supranational review as a potential source of legal ammunition for political actors.[22]

Legal Strategies and the Legal Lexicon of Practitioners

Related to this question of difference in national cultures is the presence of actors that are capable of mobilising EU law in a strategic manner. In a more international respect the question is what, if any, are the organised transnational networks of 'Euro-lawyers'? And what are the issues and clients on which they are focused? A similar question is pertinent when it comes to transnational NGOs and their legal strategies. To what extent are such strategically important interlocutors involved in the creation, and more importantly, in the subsequent enforcement of newly developed EU legislation? And to what extent do they employ legal strategies, or choose to use different means. In other words, how do the findings in this study compare to 'supranational interest representation' via other avenues, like lobbying or more institutionalised forms of 'functional participation'?[23] In what way do such other forms of interest representation differ from or coincide with efforts of legal mobilisation?

With the enforcement role of the legal profession in mind, the findings presented give indications of how EU law and norms (have) become integrated into the 'legal consciousness' of practitioners and reveal differences in both the 'litigability' of certain principles as well as the practical knowledge among practitioners when it comes to applying EU law in a meaningful way. In order to

22 See for example Cohen-Tanugi, who describes how the idea that litigation could be a powerful democratic instrument is totally foreign to French political culture. Cohen-Tanugi 1985, 158.

23 Smismans 2004.

better understand how EU law and norms find their way into the 'legal lexicon' of practitioners, future research could focus (more specifically than this study has been able to do) on how they deal with EU law on a day-to-day basis. How well are they acquainted with the jurisprudence of the ECJ, and with general principles of EU law? How significant are these norms considered to be from their perspective and how, when and why do they employ them before national courts? Special attention in this respect should be paid to differences between areas of law, both in available and applicable EU norms (non-discrimination may be relevant in trans-border tax law and social security cases, yet expectedly less so in private law) as well as in (possibly related) EU law consciousness among practitioners in different fields. To what extent are practitioners focused on EU law as a source of legal argumentation and to what extent is EU law integrated into the legal consciousness of those who are charged with decentralized enforcement in a practical sense?

A Shift Away from the Supranational Perspective

The impact of the European legal system and the way EU legislation may be employed is not limited to the supranational level. Future research would do well to shift away from focusing merely on judicial interaction and supranational jurisprudential developments and renew attention to the national, and subnational level. The focus on the judicial dialogue between the ECJ and national courts is in large part the result of outside observers taking the internal logic of the legal system at face value, all the while overlooking what goes on beyond what is 'purely legal'. Kelemen and Pavone conclude after a spatio-temporal analysis of preliminary references in Italy that "although population levels and domestic litigiousness best explain variation in reference rates, there is evidence that the domestic litigation effect is subnationally heterogeneous."[24] They recognise, in tandem with this study, that subnational mechanisms that would be proper units of analysis when studying causal factors in preliminary reference rates, e.g. cause lawyers, academic involvement in litigation, civil society organisation, EU law specialisation among practitioners. Thereby confirming the need for avenues of research that focus on the ways in which the practice of EU law is entrenched locally.

For example, this study has presented some examples of how the 'threat' of a reference may be used as a tactic as well. As such the threat of preliminary references can have effect beyond direct implementation. This leads to the inference that in Member States where national judges are relatively hesitant to refer, the incentive for lawyers and/or interest groups to employ this strategy will not

24 Kelemen & Pavone 2016, 1118.

develop as it might in countries like the Netherlands (and especially the UK, where there is for instance more extensive possibility for collective redress). We can expect to some extent a learning curve among legal professionals that can be nourished and encouraged by past successes to employ similar strategies. Further research that delves into this aspect of EU law mobilisation should, therefore, focus on the level of practical knowledge of the EU legal system at the ground level, relevant EU legislation and the awareness of opportunities among practitioners, as well as their perceptions of the importance or desirability of using EU law in court. Comparative research between national legal systems as well as between different areas of law would yield the most significant insights.

A Shift Away from the International Relations Perspective

Related to the shifting away from a jurist's perspective is the need to shift away from the political science perspective, which has dominated the study of the EU legal system in recent decades. Chapter 2 has outlined a state of the art of mainstream research into the relation between preliminary references and EU integration. The international relations tradition in the study of the EU legal system and the ECJ has limited the study of EU law largely to questions of sovereignty and compliance. This perspective, although an essential part of EU studies, has been successful partly due to the exclusion of other relevant perspectives. Recently published literature shows that the criticisms voiced and the conclusions drawn in this study do not stand alone, and newly emerging research agendas and studies conducted in tandem with this study show promising new efforts in history, sociology and socio-legal studies towards further filling in the pervasive blindspots in EU integration studies.[25]

One of the still remaining perspectives of the European legal system is the way in which EU law has penetrated domestic life. The related questions that come to mind when approaching the EU focus more on how EU law has been integrating into local legal, political and social practice. How do local bureaucracies, for instance, deal with applying EU law? How, when and why does EU law become a strategic asset in political struggle, and when is it refused or resisted, not only in legal contestation, but more broadly in political struggles? A related question is: how European is Euro-litigation? Research on litigation and European law should turn to developing a theoretical distinction in legal practice that is local and truly European. And how can a distinction be made? Based on the parties' objectives? Based on the results? Based on the functionality of the (European) legal system? Further theorizations and empirical analysis should focus on these questions. This research has shown how these two in practice are

25 Cf. Bailleux 2014, Arnholtz 2014 and Nicola & Davies 2017.

not always easily distinguishable from each other, and how often practices that are essentially focused on local and national issues are called 'European'. A better understanding of legal practice in Europe would contribute to enhancing our understanding of the ever evolving 'community based on law', not only from an institutional and legal, but also a societal perspective.

Bibliography

Alter, K.J., 'The European Court's Political Power', *West European Politics* 1996-19(3), p. 458-487.

Alter, K. J., 'Explaining National Court Acceptance of European Court Jurisprudence: A Critical Evaluation of Theories of Legal Integration', in: A.M. Slaughter, A. Stone Sweet & J.H.H. Weiler (eds.) *The European Court and National Courts: Doctrine and Jurisprudence*, Oxford: Hart Publishing 1998, p. 225-250.

Alter, K.J., 'The European Union's Legal System and Domestic Policy: Spillover or Backlash?', *International Organization* 2000-54(3), p. 489-518.

Alter, K.J., *Establishing the Supremacy of European Law. The Making of an International Rule of Law in Europe*, Oxford: Oxford University Press 2001.

Alter, K. J., 'Agents or Trustees? International Courts in their Political Context', *European Journal of International Relations* 2008-14(1), p. 33-63.

Alter, K.J., *The European Court's Political Power: Selected Essays*, Oxford: Oxford University Press 2009.

Alter, K.J., 'Private Litigants and the New International Courts', *Comparative Political Studies* 2006-39(1), p. 22-49.

Alter, K.J. & S. Meunier-Aitsahalia, 'Judicial Politics in the European Community: European Integration and the Pathbreaking Cassis de Dijon decision', *Comparative Political Studies* 1994-24, p. 535-561.

Alter, K.J., & J. Vargas, 'Explaining Variation in the Use of European Litigation Strategies: European Community Law and British Gender Equality Policy', *Comparative Political Studies* 2000-33(4), p. 452-482.

Arnholtz, J., *A 'legal revolution' in the European field of posting?: Narratives of uncertainty, politics and extraordinary events*, Doctoral dissertation, University of Copenhagen 2014.

Arnull, A., 'The Use and Abuse of Article 177 EEC', *The Modern Law Review* 1989-52(5), p. 622-639.

Azoulai, L., 'The Court of Justice and the Social Market Economy: the Emergence of an Ideal and the Conditions for its Realization', *Common Market Law Review* 2008-45(5), p. 1335-1355.

Bailleux, J., *Penser l'Europe par le Droit: L'invention du Droit Communautaire en France*, Paris: Dalloz 2014.

Banakar, R., 'Power, Culture and Method in Comparative Law', *International Journal of Law in Context* 2009-5(1), p. 69-85.

Banakar, R., 'Having One's Cake and Eating It: the Paradox of Contextualisation in Socio-Legal Research', *International Journal of Law in Context* 2011-7(4), p. 487-503.

Barnard, C., 'A European Litigation Strategy: The Case of the Equal Opportunities Commission', in: J. Shaw & G. More (eds.) *New Legal Dynamics of European Union*, Oxford: Clarendon Press 1995, p. 254-272.

Baumgärtel, M., 'Perspectives on the "User": Unpacking the Concept for Human Rights Research', *Human Rights & International Legal Discourse* 2014-8(2), p. 142-160.

Biernat, E., *The Locus Standi of Private Applicants Under Article 230 (4) EC And the Principle of Judicial Protection in the European Community*, Jean Monnet Working Paper 12/03, New York: NYU School of Law 2003.

Blankenburg, E., 'Civil Litigation Rates as Indicators for Legal Cultures', in: D. Nelken (ed.) *Comparing Legal Cultures*, Aldershot: Dartmouth 1997, p. 41-68.

Blauberger, M., 'With Luxembourg in mind ... the remaking of national policies in the face of ECJ jurisprudence', *Journal of European Public Policy* 2012-19(1), p. 109-126.

Blom, J., B. Fitzpatrick, J. Gregory, R. Knegt & U. O'Hare, '*The utilisation of sex equality litigation procedures in the Member States of the European community, a comparative study*', Report given by the Commission of the European Union, DG V, Brussels 1995.

Bonjour, S., 'Between Integration Provision and Selection Mechanism. Party Politics, Judicial Constraints, and the Making of French and Dutch Policies of Civic Integration Abroad', *European Journal of Migration and Law* 2010-12(3), p. 299-318.

Bonjour, S., 'The Power and Morals of Policy Makers: Reassessing the Control Gap Debate', *International Migration Review* 2011-45(1), p. 89-122.

Börzel, T.A., 'Guarding the Treaty: The Compliance Strategies of the European Commission', in: T.A. Börzel & R.A. Cichowski (eds.) *The State of the European Union, 6: Law, Politics, and Society*, Oxford: Oxford University Press 2003a, p. 197-220.

Börzel, T.A., *How the European Union Interacts with its Member States*, IHS Political Science Series 2003/93, Vienna 2003b.

Börzel, T.A., 'Participation Through Law Enforcement: The Case of the European Union', *Comparative Political Studies* 2006-39(1), p. 128-152.

Bouwen, P. & M. McCown, 'Lobbying versus Litigation: Political and Legal Strategies of Interest Representation in the European Union', *Journal of European Public Policy* 2007-14(3), p. 422-443.

Broberg, M. & N. Fenger, *Preliminary References to the European Court of Justice*, Oxford: Oxford University Press 2010.

Broberg, M. & N. Fenger, 'Variations in Member States' Preliminary References to the Court of Justice – Are Structural Factors (Part of) the Explanation?', *European Law Journal* 2013-19(4), p. 488–501.

Bruinsma, F., *De Hoge Raad van Onderen,* Alphen a/d Rijn: Kluwer 2010.

Brunell, T.L., C. Harlow & A. Stone Sweet, 'Litigating the Treaty of Rome: The European Court of Justice and Articles 226, 230, and 234', *New Modes of Governance Project* 2008, available at: http://www.eunewgov.org/database/DELIV/DLTFIID06a2_Litigating_Treaty_of_Rome.pdf [last accessed 12 July 2017].

Bulterman, M. & C. Wissels, 'Stategies Developed by – and Between – National Governments to Interact with the ECJ', in: M. Dawson, B. de Witte & E. Muir (eds.) *Judicial Activism at the European Court of Justice*, Cheltenham: Edward Elgar Publishing 2013, p. 264-278.

Burley, A.M., & W. Mattli, 'Europe Before the Court: a Political Theory of Legal Integration', *International Organization* 1993-47(1), p. 41-76.

Caldeira, G.A., & J.L. Gibson, 'The Legitimacy of the Court of Justice in the European Union: Models of Institutional Support', *American Political Science Review* 1995-89(2), p. 356-376.

Cappalletti, B., 'Is the European Court of Justice "Running Wild"?', *European Law Review* 1987-12, p. 3-17.

Carlin, J. & J. Howard, 'Legal Representation and Class Justice', *U.C.L.A. Law Review* 1965-12, p. 381-410.

Carrera, S., & B. Petkova, 'The Potential of civil society and human rights organizations through third-party interventions before the European Courts: the EU's area of freedom, security and justice', in: M. Dawson, B. de Witte & E. Muir, (eds.) *Judicial activism at the European Court of Justice*, Cheltenham: Edward Elgar Publishing 2013, p. 233-263.

Carrera, S., M. de Somer & B. Petkova, *The Court of Justice of the European Union as a Fundamental Rights Tribunal: Challenges for the Effective Delivery of Fundamental Rights in the Area of Freedom, Security and Justice*', Justice and Home Affairs, CEPS Papers in Liberty and Security in Europe No. 49, Brussels: CEPS 2012. Available at: http://papers.ssrn.com/sol3/papers.cfm?abstract_id= 2145891 [last accessed 12 July 2017].

Carrubba, C. J., 'The European Court of Justice, Democracy, and Enlargement', *European Union Politics* 2003-4(1), p. 75-100.

Carrubba, C.J., & L. Murrah, 'Legal Integration and Use of the Preliminary Ruling Process in the European Union', *International Organization* 2005-59(2), p. 399-418.

Chalmers, D., 'The positioning of EU judicial politics within the United Kingdom', *West European Politics* 2000-23(4), p. 169-210.

Chalmers, D., 'Law and European integration: Socio-legal perspectives', *EUSA Review* 2004-17(4), p. 3-4.

Chalmers, D. & M. Chaves, 'The Reference Points of EU Judicial Politics', *Journal of European Public Policy* 2011-19(1), p. 25-42.

Cichowski, R.A., 'Integrating the Environment: The European Court and the Construction of Supranational Policy', *Journal of European Public Policy* 1998-5(3), p. 387-405.

Cichowski, R.A., 'Introduction: Courts, Democracy, and Governance', *Comparative Political Studies* 2006a-39(1), p. 3-21.

Cichowski, R.A., 'Courts, Rights, and Democratic Participation', *Comparative Political Studies* 2006b-39(1), p. 50-75.

Cichowski, R.A., *The European Court and Civil Society: Litigation, Mobilization and Governance*, Cambridge: Cambridge University Press 2007.

Cichowski, R.A. & A. Stone Sweet, 'Participation, representative democracy and the courts', in: B. Cain, R. Dalton & S. Scarrow (eds.), *Democracy transformed? Expanding political opportunities in advanced industrial democracies*, Oxford: Oxford University Press 2003, p. 192-220.

Claes, M. & B. de Witte, 'Report on the Netherlands', in: A.M. Slaughter, A. Stone Sweet & J.H.H. Weiler (eds.) *The European Courts and National Courts – Doctrine and Jurisprudence: legal change in its social context*, Oxford: Hart Publishing 1998, p. 188-192.

Coen, D. & J. Richardson, *Lobbying the European Union: Institutions, Actor and Policy*, Oxford: Oxford University Press 2008.

Cohen-Tanugi, L., 'Le Droit sans l'État. Sur la démocratie en France et en Amérique', *Politique étrangère* 1985-50(3), p. 804-805.

Conant, L., *Justice Contained. Law and Politics in the European Union*, Ithaca: Cornell University Press 2002.

Conant, L., 'Europe's No Fly Zone? Rights Obligations, and Liberalization in Practice', in: T.A. Börzel & R.A. Cichowski (eds.) *The State of the European Union, 6: Law, Politics, and Society*, Oxford: Oxford University Press 2003, p. 235-250.

Conant, L., 'Individuals, Courts, and the Development of European Social Rights', *Comparative Political Studies* 2006-39(1), p. 76-100.

Conant, L., 'Review Article: The Politics of Legal Integration', *Journal of Common Market Studies* 2007a-45(1), p. 45-66.

Conant, L., 'Judicial Politics', in: K.E. Jørgensen, M. Pollack & B. Rosamond (eds.) *Handbook of European Union Politics*, London: Sage 2007b, p. 213-229.

Costa, O., 'The European Court of Justice and democratic control in the European Union', *Journal of European Public Policy* 2003-10(5), p. 66-97.

Craig, P. & G. de Búrca, *EU Law: Text, Cases, and Materials*, Oxford: Oxford University Press 2003.

Dalton, R.J., B.E. Cain & S.E. Scarrow, 'Democratic Publics and Democratic Institutions', in: B.E. Cain, R.J. Dalton & S.E. Scarrow (eds.) *Democracy Transformed?: Expanding Political Opportunities in Advanced Industrial Democracies*, Oxford: Oxford University Press 2003, p. 265-266.

Davies, G., 'Activism Relocated. The Self-Restraint of the European Court of Justice in its National Context', *Journal of European Public Policy* 2012-19(1), p. 76-91.

De Búrca, G., 'The Language of Rights and European Integration', in: G. More & J. Shaw (eds.) *New Legal Dynamics of the European Union*, Oxford: Oxford University Press 1995, p. 29-54.

Dehousse, R., *The European Court of Justice. The Politics of Judicial Integration*, London: Palgrave 1998.

Dehousse, R., & Weiler, J.H.H., 'The Legal Dimension', in: W. Wallace (ed.) *The Dynamics of European Integration*, London: Pinter 1990, p. 242-260.

De Waele, H., 'European Rules as "Law of the Land"? Towards Optimalisation of EU Member State Compliance', *Romanian Journal of Political Science* 2010a-10(1), p. 52-70.

De Waele, H., 'The Role of the European Court of Justice in the Integration Process : A Contemporary and Normative Assessment', *Hanse Law Review* 2010b-6(3), p. 3-26.

De Waele, H. & A. van der Vleuten, 'Judicial Activism in the European Court of Justice', *Michigan State Journal of International Law* 2010-19(3), p. 639-666.

Edward, D., 'How the Court of Justice Works', *European Law Review* 1995-20(1), p. 539-558.

Edward, D., 'Advocacy before the Court of Justice: Hints for the uninitiated', in: G. Barling, G. & Brealey, M. (eds.) *Practitioners Handbook of EC Law*, London: Trenton Publishing 1998, p. 22-45.

Engelen, F.A. & F.P.G. Pötgens, *Het keuzerecht en de buitenlandse belastingplicht in de IB en VPB*, Amsterdam: Elsevier 2001.

Eriksen, E.O., 'Democratic Legitimacy Beyond Borders. Government Without a State', in: R. Forst & R. Schmalz-Bruns (eds.) *Political Legitimacy and Democracy in Transnational Perspective*, ARENA Report 02/11, Oslo: University of Oslo 2011, p. 245-280.

Evan, W.M., *Law and Sociology, Exploratory Essays*, New York: Free Press of Glencoe 1962.

Everson, M. & C. Joerges, *Reconfiguring the politics-law relationship in the integration project through conflicts-law constitutionalism*, RECON Online Working Paper No. 2011/31, 2011. Available at:

http://www.astrid-online.it/Riforma-de/Studi-e-ri/RECON_wp_11_31.pdf [last accessed 12 July 2017].

Falkner, G., O. Treib, M. Hartlapp & S. Leiber, *Complying with Europe: EU harmonisation and soft law in the Member States*, Cambridge: Cambridge University Press 2005.

Falkner, G., M. Hartlapp & O. Treib, 'Worlds of Compliance: Why Leading Approaches to European Union Implementation are only "Sometimes-True Theories"', *European Journal of Political Research* 2007-46(3), p. 95-416.

Falkner, G. & O. Treib, 'Three Worlds of Compliance or Four? The EU-15 Compared to New Member States', *JCMS: Journal of Common Market Studies* 2008-46, p. 293-313.

Felstiner, W.L.F., R.L. Abel & A. Sarat, 'The Emergence and Transformation of Disputes: Naming, Blaming, Claiming…', *Law & Society Review* 1980-15(3/4), p. 631-654.

Fitzgerald, I. & R. Dickins, 'Disputing in legal and non-legal contexts: Some questions for sociologists of law', *Law & Society Review* 1980-15, p. 681-706.

Forst, R. & R. Schmalz-Bruns, *Political Legitimacy and Democracy in Transnational Perspective*, ARENA Report No 2/11, Oslo: University of Oslo 2011, p. 245-280.

Friedman, L.M., *The Legal System: A Social Science Perspective*, New York: Russell Sage Foundation 1975.

Friedman, L.M., 'Litigation and Society', *Annual Review of Sociology* 1989-15(1), p. 17-29.

Galanter, M., 'Why the Haves Come Out Ahead: Speculations on the Limits of Legal Change', *Law & Society Review* 1974-9(1), p. 165-230.

Galanter, M., 'The Duty not to Deliver Legal Service', *University of Miami Law Review* 1976-30(4), p. 929-951.

Galanter, M., 'The Day After the Litigation Explosion', *Maryland Law Review* 1986-45(1), p. 3-39.

Garrett, G., 'International Cooperation and Institutional Choice: The European Community's Internal Market', *International Organization* 1992-46(1), p. 533-560.

Garrett, G., 'The Politics of Legal Integration in the European Union', *International Organization* 1995-49(1), p. 171-181.

Garrett, G., R.D. Kelemen & H. Schulz, 'The European Court of Justice, National Governments, and Legal Integration in the European Union', *International Organization*, 2003-52(1), p. 149-176.

Garapon, A., *Le Gardien de Promesses: Justice et Démocratie*, Paris: Odile Jacob 1996.

Gehring, A., 'Dutch Retirement Migration to Spain and Turkey: Seeking Access to Healthcare Across Borders', *Transnational Social Review* 2016-6(3), p. 326-343.

Gibson, J.L. & G.A. Caldeira, 'The legitimacy of transnational legal institutions: Compliance, support, and the European Court of Justice', *American Journal of Political Science* 1995-39(2), p. 459-489.

Givens, T., & A. Luedtke, 'The Politics of EU Immigration Policy: Institutions, Salience, and Harmonization', *Policy Studies Journal* 2004-32(1), p. 145-165.

Goldstein, J.L., M. Kahler, R.O. Keohane & A.M. Slaughter, 'Introduction: Legalization and World Politics', *International Organization* 2000-54(3), p. 385-399.

Golub, J., 'The Politics of Judicial Discretion: Rethinking the Interaction Between National Courts and the European Court of Justice', *West European Politics* 1996-19(2), p. 360-385.

Granger, M-P., *The Influence of Member States' Governments on Community Case Law. A Structurationist Perspective on the Influence of EU Governments in and on the Decision-Making Process of the European Court of Justice*. Doctoral dissertation, University of Exeter 2001. Available at: https://www.academia.edu/10952617/The_Influence_of_Member_States_Governments_on_Community_Case_Law_A_Structurationist_Perspective_on_the_Influence_of_EU_Governments_in_and_on_the_Decision-Making_Process_of_the_European_Court_of_Justice [last accessed 12 July 2017].

Granger, M.P., 'When governments go to Luxembourg...: the Influence of Governments on the Court of Justice', *European Law Review* 2004-29(1), p. 3-31.

Granger, M.P., 'States As Successful Litigants Before the European Court of Justice: Lessons from the "Repeat Players" of European Litigation', *Croatian Yearbook of European Law and Policy* 2006-2(2), p. 27-49.

Greer, S.L., 'The Weakness of Strong Policies and the Strength of Weak Policies: Law, Experimentalist Governance, and Supporting Coalitions in European Union Health Care Policy', *Regulation & Governance* 2011-5(2), p. 187-203.

Greer, S.L. & M. Martín de Almagro Iniesta, 'How Bureaucracies Listen to Courts: Bureaucratized Calculations and European Law', *Law and Social Inquiry* 2014-39(2), p. 361-386.

Grimmel, A., 'Integration and the Context of Law: Why the European Court of Justice is Not a Political Actor', *SSRN Electronic Journal*, 2011. Available at: http://doi.org/10.2139/ssrn.1989210 [last accessed 12 July 2017].

Groenendijk, C.A., 'Commentaar op de brief van de Ministers van BZ en I&A aan de Tweede Kamer van 28 januari 2011 over de betekenis van het arrest Soysal', *Asiel & Migrantenrecht* 2011-25(1), p. 30-31.

Groenendijk, C.A., 'The Court of Justice and the Development of EEC-Turkey Association Law', in: D. Thym & M. Zoeteweij-Turhan (eds.) *Rights of Third-Country Nationals under EU Association Agreements. Degrees of Free Movement and Citizenship,* Leiden: Brill 2015, p. 39-64.

Groenendijk, C.A. & C.A.J.M. Kortmann, 'Nieuwe verhoging leges voor verblijfsvergunningen: wederom onredelijk, onverstandig en onrechtmatig', *Nederlands Juristenblad* 2003-7, p. 314-321.

Groenendijk, C.A., M. Rondhuis & M.H.A. Strik, 'Klagen bij de Europese Commissie. Effecten van Tien Jaar Juridische Belangenbehartiging door het Inspraakorgaan Turken in Nederland', *Asiel & Migrantenrecht* 2015-6(6), p. 24-35.

Guild, E., *The European Union after the Lisbon Treaty: Fundamental Rights and EU Citizenship*, CEPS Liberty and Security in Europe Series, Centre for European Policy Studies, Brussels: CEPS 2010.

Harding, C., 'The Private Interest In Challenging Community Action', *European Law Review* 1980-5, p. 354-361.

Harding, C., 'Who Goes to Court in Europe?: An Analysis of Litigation against the European Community', *European Law Review* 1992-17(2), p. 104-125.

Harding, C. & A. Gibbs, 'Why Go To Court in Europe? An Analysis of Cartel Appeals 1995-2004', *European Law Review* 2005-30(3), p. 349-369.

Harlow, C., 'Toward a Theory of Access for the European Court of Justice', *Yearbook of European Law* 1992-12(1), p. 213-248.

Harlow, C. & R. Rawlings, *Law and Administration*, London: Weidenfeld and Nicolson 1984.

Harlow, C. & R. Rawlings, *Pressure Through Law*, London: Routledge 1992.

Havinga, T. & J. Hoevenaars, 'Éliane Vogel-Polsky en de Realisatie van Vrouwenrechten: een Actor als Factor', in: R. Baas, T. Havinga, M. Laemers & H. den Tonkelaar (eds.) *Rechtspleging en Rechtsbescherming. Liber amicorum voor prof. dr. Leny E. de Groot-van Leeuwen*, Deventer: Kluwer 2015, p. 89-100.

Helfer, L.R. & A.M. Slaughter, 'Toward a Theory of Effective Supranational Adjudication', *The Yale Law Journal* 1997-107(273), p. 273-391.

Heinz, J. & E. Laumann, 'The Legal Profession: Client Interests, Professional Roles, and Social Hierarchies', *Michigan Law Review* 1978-76(7), p. 1111-1142.

Hirschl, R., 'The Judicialization of Mega-Politics and the Rise of Political Courts', *Annual Review of Political Science* 2008-11(1), p. 93-118.

Hirschl, R., *Toward Juristocracy: The Origins and Consequences of the new Constitutionalism,* Cambridge: Harvard University Press 2004.

Hofmann, A., *Legal Mobilisation and Institutional Support – The European Commission as a Catalyst in the EU's Rights Revolution*, Paper presented at the 7th ECPR General Conference, 4-7 September 2013, Bordeaux.

Hofmann, A., *Legal Rights and Practical Effect: Why the European Commission Supports Access to Justice for Interest Groups*, Paper presented at WZB workshop 'Implementation and judicial politics: Conflict and compliance in the EU multi-level system', 3-4 March 2016, Berlin.

Jaremba, U., 'At the Crossroads of National and European Union Law. Experiences of National Judges in a Multi-level Legal Order', *Erasmus Law Review*, 2013-6(3/4), p. 191-203.

Kagan, R.A., *Adversarial Legalism: The American Way of Law,* Cambridge: Harvard University Press 2001.

Kelemen, R.D., 'Suing for Europe: Adversarial Legalism and European Governance', *Comparative Political Studies* 2006-39(1), p. 101-127.

Kelemen, R.D., *Eurolegalism*, Cambridge: Harvard University Press 2011.

Kelemen, R.D., Eurolegalism and Democracy. *Journal of Common Market Studies 2012*-50, p. 55–71.

Kelemen, R.D. & T. Pavone, 'Mapping European Law', *Journal of European Public Policy* 2016-23(8), p. 1118-1138.

Kelemen, R.D. & S.K. Schmidt, 'Introduction – the European Court of Justice and legal integration: perpetual momentum?', *Journal of European Public Policy* 2012-19(1), p. 1-7.

Kennedy, D., *The Rise & Fall of Classical Legal Thought,* Washington DC: BeardBooks 1980.

Kilroy, B.A., *Integration through the Law*, Los Angeles: University of California 1999.

Kocken, J., 'Questioning Legitimacy or Why Social Scientists Find Legitimacy Where None Exists', *Recht Der Werkelijkheid* 2008(3), p. 1-19.

Komninos, A.P., 'Introduction', in: C.D. Ehlermann & I. Atanasiu (eds.) *European Competition Law Annual 2001: Effective Private Enforcement of EC Antitrust Law*, Oxford: Hart Publishing 2003, p. xxi-xlii.

Koopmans, T., *Courts and Political Institutions: A Comparative View,* Cambridge: Cambridge University Press 2003.

Kritzer, H.M., 'Studying Disputes: Learning from the CLRP Experience', *Law & Society Review* 1980-15(3), p. 503-524.

Kronenberger, V., 'Locus standi of individuals before Community courts under Article 230(4) EC : Illusions and Disillusions after the Jégo-Quéré (T-177/01) and Unión de Pequenos Agricultores (C-50/00 P) judgments', *The European Legal Forum* 2002-230(4), p. 257-264.

Kumm, M., *How does European Union Law Fit into the World of Public Law? Costa, Kadi and Three Conceptions of Public Law*, New York University Public Law and Legal Theory Working Papers No. 262, New York 2011.

Lamassoure, A., *The Citizen and the Application of Community Law*, Online Report, June 2008. Available at: https://www.tib.eu/en/search/download/?tx_tibsearch_search%5Bdocid%5D=TIBKAT%3A733250513 [last accessed 12 July 2017].

Lasser, M. de S.-O.-l'E., *Judicial Deliberations: A Comparative Analysis of Judicial Transparency and Legitimacy,* Oxford: Oxford University Press 2004.

Lee, S. & A. Vauchez, 'Politics Building Europe on a Weak Field : Law, Economics, and Scholarly Avatars in Transnational Politics', *American Journal of Sociology* 2014-118(2), p. 449-492.

Lecourt, R., *L'Europe des Juges,* Brussels: Bruylant 1976.

Lenaerts, K., *Effective judicial protection in the EU*, Online Publication, September 2013. Available at: http://ec.europa.eu/justice/events/assises-justice-2013/files/interventions/koenlenarts.pdf [last accessed 12 July 2017].

Lijphart, A., *Patterns of democracy,* New Haven: Yale University Press 1999.

Macaulay, S., 'Non-Contractual Relations in Business: A Preliminary Study', *American Sociological Review* 1963-28(1), p. 55-67.

Mancini, G.F., 'The Making of a Constitution for Europe', *Common Market Law Review* 1989-26, p. 595-614.

Mancini, G.F. & D.T. Keeling, 'Democracy and the European Court of Justice', *Modern Law Review* 1994-57(2), p. 175-190.

Mancini, G.F. & D.T. Keeling, 'Language, Culture and Politics in the Life of the European Court of Justice', *Columbia Journal of European Law* 1995-1(3), p. 397-413.

Mastenbroek, E., *The politics of compliance: Explaining the transposition of EC directives in the Netherlands,* Doctoral dissertation, Leiden University 2007. Available at: https://openaccess.leidenuniv.nl/handle/1887/11861 [last accessed 12 July 2017].

Mastenbroek E. & M. van Keulen, 'Beyond the Goodness of Fit: A Preference-based Account of Europeanization', in: R. Holzhacker & M. Haverland (eds.) *European Research Reloaded: Cooperation and Integration Among Europeanized States*, Dordrecht: Springer 2006, p. 19-42.

Mattli, W. & A.M. Slaughter, *Constructing the European Community Legal System From the Ground Up: the Role of Individual Litigants and National Courts*, EUI Working Papers No. 1996/56, Florence: EUI 1996.

Mattli, W. & A.M. Slaughter, 'Law and politics in the European Union: a reply to Garrett', *International Organization* 1995-49(1), p. 183-190.

Mattli, W. & A.M. Slaughter, 'Revisiting the European Court of Justice', *International Organization* 1998-52(1), p. 177-209.

Mazey, S.P., 'The European Union and Women's Rights: From the Europeanization of National Agendas to the Nationalization of a European Agenda?', *Journal of European Public Policy* 1998-5(1), p. 131-152.

McCammon, H.J. & A.R. McGrath, 'Litigating Change? Social Movement and the Court System', *Sociology Compass* 2015-9(2), p. 128-139.

McCann, M., 'Law and Social Movements Contemporary Perspectives', *Annual Review of Law and Social Science* 2006-2, p. 17-38.

McGuire, K.T., 'Repeat Players in the Supreme Court: The Role of Experienced Lawyers in Litigation Success', *The Journal of Politics* 1995-57(1), p. 187-196.

Micklitz, H.W., *The Politics of Judicial Co-operation in the EU – the Case of Sunday trading, Equal Treatment and Good Faith*, Cambridge: Cambridge University Press 2005.

Micklitz, H.W., 'The ECJ between the Individual Citizen and the Member States – A Plea for a Judge-Made European Law on Remedies', in: H.W. Micklitz & B. de Witte (eds.) *The European Court of Justice and the Autonomy of the Member States*, Cambridge/Antwerp/Portland: Intersentia 2012, p. 349-399.

Micklitz, H.W. & N. Reich, *Public Interest Litigation before European Courts,* Baden-Baden: Nomos 1996.

Miller, R.E. & A. Sarat, 'Grievances, Claims and Disputes: Assessing the Adversary Culture', *Law and Society Review* 1980-15(3), p. 525-566.

Nicola, F. & B. Davies, *EU Law Stories: Contextual and Critical Histories of European Jurisprudence*, Cambridge: Cambridge University Press 2017.

Nonet, P., *Administrative Justice: Advocacy and Change in a Government Agency,* New York: Russell Sage Foundation 1969.

Nowak, T., *How judgments become law and how law restricts judgments : the influence of the European Court of Justice on the legislative process of the European Community,* Doctoral Thesis, Rijksuniversiteit Groningen 2007.

Nowak, T., F. Amtenbrink, M. Hertogh & M. Wissink, *National Judges as European Union Judges,* Den Haag: Eleven International Publishing 2012.

Panke, D., 'The European Court of Justice as an agent of Europeanization? Restoring compliance with EU law', *Journal of European Public Policy* 2007-14(6), p. 847-866.

Parker, C., 'A Critical Morality for Lawyers: Four Approaches to Lawyers' Ethics' Monash University Law Review, 2004-30, p. 49-74.

Pavone, T. 'Democracy By Lawsuit: Or, Can Litigation Alleviate the European Union's Democratic Deficit?' *Constitutional Studies* 2016-2, p. 59-80.

Prechal, S., R.H. van Ooik, J.H. Jans & K.J.M. Mortelmans, '"Europeanisation" of the Law: Consequences for the Dutch Judiciary', Raad voor de Rechtspraak Research Memoranda 2, Den Haag: Sdu 2005.

Rasmussen, H., *On Law and Policy in the European Court of Justice: A Comparative Study in Judicial Policymaking,* Dordrecht, Boston, Lancaster: Martinus Nijhoff Publishers 1986.

Rasmussen, M., 'Revolutionizing European law: A history of the Van Gend en Loos judgment', *International Journal of Constitutional Law* 2014-12(1), p. 136-163.

Rasmussen, M., 'Establishing a Constitutional Practice of European Law: The History of the Legal Service of the European Executive, 1952-65', *Contemporary European History* 2012-21(3), p. 375-397.

Rawlings, R., 'The Euro-Law Game: Some Deductions for a Saga', *Journal of Law and Society* 1993-20(3), p. 309-340.

Rosenthal, D., *Lawyer and Client: Who's in Charge?,* New York: Russell Sage Foundation 1974.

Rubin, E., 'Passing Through the Door. Social Movement Literature and Legal Scholarship', *University of Pennsylvania Review* 2001-150, p. 1-83.

Sarat, A. & S. Scheingold, *Cause Lawyering: Political Commitments and Professional Responsibilities*, New York: Oxford University Press 1998.

Schaap, D., 'Leges, Een Eindstand?', *Asiel & Migrantenrecht* 2014-10, p. 429-435.

Scharpf, F.W., 'The Joint-Decision Trap: Lessons from German Federalism and European Integration', *Public Administration* 1988-66, p. 239-278.

Scharpf, F.W., 'The Asymmetry of European Integration, or Why the EU Cannot be a "Social Market Economy"', *Socio-Economic Review* 2010-8(2), p. 211-250.

Scharpf, F.W., 'Perpetual Momentum: Directed and Unconstrained?', *Journal of European Public Policy* 2012-19(1), p. 127-139.

Scheingold, S.A., *The Rule of Law in European Integration*, London: Yale University Press 1965.

Scheingold, S.A., *The Politics of Rights: Lawyers, Public Policy, and Political Change*, New Haven: Yale University Press 1974.

Schepel, H. & E. Blankenburg, 'Mobilizing the European Court of Justice', in: G. de Búrca & J.H.H. Weiler (eds.) *The European Court of Justice*, Oxford: Oxford University Press 2001, p. 9-42.

Schepel, H., 'Law and European integration: Socio-legal perspectives', *EUSA Review* 2004-17(4), p. 1-3.

Scheppele, K.L., *Enforcing the Basic Principles of EU Law Through Systemic Infringement Procedures*, Paper presented at NYU School of Law, August 2015.

Schmidt, S.K., 'Who Cares About Nationality? The Path-Dependent Case Law of the ECJ from Goods to Citizens', *Journal of European Public Policy* 2012-19(1), p. 8-24.

Scott, C., 'Regulation in the Age of Governance: The Rise of the Post-Regulatory State', in: J. Jordana & D. Levi-Faur (eds.) *The Politics of Regulation in the Age of Governance,* Cheltenham: Edward Elgar Publishing 2004, p. 145-174.

Shapiro, M., *Courts: A Comparative and Political Analysis*, Chicago: University of Chicago Press 1981.

Shapiro, M., 'The Globalization of Law', *Indiana Journal of Global Legal Studies* 1993-1(1), p. 37-64.

Shapiro, M., 'Codification of Administrative Law: The US and the Union', *European Law Journal* 1996-2(1), p. 26-47.

Shapiro, M., 'The European Court of Justice: of Institutions and Democracy', *Israel Law Review* 1998-32(3), p. 3-50.

Shapiro, M., & A. Stone Sweet, 'The New Constitutional Politics of Europe', *Comparative Political Studies*, 1994-26(4), p. 397-420.

Shaw, J., 'European Union legal studies in crisis? Towards a new dynamic', *Oxford Journal of Legal Studies* 1996-16(2), p. 231-254.

Shaw, J. & A. Wiener, 'The Paradox of the "European Polity"', in: M.G. Cowles & M. Smith (eds.) *The State of the European Union: Risks, Reform, Resistance, and Revival*, Oxford: Oxford University Press 2012, p. 64-89.

Slaughter, A.M., A. Stone Sweet & J.H.H. Weiler, *The European Courts and National Courts – Doctrine and Jurisprudence,* Oxford: Hart Publishing 1998.

Smismans, S., *Law, legitimacy, and European Governance: Functional Participation in Social Regulation,* Oxford: Oxford University Press 2004.

Smith, M., 'Inter-institutional Dialogue and the Establishment of Enforcement Norms: A Decade of Financial Penalties under Article 228 EC (now Article 260 TFEU)', *European Public Law* 2010-16, p. 547-570.

Snyder, F., 'New Directions in European Community Law', *Journal of Law and Society* 1987-14(1), p. 167-182.

Solanke, I., '"Stop the ECJ"?: An Empirical Analysis of Activism at the Court', *European Law Journal* 2011-17(6), p. 764-784.

Stein, E., 'Lawyers, Judges, and the Making of a Transnational Constitution', *The American Journal of Comparative Law* 1981-75(1), p. 1-27.

Stone Sweet, A., 'European integration and the legal system', in: T.A. Börzel & R.A. Cichowski, *The State of the European Union, 6: Law, Politics, and Society*, Oxford: Oxford University Press 2003, p. 18-47.

Stone Sweet, A., *The Judicial Construction of Europe*, New York: Oxford University Press 2004.

Stone Sweet, A., 'The European Court of Justice and the Judicialization of EU Governance', *Living Reviews in EU Governance* 2010-5(2), p. 1–54.

Stone Sweet, A. & T.L. Brunell, 'Constructing a Supranational Constitution: Dispute Resolution and Governance in the European Community', *American Political Science Review* 1998-92(1), p. 63-81.

Stone Sweet, A. & T.L. Brunell, 'The European Court and the National Courts: a Statistical Analysis of Preliminary References, 1961-95', *Journal of European Public Policy* 1998-5(1), p. 66-97.

Stone Sweet, A. & T.L. Brunell, '*Data Set on Preliminary References in EC Law*', NEWGOV Project, Robert Schuman Centre, European University Institute, 2007. Dataset available at: http://www.eunewgov.org/database/DELIV/LTFIID4b_Data_Set_Preliminary_References_Art234_1961-2006.xls [last accessed 12 July 2017].

Stone Sweet, A. & J.A. Caporaso, 'From Free Trade to Supranational Polity: The European Court and Integration', in: W. Sandholz & A. Stone Sweet (eds.) *European Integration and Supranational Governance*, Oxford: Oxford University Press 1998, p. 92-133.

Tallberg, J., *European Governance and Supranational Institutions: Making States Comply,* London: Routledge 2003.

Tamanaha, B.Z., *Law as a Means to an End: Threat to the Rule of Law,* Cambridge: Cambridge University Press 2006.

Tamanaha, B.Z., *A Concise Guide to the Rule of Law*, Legal Studies Research Paper Series, Nr. 07-0082, New York: St. John's University 2007. Available at: http://content.csbs.utah.edu/~dlevin/conlaw/tamanaha-rule-of-law.pdf [last accessed 12 July 2017].

Tridimas, T. & G. Gari, 'Winners and losers in Luxembourg: A statistical analysis of judicial review before the European Court of Justice and the Court of First Instance (2001-2005)', *European Law Review* 2010-35(2), p. 131-173.

Tridimas, G. & T. Tridimas, 'National courts and the European Court of Justice: a Public Choice Analysis of the Preliminary Reference Procedure', *International Review of Law and Economics* 2004-24(2), p. 125-145.

UNHCR, *Safe at Last? Law and Practice in Selected EU Member States with respect to Asylum-Seekers Fleeing Indiscriminate Violence*, Online Report 2011. Available at: http://www.unhcr.org/4e2d7f029.pdf [last accessed 12 July 2017].

Vago, S., *Law and Society*, New York: Routledge 2006.

Van de Mei, A.P., 'Cross-Border Access to Healthcare and Entitlement to the Complementary "Vanbraekel-Reimbursement"', *European Law Review* 2011-5, p. 431-440.

Van Gestel, R.A.J., 'The "Deparliamentarisation" of Legislation: Framework Laws and the Primacy of the Legislature', *Utrecht Law Review* 2013-9(2), p. 106-122.

Vanhala, L., *Making rights a reality? Disability rights activists and legal mobilization*. New York: Cambridge University Press 2011.

Vanhala L., 'Legal Opportunity Structures and the Paradox of Legal Mobilization by the Environmental Movement in the UK', *Law & Society Review* 2012-46, p. 523-556.

Vanhala L., 'Legal Mobilization Under Neo-Corporatist Governance: Environmental NGOs Before the Conseil d'Etat in France, 1975-2010', *Journal of Law and Courts*, 2016-4, p. 103-130.

Vanhala, L., 'Is Legal Mobilization for the Birds? Legal Opportunity Structures and Environmental Nongovernmental Organizations in the United Kingdom, France, Finland, and Italy', *Comparative Political Studies* (in press) 2017, p. 1-40.

Van Harten, H., 'Who's Afraid of a True European Judicial Culture?' *Review of European Administrative Law*, 2012-5(2), p. 131-152.

Van Harten, H.J. & H. van Eijken, 'Lookin' for a Little Green Bag…' en de werkingssfeer van het Unierecht', *Nederlands Tijdschrift voor Europees Recht* 2011-4, p. 105-113.

Van Oers, R., *Deserving Citizenship. Citizenship Tests in Germany, the Netherlands and the United Kingdom* Leiden: Martinus Nijhoff Publishers 2013.

Vauchez, A., *Embedded law. Political sociology of the European community of law: Elements of a renewed research agenda*, EUI Working Papers No. 2007/23, Florence: EUI 2007.

Vauchez, A., 'Democratic empowerment through EU law?', *European Political Science* 2008a-7, p. 444-452.

Vauchez, A., *'Integration-Through-Law': Contribution to a Socio-History of EU Political Commonsense*, EUI Working Paper No. 2008/10, Florence: EUI 2008b.

Vauchez, A., 'The Force of a Weak Field: Law and Lawyers in the Government of the European Union (For a Renewed Research Agenda)', *International Political Sociology* 2008c-2(2), p. 128-144.

Vauchez, A., 'The Transnational Politics of Judicialization. Van Gend en Loos and the Making of EU Polity', *European Law Journal* 2010-16(1), p. 1-28.

Vaughan, D. & M. Gray, 'Litigating in Luxembourg', *Jersey & Guernsey Law Review* 2007-11, p. 1-14.

Von Bogdandy, A. & I. Venzke, 'Beyond Dispute: International Judicial Institutions as Lawmakers. On the Democratic Legitimation of International Judicial Lawmaking', *German Law Journal* 2011-12(5), p. 979-1004.

Wainwright, R., 'A View from the Commission', in: M. Andenas (ed.) *Article 177 References to the ECJ Policy and Practice,* London: Butterworths Law 2010, p. 105-127.

Ward, A., *Judicial Review and the Rights of Private Parties in EC Law*, Oxford: Oxford University Press 2000.

Weatherill, S., *Cases & Materials on EU Law* (11th ed.), Oxford: Oxford University Press 2014.

Weiler, J.H.H., 'The transformation of Europe', *The Yale Law Journal* 1991-100, p. 2403-2483.

Weiler, J.H.H., 'Epilogue: The European Courts of Justice: Beyond 'Beyond Doctrine' or the Legitimacy Crisis of European Constitutionalism', in: A.M. Slaughter, A. Stone Sweet & J.H.H. Weiler (eds.) *The European Courts and National Courts – Doctrine and jurisprudence*, Oxford: Hart Publishing 1998, p. 378-383.

Wernicke, S., 'Au nom de qui? The European Court of Justice between Member States, Civil Society and Union Citizens', *European Law Journal* 2007-13(3), p. 380-407.

Wigger, A. & A. Nolke, 'Enhanced Roles of Private Actors in EU Business Regulation and the Erosion of Rhenish Capitalism: the Case of Antitrust Enforcement', *Journal of Common Market Studies* 2007-45(2), p. 487-513.

Wilman, F., *Private Law Enforcement of EU Law before National Courts. The EU Legislative Framework,* Cheltenham: Edward Elgar Publishing 2015.

Wind, M., D.S. Martinsen & G.P. Rotger, 'The Uneven Legal Push for Europe – Questioning Variation When National Courts Go to Europe', *European Union Politics* 2013-10(1), p. 63-88.

Appendices

APPENDIX A: Case Descriptions

Breeding or Fattening?

C-355/11, Judgment of 14/06/2012, OJ C 227/6
A dairy farmer challenges the cuts in premiums he received for not complying with the ban on the tethering of calves laid down in the EU Directive on minimum standards for the protection of calves. The reference to the ECJ asks whether the Directive applies only to calves kept for breeding or fattening, or for calves kept on the dairy farm. The Court states that the term 'breeding' does not have the same meaning in all EU languages. Yet, the term cannot be interpreted in a limited sense because the EU must respect animal welfare requirements in the field of agriculture. According to the Court, therefore, calves kept under the dairy farming system fall under the protection of the Directive.

Catering Employees

C-242/09, Judgment of 21/10/2010, OJ C 346/15
In this case, the Court is asked to rule on the protection of workers in the case of a transfer of undertaking in a situation where an employee has two employers within one concern. The catering employees who, with the help of a labour union, brought this case were formally employed by a so-called personnel carrier, while working in another operating company within the larger corporation. The company decided to transfer its catering activities to a third party. The question was whether the staff acquired by the new employer could claim retaining their (old) employment conditions, as this staff had no employment contract with the operating company that transferred the catering activities. So far, Dutch legal doctrine has considered the relevant EU Directive only applicable to personnel who have a contract of employment with the alienator of the activities. However, the Court considers that the protection of the Directive also applies in a situation like this one and protects the non-contractual employment relationship.

Cattle Premiums

C-170/08, Judgment of 11/06/2009, OJ C 180/18
This case was brought by a farmer in light of the European common agricultural policy and the related income support for farmers. He was excluded from grants on the ground that the number of 'animals determined' at his farm was fixed at

zero following the finding of a prohibited substance in the urine of some of his bovine animals during an inspection in 2000. When establishing the so-called 'single payment' income support for farmers in 2006, the national authorities assumed zero cattle, which led to a permanent reduction in the income support that the farmer could claim. The Court determines that for the calculation of the reference amount, account must be kept of the number of animals for which a direct payment has been or should have been granted. The Court concludes that abatements and exclusions imposed during the reference period on the basis of the European rules for market organization in the beef sector do not function permanently and should be disregarded in the calculation of the reference amount.

Compulsory Insurance

C-347/10, Judgment of 17/01/2012, OJ C 73/3
A Dutch national who worked on a drilling platform outside Dutch territorial waters, but within the Dutch continental shelf, and who had moved to Spain appeals a denial of incapacity allowance because he does not meet the residence requirement. Supported by a labour union, his case is eventually brought before the ECJ. The question put to the ECJ is whether the European Basic Regulation on Social Security and the freedom of movement for workers apply to his situation. The Court finds that national legislation which states that it is the residence criterion which determines whether or not an employee working on a drilling platform on the continental shelf adjacent to a Member State may benefit from compulsory insurance in that Member State is contrary to EU law. Moreover, it must be found that such national legislation places non-resident workers, in a less favourable position than resident workers with regard to their social security cover in the Netherlands, and therefore undermines the principle of freedom of movement secured by EU law.

Concealed Foreign Savings

C-157/08, Judgment of 11/06/2009, OJ C 180/17
This test case, brought by a large tax consultancy firm, concerns the question whether the longer tax recovery period of up to twelve years for concealed savings in another Member State, is contrary to free movement of capital and services, due to discrimination in terms of legal certainty, and by making it less attractive for taxpayers to transfer savings to another Member State and keep them there. The ECJ indeed considers the longer period a barrier to free movement because the longer recovery period makes retaining funds from income in another Member State less attractive. However, this restriction can be justified

with the aim of the effectiveness of fiscal controls and to fight tax fraud. The Court finds the measure appropriate and not disproportionate to achieve these legitimate goals. The measure is also necessary for those cases where the Member State is not aware at all of taxable assets held in another Member State.

Conditions of Residence

C-484/07, Judgment of 16/06/2011, OJ C 232/4
A Turkish national who came to the Netherlands in the context of family reunification with her parents, married a Turkish man, but remained living with her parents. After being informed about the marriage, the IND rescinded the residence permit retroactively with effect from the date of marriage. Based on Dutch policy the family relationship is supposedly broken by the wedding. The question submitted to the ECJ is whether her situation still satisfies the conditions of residence of the Association Agreement with Turkey. The Court considers that the host Member State may require that during the first three years the family member indeed live with the parents. However, the host Member State may not set other conditions. The Dutch policy is considered in violation of the Association Agreement.

Double Nationality

C-7/10, Judgment of 29/03/2012, OJ C 151/3
Two joined cases of family members of Turkish workers who face expulsion due to a criminal past. This measure is based on national rules for expulsion of aliens, the so-called 'sliding scale'. Both family members object to their expulsion and rely on the EU Association Agreement with Turkey. Besides the Turkish, their family members also have Dutch nationality. According to the Netherlands, this precludes the possibility of relying on Association law. In its judgment the ECJ does not follow this reasoning. Family members of Turkish dual-national workers may rely on the EU Association Agreement with Turkey against their expulsion for criminal convictions. Obtaining Dutch nationality does not matter. According to the Court, the expulsion of family members of Turkish workers must be done according to the rules of the EU Association Agreement with Turkey.

Export of Benefits

C-485/07, Judgment of 26/05/2011, OJ C 211/3
In a collective action against the Netherlands Turkish pensioners who had returned to Turkey appeal the withdrawal of an allowance for their invalidity pen-

sion. According to new Dutch law limiting the export of benefits, the surcharge will be paid only to beneficiaries residing in the territory of the Netherlands. The reference to the ECJ asked whether such law is compatible with the Association Agreement between the EU and Turkey. The Court considered that Article 6 of Decision 3/80 on the coordination of social security schemes for Turkish employees is directly applicable in the Member States. Furthermore, the Court ruled that the allowance for the invalidity pension could not be withdrawn at the time that beneficiaries no longer lived in the Netherlands, since Article 6 of Decision 3/80 prohibits the instalment of a residence requirement.

Extradition

C-123/08, Judgment of 06/10/2009, OJ C 282/8
This is a case concerning the possible extradition of a German national, fighting extradition to Germany, which had issued a European Arrest Warrant (EAW). Such a warrant can be refused on certain grounds. In this case Dutch grounds for refusal were stricter than those in EU law requiring a residence permit of the subject. Dutch policy denies extradition where foreigners, including EU citizens, have a permanent residence permit, which can be obtained after five years of stay. The question put to the ECJ was how this condition relates to EU law, which does not have a requirement for the duration of the stay. According to the Court, a Member State cannot require a residence permit of EU citizens, since such a document is not required for stay in the Netherlands. However, the Court also concludes that European law does not oppose a five-year requirement for refusal of extradition, since this limits the cases in which the court may refuse to carry out an EAW, by which the final goal of the intra-EU cooperation is facilitated.

Extraterritorial Dredging

C-106/11, Judgment of 07/06/2012, OJ C 217/4
The case of a Dutch national who lives in Spain and works for a Dutch company, on a dredger ship sailing under the Dutch flag in the territorial waters of, among others, China. He opposed the decision by Dutch authorities considering that he falls under the Dutch social security system and therefore has to pay a premium. The preliminary question asks whether the Dutch social security system indeed applies to his situation. The Court answered this question in the affirmative, concluding that EU law prevents a person from being excluded from the national social security system in such a situation, simply because he does not live in the Member State concerned.

Fees in Migration Law

C-242/06, Judgment of 17/09/2009, OJ C 267/8
In a case of a Turkish national whose request for a residence permit was denied due to the failure to pay the required fee, Dutch increases in fees for residence permits are questioned in light of the 'standstill clause' in the Association Agreement between the EU and Turkey. The case, supported by a well-organised group of lawyers, academics and interest groups, resulted in an alignment of the amount of fees for residence permits of Turkish nationals and EU citizens, and had spin-off effects for other groups of migrants, including third country nationals.

Free Movement of Cannabis

C-137/09, Judgment of 16/12/2010, OJ C 55/6
In a test case set up in an agreement between a coffee shop owner and a Dutch municipality, the applicability of EU law to Dutch soft drugs policy is tested. In a pilot, the municipality of a border town issued a local prohibition of admission of persons who are not residents of the Netherlands in order to combat so-called drug tourism, and fined one coffee shop owner in alleged violation of said prohibition. The coffee shop owner argued that legislation that forbids the sale of cannabis to non-residents constitutes unjustified unequal treatment of citizens of the European Union. In the context of this procedure, questions were put to the ECJ on the compatibility of the resident criterion with EU law. The Court ruled that a coffee shop owner cannot rely on Union law for the sale of cannabis. The reason for this is that, due to their nature, these substances are completely banned from imports and sales in all Member States. With regard to the 'legal' beverages and food items being sold in the coffee shop, the Court finds that restricting access to non-residents is a justified, appropriate and proportionate measure from the point of view of combating drug tourism.

'Formally Limited' Residence Permits

C-502/10, Judgment of 18/10/2012, OJ C 379/4
An Indian national, in the Netherlands on a temporary residence permit in connection with his work as a spiritual leader is denied a permanent residence permit after five years of residence in the Netherlands. His application is rejected because his residence permit, according to the Secretary of State, is a so-called 'formally limited residence permit' within the meaning of the Directive on the status of third country nationals who are long-term residents. According to the Court, the phrase 'in cases where their residence permit is formally limited' is an

autonomous European concept and must be interpreted uniformly. According to the Court, there is no formally limited residence permit within the meaning of national law, the formal limitation of which does not prevent the third country national concerned from establishing a permanent place of residence. It is up to the national court, in the light of all circumstances, to ascertain whether that is indeed the case. Upon returning to the national court, the Secretary of State repealed its appeal to a lower court's decision, which had vindicated the spiritual leader's claim.

Income Requirements

C-578/08, Judgment of 04/03/2010, OJ C 113/13
In this case, brought by a Moroccan national with a permanent residence permit wanting to be reunited with his Moroccan wife, the ECJ is asked whether or not the Netherlands can apply a requirement of an income of at least 120% of the minimum wage for family reunification. The claimant has been in the Netherlands since 1970. In 2006 the request for a provisional permit for his wife is denied based on the fact that he does not meet the income requirement laid down in Dutch law. The question is whether the Dutch income claim for family reunification is in violation of the Family Reunification Directive. The ECJ judges that the Netherlands cannot apply the rule that family reunions must always have an income of at least 120% of the minimum wage. It is to be used as a reference amount, but the income test must be accompanied by a concrete assessment of the applicant's situation. The Court further finds that the Netherlands cannot distinguish in the income test according to whether the marriage has occurred before or after the arrival of the family member to the Netherlands.

Integration Abroad

C-155/11 PPU, Order of 10/06/2011, OJ C 269/18
This urgent preliminary ruling procedure questions the compatibility of the Dutch Civic Integration Abroad Act with the Family Reunification Directive. The case is about an Afghan woman who wants to be reunited with her husband and children, all of whom are legitimately staying in the Netherlands. Based on Dutch law she is required to pass a pre-entry civic integration test. Because she has not passed the basic examination, her request is denied. Supported by academics and the interest group the Dutch Refugee Council her case is referred to the ECJ. However, because the Dutch government grants a provisional residence permit during the proceedings, the Court finds that the main action has become devoid of purpose, therefore the case does not result in a ruling on the compatibility of the Dutch law with EU law.

Lessee Entitlements

C-470/08, Judgment of 21/01/2010, OJ C 63/13
This test case was set up in an agreement between an association of lessors and an entrepreneurial and employers' organization. Under the so-called EU farmers' single payment scheme farmers can redeem income. Such grants are granted to a farmer as a tenant, but are at the same time linked to the farmland. The test case sought to answer the question what should happen with the payment entitlements when a lease agreement ends. It was unclear whether the tenant had to transfer rights at the end of a lease agreement to the lessee. The Court decides that the payment entitlements stay with the tenant, based on the aims of the common agricultural policy of providing a fair standard of living for farmers. The link between rights and land only serves to ensure income support. Speculative transfer and accumulation of rights without an agricultural basis is prevented in this way.

Mortgage Interest Deductions

C-527/06, Judgment of 16/10/2008, OJ C 313/4
A civil servant living in Belgium and working in the Netherlands brings a claim to apply a mortgage deduction on his house in Belgium to his income tax in the Netherlands. The question put to the ECJ is whether his inability to do so constitutes discrimination in light of the right to free movement of workers. The ECJ finds this to be the case because neither his state of residence nor his state of employment takes into account his personal and family situation, in this case the mortgage interest deduction, and thus his fiscal capacity. The free movement of workers opposes the fact that a taxpayer cannot deduct negative income from a property in his state of residence from his income tax in his state of employment, while such deduction is allowed to residents of the latter state.

New Restrictions

C-300/09, Judgment of 09/12/2010, OJ C 55/11
These joined cases of two Turkish nationals who had lived legally in the Netherlands with their legally residing spouses for more than one but less than three years. Both their requests for an independent permit were denied due to the breaking of the marital bond before reaching three years of legal stay, a requirement that had been relaxed to one year in 1983 but had been reinstated in 2000. Both parties invoke the 'standstill clause' in the Association Agreement between the EU and Turkey, which precludes Member States from creating new restrictions regarding access to employment of legally resident Turkish workers

and their family members after 1980. While the Dutch government argued that there is no new restriction since the temporary easing of policy has only been reversed, the ECJ ruled differently. According to the Court, a relaxation for Turkish employees can no longer be reversed, as this creates a new constraint.

Pensioners Abroad

C-345/09, Judgment of 14/10/2010, OJ C 346/17
This is a case of pensioners living abroad opposing payment of a premium deducted from their pensions after the transition to a new Dutch health care system. According to them, the premium is in violation of EU law. The question is about the ratio of the compulsory care premium with EU law. According to the Court, the EU rules on social security and the freedom of movement and residence within the EU do not obstruct the mandatory deduction of care premiums. However, it is up to the national court to determine whether the transition to the new health care system resulted in different treatment of residents and pensioners already living abroad. The national court subsequently concluded that the alleged difference in treatment between residents and non-residents – constituting discrimination – did not exist.

Proportional Tax Deductions

C-594/10, Judgment of 16/02/2012, OJ C 98/8
A tax advisor appeals the lump sum correction to the VAT tax deduction, which he had received for use of two cars for business purposes, due to the personal use of said cars. The preliminary questions asked whether this Dutch scheme is compatible with requirements for a deduction limitation scheme laid down in the EU's Sixth VAT Directive. According to the Court, there is no provision for the limitation of deductions. The Court concludes that the Directive contravenes a national tax regime based on a flat-rate method of calculation for expenditure related to private use, if it does not take into account proportionally the actual extent of that use. The correction should therefore be proportional to the use.

Retroactive Withdrawal

C-187/10, Judgment of 29/09/2011, OJ C 340/3
A Turkish employee receives a temporary residence permit under condition of stay with his partner in the Netherlands. This residence permit is accompanied by permission to work without a work permit, which he does. One and a half years after commencement of his work, he requests a change in his residence permit from the 'stay with partner' to 'continued residence'. Moreover, his resi-

dence permit is withdrawn with retroactive effect due to the discontinuation of his relationship. The question put before the ECJ was whether Association law stands in the way of this withdrawal with retroactivity. The Court finds that this is the case, as a Turkish employee who has worked legally for one year has built up rights under Association law. These rights do not depend on the survival of the circumstances on the ground on which they originated. The Court concludes that it is contrary to Association law, as well as to the general principle of the respect for acquired rights, to withdraw a residence permit with retroactive effect after one year of legal work.

Self-Employed Tax Deductions

C-440/08, Judgment of 18/03/2010, OJ C 134/6
This test case, brought by a small accountancy firm sought to answer the question whether or not the Dutch self-employment deduction scheme is in accordance with EU law. According to this arrangement, a Dutch resident has a right to deduct if he works more than 1,225 hours in his Dutch and/or foreign company. A foreign taxpayer is only entitled to deduction after working at least 1,225 hours in the Netherlands. A case was brought in the name of one of the clients of the accountancy firm who operates a company in both Germany and the Netherlands and who has worked in Germany for more than 1,225 hours, but not in the Netherlands. The Court is asked to examine the scheme in light of the freedom to provide services and considers that it indeed discriminates based on residence. Domestic and foreign self-employed persons are in an objectively similar situation, which does not justify the difference in treatment.

Student Finance

C-158/07, Judgment of 18/11/2008, OJ C 6/4
A German national studying in the Netherlands appealed a decision by the Dutch 'IBG' (the administrative body charged with the enforcement of Netherlands legislation relating to the financing of studies) to annul her maintenance grant and a request to repay excess sums. The IBG considered that she was not complying with requirements for legal stay and integration in the Netherlands, which were a prerequisite for the maintenance grant. The ECJ finds that since the granting of student grants to students from other Member States should not become an unreasonable burden, Member States may require that the students in question have shown a degree of integration. The Court finds that a term of residence is an appropriate, and not excessive, means to ensure that the student in question is integrated into the host country.

Subsidiary Protection

C-465/07, Judgment of 17/02/2009, OJ C 90/4
Two Iraqi nationals were denied an asylum claim to a temporary residence permit based on the dangers they faced from indiscriminate violence in Iraq. The reference of their case to the ECJ (which was subsequently supported by a small group of cause lawyers and academics) sought an interpretation of the new EU Qualification Directive on asylum, stipulating the qualification for subsidiary protection. The ECJ was asked to answer the question whether, the Directive offered supplementary or other protection, potentially broadening the scope of the protection that asylum seekers enjoy under EU law, and therefore providing an interesting target for champions of the rights of asylum seekers. The ECJ concludes that the Directive does not require the applicant to be specifically targeted and that the more the applicant is able to show that he is specifically affected, the lower the level of indiscriminate violence required for him to be eligible for subsidiary protection.

Suckler Cow Premiums

C-446/06, Judgment of 28/02/2008, OJ C 107/5
Case of a Dutch farmer who challenges the cuts in premiums he received for his suckle cows. His case evolves into a question of whether or not Member States may place conditions on the right to EU premiums based on usual animal husbandry practice. While the European Commission argues against it, the Court finds that the term ‘suckler cow’ is not defined accurately enough in the implementing regulation. Therefore, Member States are free to determine conditions based on common animal husbandry practices within their territory.

Tethered or Chained?

C-187/07, Judgment of 03/04/2008, OJ C 128/14
A Dutch farmer who houses his calves in individual half-open boxes while tying them with a rope of around three metres, challenges a fine he received based on tying the young calves in place in violation of rules laid down in the EU Directive on minimum standards for the protection of calves. He argues that the calves are not bound within the meaning of the Directive. The Court looked to the general and common meaning of the word ‘tethered’ and the different language versions of the Directive. The Court found that a calf was bound in the sense of the Directive when held in place with a tethering device, regardless of the nature and length thereof and regardless of the reason for tying.

APPENDIX B: References According to Member State

Member State	Total Number of Preliminary References since 1961	Ranking according to Total Number of References	Number of References between 2008-2012	Ranking in period 2008-2012
Austria	490	7	39	11
Belgium[1]	**820**	**5**	**156**	**3**
Bulgaria	101	17	54	8
Croatia	8	26	0	27
Cyprus	7	27	0	27
Czech Republic	53	21	21	18
Denmark	184	9	33	15
Estonia	18	24	10	24
Finland	102	16	25	17
France	**954**	**4**	**119**	**5**
Germany	**2300**	**1**	**352**	**1**
Greece	178	10	36	14
Hungary	136	12	53	9
Ireland	91	18	18	19
Italy	**1388**	**2**	**226**	**2**
Latvia	55	20	11	22
Lithuania	45	22	11	22
Luxembourg	**91**	**19**	**18**	**19**
Malta	3	28	1	26
Netherlands	**975**	**3**	**148**[2]	**4**
Poland	108	15	39	11
Portugal	153	11	39	11
Romania	123	14	45	10
Slovakia	38	23	18	19
Slovenia	17	25	4	25
Spain	437	8	93	7
Sweden	126	13	30	16
United Kingdom	612	6	113	6
Total	9613		1712	

Data collected from the ECJ's yearly statistics, available at: https://curia.eu.

1 Member States in bold are the original Members of the European Communities.
2 These are the total of new references lodged at the ECJ in the selected five-year period. Hence, the different number from that of the selection for this research that included the cases dealt with by the Court in the same period.

Curriculum Vitae

Jos Hoevenaars, born in 1986 in Rotterdam, studied Sociology at the Erasmus University in Rotterdam and obtained his master's degree in 2011. From 2012 he worked as a PhD researcher and lecturer at the Institute for Sociology of Law and the Centre for Migration Law of the Radboud University Nijmegen. From 2012 to 2017 he performed his study on private party litigation before the Court of Justice of the European Union, combining legal and political science perspectives on this so-called 'Euro-litigation' with a sociological approach and methodology. As of September 2017, he works as a postdoc researcher at the Erasmus School of Law, Erasmus University Rotterdam, on the project 'Self-Representation in Civil Justice' as part of the ERC funded research programme 'Building EU civil justice: challenges of procedural innovations bridging access to justice'. Apart from academic work, he is co-founder and editor of the Rotterdam-based journal *Het Potentieel.*